GOLF VACATIONS

EVEN NON-GOLFERS

WILL ENJOY

Myrtle Beach, SC
Photo courtesy of Myrtle Beach Area Chamber of Commerce

GOLF VACATIONS

EVEN NON-GOLFERS

WILL ENJOY

SOUTHEASTERN UNITED STATES

Julie L. Moran

 John F. Blair, Publisher   *Winston-Salem, NC*

*This paper meets the guidelines
for permanence and durability of the
Committee on Production Guidelines
for Book Longevity of the Council
on Library Resources.*

Design by Liza Langrall
Cover design by Debra Long Hampton and Liza Langrall
Cover photographs:

> *Background cover photo*—Wintergreen Resort, VA, courtesy of VA Division of Tourism
>
> *Inset photos (top to bottom)*—Hilton Head, SC, by David S. Soliday, courtesy of Hilton Head
> Island Chamber of Commerce; Myrtle Beach Pavilion roller coaster, courtesy of Myrtle
> Beach Area Chamber of Commerce; Naples Beach, courtesy of Naples Area Chamber of
> Commerce.

Library of Congress Cataloging-in-Publication Data:
Moran, Julie L., 1963–
    Golf vacations even non-golfers will enjoy : southeastern United
States / Julie L. Moran.
        p.   cm.
    Includes index.
    ISBN 0-89587-153-X (alk. paper)
    1. Golf resorts—Southern States—Guidebooks. 2. Golf courses—
Southern States—Guidebooks. 3. Travel—Southern States—Guidebooks.
4. Restaurants—Southern States—Guidebooks.
I. Title.
GV982.S67M67   1996
796.352'0975—dc20   96-28706

For my beloved husband Sean, who made
me a golf widow, and thus spawned
the idea for this book;

for Katie and Sean, Jr., my inspirations;

and for my mother (my other traveling
buddy) and my father

CONTENTS

Acknowledgments

My husband, Sean M. Moran, a tax attorney in New York City and three-time club champion at Leewood Golf Club (a 1922 Devereux Emmet layout in Eastchester, New York), is the author of the golf course reviews in this book.

I'd like to thank the following people for their invaluable input, and without whom this book would not have been possible:

I'd like to thank PGA professional Timothy Nevin for his suggestions and critiques of the course reviews; PGA professional Steven Purviance for his suggestions; and my father-in-law, J. Patrick Moran, for his research efforts.

I'd also like to express my appreciation to the following individuals for their contributions to this project: My mother-in-law, Patricia Moran, who cared for the grandchildren while I traveled southward; and, for providing research and information for the book, thanks go to Judy Thompson of the National Golf Foundation; Andrew Leibowitz; Nicole Olivo; my mother and father, Lee and Mona Lumpkin; Lee and Lisa Lumpkin; Bill Lumpkin; Megan Avakian; Patty Lee; Tom, Tom, Jr., and Sonia Monahan; and Jakki Fox.

Sincere thanks also go to the many state and local organizations who provided significant assistance with the project, especially Karen Parker and

Christine Mackey of the North Carolina Division of Travel and Tourism, as well as the following people and their respective area chamber of commerce or convention and visitors bureau: Diane Bechtol, Alexandria; Gail Doyle and Anne Atkinson, Richmond; Louise Barnes, Norfolk; Pam Baker, Newport News; Amy Jonak, Hampton; Pat Hamm, Virginia Beach; Bobbye Saunders, Charlottesville; Jean Clark, Lexington; Rebecca Moore, Outer Banks; Jane Petersen, Wilmington; Kelley Sellers, Bald Head Island; Laurel Stannel, Pinehurst; Von Spivey and Margaret Pike, Winston-Salem; Gail Murphy, Greensboro; Rae Hunter and Charlotte Young, High Point; Marla Tambellini and Michelle Clifton, Asheville; Judi Scharns, the Boone area; Liz Mitchell and Steve Greene, Myrtle Beach (and Doug Bell, formerly of that office); Victoria Bryant, Charleston; Darla Davis, Hilton Head Island; Grace Belangia, Augusta; Jenny Stacy, Savannah; Kathy Ansley, Brunswick and the Golden Isles; Mary Kay Vollrath, Atlanta; Jeff Henderson, Lake Lanier Islands; Shelby Guest, Columbus; Laura Brooks, Jacksonville; Amy Rankin of St. John and Partners, Amelia Island; Dan Ryan and Kerri, Daytona Beach; Vic Colvin and Angie Garcia del Busto, Orlando; Stacie Faulds, Greater Fort Lauderdale; Tim Dougher, Palm Beach; Lee Daniels, St. Petersburg/ Clearwater; Michelle Brent, Tampa; and to others whose names I do not know, but who took the time to provide information and answer my questions. For the photographs supplied for the book, I'd like to thank the following audiovisual librarians from each respective state: Jay Hollomon, Virginia; Bill Russ, North Carolina; Bob Busby, Georgia; and Dixie Nims, Florida; and the individuals from the chambers of commerce and convention and visitors bureaus named above who also supplied photos.

For their help in providing maps to use as models for the maps in this book, I'd like to thank the following individuals in their respective state's department of transportation: Donna Purcell Mays, Virginia; A. Poe Cox, North Carolina; John Swiderski, Georgia; Tom Duffy, Florida. Finally, I'd like to thank my editor, Andrew Waters, for his invaluable assistance with this project.

Introduction

I became a widow the day I married . . . a golf widow, that is. I knew what I was getting into when our June wedding had to be scheduled around the U.S. Open. And every vacation since then has had to be at a location with accessible, quality golf nearby.

Counting only travel and lodging costs, and excluding golf fees, dining, and other spending, golf travel is a more than 8 billion dollar annual industry in the United States alone (the single largest component of the golf economy). In 1994, of the approximately 25 million golfers in the United States, 79.4% were men and 20.6% were women. Ten and a half million of these golfers traveled to play 62 million rounds of golf. Moreover, these numbers appear to be increasing steadily. Therefore, it stands to reason that there are many women and men out there who, like me, travel with an avid golfer. And while traveling with a golfer may by definition limit your choices of vacation spots, there are many exciting destinations that are well suited for both golfers and their non-golfing companions. This is especially true in the southeastern United States, which has an abundance of great golf courses, many at or near vacation destinations that appeal to those interested in things other than golf. However, to date, travel books for golfers provide little or no information to help their non-golfing companions decide whether they'll enjoy certain destinations based on an area's offerings and attractions. On the other hand, the many general travel guides available may sometimes list golf courses in certain areas, but do not provide detailed reviews or information on area courses. This book is intended to fill the needs of this large and growing group of travelers who need information on both topics.

HOW TO USE THIS BOOK ....

The book encompasses destinations within Virginia, North Carolina, South Carolina, Georgia, and Florida that offer terrific golf opportunities, and which have characteristics that would appeal to non-golfers with a variety of interests. Florida's panhandle was excluded, as it is more appropriately covered in a golf travel guide encompassing Alabama, Louisiana, and other destinations west.

Destinations were first selected on the availability of at least two great golf courses accessible to the public, although certain areas may have an abundance of such courses. Of the resort courses included, a few are restricted to guests, but the vast majority allow access by non-resort guests. In selecting courses, great backdrops such as oceans, marshes, lush valleys, mountains, and forests that greatly enhance a golfer's experience were also kept in mind. Places that offered less than two terrific public courses or those that did not offer plenty for non-golfers were eliminated. There were two exceptions

that cater somewhat more to golfers than non-golfers: Pinehurst, North Carolina, and Augusta, Georgia. However, as both places are golf meccas in their own right, they necessitated inclusion. These two locations are noted for their great golf, not their abundance of other activities. As you'll see, though, both destinations do offer a respectable number of activities for non-golfers. As for places being selected with a minimum of two great courses, only one exception exists: St. Marys, Georgia. It was included because it does have an outstanding course, and it has a unique vacation spot (Cumberland Island), which seemed too special to leave out.

While some of the areas included have golf courses right near non-golf attractions, others are a bit more spread out. The upper limit for courses considered to be within an area was an hour's drive from the main destination (though a majority of golf courses covered are within ten to fifteen minutes' drive, or less). Also added, although generally as side trips, were any isolated, but outstanding, golf courses that were somewhat near chosen destinations.

To appeal to non-golfers, a wide spectrum of locations was selected. Some were chosen for their natural surroundings, such as mountains or beaches, and some were included because they encompass interesting cities and towns. In general, the places selected offer a wide variety of non-golf activities such as historic sites; art, science, culture, history, and other museums; theme parks; sports other than golf; military sites and historic homes; great festivals; and more. Given these criteria, it was sometimes difficult to find destinations with a perfect balance between golf and non-golf activities. Some areas may have more to offer non-golfers than golfers (again, with a minimum of two fine courses within each destination), and while most of the areas included make satisfying trips of a week or more, a few may only make for an ideal weekend trip or stopover to or from a major destination. These shorter trips or stopovers are noted in the introductions of the chapters (e.g., St. Marys and Cumberland Island, Georgia, which is a short distance from Amelia Island off the coast of Jacksonville, Florida).

Once the areas were selected, they were organized clockwise within each state from the northeast section, down the coast and, in states where it applies, inland toward the southwest and back up to northwest sections.

GOLF INFORMATION ....

In each area, whether one with dozens of accessible courses, or one with only a couple of terrific courses, the golf section always describes in detail at least two flagship courses. The courses were selected by Sean Moran (with input from PGA professionals Tim Nevin, Steve Purviance, and others) for their quality, playability, and natural surroundings. Many of these courses are also rated as being among the nation's or the state's best according to *Golf Digest*, *Golf*, *GolfWeek*, and other golf publications. Also cited on occasion is the star system set forth in *Golf Digest's Places to Play*: one star = basic golf; two stars = good (not great, but not a rip-off, either); three stars = very good (tell a friend it's worth getting off the highway to play); four stars = outstanding

(plan your next vacation around it); and the rare five stars = golf at its absolute best (pay any price at least once in your life). Half stars are used for courses that fall between categories.

Yardage numbers for courses are given throughout this book. In many cases, we provide the yardage from all the sets of tees. But when only two yardage numbers are given for the tees, they represent the longest, or maximum, length of the course and the shortest, or minimum, length. Some courses have up to six different sets of tees and it gets burdensome to list the yardage for each set.

You'll also note that rating and slope information is provided for the course being reviewed. Rating/slope are two different methodologies used by the United States Golf Association (the "USGA") to comparatively evaluate a course using a universal standard. The rating of a course, based primarily on a course's length, indicates the number of shots a professional player would take to play the course. The slope is primarily based on the obstacles presented by a course, and it allows players to adjust their handicap according to the degree of difficulty of the course they are playing with the use of a conversion chart prepared by the USGA. Higher slopes indicate more difficulty, while lower slopes indicate less difficulty. Though it's normally stated in what appears to be a ratio, as we have done here, it's actually not a ratio.

Every effort has been made to provide current cart and tee-time policies and greens fees for the courses reviewed, but some fees and policies may have changed since press time, as they tend to fluctuate frequently. Many courses have increased fees during the high season. In cases where low season fees were not available, the high season fees were listed. When they were available, both high and low season fees were provided. In any case, before traveling, you may wish to call courses to confirm greens fees and tee-time policies.

TEMPERATURES AND HIGH SEASONS ....

The normal monthly temperatures stated in each chapter were provided by the National Weather Service. In some instances where the National Weather Service does not measure temperatures in a certain location, I have instead provided the temperatures of the nearest city with comparable normal monthly temperatures (as recommended by the National Weather Service). The most popular season for visitors has been provided, though some areas have more than one listed because the peak golf season may differ from seasons that draw visitors for other reasons (e.g., to the beaches or for skiing). In these cases, other peak seasons are provided to help visitors (in conjunction with the temperatures and, in some cases, special seasonal events) decide when a vacation may be best planned for both golfers and non-golfers.

ACCOMMODATIONS AND RESTAURANTS ....

The accommodation and restaurant listings in this book are not meant to be comprehensive. Most destinations covered here have many quality accommodations and restaurants to choose from, and I was limited by time and space constraints from including them all. However, for each destination I have attempted to suggest some quality accommodations within various price ranges, as well as good restaurants encompassing both fine and casual dining.

As for accommodations, all listings given are either hotels, motels, resorts offering a variety of lodgings, or bed-and-breakfast inns, and in few cases, campsites. No rental properties or real estate agents have been listed; however, if you wish to rent a cottage, home, or apartment, check with local tourism offices listed under the General Information category in each chapter. Hotel listings are divided by Expensive, Moderate, and Inexpensive with some areas offering only moderate to inexpensive selections (most commonly, hotels in or near beach resorts). Prices within the three categories correspond to the following pricing legend (based on a per-night double occupancy rate): Expensive is $125 and up (although some resorts and exclusive hotels can cost up to several hundred dollars per night); Moderate is between $70 and $120; and Inexpensive is between $45 and $70, although there are some campsites listed that are generally much less, and sometimes even free. In addition, Moderate/Inexpensive selections generally have accommodations that are between $70 and $95. Again, these are listed in areas where less expensive, quality accommodations are difficult to come by. Some of the more expensive resort areas have been noted within the text of those chapters. In these more expensive areas, the inexpensive accommodations tend to be in a less optimal location (e.g., off the beach by several blocks or a short drive away), and the less expensive selections tend to be no-frills across the board (while in less expensive destinations, guests at the inexpensive or moderate selections tend to get more desirable locations and/or more amenities for the same price).

As for restaurants, they have been divided into the categories of fine dining and casual dining. Some cities selected (e.g., Atlanta and Miami) have many fine restaurants with world-class chefs, while others, mainly beach and a few mountain or inland areas, have little dining that would require a jacket and tie or have famous chefs. You will find that at the head of some of the restaurant sections, I have noted the availability of fine dining or other information such as local specialties. Again, the list of restaurants is not meant to be comprehensive, and most areas have many other excellent choices. In any event, we suggest some of the finest dining available within each area.

Restaurants were chosen and recommended on the basis of the following factors (in addition to some being personal favorites of the author): Reputation, as based on restaurant reviews published in local newspapers or magazines; recommendations from locals who frequent restaurants; and the popularity of a place as shown by frequent publicity and/or its longstanding existence in an area. While the distinction between fine and casual dining can be a tough call, we have tried to base our listing on the following criteria: decor, local reputation of the chef and the cuisine, and prices. In some cases, whether the restaurant required a jacket and tie was also a consideration, although restaurants in many vacation areas have done away with this distinction in order to create a casual, relaxed atmosphere for vacationers.

GOLF VACATIONS

EVEN NON-GOLFERS

WILL ENJOY

Part One

VIRGINIA

Oatlands Plantation, near Leesburg
Photo courtesy of the Virginia Division of Tourism

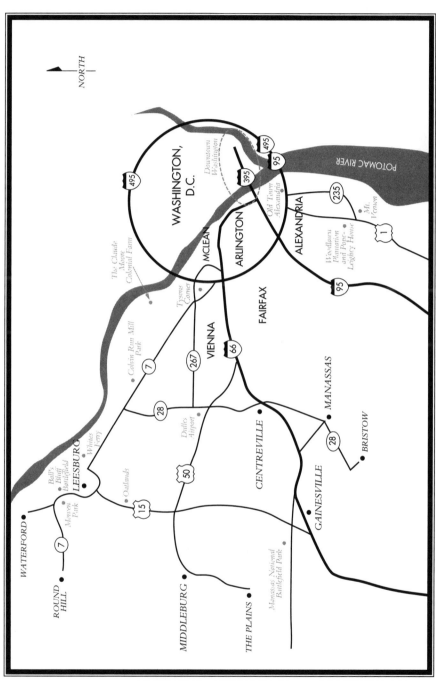

LEESBURG, ALEXANDRIA, and VICINITY, VA.

Leesburg, Alexandria, and vicinity

INCLUDING MANASSAS, ARLINGTON,

McLEAN, AND WASHINGTON, D.C.

AREA CODES:

202 (WASHINGTON, D.C.);

703 (ALL OTHERS)

INTRODUCTION ....

This area of northern Virginia, just over the Potomac River from the nation's capital, is a hotbed of American history. While few, if any, visitors come to northern Virginia and Washington, D.C., for the sole purpose of playing golf, this region is a popular tourist destination (attracting nearly 20 million visitors each year to D.C. alone), and thus, many golfers find themselves here at one time or another. Fortunately for them, accessible quality courses, in-

cluding one of the nation's finest golf resorts, can be found in the area in Leesburg, 35 miles from D.C., and just across the Potomac River in Arlington, Alexandria, McLean, and Manassas.

Leesburg, one of Virginia's oldest towns, has a population of about 10,000. The city is believed to be named after Francis Lightfoot Lee, a signer of the Declaration of Independence. The city served as an outpost in the French and Indian War, and during the War of 1812, it was where James and Dolley

Madison fled with precious original documents (the Declaration of Independence among them) during the burning of the District of Columbia. The town is nestled within Virginia's beautiful, hilly countryside, creating a perfect setting for raising and training the region's famed thoroughbred horses. Aside from being known for equestrian events, including a prestigious steeplechase, Leesburg offers quality golf, wineries, a historic district, hiking, and hunting. It's an excellent home base for golfers and non-golfers, not only because of its beautiful location and relaxed southern atmosphere, but for its proximity to literally hundreds of cultural and historical attractions. Arlington and Manassas (Bull Run) in Virginia, and Washington, D.C., are all under an hour's drive away (rush-hour traffic aside).

Another, less-crowded place to stay is Alexandria's Old Town, a historic district of quaint streets, churches, cemeteries, and museum houses; although visitors should avoid some other areas of the city, especially after dark. Just 10 miles from D.C., and about 30 miles from Leesburg, Alexandria is an old trade city that was surveyed by George Washington before it was later established in 1749. It was given to D.C. by Virginia in 1789, but then taken back after 57 years with the permission of Congress. Alexandria was captured by Union troops during the Civil War, yet many of her old buildings remain intact.

Winter months in this area are often too cold for golf. The high season is during spring (especially April, when the cherry blossoms are in bloom), and summer. As measured in Manassas, the normal monthly temperatures are: January, 33; February, 36; March, 46; April, 55; May, 64.5; June, 72.9; July, 77.2; August, 75.7; September, 69; October, 57.4; November, 47.8; December, 37.5.

GOLF INFORMATION ....

LANSDOWNE COUNTRY CLUB, LEESBURG (703) 729-8400 OR (800) 541-4801

Lansdowne is set in the rolling green hills of the lovely Potomac River Valley. This 1991, Robert Trent Jones, Jr., layout has been recognized by *Golf Digest* for its excellent design and conditioning. As is the case with many of this younger Jones's excellent courses, Lansdowne is intended to offer a challenge for all levels of play. It does this by offering multiple tees, ranging from 5213 yards to over 7000 yards, with a rating/slope ranging from 73.3/126 to 75/134. Jones also preserves the physical attributes of the natural landscape, while at the same time presenting obstacles and hazards that the player must mentally and physically negotiate. At Lansdowne, Jones has created a completely different feel between the wide-open front nine and the tree-lined back nine. On the front nine, the rolling terrain, prevalent wind, and the yardage of the holes are the dominant features. For example, the sixth, the number-one handicap hole on the course, is an uphill, 442-yard par 4 that generally plays into the wind. If that's not enough, the tee shot must avoid three bunkers in the landing area. Jones, obviously aware that players often try to draw the ball when extra distance is needed, presents a dilemma with these three bunkers that must be resolved even before you take

Mount Vernon, Fairfax County
Photo courtesy of the Virginia Division of Tourism

your first shot. To make sure your hitting shoes are on, the warm up for the sixth is the 610-yard, par 5 fifth. On the back side, the course features more hills and winds its way through forests, lakes, streams, and even stone walls. Possessing almost all of these features is the sixteenth hole, a 417-yard, par 4 dogleg. The hole is well treed, bordered by a stream on the left, and plays up a steep hill to the green.

Carts: Mandatory. *Greens Fees:* $55 November-March; rest of year, $80 weekdays, $90 weekends/18 holes, including cart. *Tee Time Policy:* Can be reserved forty-eight hours in advance.

PENDERBROOK GOLF CLUB, FAIRFAX
(703) 385-3700

Penderbrook, designed by Ault,

Clark and Associates, opened in 1985. Although relatively short, measuring only from 5042 to 6152 yards, Penderbrook is no pushover—it has a slope of 130 from the back tees. A great stretch of holes starts with the short, par 4 eighth and finishes with the 415-yard, par 4 twelfth (a hole that has been named one of the toughest in the Washington, D.C., area and the state of Virginia). The eighth hole requires a well-placed tee shot so that the approach, which must be played over a lake, has a chance of holding the wide, shallow green, which is protected to the left and in the rear with bunkers. The par 4 ninth plays back over the lake from the tee and, again, requires a well-placed tee shot so that the approach can get anywhere near the pin. The tenth is a 220-yard par 3 that plays, yet again, over the same lake to a large green protected front and back with bunkers. The short, par 4 eleventh is a change up that plays through the woods. The twelfth is a rough par 4 that requires a long tee shot, preferably played up the left side of the fairway. Depending on the length of the drive, the player can play for the green, protected on the right with two large bunkers, or can lay-up short of the lake and around the corner of a dogleg for a short pitch to the green. Regardless of how you play these holes, they are a memorable stretch that should not be missed.

Carts: Not required. *Greens Fees:* $32 Monday-Thursday, $42 Friday-Sunday/18 holes; carts: $13 per person. *Tee Time Policy:* Can be reserved three days in advance; same day reservations can be made if available.

VIRGINIA OAKS GOLF AND COUN-
TRY CLUB, GAINESVILLE
(703) 754-7977

Virginia Oaks is a Pete Dye course that opened in 1995 and is situated in a golf course community on the border of beautiful Lake Manassas. The course offers four sets of tees that range from 4852 to 6928 yards, with a rating/slope from the back tees of 73.3/133. An excellent stretch of holes is the 471-yard, par 5 third, the 432-yard, par 4 fourth, and the 205-yard, par 3 fifth. The holes, set on a peninsula surrounded by the lake, are stern tests, requiring length and accuracy. The back nine winds its way through the community with some real tough holes. For example, the par 5 tenth is 621 yards, requiring a strong drive, a long lay-up, and an accurate approach to a green

backed by the lake. An exciting and classic Pete Dye hole is the 310-yard, par 4 twelfth. The tee shot must be played over a lake, and the approach is to a smallish green protected by a cavernous bunker more than 10 feet deep (affectionately called "Big Bertha").

Carts: Required weekends until twilight. *Greens Fees:* $47 Monday-Thursday, $58 Friday-Sunday, in high season/18 holes, including cart. *Tee Times:* Can be reserved up to seven days in advance.

BRISTOW MANOR GOLF CLUB,
BRISTOW (703) 368-3558

Bristow Manor, named after the historic southern mansion on the property, is a Ken Killian, links-style design that opened in 1994. Sitting alongside the Kettle Run River, this course features water on twelve holes. Par is 72, and the tees range from 5154 to 6770 yards, with a rating/slope ranging from 70.1/122 to 71.6/128. A pretty, but brutal, hole is the 455-yard, par 4 seventh, which is a dogleg right. Although an accurate tee shot is required to avoid a lake skirting along the right side of the fairway, length cannot be sacrificed if the player wants a shot of reasonable length to the green. The approach shot must then carry a second lake to reach a narrow, deep green that is protected with two bunkers on the right and one on the left. Another excellent hole is the 419-yard, par 4 eighteenth. The excitement on this dogleg left begins with the approach, which must be played over a lake to a wide, shallow green.

Carts: Mandatory only Friday-Sunday before twilight. *Greens Fees:* $35 weekdays, $45 weekends/18 holes; carts: $12 per person. *Tee Time Policy:* Call for times (this is a public course).

OTHER EXCELLENT COURSES
IN THE AREA:

Meadows Farms, Locust Grove (540-854-9890), sports an 841-yard par 6, as well as oversized, hilly greens, such as the 10,000-square-foot, triple-tiered eighteenth green. **Stoneleigh Golf Club**, Round Hill (540-338-4653), was designed by Lisa Maki, a student of Scottish designs, so it features a hilly, links-style layout that reaches 6903 yards. This course opened in 1993 and is open to the public for daily fee play for a limited time (i.e., until all full memberships are sold). **Goose Creek Golf Club**, Leesburg (703-729-2500), was designed by Bill Gordon in 1952, but the 6400-yard layout has been renovated recently by Billy Casper Golf Management of Vienna. **Reston National**, Reston (703-620-9333), was designed by Al Jameson et al. The course stretches to 6871 yards and is considered to be one of the best daily-fee courses in the area. **Brambleton Regional Park Golf Course**, Ashburn (703-327-3403), opened in 1994 and features a 6764-yard layout that requires a player to negotiate rocks, water, heather, and tree-lined fairways. **Lee's Hill**, Fredericksburg (540-891-0111), opened in 1993 and was designed by Bill Love. The 6805-yard layout has a Civil War motif, as the course features preserved Confederate trenches and uses tee markers that are cannons, rifles, sabres, and pistols.

ATTRACTIONS ....

TOURS

In Leesburg, visitors can obtain self-guided tour maps for $1.00 from the **Loudoun Museum**, at 16 West Loudoun Street, and enjoy a stroll down brick streets lined with stately old homes and buildings. Guided walking tours can also be arranged through the museum by prior appointment. Call 703-777-7427.

All About Town, at 519 Sixth Street NW in Washington, D.C., schedules full and half-day tours of Washington, Georgetown, Mount Vernon, and Arlington in air-conditioned motorcoaches. Call 202-393-1618. **Gray Line of Washington**, at 5500 Tuxedo Road in Tuxedo, Maryland, offers day trips to D.C., Arlington, Alexandria, and other locations. Call 301-386-8300.

Boat tours

The Dandy Restaurant **Cruise Ship** cruises around D.C. or Alexandria on the Potomac River. Call 703-683-6076, or 703-683-6090 (for a recorded message). **Spirit Cruises** takes visitors on lunch and dinner cruises to Mount Vernon. Call 202-554-8000. **The Potomac Riverboat Company** gives narrated tours of Alexandria and of D.C.'s monuments from April through October. Call 703-684-0580.

The Whites Ferry, in operation since 1824, is the only working ferry left on the Potomac River. Visitors can take the short ride from a point 2 miles northeast of Leesburg to Whites Ferry, Maryland, between 6 A.M. and 11 P.M. daily. Call 301-349-5200.

HISTORIC PLACES

This entire area is packed with historic places. The following suggestions are just a tiny portion of what you can find.

Morven Park, located a mile north

of Leesburg on Old Waterford Road, was once owned by former governors of Maryland and Virginia. On the sprawling, 1500-acre grounds you can tour the restored, Greek Revival–style mansion, as well as an antique carriage museum with over a hundred items (including a funeral hearse and a charcoal-burning fire engine). Also on the grounds is the Museum of Hounds and Hunting, which showcases the history and equipment of fox hunting. Horse lovers may want to attend some of the many events held at the **Morven Park International Equestrian Institute.** Morven Park is open daily except Monday from April through October. Admission is charged. Call 703-777-2414.

Oatlands Plantation Mansion is on a 261-acre estate located 6 miles south of Leesburg on U.S. 15. The mansion was built by George Carter in 1803, and has been restored and decorated with antique American and French artworks and furnishings owned by the William Corcoran Eustis family, the former owners of the estate. The grounds have terraced gardens and large fields, and they are used for horse shows, a foxhound show, and other special events. Open daily except Monday from April through December. Admission is charged for both house and gardens. Call 703-777-3174.

Waterford, located on VA 662, is a restored village originally settled by Quakers in the eighteenth century. Visitors can walk around the historic area, although the homes are closed to the public and there are no stores here. No admission is charged, but walking-tour maps are for sale from the Waterford Foundation. Call 540-882-3018. Dur-ing the first full weekend in October, Waterford holds its popular **Annual Homes Tour** which features music, crafts sales, and demonstrations.

Ball's Bluff Battlefield, northeast of Leesburg on U.S. 15, is where the Union suffered many casualties in the third armed battle of the Civil War in 1861, and where future Supreme Court Justice Oliver Wendell Holmes was wounded. The battlefield is marked by a national cemetery. No admission is charged.

Alexandria's sizeable Old Town historic district includes a number of quaint streets, churches, cemeteries, and museum houses. Some sites you should see are the boyhood home of Robert E. Lee, the Lee-Fendall house, and the Gadsby's Tavern Museum (admission is charged at all three). Most sites here can be covered via a walking tour, and free maps are available at the Alexandria Convention and Visitors Bureau in the Ramsay House at 221 King Street. Call 703-838-4200.

Mount Vernon, on Mount Vernon Memorial Parkway, is located 16 miles from D.C. and 9 miles from Alexandria. The home was built by George Washington's father, and George inherited it upon his half brother's death. He brought the mansion to its current grandeur during his many years there with Martha and his two stepchildren from her prior marriage. He and Martha are buried on the grounds. Open daily. Admission is charged. Call 703-780-2000.

Gunston Hall Plantation, is in nearby Mason Neck (in Lorton), 14 miles south of Mount Vernon along the Potomac River. This 1755 mansion with formal gardens was owned by

George Mason, who helped create the Bill of Rights. Open daily. Admission is charged. Call 703-550-9220.

Located between Mount Vernon and Gunston Hall Plantation are **Woodlawn Plantation**, built by a stepdaughter of George Washington, and Frank Lloyd Wright's **Pope-Leighey House**, both located at 9000 Richmond Highway. Admission is charged for individual houses, or combination tickets are available. Open daily; weekends only in January. Call 703-780-4000.

MUSEUMS/SCIENCE CENTERS

Loudoun Museum, at 16 West Loudoun Street in Leesburg, has exhibits and an audio-visual presentation spanning the county's more than 200-year history. Open daily. Donations are suggested. Call 703-777-7427.

Gadsby's Tavern Museum, at 134 North Royal Street in Alexandria, is an authentic eighteenth-century hostelry known for its architecture and connection with George Washington (who was a patron). The museum showcases the look and function of the tavern in daily colonial life. Call 703-838-4242.

Stabler-Leadbeater Apothecary Museum and Shop, at 105-107 South Fairfax Street in Alexandria, is an old apothecary that houses the largest collection of early pharmaceutical artifacts in the United States, including prescriptions, bottles, scales, and medicines. Prominent customers included Washington, John C. Calhoun, and Robert E. Lee. Admission is charged. Call 703-836-3713.

George Washington Masonic National Memorial, at 101 Callahan Drive in Alexandria, was built by the American Freemasons (Washington was

a member and the lodge's first master). The memorial is an impressive, church-like structure, and inside is a large collection of objects that once belonged to Washington. Open daily. Admission is free. Call 703-683-2007.

Fort Ward Museum and Historic Site, at 4301 West Braddock Road in Alexandria, has a restored bastion from part of the original Civil War fort, and a museum dedicated to the Civil War experience. Open daily. Admission is free. Call 703-838-4848.

CULTURAL OFFERINGS

There are several winery tours in and around Leesburg, as well as in Middleburg, 15 miles southwest of Leesburg. In Leesburg, you can visit **Tarara Vineyards and Winery**, at 13648 Tarara Lane (call 703-771-7100); **Willowcroft Farm and Vineyards**, on Route 2 (call 703-777-8161), and **Loudoun Valley Winery** in Waterford, (call 540-882-3375). In Middleburg, there's **Meredyth Vineyards**, on VA 628, (call 703-687-6277), and the **Piedmont Vineyards**, on VA 626 (call 703-687-5528). Most wineries are open daily and offer free admission.

The Alexandria Symphony Orchestra, (call 703-845-8005), **Opera Americana** (call 703-836-0621), and the **Alexandria Royal Fifes, Drums, Trumpets and the Sound of America Show** (a musical revue of the colonial and World War I and II eras; call 703-768-8295), all perform year round at various locations in Alexandria. Call the individual organizations for schedules.

Torpedo Factory Art Center, at 105 North Union Street in Alexandria, was once a torpedo factory but now houses studios and sales galleries for local artists. Open daily. Admission is free. Call 703-838-4565. Also at the Torpedo Factory Art Center is **Alexandria Archeology**, a museum and working research laboratory. Open daily except Monday. Admission is free. Call 703-838-4399.

For information on current performances and exhibitions throughout northern Virginia, contact the Fairfax County Council of the Arts at 703-642-0862. Alexandria has a 24-hour event line, which can be reached at 703-838-5005. In D.C., call the Convention and Visitors Association at 202-789-7000 for information on cultural offerings.

RECREATION

For spectator sports, there are three major professional teams in the area. The **Washington Bullets** play NBA basketball (call 301-622-3865 for tickets) and the **Washington Capitals** play NHL hockey (call 301-386-7000 for tickets) at the USAir Arena in Landover,

Stone House, Manassas
National Battlefield Park
Photo Courtesy of the Virginia Division of Tourism

Maryland (call 301-350-3400). The **Washington Redskins** play NFL football in RFK Stadium, at 2400 East Capitol Street SE in Washington, D.C., though only preseason tickets are available. Call 202-546-2222.

In Leesburg, contact the chamber of commerce at 703-777-1758 for information on hunting and hiking. For horseback riding in Leesburg, call **Greenway Stables** at 703-327-6117.

SEASONAL EVENTS

In February, George Washington gets a big birthday celebration in Alexandria, with a Revolutionary War pageant, races, and a parade. For information, contact the Alexandria Convention and Visitors Bureau at 703-838-4200

The Alexandria Red Cross Waterfront Festival takes place in June, with cruises, races, a fair, and the annual blessing of the fleet. Admission is charged. Call 703-549-8300.

Among Leesburg's most famous events is **August Court Days**, held in August. The colonial celebration features a reenactment of the opening of the court, which was a significant social and cultural event during the late 1700s. The festival also features crafts, games, and costumed colonial interpreters.

In December, Alexandria has the **Scottish Christmas Walk**, with a tour of historic homes and a parade. Call 703-549-0111. There are also **Scottish Games** in July, with games, music, and food. For information, contact the Alexandria Convention and Visitors Bureau at 703-838-42000.

Many equestrian events take place throughout the year in Leesburg at **Oatlands** (call 703-777-3174) and **Morven Park** (call 703-777-2414).

Events include horse trials, race meets, and more. Contact the individual estates, or call the Leesburg Chamber of Commerce at 703-777-1758 for a copy of the current steeplechase-racing calendar.

ACCOMMODATIONS ....

If you're staying in Alexandria, the Alexandria Hotel Association is a free reservation service. Call 800-296-1000.

EXPENSIVE

Lansdowne Resort, at 44050 Woodridge Parkway, 4 miles from Leesburg in Lansdowne, is a peaceful, countryside sanctuary. Aside from having one of the best championship golf courses in the state (See Golf Information), the resort has two pools, tennis, lawn games, concierge service, and supervised children's activities in summer. Rooms have private balconies overlooking the manicured lawns, lakes, and wooded acres surrounding the resort. Call 800-541-4801.

Norris House, at 108 Loudoun Street SW in Leesburg, is in a 1760, Federal-style home. The charming rooms all come with fireplaces, antiques, and canopied, feather beds. There's also a veranda and garden area. Full breakfast and afternoon tea are served. Call 800-644-1806.

Morrison House, at 116 South Alfred Street in Alexandria, is a delightful inn with an old European ambience. The inn is packed with old-fashioned charm, from the mahogany-paneled library and costumed butlers to the canopied, fourposter beds to the fireplaces in each individually appointed room.

Tea is served daily. Call 703-838-8000 or 800-367-0800.

MODERATE

Tysons Corner Marriott, at 8028 Leesburg Pike in Vienna, is located off I-495. This modern, high-rise hotel has a pool and plenty of other amenities, and it is located next to the Tysons Corner shopping mall (See Shopping). Call 703-734-3200.

Best Western Leesburg, at 726 East Market Street in Leesburg, allows small pets, has free cable and an outdoor pool, and offers moderate to inexpensive rates. Call 703-777-9400.

INEXPENSIVE

Days Inn, at 721 East Market Street in Leesburg, is a comfortable, economic choice located near the Lansdowne Resort and Goose Creek Golf Course. Call 703-777-6622.

Howard Johnson Olde Towne, at 5821 Richmond Highway in Alexandria, has exercise facilities, free airport transfers, an indoor pool, game room, beauty shop, valet service, jacuzzi, and sauna—all for reasonable rates. The motel also accepts pets and is convenient to Alexandria's Old Town district. Call 703-329-1400.

SHOPPING ....

Antique lovers will enjoy downtown Leesburg's several antique malls, and Alexandria's variety of antique shops and art galleries.

The East Coast's largest shopping mall, featuring 230 stores, is at **Tysons Corner**, at 1961 Chain Bridge Road in upscale McLean, Virginia (See Side Trips). This spacious complex has

Iwo Jima Memorial, Arlington
Photo courtesy of the Virginia Division of Tourism

plenty of great stores and picturesque details, such as a palm-lined fountain and A-frame skylights. The shopping center is located at the intersection of VA 7 (Leesburg Pike) and VA 123, just off I-495. For information, call 703-893-9400. Also nearby is the **Galleria at Tysons II**, located at 2001 International Drive. Call 703-827-7700.

For bargain shopping, try the **Potomac Mills Outlet Mall** in Dale City, Virginia. For information, call 800-VA-MILLS.

RESTAURANTS ....

DINNER THEATERS

Alexandria's **West End Dinner Theater**, in the Foxchase Shopping Center at 4615 Duke Street, has shows throughout the year. Call 703-370-2500 or 800-368-3799.

FINE DINING

Tuscarora Mill Restaurant, at 203 Harrison Street SE in Leesburg, is popular with locals and visitors alike. It serves classic American cuisine, and popular dishes include sesame-roasted salmon and rack of lamb. They have twenty-one beers on tap and an award-winning wine list. Serves lunch and dinner daily. Call 703-771-9300.

La Bergerie is at 218 North Lee Street in the restored Crilley Warehouse in Alexandria's Old Town district. The cuisine leans toward French Basque, with duck and seafood dishes a specialty. Reservations are required on weekends. Open for lunch and dinner; closed Sundays (except Mother's Day). Call 703-683-1007.

CASUAL DINING

Laurel Brigade Inn, at 20 West Market Street in Leesburg, has a section dating from 1759. The theme and decor are colonial, with stone walls and an old fireplace. Popular items are fried chicken and seafood. Open daily for lunch and dinner. Call 703-777-1010.

Green Tree, at 15 South King Street in Leesburg, is a restaurant specializing in authentic dishes from the 1700s, like Jefferson's Delight (made with calf liver) and colonial desserts such as bread pudding. Open daily for lunch and dinner; Sunday brunch served from 11:30 A.M. to 4:00 P.M. Call 703-777-7246.

Lansdowne Resort, at 44050 Woodbridge Parkway in Lansdowne, has two good restaurants: the **Potomac Grill**, serving dinner Tuesday through Saturday, and the **Riverside Hearth**, open daily from 6 A.M. until 10 P.M. Call 800-541-4801.

Gadsby's Tavern Restaurant, at 138 North Royal Street in Alexandria, is a colonial restaurant where costumed servers bring guests colonial favorites and provide music and entertainment. Reservations recommended. Open for lunch, dinner, and Sunday brunch. Call 703-548-1288.

JUST FOR KIDS ....

Lansdowne Resort has a **Resort Rascals** program from Memorial Day through Labor Day for ages three through twelve. The program offers crafts, bike riding, nature walks, movies and pizza, and golf and tennis clinics.

There are several worthwhile side trips to Washington, D.C., that children will enjoy. **The National Zoological Park**, at the 3000 block of Connecticut Avenue NW, has over 5,000 animals. A popular new attraction at the zoo is the giant panda. Open daily. Admission is charged. Call 202-673-4800. **The National Aquarium**, at Fourteenth Street and Constitution Avenue NW, is the nation's oldest aquarium, and among its best. Open daily. Admission is charged. Call 202-482-2826. **The Capital Children's Museum**, at 800 Third Street NE, covers technology, science, and culture, with exhibits designed for children's involvement. Open daily. Admission is charged. Call 202-543-8600. **The Washington Dolls' House and Toy Museum**, at 5236 Forty-fourth Street NW, has antique dolls, games, and toys. Open Tuesday through Sunday. Admission is charged. Call 202-244-0024.

SIDE TRIPS ....

Arlington National Cemetery, about 5 miles from Alexandria, is where such famous Americans as President John F. Kennedy, Jacqueline Kennedy Onassis, boxer Joe Lewis, and Supreme Court Justice Thurgood Marshall are buried. Visitors should be sure to see the changing of the guard at the Tomb of the Unknown Soldiers, which occurs hourly from October through March, and every half hour from April through September. The cemetery is open daily. Admission is free; charge for parking and tour tram. Call 703-692-0937 for information. Also on the site is **Arlington House**, where Robert E. Lee once lived. Open daily. Admission is free. Call 703-557-0613.

McLean is a posh area of Virginia, located northwest of Arlington on VA 193 (where it meets VA 123), that is home to senators and other illustrious locals. A popular tourist site in McLean is the **Claude Moore Colonial Farm at Turkey Run**, located at 6310 Georgetown Pike. The site is a living museum of a late eighteenth-century farm featuring costumed employees demonstrating actual farming techniques of the era. Admission is charged. Call 703-442-7557. Also in McLean is **Tysons Corner** (See Shopping and Accommodations). Farther north on VA 7, heading toward Leesburg, is **Great Falls**, where you can visit the **Colvin Run Mill Park**, on Colvin Run Road. The park features a miller's house, a mill, a small museum, and a general store. Admission to the grounds is free. Call 703-759-2771. Also in Great Falls is one of the area's finest restaurants, **L'Auberge Chez Francoise**, located at 332 Springvale Road. Dinner is served daily except Monday. Jacket and reservations required. Call 703-759-3800.

The Manassas National Battlefield Park, also known as Bull Run, is at the junction of VA 234 and U.S. 29, about 25 miles southwest of Alexandria. The battles fought here were among the earliest and most notable of the Civil War, and this is where General "Stonewall" Jackson earned his nickname. There's a visitors center, and the battlefield can be toured by car or on foot. Guided tours are available in summer. Open daily. Admission is charged. Call 703-361-1339. A few miles away, the **Manassas Museum**, at 9101 Prince William Street, covers the history and culture of Manassas and the northern Virginia piedmont region, from prehistoric times through the present. Open daily except Monday. Admission is charged. Call 703-368-1873. Moreover, the Manassas area has two excellent daily-fee golf courses, Virginia Oaks Golf and Country Club in Gainesville, and the Bristow Manor Golf Club in Bristow (See Golf Information).

GENERAL INFORMATION ....

For more information about Leesburg, contact the Loudoun County Convention and Visitors Bureau at 703-777-0519 or 800-752-6118, or contact the Leesburg Chamber of Commerce at 703-777-1758. For information on Alexandria, contact the Alexandria Convention and Visitors Bureau at 703-838-4200. For information about Arlington, contact the Arlington County Visitors Center at 800-677-6267. For information about Washington, D.C., contact the District of Columbia Convention and Visitors Association at 202-789-7000.

Publications of general interest include the *Washington, D.C. Visitors Guide*, and the seasonally published calendar of events, both available from the District of Columbia Convention and Visitors Association. The Alexandria and Loudoun County Convention and Visitors Bureau each offer a *Visitors Guide*. From the Fairfax County Visitors Center, you can obtain a calendar of events, a pocket guide, and the *Northern Virginia Visitors Guide*.

Some local publications feature golf information. Fairfax County offers the *Tee Up!* pamphlet. Loudoun County's *Visitors Guide* has golf information, and most information centers offer a general publication called *Virginia Golf*.

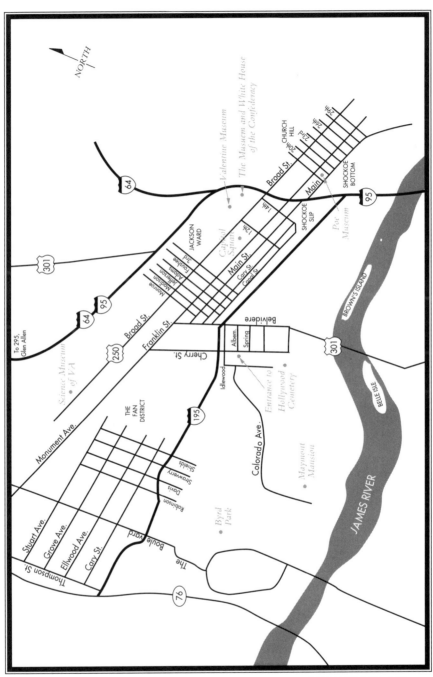

RICHMOND, VA.

Richmond and vicinity

AREA CODE: 804

INTRODUCTION ....

Richmond is a city for history and museum lovers, military history buffs, and lovers of fine architecture. And although it is not a place golfers choose strictly for golf, there are excellent courses all around the Richmond area (with a total of thirteen public courses). It's also a convenient stop on the way to or from Williamsburg, as they're about 40 miles from one another.

After serving as Virginia's capital since 1780, and the capital of the Confederacy from 1861 to 1865, Richmond is a treasure-trove of state and United States history. In the eighteenth century, the area was engulfed in a war between the native Seminoles and the settlers, which ultimately was won out by the settlers. Later that century, in 1775, Patrick Henry gave his famous "Give Me Liberty or Give Me Death" speech in Richmond (though you can also see it reenacted in Colonial Williamsburg). The city saw much destruction during the ensuing Revolutionary War, and again, a century later, in the Civil War; however, during both conflicts, Richmond managed to retain much of its industry, architecture, and prestige.

Today, Richmond is both historic and modern, and sometimes even trendy. The James River splits the city in half, though the historic district and most attractions covered in this book lie to the north of the river. Visitors will find large, historic buildings—some found along old, brick-paved streets—near a variety of more recent, yet no less elegant, structures. This pristine city thrives with industry and culture, enriched by the three major state universities found here.

Normal monthly temperatures are: January, 35.7; February, 38.7; March, 48; April, 57.3; May, 66; June, 73.9; July, 78; August, 76.8; September, 70; October, 58.6; November, 49.6; December, 40.1. Peak times for visitors are April through July.

GOLF INFORMATION ....

THE CROSSINGS GOLF CLUB, GLEN ALLEN (804) 261-0000

The Crossings, opened in 1979, is a classic Joe Lee design that has consistently ranked in the top ten listing of Virginia courses. It has also hosted both U.S.G.A.'s Publinks Championship and Nike Tour qualifying events. The course's name derives from its location as a troop crossing during the Civil War. The layout has four sets of tees measuring from 5625 to 6619 yards, and features a rating/slope ranging from 70.7/126 to 73.2/128, making it enjoyable and playable by all levels of golfer. Features include: six elevated tee

boxes, three lakes, tree-lined fairways, seventy-two bunkers, and large and undulating greens. An excellent hole is the par 4 fourteenth, the number-two handicap hole. The hole, a slight dogleg left that stretches to 412 yards, is bordered on the left side of the fairway by a lake running almost from the tee to the green, forcing the golfer to decide on the tee how much of the lake he/she wishes to traverse. There is no relief once you reach the fairway because the approach shot must carry a second lake that fronts a long, narrow green protected with a bunker on the right. A par here is a fine accomplishment.

Carts: Required certain times; walking restricted during peak season. *Greens Fees:* $39 weekdays, $45 weekends, in high season (including cart); $30 weekdays, $35 weekends, in offseason (carts extra)/18 holes. *Tee Time Policy:* Can be reserved seven days in advance (earlier for groups).

RIVER'S BEND GOLF AND COUNTRY CLUB, CHESTER (804) 530-1000

This course opened in 1990 and is set on the lovely, historic James River. River's Bend was designed by Steve Smyers, with the help of PGA Tour pro Bobby Wadkins. With a par of 71, the course has tees that measure from 4932 to 6671 yards and a rating/slope that ranges from 67.8/117 to 71.9/132. The front nine is tight and requires a golfer to play each shot at a defined target. The back nine is more open and hilly. Bring your sand game to River's Bend, because this course boasts an amazing 112 bunkers. The tenth and eighteenth holes feature lovely scenery that appears to stretch for miles.

Carts: Walking allowed during weekdays and after 1 P.M. on weekends and holidays. *Greens Fees:* $37 weekdays, $42 weekends/18 holes, including cart. *Tee Time Policy:* Can be reserved seven days in advance.

OTHER EXCELLENT AREA COURSES:

Belmont Park, Henrico County (804-266-4929), is now a municipal course but was once known as Hermitage Country Club. This par 71, A.W. Tillinghast design was opened in 1916 and renovated by Donald Ross in 1940. In 1949, it hosted the PGA Championship won by Sam Snead, and the course still possesses plenty of class and character. **Royal Virginia Golf Club**, Hadensville (804-457-2041 or 800-238-0055), is a 1993 course that sports tees reaching over 7100 yards, with a slope of 131. **Sycamore Creek Golf Course**, Manakin-Sabot (804-784-

3544), is a 6256-yard, par 70 course that is rated 3 stars by *Golf Digest's Places to Play.*

ATTRACTIONS ....

TOURS

Historic Richmond Tours (part of the Historic Richmond Foundation) conducts high-quality motorized tours and Sunday walking tours. They offer tours that provide an overview of the city's history and architecture, and a tour that focuses on the Civil War. Reservations required. Call 804-780-0107.

Richmond Discoveries has several full and half-day trips to local places of interest, including specialized (e.g., Civil War) tours. For information, call 804-795-5781.

Annabel Lee is a replica of a nineteenth-century riverboat. Tours include

Agecroft Hall Gardens, Richmond
Photo courtesy of the Virginia Division of Tourism

lunch, dinner, brunch, party, and plantation cruises, and run April through October. Departures are from 4400 East Main Street. Call 804-644-5700.

HISTORIC PLACES

Capitol Square is a lovely, hilltop complex surrounded by a wrought-iron fence and bounded by Ninth, Bank, Governor, and Broad Streets. The complex consists of the Capitol, the Governor's Mansion, and the Virginia State Library and Archives.

The Capitol is a striking, white-columned building designed by Thomas Jefferson (inspired by La Maison Carre, an ancient Roman temple in France). Visitors can tour the Rotunda, featuring Houdon's statue of George Washington, among others, as well as the museum in the Hall of the House of Delegates, where the Confederate Congress met, and where Aaron Burr was tried for treason. Open Monday through Saturday from April through November. Admission is free. Visitors can take free tours of the Governor's Mansion, the oldest continuously occupied executive mansion in the country. Tours are by appointment only. For information, call 804-371-2642. **City Hall**, at Broad and Ninth Streets near Capitol Square, features an observation deck on the eighteenth floor that offers great views of the city. The observation deck is open daily. Call 804-780-7000.

Hollywood Cemetery, at 412 Cherry Street, is a graveyard whose inhabitants read like a who's who of American history, including Presidents James Monroe and John Tyler and Confederate President Jefferson Davis. Open daily; an eighteen-minute orientation film runs weekdays from

Interior of Virginia's Capitol, Richmond

Photo courtesy of the Virginia Division of Tourism

8:30 A.M. to 4 P.M. Admission is free, but self-guided tour maps cost $1.00. Call 804-648-8501.

Several historic neighborhoods in Richmond make for a scenic walk or drive. **The Church Hill Historic District**, located east of Capitol Square and bordered by Twenty-first, Main, Twenty-ninth, and Broad Streets, is noted for its antebellum homes, many of which are open for public tours during April's Historic Garden Week (See Seasonal Events). However, this district's most famous site is **St. John's Episcopal Church**, at 2401 East Broad Street, which is where Patrick Henry delivered his famous "Give Me Liberty or Give Me Death" speech before the Second Virginia Convention. The church is open daily year round; reenactments of the speech are given at 2 P.M. on Sundays in summer. Admission is charged. Call 804-648-5015. While enjoying scenic and historic areas, be sure to head down **Monument Avenue**, which has a series of likenesses of Civil War heroes in the street's center dividers. In 1996, a statue of Arthur Ashe was added to the boulevard. The **Fan District**, located within Franklin Street, Monument Ave-nue, the Boulevard, Main Street, and Belvidere Street, is noted for its antebellum and late Victorian architecture. The neighborhood gets its name because these streets all fan out from Monroe Park to the west. The **Jackson Ward District**, bordered by I-95, Seventh, Broad, and Belvidere Streets (in the northeast part of the city), is known for its eighteenth-century Victorian and Greek Revival homes (as well as homes of other architectural styles), and for its importance in Richmond's African-American history.

Richmond National Battlefield Park has a visitors center at 3215 East Broad Street in Chimborazo City Park. The center provides background information and maps which tourists may find useful before touring the Civil War battlegrounds. Admission is free. Call 804-226-1981. Civil War buffs can also tour Petersburg National Battlefield, about 20 miles south of Richmond, where some 70,000 casualties occurred. Open daily; special reenactments in summer. Admission is free. Call 804-732-3531.

There are many historic homes in Richmond that can be toured. A few notable examples include:

The Museum and White House of the Confederacy, at 1202 East Clay Street, is where Jefferson Davis lived while he was president of the Confederacy, though the house itself is gray. The museum features the country's largest Confederate Civil War collection. Admission is charged. Call 804-649-1861.

John Marshall House, at Ninth and Marshall Streets, was built by Supreme Court Justice John Marshall in 1790. This neoclassical- and Federal-style structure contains colonial furnishings, including original family heirlooms. Open daily except Monday; hours vary seasonally. Admission is charged. Call 804-648-7998.

Agecroft Hall, at 4305 Sulgrave Road, was a fifteenth-century Tudor home originally built in England. The home was disassembled and brought to Richmond in 1925, along with many fifteenth- and sixteenth-century furnishings. The formal English gardens overlook the James River. Open daily. Admission is charged. Call 804-353-4241.

Wilton, at 215 South Wilton Road, is the 1753 home of William Randolph III, and headquarters of the National Society of Colonial Dames in Virginia. The house contains family portraits and colonial furnishings. Open daily except Monday. Admission is charged. Call 804-282-5936.

Maymont Mansion, at 1700 Hampton Street, is a late Victorian mansion containing antique paintings and artworks. There are also formal gardens, a wildlife habitat and arboretum, antique carriages, and a petting farm. Grounds open daily. House, nature center, and barn open from noon to 5 P.M. daily except Monday. Admission is charged. Call 804-358-7166.

MUSEUMS/SCIENCE CENTERS

Edgar Allen Poe Museum, at 1914 East Main Street, has a stone portion built in 1737, which is believed to be the oldest remaining structure in Richmond. Though Poe never lived here, the museum contains exhibits from the author's life during his residency in Richmond, including a model of Richmond as it existed during that time, raven statues, and manuscripts. Open daily. Admission is charged. Call 804-648-5523.

The Science Museum of Virginia, at 2500 West Broad Street, is housed in an old railroad station. Exhibits focus on the physical sciences, from a Foucault pendulum to computerized flight simulators. There's also an Omnimax Planetarium. Open daily. Admission is charged. Call 804-367-1080 or 804-367-1013.

The Valentine Museum, at 1015 East Clay Street, focuses on the history of Richmond. One of the main buildings here is the 1812 Wickham House, designed by the same architect who designed Boston's Faneuil Hall. Wickham was Richmond's wealthiest man in his time, and entertained such illustrious guests as Daniel Webster and President Zachary Taylor. Slave quarters also can be toured, and the museum's collections show many artifacts of the period such as costumes, textiles, furnishings, and artworks. Open daily. Admission is charged. Call 804-649-0711.

Virginia Museum of Fine Arts, at 3800 Grove Avenue in the Fan District, has exquisite pieces including Fabergé eggs, Roman and Egyptian statues, and paintings by Van Gogh, Monet, Goya, and Renoir. Open daily except Monday. Admission is charged. Call 804-367-0844.

Meadow Farm Museum, on Woodman Road off I-295, 12 miles northwest of Richmond, is a living history museum where life continues as it did in rural Virginia during the 1860s. There's an orientation center, farmhouse, barn, crop fields, a doctor's office, and other buildings. Surrounding the museum is the 150-acre General Sheppard Crump Memorial Park, which has a playground. Admission is free except during special events. Call 804-672-9496.

CULTURAL OFFERINGS

Theatre Virginia is known for its dramatic productions, often presented in the Virginia Museum of Fine Art's theater, at 3800 Grove Avenue. The museum theater has additional productions each year ranging from Broadway to Shakespeare. The season runs from September through April. Call 804-353-6161 for information or 804-353-6100 for tickets. The **Carpenter Center**, at 600 East Grace Street, presents ballets, operas, symphonies, and special shows. Call 804-782-3900. **The Landmark Theater**, at Main and Laurel Streets, is a Moorish theater with performances from jazz concerts to Broadway plays throughout the year. Call 804-780-4213.

The Richmond Symphony is well respected internationally and draws well-known guest vocalists and musicians. For information, call 804-788-1212. **Concert Ballet (of Virginia)** is a well-versed troupe that performs a variety of styles, from classics to the cutting edge. Call 804-780-1279.

RECREATION

Paramount King's Dominion Wildlife and Amusement Park is located 20 miles north of Richmond off I-95 in Doswell. The park features over a hundred attractions, shows, and rides, including heart-stoppers like "The Hurler" (in the section of the park based upon Paramount's *Wayne's World* movies, where you can party on, dude). The park also has other attractions based on well-known Paramount characters and themes. Open April to October; hours change seasonally. Admission is charged. Call 804-876-5000.

The city offers several large parks, including: **William Byrd Park**, with an impressive pink bell tower commemorating Richmond's World War I dead; **Bryan Park**, known for its large azalea gardens and outstanding variety of other native plants; and **James River Park**, with canoeing and tubing, a wildlife sanctuary, and a visitors center (fees for activities). For information on these city parks, call the Richmond Department of Parks and Recreation at 804-780-5695. **Pocahontas State Park**, south of Richmond on VA 655, has a pool, camping facilities, and a nature center. Fees charged for some activities. Call 804-796-4255.

Professional auto racing takes place September through March at the **Richmond Fairgrounds Raceway**, off I-64 on Laburnum Avenue. Call 804-329-6796 or 804-329-7223.

The Richmond Coliseum hosts many spectator sports, such as wrestling, skating shows, basketball, and tennis. For information, call 804-780-4956. **The Richmond Braves**, the Atlanta Braves AAA minor-league team, play at the Diamond, located in the 3000 block of the Boulevard. For information, call 804-359-4444.

White-water rafting fans can head down the James River—right through the center of town. Day trips are available. Reservations are suggested. For information, contact **Richmond Raft** at 804-222-7238.

SEASONAL EVENTS

Historic Garden Week is a statewide event allowing the public to tour lovely private homes from late April through early May. For information on the event in Richmond, call 804-644-7776 or 804-643-7141. At Christmas, Richmond has a similar festival, the annual **Open House Tour**. Call 804-649-3519 or 804-355-0892.

The **Virginia State Fair** takes place at the State Fairgrounds in Strawberry Hill (off I-95 and I-295) and runs from late September through early October. At the event you'll find activities like rides, games, agricultural contests, and a horse show. Call 804-0228-3200.

ACCOMMODATIONS ....

EXPENSIVE

The historic, five-diamond **Jefferson Hotel**, at Franklin and Adams Streets, emanates with Victorian elegance. The interior features a statue of Thomas Jefferson, a central staircase, and a dome with a stained-glass interior. Rooms have refrigerators and pretty furnishings, and a concierge service is available. Call 804-788-8000 or 800-424-8014.

Omni Richmond, at 100 South Twelfth Street, is located downtown near Shockoe Slip (See Shopping). This lovely hotel has a marble-and-velvet interior with large modern rooms. Amenities such as a concierge service, indoor and outdoor pools, an indoor track, and other exercise facilities are offered. Call 804-344-7000 or 800-843-6664.

Residence Inn by Marriott, at 2121 Dickens Road, offers guests comfortable rooms, free continental breakfast, valet service, and pool privileges. Call 804-285-8200.

Holiday Inn Koger Center South, at 10800 Midlothian Turnpike, has large rooms, an outdoor pool, and good prices. Families will appreciate the park with nature trails, a playground, and tennis facilities next door. Call 804-379-3800 or 800-HOLIDAY.

No-frills travelers will like the **Massad House Hotel**, at 11 North Fourth Street, where for a fair price you get comfortable rooms in a downtown location, just blocks from Capitol Square. Call 804-648-2893.

Red Roof Inn, at 4350 Commerce Road, is south of the downtown area, but their prices are reasonable. It's nothing fancy, but it's clean and economical for those on a budget. Call 804-271-7240.

SHOPPING ....

Shockoe Slip, on East Cary Street, between Twelfth and Fourteenth Streets, was once a group of tobacco warehouses, but now it is a section of chic boutiques, upscale stores, cafés, and restaurants.

Seventeenth Street Market is a farmer's market on Seventeenth Street between Market and Main Streets. Fresh produce and holiday greens are sold daily to the public at wholesale prices. Nearby are several boutiques and antique shops.

Two other shopping areas are the **Sixth Street Marketplace**, on Sixth Street between Grace and Coliseum Streets, which consists of a restored section with specialty shops, boutiques, and restaurants; and **Carytown**, an eight-block shopping-and-entertainment district next to the Fan District.

RESTAURANTS ....

The first dinner theater in the United States, the **Barksdale Dinner Theater at Hanover Tavern**, in Hanover on U.S. 301 (across from the Hanover County Courthouse), has evening performances Wednesday through Saturday, and Sunday matinees. Dinner is served in lovely candlelit colonial dining rooms. Call 804-537-5817. In Colonial Heights (about 40 minutes north of Richmond), **The Swift Creek Mill Playhouse**, on 17401 Jefferson Davis Highway, is a popular dinner theater located inside a seventeenth-century gristmill. Call 804-748-5203.

La Petite France, at 2108 Maywill Street, is an elegant dining spot with emerald walls, white tablecloths, and eighteenth century–style wall portraits. The French menu has specialties like Dover sole, Châteaubriand, and lobster whiskey. Jacket, tie, and reservations suggested. The restaurant serves lunch and dinner; closed Sunday, Monday, and last two weeks in August. Call 804-353-8729.

Mr. Patrick Henry's Inn, at 2300 East Broad Street, is a restaurant and three-suite inn in the Church Hill Historic District that has been constructed by combining two restored houses. The menu features a variety of cuisines. There's a colonial-style, fireside dining room upstairs where jacket and tie are required, a less-formal tavern downstairs, and outdoor dining in the garden. Historic specialties are roast duckling with plum sauce and crab cakes. Open for lunch and dinner; closed Sundays. Call 804-644-1322.

CASUAL DINING

LeMaire, in the Jefferson Hotel at Franklin and Adams Streets, offers fine dining in elegant surroundings, though dress is casual. Open for lunch and dinner daily, and Sunday brunch. Call 804-788-8000. Also at the Jefferson Hotel is **TJ's Bar and Grille**, offering American continental selections in a lively atmosphere. Call 804-788-8000.

Richbrau Brewing Company, at 1214 East Cary Street in Shockoe Slip, is a brewpub serving homemade beer and great accompaniments like Cajun foods and sausages. Serves lunch and dinner daily. Call 804-644-3018.

Bob's Sports Bar and Grill, at the Holiday Inn on 6531 West Broad Street, serves seafood, sandwiches, and salads in a tavern setting with a sports theme. Call 804-285-9951.

JUST FOR KIDS ....

Richmond Children's Museum, at 740 North Street, is geared toward children ages two to twelve, with a simulated cave, dress-up area, sound stage, TV studio, kids artroom, and a special toddler area. Admission is charged. Call 804-788-4949. The museum also has a recorded message line for current activities. Call 804-643-KIDO. Children will also enjoy the Science Museum of Virginia (See Museums/Science Centers).

Older kids might enjoy the **Softball Hall of Fame**, at 3935 South Crater Road in Petersburg, 20 miles south of Richmond. The museum has clips of famous games and mementos of inducted players. Call 804-733-1005.

GENERAL INFORMATION ....

For information on Richmond, call the Metro Richmond Convention and Visitors Bureau at 800-365-7272. The visitors centers in Richmond are at 1710 Robin Hood Road (at Exit 78 off I-95), at the airport, and in the Sixth Street Marketplace.

For current events information, ask the visitors center for a copy of the *Metropolitan Richmond Visitors Guide*.

Annabel Lee, *Richmond*
Photo courtesy of the Virginia Division of Tourism

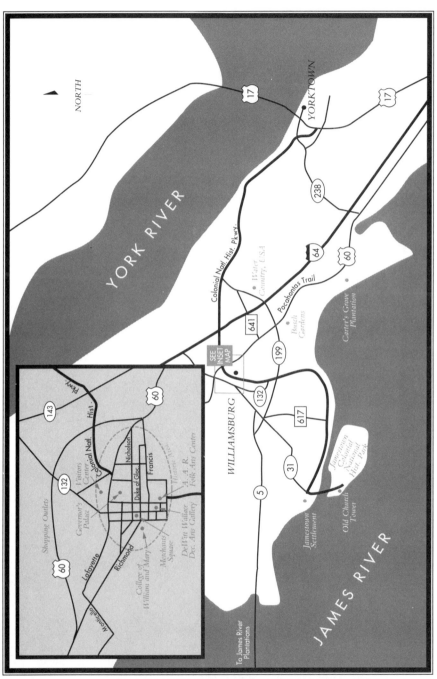

WILLIAMSBURG and the TIDEWATER AREA, VA.

Williamsburg and the Tidewater Area

AREA CODE: 757

(NOTE: SOME NEARBY

AREA CODES REMAIN

804, AS INDICATED)

INTRODUCTION ....

Known for its historic, and other, attractions, as well as for its fabulous golf, Williamsburg is among the top five domestic tourist destinations in America. The area's main attraction is Colonial Williamsburg, an artfully preserved living museum of American history. But Colonial Williamsburg is not the only historically significant site in the area. It joins with the Jamestown Settlement, the first permanent English settlement in the United States, and Yorktown, where the Battle of Yorktown was fought, to form the National Historical Park (also known as the Historic Triangle), a veritable treasure-trove for American history enthusiasts.

The Williamsburg area, once known as Middle Plantation, was built up around a palisade that colonists constructed between the York and James Rivers after an Indian massacre in 1622. Eventually, the area became a bustling English colony and was renamed

Duke of Gloucester Street, Williamsburg
Photo courtesy of the Virginia Division of Tourism

Williamsburg after King William II of England. In 1693, the College of William and Mary was established here, and over the course of the school's illustrious history, it has been attended by Presidents John Tyler, James Monroe, and Thomas Jefferson, and was the birthplace of the Phi Beta Kappa honor society. Williamsburg soon became a social, cultural, and political center in the British colonies, and many of the ideas and movements which led to the fight for independence from England were born in the city. For example, George Mason's "Declaration of Rights," written in Williamsburg, inspired the Bill of Rights to the Constitution of the United States.

The city eventually grew up, and the colonial section was in danger of falling into disrepair. However, in the 1920s, John D. Rockefeller and Dr. W.A.R.

Goodwin, then rector of the Bruton Parish Church (which has the oldest communion silver in the United States), took a personal interest in restoring and preserving the area. The massive project required extensive research and renovation to assure accurate restoration, and it is only recently nearing completion.

The colonial section is now a 173-acre living museum known as Colonial Williamsburg. If you've ever wished you could slip back in time to see what early American life was like, this is as close as it gets. The authenticity has been painstakingly recreated, and the effect is convincing, to say the least.

Yet Colonial Williamsburg and the rest of the Historic Triangle are only a few of the many compelling attractions here. Golfers, in particular, will find the area immensely enjoyable. Williamsburg's verdant meadows, rolling hills, and pleasant climate, along with the spectacular layouts by top designers, are the reasons many people equate Williamsburg with some of the best golf in America. And all visitors can enjoy Williamsburg's unique shopping, museums, and theme parks like Busch Gardens.

Average air temperatures are as follows: January, 37.3; February, 39.9; March, 48.4; April, 57.2; May, 66; June, 73.5; July, 77.5; August 76.5; September, 70.5; October, 59.7; November, 51; December, 41.7. Although peak tourist seasons are in spring and summer, golfers can play year round, weather permitting.

GOLF INFORMATION ....

There's a new golf association in Williamsburg made up of seventeen area hotels and all eleven area golf courses (including the newest courses, Stone House and Royal New Kent, which opened in 1996). This non-profit association will send a catalog with information about accommodations and golf courses, and visitors can then call selected accommodations and arrange golf packages tailored to their needs and interests. For more information, call 800-FOR-GOLF.

FORD'S COLONY COUNTRY CLUB, WILLIAMSBURG (757) 258-4130

Designed by architect Dan Maples, Ford's Colony sports 36 holes (with 18 more holes on the way). The club consists of the par 72 Red/White course, which reaches 6755 yards, and the par 71 Blue/Gold course, which reaches 6789 yards. Both courses wind through rolling, mature hardwood forests dot-

ted with lakes, ponds, and creeks. An excellent, yet difficult, hole on the Red/White course is the 475-yard (452 yards from the whites), par 4 seventh, a hole that Fuzzy Zoeller (a resident of Ford's Colony) says is his favorite. It's a sharp dogleg right that plays up to the crest of a hill, then drops steeply to a forward-sloping green with a monstrous trap on the front right. The number-one handicap hole on the Blue/Gold course is the 538-yard, par 5 fourth hole. The tee shot plays down a narrow, tree-lined fairway. The short way to the green is on the right side, but your approach must then be played over a lake and a massive bunker. The left side is more open, and safer. The green is slightly elevated with a deep bunker on the right that must be avoided.

Carts: Mandatory. *Greens Fees:* $95 weekends, $85 weekdays, high season/18 holes, including cart. *Tee Time Policy:* Can be reserved seven days in advance.

GOLDEN HORSESHOE GOLF CLUB, WILLIAMSBURG (757) 220-7696

Playing the Gold course at Golden Horseshoe is a must if you are in the Williamsburg area. Opened in 1963, it is a classic Robert Trent Jones, Sr., layout. The course has received just about every accolade possible, including being considered among the best resort courses in the country by *Golf* and *Golf Digest.* Moreover, *Golf Digest's Places to Play* gives it a 4½-star rating. It encompasses 125 acres of rolling fairways that stretch over a 5-acre lake, across ravines, and through woodland glens. Par is 71, the tees range from 5159 to 6700 yards, and the rating/slope ranges from 66.2/120 to 73.1/137. As is often the case with the elder Jones's courses, the par

3s are excellent, and were honored as the best par 3s in the South by *Southern Links*. The 190-yard third hole is a beautifully designed hole that plays from the top of a hill down over a pond to a green running diagonally along the pond. Similarly, the 207-yard seventh hole plays from elevated tees over a pond, but this time the green—guarded left, back, and right by sand—is nestled into a hillside 25 feet above the water line. The 185-yard twelfth hole is exquisite. The green, some 40 feet below the tee on the far bank of a lake, is located in front of a hillside covered with mature oak and pine trees. Finally, the 160-yard sixteenth hole plays to a 25,000-square-foot island (obviously water is a major theme on these holes) centered by a bunker-flanked green. Surprisingly, all things considered, the bunkers on this hole do not seem all that uninviting. Golfers should savor playing each of these holes.

As if Golden Horseshoe needed anything else, it also offers the Green course, which was considered among the top five new resort courses by *Golf Digest* in 1992. This layout was designed by Rees Jones (creating the first father-son tandem at a resort) and is set over rugged land with lots of ravines and draws. The course, cut through 105 acres of mature, hardwood forest, reaches over 7100 yards from the championship tees. Like his father, Rees Jones is skilled in creating excellent par 3s, and the Green course has a very fine collection of short holes. For example, the ninth is a 196 yarder that requires a carry over a ravine and a bunker at the front of the green. The 195-yard eleventh hole is a near-perfect par 3 that has been described as dramatic, beauti-

ful, and intimidating. From the elevated tees, the player is faced with a shot that must carry a pond on the front and left sides of an amphitheater green, while at the same time avoiding the four treacherous pot bunkers at the rear and right of the green.

Carts: Generally mandatory (some exceptions in winter). *Greens Fees:* $95 for guests of a Colonial Williamsburg hotel; for others, $125 gold course, $115 Green course, in high season/18 holes, including cart. *Tee Time Policy:* Hotel guests can book times when making hotel reservation; others can book seven days in advance.

KINGSMILL RESORT, WILLIAMSBURG (757) 253-3906

Kingsmill offers three excellent courses, which may be among the most historic courses in America. For example, during the building of the River course, a number of Native American and Colonial archaeological sites were discovered. Additionally, the course is set among plantation house ruins, a tribal village site, and colonial artillery emplacements that once defended the James River. The River course, opened in 1975 and designed by Pete Dye, is the home of the PGA Tour's Michelob Classic. The course ranges from 4606 to almost 6800 yards, with a rating/slope ranging from 67.4/109 to 73.3/137. True to form, Dye rewards accuracy and good shotmaking. The course is set among pure Virginia terrain, with rolling hills, thick woods, creeks, ponds, and lakes. The famous, 177-yard seventeenth, located on the James River, is beautiful and terrifying, all at the same time. Anything to the right is history (sorry, couldn't help it).

The Plantation course, opened in 1986 and designed by Arnold Palmer and Ed Seay, is a little less demanding than the River course. On this 6605-yard course (tees begin at 4880 yards), driving the ball straight is less important than hitting good approaches to the medium-to-small, undulating greens.

The Woods course, opened in 1995, is a Tom Clark/Curtis Strange design that was considered among the top ten new public courses by *Golf*. With four sets of tees, the longest reaching 6784 yards, this track is hand-cut through towering oak and beech trees. The layout works its way around ravines, over and along hilltops, and through lovely lakes and wetlands. The number-one handicap hole is the 542-yard, par 5 fifth—a double dogleg. Its huge green is protected by a massive wasteland that must be played over if you want to reach the green in two. The 195-yard, par 3 twelfth and the 388-yard fifteenth share a huge double green with a bunker in the middle (which is pretty neat).

Carts: Mandatory. *Greens Fees:* $110 non-guests, $80-$90 for resort guests, in high season/18 holes. *Tee Time Policy:* Resort guests can book at time room reservation is made; others should call a day in advance.

TIDES INN (804) 438-5501 AND TIDES LODGE (804) 438-6200, IRVINGTON

Golden Eagle at Tides Inn is a 6963-yard (tees start at 5384 yards) course designed by George Cobb and opened in 1976. It consistently has been ranked among the top courses in Virginia, and it hosted the 1987 and 1991 state amateur championships. The course, which meanders around Lake Irvington, is located on gently rolling and densely wooded terrain featuring oaks, pines, cedars, and dogwoods. The number-one handicap hole is the par 4 fifth, a dogleg left that can reach 463 yards. It is bordered on the left side by the lake. An aggressive tee shot can shorten the hole significantly, which is awfully helpful because the left side of the green is on the bank of the lake, while the right side is protected by two giant traps.

The Tartan Course at Tides Lodge is a par 72 course that offers tees ranging from 5121 to 6586 yards. The front nine was designed in 1959 by Sir Guy Campbell, then resident architect of St. Andrews Royal and Ancient. George Cobb completed the back nine in 1968. The course, which winds over and along historic Carter Creek, is cut through towering Virginia pines, oaks, dogwoods, azaleas, and mountain laurels.

Carts: Not required. *Greens Fees:* At Tides Inn, $65 for non-guests, $38 for guests, in high season; At Tides Lodge, $45 for non-guests, $30 hotel guests, in high season/18 holes. *Tee Time Policy:* At Tides Inn, guests can reserve when making room reservation, non-guests should call in advance. At Tides Lodge, guests can reserve when making room reservation; non-guests should call seven days in advance.

OTHER EXCELLENT AREA COURSES:

The Colonial Golf Course, James City County (757-566-1600), was designed by Lester George with the help of PGA touring pro Robert Wrenn. This course rambles over 210 acres of hardwoods, holly trees, and mountain laurel. **Williamsburg National**,

Williamsburg (757-258-9642 or 800-826-5732), is a 6928-yard, par 72 championship course opened in the summer of 1995. It was designed by Jack Nicklaus Associates and Jim Lipe.

ATTRACTIONS ....

TOURS

Walking Tours

Interpre-Tours has guided tours, from mainstream historic tours to theme tours including a History Mystery Evening, Myths and Legends of Williamsburg tour, and Hauntings of Old Town tour. Call 800-486-9624. **Maximum Guided Tours, Inc.**, is another company offering a guided walking tour, called the "Ghosts of Williamsburg" tour. Call 757-253-2094.

Motorized Tours

Tidewater Touring, Inc., has local sightseeing tours and day-trips to Washington, D.C., Norfolk, and other cities. This company also offers boat tours on the James River. Call 757-872-0897.

Carriage Tours

Carriage tours can be reserved (weather permitting) for an additional charge (less for visitors who have paid admission to Colonial Williamsburg). Make reservations in person on the day you wish to ride at the Lumber House or the Colonial Williamsburg Visitors Center.

Air Tours

Historic Air Tours flies over plantations, battlefields, naval shipyards, and sites within the Historic Triangle. For information, call 757-253-8185.

HISTORIC PLACES

Colonial Williamsburg is a restored community that once was the largest city in Britain's thirteen colonies. The streets, homes, taverns, and buildings have been restored or rebuilt with painstaking historical accuracy. Visitors can also see restored gardens, including one with colonial lawn games. The site includes more than 500 buildings, homes, and taverns, about 90 of which are completely restored and can be toured. In this historical time warp, live actors play the parts of colonial men, women, and children, as well as historic characters like Thomas Jefferson and Jefferson's slave, Jupiter. Many of the actors even emulate colonial speech. There are also craftsmen who demonstrate more than thirty colonial trades and crafts, from silversmithing and wig-making to weaving and pottery. One outstanding site, with its own separate admission charge, is the elegant Governor's Mansion and Gardens, at the north end of Palace Green. Visitors don't need tickets to walk around the historic area, but they do to enter restored buildings or ride the tram. Tickets, maps of the historic area, and additional information are available at the Colonial Williamsburg Visitors Center at VA 132 and Colonial National Historic Parkway. Admission is charged. Call 757-220-7645 or 800-HISTORY.

Yorktown Battlefield, 14 miles southeast of Williamsburg on the Colonial National Historic Parkway, is where America defeated the British in October of 1781, thus securing United

States' independence from the British crown. The site includes a road tour showing Washington's headquarters, the sites of major events during the battle, Surrender Field, and the Moore House, where the final surrender was negotiated. Nelson House (home of a signer of the Declaration of Independence) is also here, as is a monument to the victory. Open daily. Admission is free. 757-898-3400.

The Yorktown Victory Center, at VA 238 and Colonial National Historic Parkway, adjacent to the battlefield, is a museum about the Revolutionary War. The vivid displays recount the war through the eyes of well-known heroes and everyday people. Exhibits include a reconstructed eighteenth-century farm and a Continental Army encampment. Open daily. Admission is charged. Call 757-887-1776.

Jamestown Settlement, at VA 31 and the Colonial National Historic Parkway, is a reconstructed living museum, built in 1957, to commemorate the 300-year anniversary of Jamestown, America's first permanent English settlement. Among the fascinating sites are three life-size replicas of the ships that landed here in 1607, a fort and Indian village where costumed actors reenact daily life in the settlement, and a museum. Open daily. Admission is charged. Call 757-253-4838.

The College of William and Mary, located in Williamsburg's historic district on the west end of Duke of Gloucester Street, was founded in 1693, making it second only to Harvard among the nation's oldest colleges. The campus boasts lovely early architecture, including a building by the English architect, Christopher Wren,

who designed St. Paul's Cathedral in London.

MUSEUMS/SCIENCE CENTERS

The DeWitt Wallace Decorative Arts Gallery, which adjoins the Public Hospital in Colonial Williamsburg, exhibits British and American decorative arts from the seventeenth through the nineteenth centuries. Admission is charged. Call 757-229-7724.

Watermen's Museum, at 309 Water Street in Yorktown, documents the lives of mariners of the Chesapeake Bay and the surrounding rivers. On display are ship models, paintings, life-like depictions, photographs, and artifacts, including some outdoor exhibits demonstrating this ancient, though nearly extinct, occupation. Open April through mid-December. Admission is charged. Call 757-887-2641.

America's Railroads on Parade, at 1915 Pocahontas Trail (in the Village Shops of Kingsmill), encompasses 4,000 square feet and displays more than forty-five trains using computerized lighting, special effects, and animation. Open daily. Admission is charged. Call 757-220-TRAK.

CULTURAL OFFERINGS

Abby Aldrich Rockefeller Folk Art Center, on York Street, a half-block from the Capitol, has one of the finest collections of American Folk Art in the United States. Admission is charged. Call 757-220-7698.

Kingsmill Art Studio, off U.S. 60 near Busch Gardens, has paintings, prints, glasswork, and other fine arts for display and for sale. Call 757-220-8392.

Plays and comedies from the

eighteenth century and historical re-enactments, such as *Cry Witch!*, are performed in Colonial Williamsburg throughout the year by costumed professional players. Admission is charged. For a schedule of performances, contact the Colonial Williamsburg Foundation at 800-HISTORY.

The Old Dominion Opry, at 3012 Richmond Road in Williamsburg, has a variety of live entertainment with a southern flare. Shows start at 8:00 P.M., Monday through Saturday. Closed early January. Admission is charged. Call 757-564-0200.

RECREATION

Busch Gardens Williamsburg is 3 miles from Colonial Williamsburg on U.S. 60. This family oriented theme park has an Old World European atmosphere, with simulated seventeenth-century villages from Germany, Scotland, England, France, and other countries. There are more than thirty rides, including several in which you'll get wet. Thrill-seeker types will enjoy the "Drachen Fire" roller-coaster and the new "Escape from Pompeii," which simulates the eruption of Mount Vesuvius and the resulting ruins of Pompeii. There are also milder kiddie-rides and a petting zoo. A monorail and skyride take visitors around the park. There's a variety of entertainment, such as a 3-D theater with a movie called *Haunts of the Olde Country* and live concerts. Admission is charged. Visitors can take self-guided tours of the on-site Anheuser-Busch Hospitality Center and sample their famed brau (theme-park tickets aren't necessary to tour the hospitality center). For information on Busch Gardens Williamsburg, call 757-253-3350.

Water Country USA, at Exit 242B off I-64, 3 miles east of Williamsburg, is a water park with 40 acres of water rides, pools, slides, designated areas for kids of varying ages, and entertainment. Open Memorial Day through Labor Day. Admission is charged. Call 757-229-9300.

Tennis courts are available at several area hotels. Contact the hotel reservation service or the Colonial Williamsburg Area Convention and Visitors Bureau at 757-253-0192 or 800-368-6511.

For boating, fishing, hiking, and picnicking, there is **York River State Park**, northwest of Williamsburg on VA 606E off VA 607 (call 757-566-3036).

Family Funland, 801 Merrimac Trail at the James York Plaza, is an indoor recreation center with miniature-golf, laser tag, an arcade, and a playground. Call 757-220-1400. **Kidsburg**, a playground in MidCounty Park on Ironbound Road in James City County, has child-designed gym equipment for climbing. For information, call the James City County Recreation Department at 757-565-6920.

SEASONAL EVENTS

Several seasonal events take place at Colonial Williamsburg each year. **Colonial Weekends** are offered from January through March, featuring banquets, lectures, and tours centered around a certain theme. February brings an **Antiques Forum** to Colonial Williamsburg, as well as a celebration of Washington's birthday later in the month. May 15 is the **Prelude to Independence**, which commemorates the day in 1775 when the Virginia Convention proposed American Independence. For informa-

Ships of Jamestown Settlement
Photo courtesy of the Virginia Division of Tourism

tion, call 757-220-7645. From mid-March to October, weekly costumed military drills take place on the Market Square Green. November brings a four-day Thanksgiving celebration, and December brings a wealth of Christmas celebrations. For information on these and other events, contact Colonial Williamsburg Visitors Center at 757-220-7645, or contact the Colonial Williamsburg Foundation at 800-HIS-TORY.

Nearby Yorktown celebrates the anniversary of the **Surrender at Yorktown** in October. For information, call the Yorktown Battlefield at 757-898-3400 and the Yorktown Victory Center at 757-887-1776.

In early November at Berkeley Plan-

tation (See Side Trips), interpreters re-enact what some people claim was the actual first Thanksgiving—a celebration that occurred here some three years prior to the Thanksgiving celebration at Plymouth. Admission is charged. Call 804-829-6108.

Jamestown Settlement also offers special Christmas events during December. For information, call 757-229-1607.

ACCOMMODATIONS ....

The Williamsburg Hotel and Motel Association is a free service that can help you select and arrange accommodations at over seventy area hotels and arrange golf packages. For information, call 800-446-9244.

EXPENSIVE

Kingsmill Resort, at 1010 Kingsmill Road, is one of America's finest golf resorts. This Colonial-style resort hotel has extensive exercise facilities, tennis courts, lawn games, a beauty salon, babysitting service, supervised children's programs, and more. Call 757-253-1703 or 800-832-5665.

Williamsburg Inn, on Francis Street, is a splendid hotel in the historic district. Rooms have fireplaces, balconies, and Regency-style furnishings. Golfers will enjoy the championship 9-hole course and the two 18-hole courses. Non-golfers will appreciate the exercise facilities, lawn games, pools, tennis, children's program in summer, and the concierge service. The inn offers rooms in the hotel or in colonial houses and taverns. Call 757-220-1000 or 800-447-8679.

MODERATE

Williamsburg Hospitality House, at 415 Richmond Road, has a concierge service, a heated pool, golf privileges, and a lounge with entertainment and dancing. Call 757-229-4020 or 800-932-9192.

Williamsburg Woodlands, located off I-64, behind the Colonial Williamsburg Visitors Center, is a family-oriented hotel with a playground, two pools, a wading pool, children's summer program, babysitting services, miniature-golf, and lawn games. Call 757-229-1000 or 800-447-8679.

INEXPENSIVE

Captain John Smith Motor Lodge, at 2225 Richmond Road, is located near popular area attractions. Rooms are equipped with microwaves, refrigerators, and coffeemakers. Call 757-220-0710 or 800-933-6788.

Colonial America Inn, at 216 Parkway Drive, is a comfortable motel that's undergone recent renovations. Aside from being only three blocks from the historic district, this family-oriented motel has a picnic area and other amenities. Call 757-253-6450 or 800-296-7829.

Best Western has several motels in Williamsburg, some next to the historic district and others a reasonable drive away. All offer comfortable, reasonably priced lodgings, and most offer a playground, pool, and children's pool. For information, call 800-446-9228.

Colonial militia drill, Williamsburg

Photo courtesy of the Virginia Division of Tourism

Golf Vacations Even Non-Golfers Will Enjoy

SHOPPING

There are a series of outlet malls located along U.S. 60, a short drive west from Williamsburg. These include: the **Pottery Outlet Shops**, with crafts, clothing, and more (call 757-564-3326); the **Berkeley Commons Outlet Center**, with several designer-name stores (call 757-565-0702); the **Williamsburg Outlet Mall**, with over fifty-five stores (call 757-565-3378); and the **Lenox Outlet** (call 757-565-0800).

Williamsburg House of Crafts, at 5965 Richmond Road, features over 200 craftsmen exhibiting and selling handmade crafts. Call 757-564-0308. For art, check out the **Kingsmill Art Studio** (See Cultural Offerings).

For handmade porcelain dolls, doll and dollhouse accessories, and stuffed animals, check out the **Williamsburg Doll Factory**, at 7441 Richmond Road. You can also watch the dolls being made. Call 757-564-9703.

Another place to shop and watch craftspeople at work is the **Williamsburg Soap and Candle Factory**, on U.S. 60, which has a film and live demonstrations. Call 757-564-3354.

Merchants Square, next to the Colonial Williamsburg area, has many stores and restaurants, including shops with College of William and Mary merchandise, famous Colonial Williamsburg Christmas ornaments, sportswear with the Colonial Williamsburg logo, and colonial-style furniture and decorative items.

For colonial foods and kitchen items, stop in the **M. DuBois Grocer's Shop**, where you can find Sally Lunn cake mix, King's Arms Tavern root beer, spices, jellies, and more. The shop is located on Duke of Gloucester Street next to the Colonial Post Office. Call 757-229-1000.

If you like shopping for baskets or antiques, a trip to the nearby town of **Toano**, located 7 miles west of Williamsburg on U.S. 60, may be worth your while. Here you'll find **Basketville of Williamsburg**, with baskets, dried flower arrangements and other decorative items (call 757-566-8420), and the **Colonial Antique Center**, offering, among other things, porcelain, glassware, dolls, furniture, clocks, and a clock-repair service (call 757-229-2082).

RESTAURANTS

FINE DINING

Bray Dining Room, in the Kingsmill Resort at 1010 Kingsmill Road, offers a panoramic view of the James River. Southern and European selections are a specialty, as are their Sunday brunch and Friday evening seafood buffets. Reservations recommended. Call 757-253-3900.

Regency Room, in the Williamsburg Inn on Francis Street, serves breakfast, lunch, dinner, and Sunday brunch. Their most noted dishes are the rack of lamb, the snapper, and veal stuffed with crab meat. There's also an outdoor patio. Jacket required. Call 757-229-1000.

CASUAL DINING

Visitors to the historic area should try at least one colonial tavern, as they serve authentic colonial and regional specialties. One suggestion is **Christiana Campbell's Tavern**, located on Waller Street, which was a favorite place of George Washington. Another great choice is the **King's Arms Tavern**, on Duke of Gloucester Street, which is an eighteenth-century tavern featuring selections like filet mignon stuffed with oysters, Virginia ham, colonial game pie, and peanut soup. **Chownings Tavern**, in the Williamsburg Inn on Francis Street, has colonial "Gambols" (games, music, and entertainment by costumed actors) in the Tap Room starting at 9 P.M. Reservations recommended. For information on all three taverns, call 757-229-2141 or 800-828-3767.

Aberdeen Barn, at 1601 Richmond Road, has won several awards, including being selected the most outstanding steakhouse in Virginia. The prime rib and seafood are also excellent. Call 757-229-6661.

The Jefferson Inn, at 1453 Richmond Road, is a family owned restaurant that has been in operation since the 1950s. They serve continental selections, Italian dishes, seafood, steak, and southern traditional favorites. Dinner is served daily. Call 757-229-2296.

JUST FOR KIDS ....

This is where kids will have so much fun they won't even realize they're learning. They'll especially enjoy the costumed children and teen interpreters at Colonial Williamsburg, who perform as free and slave children going about typical daily chores. These child interpreters can be found mainly at the Geddy House, the Powell House, and the Wetherburn's Tavern. Children will also love playing colonial lawn games, such as quoits (similar to horseshoes) and hoops, at **Palace Green** and on Market Square. Colonial Williams-

burg also schedules special tours and events for children. For information, call 800-HISTORY.

Several resorts have children's activities, especially in summer, including Kingsmill Resort, Williamsburg Woodlands, Williamsburg Inn, and Governor's Inn (which shares facilities with Williamsburg Woodlands), though the programs are generally not given to children under age five. For information on these and other programs, call the hotel and motel reservation service at 800-446-9244.

SIDE TRIPS ....

Though part of Colonial Williamsburg, **Carter's Grove Plantation** is 8 miles southeast of town on U.S 60. It encompasses the Winthrop Rockefeller Archeology Museum, an early eighteenth-century slave quarter, Wolstenholme Town (a partially reconstructed plantation colony), and a 1755 riverfront mansion restored to its 1930s appearance. Open Tuesday through Sunday from mid-March through December. Admission is charged.

There are several colonial and antebellum plantations on the James River near Charles City, about 25 miles west of Williamsburg on VA 5. The following are open to the public (all charge admission):

Berkeley Plantation, at 12602 Harrison Landing Road in Charles City, was the location of a Thanksgiving celebration held in 1619. Whether this event, or the one in Plymouth in 1621, was the true first Thanksgiving is, to some, a matter of historical debate. The plantation house is where

Benjamin Harrison, a Virginia governor and signer of the Declaration of Independence, was born. It's also where the bugle tune "Taps" was composed. Visitors should be sure to check out the lovely terraced gardens. Open daily. Call 804-829-6018.

Sherwood Forest Plantation, on VA 5, was the home of President John Tyler. The house, furnished with original family possessions, has America's longest frame, spanning 300 feet. Call 804-829-5377.

Shirley Plantation, on VA 5, was settled in 1613 and is still home to the Hill-Carter family. The eighteenth-century mansion on the premises has an amazing hanging staircase, as well as antique furnishings. Open daily. Call 804-829-5121.

Evelynton Plantation, on VA 5, was formerly part of the Westover Plantation, but was acquired in 1847 by the family of Edmund Ruffin, who fired the first shot in the Civil War. Features include antiques and formal gardens. Call 757-473-5075.

GENERAL INFORMATION ....

Contact the Colonial Williamsburg Area Convention and Visitors Bureau at 757-253-0192 or 800-368-6511, or contact the Colonial Williamsburg Foundation at 800-HISTORY. You can contact the Colonial Williamsburg Visitors Center at 804-220-7645. The Colonial Williamsburg Foundation will provide you with a copy of the *Colonial Williamsburg Vacation Planner*. The Williamsburg Motel and Hotel Reservation service provides a glossy publication called *Williamsburg Great Entertainer Magazine*. To receive a copy, call 800-446-9244.

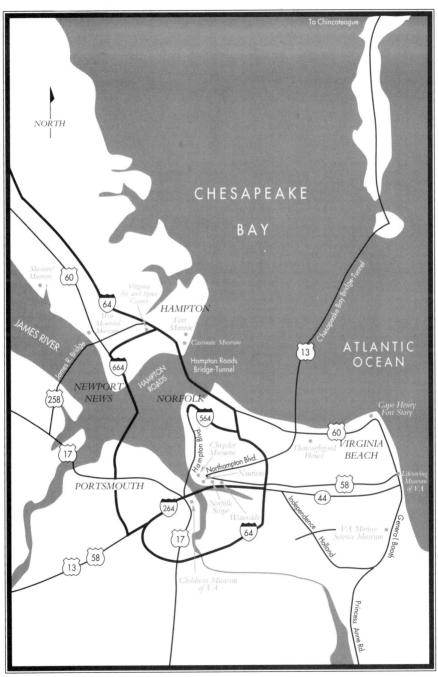

NORFOLK, VIRGINIA BEACH, HAMPTON, and NEWPORT NEWS, VA.

Norfolk, Virginia Beach, Hampton, and Newport News

INTRODUCTION

The Port of Hampton Roads is made up of four separate cities: Hampton and Newport News on the north side of the James River, and Norfolk and Portsmouth (sister cities connected by a bridge-tunnel) on the south side. Situated where the James River meets the Chesapeake Bay, Hampton Roads' strategic location has encouraged the arrival of explorers, settlers, merchants, and others to its shores over the past three centuries, and has assured the region's prestige in military and maritime history.

In 1607, English colonists rounded Cape Henry, sailed past what would become Hampton Roads, and continued on up the river to establish Jamestown. But the area would not be passed over for very long. During the colonial era, Hampton Roads became an important port that was crucial for the delivery of supplies during both times of peace and war. However, during the Revolutionary and Civil Wars,

Norfolk and the nearby towns suffered many losses (Norfolk fell to Union forces in 1862). The area has also suffered through a variety of natural disasters, including fires and hurricanes. Despite these odds, the region has always bounced back. Today, Norfolk has the world's largest naval base and boasts three universities; Hampton is the location of important space and military development, and Newport News has the world's largest privately owned shipyard. Virginia Beach has grown rapidly over the last few decades and is now the state's most populous city.

While several museums and historic sites in the area attract large numbers of tourists, perhaps the major draw here is the 25 miles of fabulous beaches found at Virginia Beach, not to mention the great golf, hunting, and fishing there. Additionally, the area is only a short drive from the National Historical Park (See Williamsburg and the Tidewater Area chapter), making the Virginia Beach and Williamsburg areas a great vacation combination for golfers, non-golfers, and their families. While the golf near Virginia Beach is less about quantity than quality, the championship courses listed below are certain to keep golfers happy. And, while the beaches here attract many college students, Virginia Beach offers, as its motto says, "good, clean fun," including several beaches that are family oriented.

The normal monthly temperatures, as measured in Norfolk, are: January, 39.1; February, 41; March, 48.6; April, 57; May, 66.1; June, 74.1; July, 78.2; August, 77.2; September, 71.9; October, 61.2; November, 52.5; December, 43.8. The high seasons are during spring and summer.

GOLF INFORMATION ....

HELL'S POINT GOLF CLUB, VIRGINIA BEACH (757) 721-3400

Hell's Point is a Rees Jones, par 72 layout that opened in 1982. It was chosen as one of the best new courses by *Golf Digest*, and was considered one of the best-designed courses in 1984 and 1987 by the American Society of Golf Course Architects. Located only a mile from the ocean, the course winds its way through pine and hardwood forests. It features lakes, marshes, canals, and over sixty sculptured bunkers (a Rees Jones hallmark). The four sets of tees measure from 5003 to almost 7000 yards, with a rating/slope ranging from 71.2/116 to 73.3/130, making it possible for a player to choose his or her comfort (or challenge) zone. Not only will you find Hell's Point to be a fine course, its pro shop was named one of America's hundred best by *Golf Digest* in 1988 for its quality service and merchandise.

Carts: Not required. *Greens Fees:* $26-$49/18 holes, including cart. *Tee Time Policy:* Non-members can call up to a week in advance (earlier if staying at Ramada Plaza Resort).

KILN CREEK GOLF AND COUNTRY CLUB, NEWPORT NEWS (757) 988-3220

This 27-hole layout, consisting of an 18-hole course and a 9-hole course, opened in 1989 to rave reviews and ranked in the top five courses in Virginia. The additional 9 holes opened in 1996. Kiln Creek is a Tom Clark design and its white tees, only 6181 yards, and the blue tees, reaching 6630 yards, each have high course slopes of 133 and 137, respectively, with the course rating on the blue tees reaching almost 74. The course is well bunkered, to say the least (it has 105 bunkers), so bring your sand game. The fairways are nicely maintained, and the greens are quick and in good condition. The mature landscaping and natural lakes make this course challenging, fun, and beautiful. The 416-yard, par 4 eighth hole has the notoriety of consistently being ranked as one of the most difficult and picturesque holes in the state. The tee shot must somehow find a fairway bordered on the left with a series of traps and on the right with a 50-yard bunker and water. The approach is to a small green surrounded by three traps.

Carts: Mandatory. *Greens Fees:* $64 Monday-Thursday, $74 Friday-Sunday, in high season/18 holes, including cart. *Tee Time Policy:* Advance reservation is required; non-members can book seven days in advance.

OTHER EXCELLENT AREA COURSES:

Newport News Golf Club (formerly Deer Run), Newport News (757-886-7925), offers 36 holes. The Deer Run Course is long at over 7000 yards from the back tees and 6757 from the white tees. **Sleepy Hole Golf Course**, Suffolk (757-538-4100), is a 1972, Russell Breeden course that formerly hosted the LPGA Crestar Classic.

ATTRACTIONS ....

TOURS

Trolley Tours
The Norfolk Trolley operates from May through September along a down-town route that stops at major points of interest. Passengers can get on and off as often as they wish throughout the day. Call 757-627-2896. Portsmouth's trolley system, the **Olde Town Trolley Tour**, leaves from the city visitors center between noon and 4 P.M. daily from May through September. Call 757-393-5111.

Driving Tours
This region has self-guided driving tours with road markers posted at historic sites. Maps of routes are available from the area visitors centers. Call 757-437-4882 or 800-822-3224 for the Virginia Beach tour; call 757-441-5266 for the Norfolk tour; and call 757-727-1102 for the Hampton Circle Tour of Hampton.

Boat Tours
Harbor Cruises, at Waterman's Wharf in Newport News, currently offers the only cruise covering the entire Hampton Roads area. Cruises run seasonally. Call 757-245-1533. **The Discovery Cruise** takes passengers on sightseeing tours of Virginia Beach's bay. Call 757-422-2900. **Wharton's Tours** offers boat tours of the area on different routes, including ones along Hampton Harbor, the James River, and other local waterways. Call 757-245-1533. *The Carrie B* is a reproduction of a Mississippi riverboat that gives narrated, historic Civil War tours. Call 757-393-4735. *The Spirit of Norfolk* has sightseeing, dinner, and lunch cruises (call 757-627-7771), and **American Rover Sailing** tours gives narrated schooner rides focusing on local military and maritime events (call 757-627-7245). *The Miss Hampton II* provides

sightseeing tours around Hampton Roads and includes a stop at Fort Wool. Tours depart from the dock next to the Hampton Visitors Center. Call 757-727-1102 or 800-800-2202.

HISTORIC PLACES

The restored **St. Paul's Church and Graveyard** (circa 1739), at St. Paul's Boulevard and City Hall Avenue in Norfolk, is the lone surviving structure from a cannonball attack on the city in 1776. Open Tuesday through Friday. Donation suggested. Call 757-627-4353.

The Moses Myers Home, at 331 Bank Street in Norfolk, was built in 1792 by Moses Myers, the first permanent resident of the city. Most of the furnishings are original family possessions, including a collection of silver Kaddish cups and fine China. Open daily except Monday (closed Sundays from January through March). Hours vary seasonally. Admission is charged. Tickets also allow access to the Willoughby-Baylor and Adam Thoroughgood Houses. Call 757-664-6283.

The Georgian- and Federal-style **Willoughby-Baylor House,** at 601 East Freemason Street in Norfolk, was built in 1734 by Captain William Willoughby. Its contents, though not originals, match an inventory taken of the captain's estate. The grounds also feature a garden. Open Tuesday through Saturday by appointment. Admission is charged. Call 757-664-6283.

The four-room **Adam Thoroughgood House**, at 1636 Parish Road in Virginia Beach, was built around 1680, some forty years after its namesake had died (though he had owned the land). Open Tuesday through Saturday year round; also open Sunday from April through December. Admission is charged. Call 757-664-6283.

Francis Land House and Gardens, at 3131 Virginia Beach Boulevard in Virginia Beach, was built by a wealthy, eighteenth-century Dutch family. The home contains a collection of period furnishings. Open daily except Monday. Admission is charged. Call 757-431-4000.

The moat-enclosed **Fort Monroe**, on U.S. 258 in Hampton, is the largest stone fort in the United States. It was completed in 1834. The adjoining **Casemate Museum** includes a wall chamber where Jefferson Davis and others were imprisoned during and after the Civil War. On display are wartime memorabilia, from uniforms to weapons. Open daily. Admission is free. Call 757-727-3391.

The Douglas MacArthur Memorial is at Bank Street and City Hall Avenue in Norfolk. This former city hall is MacArthur's burial site. The buildings here house a museum and archives on the life and military accomplishments of this five-star general. Open daily. Admission is free. Call 757-441-2965.

The Norfolk Naval Base and Naval Air Station, at Hampton Boulevard and I-564 in Norfolk, is the world's largest naval installation. The public can tour some naval ships and take bus tours of the base. For days, times, and departure points, contact the base's tour and information office at 9809 Hampton Road. Admission is charged. Call 757-444-7955.

MUSEUMS/SCIENCE CENTERS

The Mariners' Museum, at 100

Museum Drive in Newport News, has an extensive collection of boats, including over fifty full-scale models (from bark canoes to submarines) and miniature models (some detailed enough to require a magnifying glass). There are also ships in bottles, scrimshaw, and other relics of maritime life in the Chesapeake Bay area. Open daily. Admission is charged. Call 757-595-0368.

The War Memorial Museum of Virginia, at 9285 Warwick Boulevard in Huntington Park, Newport News, houses over 60,000 military artifacts, dating from the Revolutionary War through Desert Storm. There are special women's and African-American exhibits, and a Vietnam War Memorial is on the grounds. Open daily. Admission is charged. Call 757-247-8523.

The United States Army Transportation Museum is in Fort Eustis, about 10 miles west of Newport News off I-64. Visitors can take self-guided driving tours of the fort, and the museum depicts military transportation from the Revolutionary War through the present. Open daily. Admission is free. Call 757-878-1182.

Virginia Air and Space Center, at 600 Settlers Landing Road, off I-64 on the waterfront in downtown Hampton, has an IMAX theater and houses more than a hundred exciting aeronautic and space exhibits, ranging from real launch capsules to moon rocks. The Virginia Air and Space Center is also the official visitors center for the NASA Langley Research Center. **The Hampton Roads History Center**, also located at the Virginia Air and

Virginia Air and Space Center, Hampton
Photo courtesy of the Virginia Division of Tourism

Norfolk, Virginia Beach, Hampton, and Newport News, VA

Space Center, has artifacts relating to local events like the capture and beheading of the pirate Blackbeard and the Civil War battle of Hampton Roads. Open daily. Admission charged for both attractions. Call 800-296-0800.

Hermitage Foundation Museum, at 7637 North Shore Road in Norfolk, is housed in a seventeenth-century, Tudor-style home. The museum focuses on oriental art, from paintings to ivories to a large marble Buddha, yet there are pieces, mainly decorative arts, from all over the world. Open daily. Admission is charged. Call 757-423-2052.

The Chrysler Museum, at 245 West Olney Road in Norfolk, is among the top art museums in the United States. Its collection includes paintings from European masters like Picasso, Renoir, and Rubens, and American greats like Pollack. The decorative arts collection contains Tiffany glass and porcelains. Open daily. Donation suggested. Call 757-664-6200.

Nauticus, the National Maritime Center, at One Waterside Drive in Norfolk, is a technologically advanced interactive museum. The more than seventy marine-related exhibits are spread on three decks. Examples of exhibits include a replica of a drilling rig, a virtual reality underwater voyage, and a shipbuilding exhibit where you help design a ship. The wide-screen theater shows an Academy Award–nominated documentary film titled *The Living Sea*. Open daily. Admission is charged. Call 757-664-1000.

Portsmouth Naval Shipyard Museum, at 2 High Street, is a naval history museum on the waterfront in Portsmouth. The museum's exhibits include a Coast Guard ship kids can climb on and explore. Open daily except Monday. Admission is charged. Call 757-393-8591.

Lifesaving Museum of Virginia, at Twenty-fourth Street and Atlantic Avenue in Virginia Beach, is inside a 1903 lifesaving station. The museum contains equipment used for lifesaving and artifacts from local shipwrecks and related sea battles. Closed Mondays from October through Memorial Day. Admission is charged. Call 757-422-1587.

The Virginia Living Museum, at 534 J. Clyde Morris Boulevard in Newport News, has native wildlife, from birds to bobcats, in their natural habitats. There's also an aquarium, botanical garden, planetarium, and observatory. Open daily (hours vary seasonally). Admission is charged. Call 757-595-1900.

Association for Research and Enlightenment, at Sixty-seventh and Atlantic Avenue in Virginia Beach, is where psychic Edgar Cayce researches psychic phenomena. The facility has exhibits, movies, and an ESP testing machine. Open daily. Admission is free. Call 800-333-4499.

Virginia Marine Science Museum, at 717 General Booth Boulevard in Virginia Beach, is an interactive museum with an IMAX theater and over 200 sea-related exhibits, including a simulated underwater submarine, computerized weather predictor, and a touch tank. Open daily except Sunday. Admission is charged. Call 757-425-FISH (3474).

CULTURAL OFFERINGS

The Virginia Opera, which has played throughout the United States and abroad, gives performances from

October through March. Call 757-623-1223. **The Virginia Symphony** performs classical and pops concerts, mainly in the Chrysler Hall, at 201 East Brambleton Street, next to the Norfolk Scope. Call 757-623-2310. **The Virginia Stage Company** performs a variety of productions. Call 757-627-1234.

The Wells Theater in Norfolk, at 118 Tazewell Street, (call 757-441-2764), and **Chrysler Hall**, at 201 East Brambleton Street (call 757-441-2161), host plays, symphonic concerts, and more. **Hampton Coliseum**, at 1000 Coliseum Drive in Hampton, has music concerts ranging from rap to country to rock. Call 757-838-4203. Another popular concert place is the **Norfolk Scope**, at 1 Scope Plaza in Norfolk. Call 757-441-2161.

In Virginia Beach, the **Center for the Arts**, at 2200 Park Avenue, displays artworks and hosts a variety of performing arts. Open daily except Monday. Call 757-425-0000.

Peninsula Fine Arts Center, at 101 Museum Drive (near the Mariners' Museum) in Newport News, displays works by regional and national artists and hosts special arts events. Open daily except Monday. Donation suggested. Call 757-596-8175.

RECREATION

Scuba diving is popular here. For gear, lessons, and guided expeditions in Virginia Beach, try **Lynnhaven Dive Center.** Call 757-481-7949. For windsurfing rentals and lessons, try **Chick's Beach Sailing Center.** Call 757-460-2238.

Fishermen can head for the **James River Fishing Pier** in Newport News,

which is open year round, though hours are limited offseason. Call 757-247-0364. For charter fishing, contact **Chesapeake Charter Service** in Hampton. Call 757-723-0998.

As for spectator sports, **Langley Raceway**, at 3165 North Armistead Avenue in Hampton, has stock-car racing from March to October. Call 757-865-1992. The **Norfolk Tides** are a AAA minor-league baseball team affiliated with the New York Mets. They play at Harbor Park, on 150 Park Avenue in Norfolk, from April through September. Call 757-461-5600. The **Peninsula Poseidons** are a semi-professional football team that can be seen at Todd Stadium, located at 12465 Warwick Boulevard in Newport News. Call 757-873-1113. **Hampton Roads Admirals** play hockey in the Norfolk Scope, at 1 Scope Plaza, from October through March. Call 757-640-1212.

The Norfolk Botanical Gardens are located next to the airport on Azalea Garden Road. The 175-acre facility has several gardens, from rose gardens, to colonial, ethnic, international, and fragrance gardens. There's a visitors center, and narrated boat and train rides run seasonally. Open daily (though blooms are best from April through October). Admission is charged. Call 757-441-5830.

Virginia Zoological Park, at Thirty-third and Granby Streets in Norfolk, has animals, a conservatory, tennis, a playground, basketball, and boating. Open daily. Admission is charged. Call 757-441-2706 (recorded message) or 757-441-5227.

Ocean Breeze Fun Park, at 849 General Booth Boulevard, is a waterpark and motorway, with waterslides, rides, pools, miniature-golf, go-carts, and batting cages. Open seasonally. Admission is charged. Call 757-425-1241.

The Great Dismal Swamp begins at Chesapeake, just south of Portsmouth. This National Wildlife Refuge covers over 106,000 acres, allowing the bears, bobcats, and other native wildlife to roam free. This overgrown, somewhat eerie swamp is mainly accessed by private boat from Chesapeake. No services are available. Open daily. Call 757-986-3705.

Old Cape Henry Lighthouse, off I-64, near the mouth of the Chesapeake Bay, is where colonists stopped in 1607 en route to Jamestown. The old lighthouse is open (the new one is closed to the public). Open daily from mid-March through October. Admission is charged. Call 757-422-9421.

SEASONAL EVENTS

In April, the Norfolk Botanical Garden has the **Azalea Festival**, an international celebration in honor of NATO. There's a coronation, a parade, an air show at the naval base, live entertainment, and a fair. Also in April is the Norfolk **British and Irish Festival**, where the British Isles are represented in traditional dress, games, food, and music. In June, the **Harborfest** is held on the Norfolk waterfront, with water shows, sky shows, naval demonstrations, and children's events. For more information on these events, call the Norfolk Convention and Visitors Bureau at 757-664-6620 or 800-368-3097.

The four-day **Boardwalk Art Show** is held in Virginia Beach in June. It features more than 350 artists from all over the world exhibiting their

works. In August, the **East Coast Surfing Championships** are held in Virginia Beach, and in September, the **Neptune Festival** takes place there, with seafood and entertainment. For more information on these events, call the Virginia Beach Information Center at 757-437-4888 or 800-822-3224.

In Hampton, late June brings the **Hampton Jazz Festival** at the Hampton Coliseum. For tickets, call 804-838-4203. In August, hydroplanes race for the **Hampton Cup**. **The Hampton Bay Days** festival in September has live entertainment, Chesapeake Bay seafood, midway rides, fireworks, and sporting and water exhibits. Call 757-727-6122. For more information on these events, call the Hampton Visitors Center at 757-727-1102 or 800-800-2202.

ACCOMMODATIONS ....

EXPENSIVE

Cavalier Hotels, at Forty-second Street and Atlantic Avenue in Virginia Beach, is an oceanfront hotel on 18 acres, with additional rooms nearby that require brief travel to the beach. The oceanfront hotel has a private beach, summer children's programs, exercise facilities, and indoor and outdoor pools. Call 757-425-8555 or 800-446-8199.

Omni Waterside, at 777 Waterside Drive in Norfolk, is a waterfront hotel with rooms, suites, and a luxury level. Perks include health club privileges, balconies, bars, restaurants, a pool with poolside bar, and harbor views. Call 804-622-6664.

Radisson Hampton is located at 700 Settlers Landing Road on the Hampton River in Hampton. This first-

The Mariners' Museum,
Newport News
Photo courtesy of the Virginia Division of Tourism

class hotel has magnificent views of the waterfront, exercise facilities, a pool, airport transfers, restaurants, and a lounge. Call 757-727-9700.

Page House Inn, at 323 Fairfax Avenue in Norfolk's historic district, is a restored Georgian-style home with impeccable service, free breakfast, and afternoon refreshments (although the inn is not appropriate for children under twelve). Call 757-625-5033.

Courtyard by Marriott, at 1917 Coliseum Drive in Hampton, has comfortable rooms with free in-room coffee, an outdoor pool, valet service, and exercise facilities. Call 757-838-3300.

Best Western Oceanfront, on Atlantic Avenue at Eleventh Street in Virginia Beach, offers ocean-view rooms with balconies, as well as a pool, restaurant, lounges, and valet service. Call 757-422-5000.

MODERATE/INEXPENSIVE

Holiday Inn Oceanside, at Twenty-first Street and Atlantic Avenue in Virginia Beach, has an indoor pool and rooms with private balconies overlooking the ocean. Call 757-491-1500.

Holiday Inn Sunspree, at Oceanfront Drive and Thirty-ninth Street in Virginia Beach, has a wide range of rates, many quite reasonable if you book early. Supervised children's activities are provided in the summer. Oceanfront rooms have private balconies. Call 757-428-1711.

SHOPPING ....

The Waterside, at 333 Waterside Drive in Norfolk, is a large shopping and dining complex along the waterfront. There's also a park and marina with passenger boats nearby. Also in Norfolk, the **Ghent Area** is a charming shopping district at Colley Avenue and Twenty-first Street.

The d'Art Center, at 125 College Place in Norfolk, has studios where you can watch artists work and purchase pieces from their galleries. Call 757-625-4211.

Rowena's Jam and Jelly Factory, at 758 West Twenty-second Street in Norfolk, gives factory tours Monday through Wednesday with advance reservations, and sells jams and other goodies. Call 757-627-8699.

The Great American Outlet Mall, at 3750 Virginia Beach Boulevard in Virginia Beach, has over forty outlet stores. Call 757-463-8665.

RESTAURANTS ....

FINE DINING

Le Chambord, at 324 North Greatneck Road in Virginia Beach, offers great veal chops and rack of lamb, among other fine French and Continental selections. The decor is Mediterranean, and the building was once a post office. Open daily for lunch and dinner. Reservations are required on weekends. Call 757-498-1234.

CASUAL DINING

Doumar's Drive-In, at 1919 Monticello Avenue in Norfolk, is a landmark because, aside from its friendly atmosphere, wholesome sandwiches, and good ice cream, you can view the machine, which is still operable, used to make the first ever ice cream cones. The restaurant's founder, Abe Doumar, invented the ice cream cone in 1904. Call 757-627-4163.

Freemason Abbey, at 209 West Freemason Street in Norfolk, is located in a renovated 1873 church and furnished with antiques. Standard fare includes excellent prime rib and lobster. Open for Sunday brunch and daily for lunch and dinner. Call 757-622-3966.

Grate Steak, at 1934 Coliseum Drive in Hampton, has a common barbecue grill where diners can choose pre-marinated chicken or seasoned steaks and do the grilling themselves, but the prime rib is cooked by the chef. There's also a salad bar. Call 757-827-1886.

h Virginia Beach, try the **Lynnhaven Fish House**, located at 2350 Starfish Road. Seafood is the theme, and there's a raw bar and live lobster tank. For dessert, try the whis-

key pudding made from an old European recipe. Call 757-481-0003.

JUST FOR KIDS ....

Of special interest is the **Portsmouth Children's Museum**, at High and Court Streets. Located in the 1846 Courthouse, the museum teaches scientific concepts through interactive play. Open daily. Admission is charged. Call 757-393-8393. Children will also enjoy the **Hampton Carousel**, a real wooden horse carousel from 1920 that has been restored to its original state. It's located at the downtown waterfront in Hampton off Settlers Landing Road. The carousel operates from April to December, with varying hours. There is a small fee for the ride. Call 757-727-6381. The Portsmouth Naval Shipyard Museum (See Museums/Science Centers) and the Virginia Zoological Park (See Recreation) will also appeal to children.

SIDE TRIPS ....

Chincoteague is a charming barrier island near the border of Maryland and Virginia (approximately 80 miles north of Virginia Beach), which is easily reached via the 17½-mile-long Chesapeake Bay Bridge-Tunnel—an engineering marvel. The island has terrific beaches and is known for the wild ponies that live on nearby Assateague Island. The island is also renowned for being the home of the **Channel Bass Inn**, at 6228 Church Street. The restaurant at the inn is exquisite in every detail, from the antique chairs and fine artworks, to the professional service and delectable gourmet dishes with French and Spanish influences. Reservations are secured by a credit card (there's a charge if you don't show), but guests have all evening to savor their meals. The food is expensive, yet top notch. Dress is neat-casual. Call 757-336-6148. For more information on Chincoteague, call the Chincoteague Chamber of Commerce at 757-336-6161.

GENERAL INFORMATION ....

For more information, contact the following: Hampton Visitors Center at 757-727-1102 or 800-800-2202; Norfolk and the Virginia Waterfront at 757-664-6620 or 800-368-3097; the Newport News Tourism and Conference Bureau at 800-333-7787; and the Virginia Beach Information Center at 757-437-4888 or 800-822-3224. Each city will be happy to send you a free copy of their visitors guide.

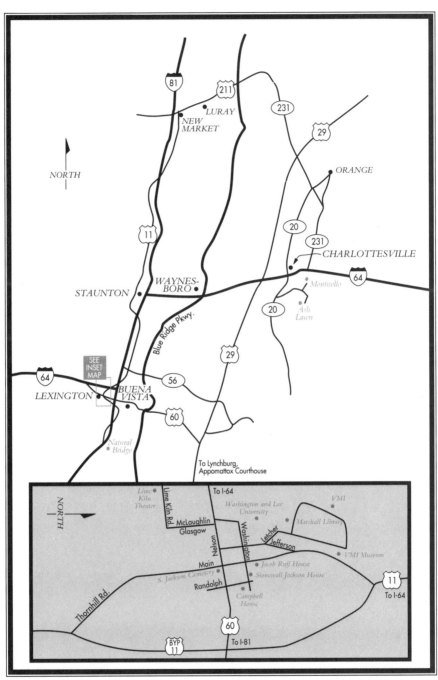

LEXINGTON and VICINITY, VA.

Lexington and vicinity

INCLUDING HOT SPRINGS,

NATURAL BRIDGE, SALEM,

AND APPOMATTOX

AREA CODE: 540

INTRODUCTION ....

Lexington is in the lower region of the Shenandoah Valley, the picturesque region between the Blue Ridge and Allegheny Mountains. The city brims with historic significance and is a convenient distance from great golf, other outdoor sports, and natural phenomena—most notably the Natural Bridge, one of the seven natural wonders of the world.

The area around Lexington was once home to Cherokee and Monacan Indian tribes, and European colonists began settling here during the 1730s. However, it's best known as a small, but mighty, melting pot of military and political history, as it claims either as a hometown or alma mater such generals as Thomas "Stonewall" Jackson, Robert E. Lee, George C. Marshall, and George Patton. During the Civil War, Lexington suffered terrible losses, but many of the buildings and institutions founded within the previous three centuries have survived, giving the city a very historic feel.

Aside from Lexington's architectural beauty and the lush, scenic backdrop of the Shenandoah Valley, this tranquil hamlet of about 7,000 people is known very much as a college town, since two major institutions—Washington and Lee University and the Virginia Military Institute—are located here. The colleges are not only bustling centers of education, but are inexorably intertwined with the town's, and the nation's, history, and both have become tourist attractions in their own right. These two schools offer museums and tours, and at VMI, the traditional Friday afternoon full-dress parade by cadets has become a major draw for visitors.

An area mecca for both golfers and non-golfers is the internationally known resort called the Homestead. Located in Hot Springs, about an hour's drive from Lexington, the resort was built in 1766 near natural waters prized for their therapeutic properties. Guests at this magnificent, red-brick hotel have included Thomas Jefferson and George Washington, and the golf courses here are among the finest in the world. While the resort and greens fees are expensive, daily fee play is allowed. Aside from the Homestead, other excellent courses in the region include the Greenbrier resort, just over the West Virginia border, and the Hanging Rock Golf Club in Salem, Virginia, about 50 miles south of Lexington.

Normal monthly temperatures for Lexington are as follows: January, 33.6; February, 36.7; March, 46.3; April, 55.3; May, 63.9; June, 71.1; July, 74.8; August, 73.8; September, 67.1; October, 56.1; November, 46.4; December, 37.3. Most visitors come in summer, but skiing is popular in winter (though it is generally too cold for golf then).

GOLF INFORMATION ....

THE HOMESTEAD, HOT SPRINGS (PHONE NUMBERS LISTED BELOW)

For almost seventy years, the Cascades course (call 540-839-3083) at the Homestead has hosted major championships. In 1928 and 1994, it was the site for the USGA Women's Amateur Championship; in 1980 and in 1988, it hosted the USGA's Senior Men's and Men's Amateur Championships; in 1932, it held the National Intercollegiate Championship; in 1966, it was the home of the Curtis Cup; and in 1967, it hosted the Women's National Open. Not only is Cascades considered the best course in Virginia, and among the top courses in the United States, it is where Sam Snead caddied as a youngster and learned the game of golf. It was designed by William Flynn, the same architect who designed the renowned Cherry Hills, Shinnicock Hills Golf Club, and Merion courses. The famed therapeutic hot springs run near the course, which is set amidst the beautiful Allegheny mountains. Its nineteenth hole is Sam Snead's Tavern (See Restaurants). It has quick greens and thick pine trees that give no quarter. From the longest tees, it reaches 6566 yards, with a slope of 136 and a par of 70. It has it all. Go play it.

In the category of "tough acts to follow," the Homestead also has the Lower Cascades (call 540-839-7995) and the Homestead courses (call 540-839-7739). The Lower Cascades, opened in 1962 and designed by Robert Trent Jones, Sr., is a fine, 6663-yard layout that hosted the 1988 USGA Men's Amateur Championship. This course is user-friendly, with fairways that are more wide open than the Cascades' fairways, but its greens are equally fast and bunkers are prevalent throughout. The Homestead Course, designed by Donald Ross in 1892, is almost 5800 yards and is said to have the longest "continuously operating tee in America."

Carts: Cart or caddie required at all times. *Greens Fees:* $85-$125/18 holes. *Tee Time Policy:* Resort guests can book when making room reservation; nonguests can reserve seven days in advance.

HANGING ROCK GOLF CLUB, SALEM (ABOUT 50 MILES SOUTHWEST OF LEXINGTON; NEAR ROANOKE) (540) 389-7275

Hanging Rock is the first new public course in southwest Virginia in the last twenty-five years. The course is set in a superb mountain location surrounded by mountain streams, boulders, and pristine forests. This Russell Breeden design offers seventy-five tee boxes and ranges in length from 4691 to 6828 yards, with a rating/slope reaching 72.3/125. The greens are immense and test most players with unusually long lag putts. You may hit all of these greens, but you will do well to keep your putt count in the 30s. In the category of "what will they think of next," and putting to rest the erratic player's promise of "I'll see you on the green," the fifth hole at Hanging Rock offers two different greens. One of the greens plays straight from tee to green while the other is a dogleg right. Both

approach shots are roughly the same; although it's not clear whether etiquette requires a player to call which green he or she is playing for before the shot.

Carts: Required weekends and holidays before 1 P.M. *Greens Fees:* $32 weekdays, $37 weekends and holidays/18 holes, including cart. *Tee Time Policy:* Advance tee time required. For weekdays, call a day in advance; for weekends and holidays, call the Wednesday in advance.

OTHER EXCELLENT
AREA COURSES:

The Greenbrier, White Sulphur Springs, West Virginia (304-536-7851 or 800-624-6070), has three 18-hole courses, the Greenbrier and the Old White Courses being considered the best (but all three are terrific). Both the Greenbrier and the Old White are considered among the top seventy-five best courses in the United States by *Golf Digest.* The Old White is a 1913, C.B. MacDonald course. The Greenbrier opened in 1925, but was revamped by Jack Nicklaus in 1979. It stretches to over 6681 yards, sits in an upland valley of the Allegheny mountains, and was the site of the 1979 Ryder Cup matches.

ATTRACTIONS ....

TOURS

Maps of walking tours are available at the Lexington Visitors Center, at 106 East Washington Street. Themed tours include a military tour, Washington and Lee University tour, and historic homes tour. Call 540-463-3777.

Lexington Carriage Company

The Homestead, Hot Springs
Photo courtesy of the Virginia Division of Tourism

gives forty-five-minute horse-drawn carriage tours from April 1 through October 31. Carriages depart between 9:30 A.M. and 4:30 P.M. from the corner of Washington Street and Varner Lane, across from the Lexington Visitors Center. Call 540-463-5647.

HISTORIC PLACES

The General Thomas J. "Stonewall" Jackson Home is at 8 East Washington Street in Lexington. Jackson, who earned his nickname for his fierce stand at First Manassas, lived here for many years prior to the Civil War. The furnishings exactly match his estate inventory, although only some of the pieces actually belonged to him. Tours are given on the hour and half hour throughout the year. Call 540-

463-2552. On South Main Street is the **Stonewall Jackson Cemetery**, where he and more than a hundred Confederate veterans are buried. Open from dawn until dusk. Free admission. Maps of gravesites are available at the entrance.

MUSEUMS/SCIENCE CENTERS

Lee Chapel and Museum, on the Washington and Lee University campus, was built in 1867 under Robert E. Lee's supervision, and is where Lee and his family are buried. It houses the general's office, several family portraits, and other items owned by Lee's family. General Lee's horse, Traveller, is buried outside the chapel. Open daily; hours vary seasonally. Admission is free. Call 540-463-8768.

VMI has two noteworthy military

museums on campus. **Virginia Military Institute Museum**, located in the Jackson Memorial Hall, is the state's oldest museum and chronicles the history of the institute. Artifacts include items belonging to military leaders, antique firearms, uniforms, and Civil War items. Open daily; closed December 24 through January 1. Admission is free. Call 540-464-7232. **The George C. Marshall Museum**, at the southernmost end of the VMI Parade Grounds, chronicles the life and career of the illustrious World War II general and chief of staff. Of special interest are his Nobel Peace Prize gold medallion, a World War II jeep that children can climb on, and military documents of historical significance. Open daily; hours vary seasonally. Admission is charged. Call 540-463-7103.

CULTURAL OFFERINGS

The Theater at Lime Kiln, at 14 South Randolph Street, is an outdoor theater situated in an old lime quarry. It features a real kiln and stone ruins decked with ivy and wildflowers, giving an eerie reality to such performances as the Civil War drama, *Stonewall Country*. A variety of musicals, plays, and concerts are performed here from Memorial Day through Labor Day. For information and tickets, call the box office at 540-463-3074.

The Lenfest Center for the Performing Arts, on West Nelson Street at Washington and Lee University, has an art gallery and two theaters where student and professional productions take place. For information, call 540-463-8000.

RECREATION

The Virginia Horse Center, on VA 39, has shows and events throughout the year, including a horse festival (though riding rentals are not available). For a schedule and ticket information, call 540-463-2194. For horseback rides through the valley and mountains, contact **Virginia Mountain Outfitters** near Buena Vista. Call 540-261-3841.

Goshen Pass, located on VA 39 near Goshen, is a 3-mile mountain gorge where you can swim, canoe, fish, picnic, and hike along a riverside trail. In the nineteenth century, VMI Professor Matthew Fontaine Maury declared Goshen Pass the loveliest spot in Virginia (there's a memorial to him here). Other outdoor recreation areas include the **Sherando Lake Recreation Area,** located on the Blue Ridge Parkway in the George Washington National Forest, which has swimming, fishing, seasonal theater productions, and camping from April through October. Call 540-564-8300. There's also **A. Willis Robertson Lake**, near Lexington, with camping, fishing, tennis courts, and other sports facilities Call 540-463-4164. In Lexington, nature-lovers will enjoy the **Chessie Nature Trail**, with sites including locks, bridges, and historic homes; and **Woods Creek Park**, which is only two miles long but has some of the area's prettiest scenery.

For skeet shooting, **Quail Ridge Sporting Clays**, on Murat Road in Lexington, has a half-mile course with thirteen stations. Closed Tuesdays. Call 540-463-1800.

Canoeing and white-water canoeing can be arranged through **James River Basin Canoe Livery**. Open daily from May through September, other times by appointment. Call 540-261-7334.

In late April, there's an annual tour of area homes and gardens. For dates and information, call 540-463-3777. In early December, the annual **Holiday in Lexington Festival**, a family oriented event featuring children's programs, a parade, and plays, is held. Call 540-463-3777. For a current list of events throughout the area, contact the Shenandoah Valley Travel Association at 540-740-3132.

ACCOMMODATIONS ....

EXPENSIVE

The prestigious, 15,000-acre **Homestead Resort**, on U.S. 220, dates from 1766 and has hosted eight United States presidents, beginning with Jefferson. The structure itself is a gorgeous, red-brick hotel, and the expansive grounds have fabulous scenery and world-class golf, as well as outdoor pools, horseback riding, seven restaurants, nineteen tennis courts, a bowling alley, and a luxury spa facility (including, of course, hot springs treatments). Call 540-839-1766, or 800-336-5771 (outside Virginia) and 800-542-5734 (in Virginia).

Sugar Tree Inn, on VA 56 in Steeles Tavern, 19 miles northeast of Lexington, is a beautiful country inn complete with a porch and rockers. Guests enjoy stunning mountain views, fireplaces, and private baths in each room, and some rooms even have whirlpools and VCRs. Children under certain ages are not encouraged. Rates include full breakfast for two. Call 540-377-2197.

MODERATE

McCampbell Inn, at 11 North Main Street in Lexington, is a circa 1809, four-story inn in the historic downtown district. Rooms contain antique furnishings, private balconies and patios, and refrigerators. Guests receive complimentary continental breakfast, tea and sherry, and pool and tennis privileges. Call 540-463-2044.

The Natural Bridge Hotel, located 12 miles south of the Lexington Visitors Center on U.S. 11, has provided southern hospitality to travelers for centuries. The facilities include the Classic Hotel and the Stonewall Inn, with 180 rooms in all. Families are welcome. The Colonial Dining Room serves authentic regional cuisine. Call 540-291-2121 or 800-533-1410.

INEXPENSIVE

The Thrifty Inn, at 820 Main Street, about a mile south of Lexington, offers reasonable rates and is close to downtown attractions. The motel allows pets and provides free breakfast and local calls. Call 540-463-2151.

The Roseloe Motel, on U.S. 220 in Hot Springs, is a homey country motel with comfortable rooms at reasonable rates, and it is situated only a few miles from the famous Homestead resort. Call 540-839-5373.

SHOPPING ....

Just north of Lexington on U.S. 11 is the **Lexington Antique and Craft Mall**, a 40,000-square-foot mall containing shops selling furnishings, dolls, toys, Civil War memorabilia, jewelry, quilts, and other items. Open daily. Call 540-463-9511.

Country store fans may enjoy the **General Store** in Buena Vista. The store was established in 1891 and offers nostalgic and hard-to-find old-fashioned goods. Call 540-261-3860. **Wade's Mill** (circa 1750) is a working flour mill with a shop selling fresh flour and gift items. It's located on VA 606 (exit 205 off of I-81) in Raphine. Call 540-348-1400.

RESTAURANTS ....

FINE DINING

Willson-Walker House, at 30 North Main Street in Lexington, is an 1820, Greek Revival–style home in the historic downtown district. The restaurant serves creative American cuisine, with an emphasis on veal, pasta, and seafood. Outdoor dining is available in good weather. Open for lunch and dinner from Tuesday through Sunday. Call 540-463-3020.

Maple Hall Dining Room, located 7 miles north of Lexington on U.S. 11 off of I-81, is in a restored 1850 inn situated on 56 scenic acres. The restaurant serves gourmet food in elegant surroundings. Open daily for dinner. Reservations are recommended. Call 540-463-4666.

CASUAL DINING

Southern Inn and Diggers Pub, at 37 Main Street in Lexington, has been around since 1932. They serve homemade soups, breads, sandwiches, and a full dinner menu. Open for lunch and dinner daily. The pub serves Virginia wines and a variety of beers from around the world. Call 540-463-3612.

For down-home cooking, try **Vir-**

ginia House at 722 Main Street in Lexington. The menu features real stick-to-your-ribs dishes like fried or baked Virginia ham and biscuits served up in generous portions. Open daily for breakfast, lunch, and dinner. Call 540-463-3643.

Sam Snead's Tavern, on Main Street in Hot Springs, is a must for golf lovers. The restaurant has a lovely, rustic, mountain decor and setting (see the other listing in Myrtle Beach, South Carolina). House specialties are steaks and fresh fish. Reservations are required. Call 540-839-7666.

JUST FOR KIDS ....

Kids love the full-dress military parades given by VMI cadets on Friday afternoons while the school is in session.

At the **General Thomas J. "Stonewall" Jackson Home**, kids are encouraged to participate in the tour. They're

Goshen Pass, near Lexington
Photo courtesy of the Virginia Divison of Tourism

given slates listing household items that children can circle as they spot them. (See Historic Places.) **The George C. Marshall Museum** holds scavenger hunts, and for groups of children, the museum will schedule a "Try on a Piece of History" program, using parts of military uniforms. (See Museums/Science Centers.)

The Theater at Lime Kiln has children's productions in summer. For information or tickets, call the box office at 540-463-3074. (See Cultural Offerings).

SIDE TRIPS

Natural Bridge, located 12 miles south of Lexington off I-81, has several interesting attractions. The chief one is the **Natural Bridge** itself, one of the seven natural wonders of the world, which was once owned by Thomas Jefferson and still has visible initials carved by George Washington. The bridge has a nighttime light-and-sound show called "The Drama of Creation." The nearby **Natural Bridge Caverns** are a quiet world of hanging gardens, stalagmites, stalactites, and waterfalls, located more than 350 feet below the ground (remember to bring a sweater). Caverns are open daily from mid-March through the end of November. Open daily; hours vary seasonally. Call 540-291-2121 or 800-533-1410. (Note: This number is for the Natural Bridge Hotel, which will connect you to the Natural Bridge). In addition, there's a wax museum, where scenes come eerily to life using wax figures, animation, electronics, sound, and light. Visitors also can tour the wax factory. Open year round with seasonal hours.

Call 540-291-2426. In the warmer months, visitors can see the **Natural Bridge Zoo**, which has more than 400 reptiles, birds, and mammals, with a special petting area for kids. Call 540-291-2420. For more information on Natural Bridge, call 800-533-1410.

Appomattox Court House National Historic Site is on VA 24, about 3 miles northeast of Appomattox. Though it is a good 70 miles from Lexington, the site is a must-see for Civil War buffs. The area is a living museum with costumed interpreters, restored to the way it appeared in 1865 when Robert E. Lee surrendered to Ulysses S. Grant, thus ending the Civil War (in spirit, if not in substance). Exploration here is on foot, as no cars are allowed. The visitors center in the courthouse provides orientation slide shows, exhibits, and pamphlets. You can enter most of the more than two dozen buildings, including the house in which the articles of surrender were signed, and Lee's headquarters. Open daily; hours vary seasonally. Call 804-352-8987.

GOLFER'S SIDE TRIP: LAUREL FORK

(Note: This course is about 95 miles southwest of Lexington, but worth the trip for some avid golfers.)

OLDE MILL GOLF COURSE, LAUREL FORK (540) 398-2211 OR (540) 398-2638

Located in the shadow of Groundhog Mountain, this Ellis Maples layout opened in 1973 and is a treat. The course rolls and winds through mountainous terrain and around a 67-acre lake. Holes not on the lake generally are bordered by mountain streams. Although the course can stretch to over 6800 yards (the red tees are 4876 yards, the gold tees are 5453 yards, and the white tees are 6185 yards), accuracy is required at Olde Mill. The first three holes, and holes ten through fourteen, literally wrap around and across the lake. The bent-grass greens are medium in size and well protected by bunkers (in some cases, on all sides). Not only will the course excite you, the groves of white pine, dogwood, rhododendron, and laurel provide for enjoyable sightseeing.

Carts: Mandatory. *Greens Fees:* $26 Monday-Thursday ($14 for 9 holes), $36 Friday-Sunday ($19 for 9 holes)/ 18 holes, including cart. *Tee Time Policy:* Call in advance for weekend tee times; advance tee times recommended on weekdays.

GENERAL INFORMATION ....

For more information, contact the Lexington Visitors Center at 540-463-3777. They can send you brochures and a glossy publication entitled *Visiting Lexington and the Rockbridge Area.* For information on the Shenandoah Valley and its attractions, contact the Shenandoah Valley Travel Association at 540-740-3132. They can send you a copy of the *Shenandoah Valley Travel Guide and Calendar of Events.*

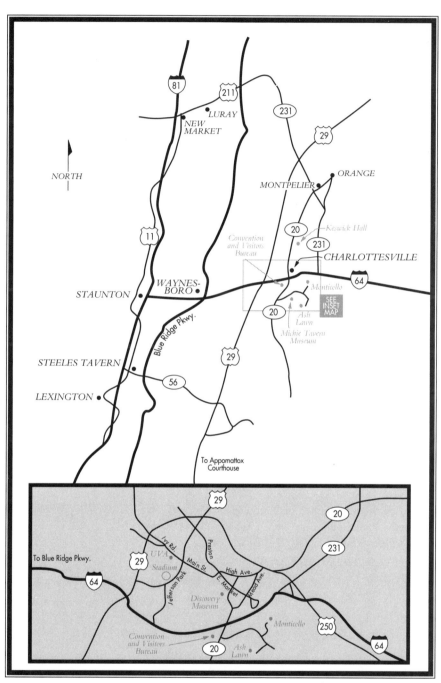

CHARLOTTESVILLE and VICINITY, VA.

Charlottesville and vicinity

INCLUDING LURAY, NEW MARKET,

STAUNTON, AND ORANGE

AREA CODES:

804 (CHARLOTTESVILLE);

540 (ALL OTHER AREAS)

INTRODUCTION ....

Charlottesville is set in the lush foothills of the Blue Ridge Mountains bordering the Shenandoah Valley in central Virginia. The word *Shenandoah* is an Indian term believed to mean either "daughter of the stars" or "river of the high mountains," and somehow, the word perfectly captures the beauty of this picturesque region nestled between the Blue Ridge and Allegheny Mountains. Aside from the stunning scenery, the area is also known for its abundance of important historic and cultural sites, parks and outdoor recreation, and outstanding natural formations (including the Luray Caverns, the largest caverns in the eastern United States). Perhaps the most popular attraction in the area is the Shenandoah National Park, which encompasses 300 square miles and receives about two million visitors annually.

The tranquil college town of Charlottesville has a nice mix of southern history and new development.

Perhaps the most important historical fact about the town is that the city was the home of Thomas Jefferson, whose admiration for the scenery here led him to call these mountains "the Eden of the United States." His influence is still evident, from his home, the architectural masterpiece known as Monticello, to the buildings at the University of Virginia. Jefferson's love for Charlottesville seems to be contagious since the city is undergoing a wave of expansion and attracting a new kind of celebrity—like Sissy Spacek, Jessica Lange, and others—who have come to the area seeking quiet country homes in this unspoiled mountain setting.

Most notable for golfers are the two remarkable courses at the Wintergreen Resort, located 43 miles southwest of Charlottesville. Both courses offer spectacular scenery, and one is at an elevation of 3,850 feet—the highest golf course in Virginia. Another nationally recognized course is at the Caverns Country Club Resort in Luray—a city that is known for the huge Luray Caverns and for other family friendly attractions. Charlottesville itself is near the fabulous golf course at Keswick Hall, though the course is open only to guests of the resort (See Accommodations).

The normal monthly temperatures in Charlottesville are: January, 34.5; February, 37.1; March, 46.6; April, 56.4; May, 64.9; June, 72.6; July, 76.4; August, 75; September, 68.9; October, 58.1; November, 49; December, 38.3. Although ski season brings visitors even in cold weather, golfers and their families generally come between April and October.

GOLF INFORMATION ....

WINTERGREEN RESORT, WINTERGREEN (PHONE NUMBERS LISTED BELOW)

Wintergreen features two very fine courses—Stoney Creek, a Rees Jones design opened in 1988, and Devils Knob, an Ellis Maples course opened in 1976. Stoney Creek (call 804-325-8250) has received numerous accolades since its opening. It was *Golf Digest's* runner-up as the best new resort course, is listed among *Golf Digest's* top resort courses in the United States, is rated in the top five courses in Virginia, and is a 4-star course according to *Golf Digest's Places to Play*. The course offers tees ranging from 5500 to 7003 yards, with a rating/slope ranging from 71/125 to 74/132. Brooks and streams run down from the mountains and border and cross many of the holes on the course, while oaks, dogwoods, sycamores, and beeches frame the fairways and greens. Tees are elevated and the greens vary in size, with some possessing undulations with large breakers. There is no shortage of sand on the course, with more than a hundred bunkers creating havoc in the fairways and around the greens. The par 3s are excellent, as they involve lakes, streams, cavernous bunkers, extreme elevation changes, and overhanging trees. The par 4s can be monstrous—the tenth is 440 yards, while the eighteenth is 450 yards. And the par 5s provide no relief—the par 5 thirteenth is the number-one handicap hole on the course. It measures 575 yards, doglegs left, and has bunkers everywhere. If you're in these parts, don't miss this course.

A few thousand feet up the moun-

Luray Caverns, VA
Photo courtesy of the Virginia Division of Tourism

tain, you will find Devils Knob (call 804-325-8240). At 3850 feet, it is the highest course in the state, and it provides unmatched and unlimited views of the Shenandoah Valley. Devils Knob has tees ranging from 5101 yards to 6576 yards, but you might as well throw out your yardage book because the elevation results in much longer carries. The constant wind will either further exaggerate or offset the impact of the elevation on your shots. A fascinating and difficult hole is the double dogleg, par 5 seventh. The hole can stretch to 600 yards and requires two carries over water to reach a small green protected on both sides with bunkers.

Carts: Mandatory. *Greens Fees:* $65–$90, depending on course and season/18 holes; cart: $18 per person. *Tee Time Policy:* Can be reserved up to thirty days in advance for Monday-Thursday times, fourteen days in advance for Friday-Sunday times.

CAVERNS COUNTRY CLUB RESORT, LURAY (SEE SIDE TRIPS) (540-743-7111)

High above the banks of the Shenandoah River in the shadows of the Blue Ridge and Massanutten Mountains, you will find this Hal and Mark Purdy (father/son) 1976 course. The course reaches 5499 yards from the red tees, 6307 yards from the white tees, and just under 6500 yards from the blue tees. This mountainous layout winds through a mature deciduous forest and provides the player with lovely panoramic views. Right from the 490-yard first hole you know you are in for a treat at the Caverns. The hole has a sharp vertical drop to a narrow, tree-lined fairway that features the largest of the course's several cave openings right in the middle of the fairway.

Carts: Not required. *Greens Fees:* $18, Monday-Thursday, $26 Friday-Sunday/18 holes. *Tee Time Policy:* Can be reserved seven days in advance.

OTHER EXCELLENT AREA COURSES:

Bryce Resort Golf Course, Basye (540-856-2124), is set at the foot of ski slopes and is a challenging 6200-yard course with a slope of 122. **Shenandoah Valley Golf Club**, Front Royal (540-636-2641), was redesigned by Rees Jones. This 27-hole course has played host to the Kemper Open Qualifier, the Virginia State Junior Championships, and the Virginia State Senior Championships. **Birdwood Golf Course**, Charlottesville (804-293-4653), is a 1984 course designed by Lindsay Ervin (who also designed the top flight second 18 at White Deer in Pennsylvania and the Queens Town

Monticello, near Charlottesville
Photo courtesy of the Virginia Division of Tourism

Harbor course in Maryland). This mountainous, par 72 course can stretch to over 6800 yards, with a rating/slope ranging from 65.2/116 to 72.8/132. **Lakeview Golf Course**, Harrisonburg (540-434-8937), features three, 9-hole courses designed by Ed Ault. The rolling courses are an excellent value and feature a very brisk pace of play. **Keswick Club of Virginia at Keswick Hall**, Keswick (540-979-3440), features an Arnold Palmer/Ed Seay redesigned course that rambles over gently rolling hills and through wooded glens. (Open only to resort guests; see Accommodations).

ATTRACTIONS ....

TOURS

Maps for self-guided walking tours of Charlottesville's historic district—with sites like the Albemarle County Courthouse—are available from the Charlottesville/Albemarle County Convention and Visitors Bureau, housed in the Monticello Visitors Center building on VA 20, 2 miles from Monticello. The center has a film and an exhibition about Jefferson's life. Open daily. Call 804-977-1783.

HISTORIC PLACES

Monticello, 4 miles southeast of Charlottesville on VA 53, was the home of Thomas Jefferson. This masterpiece, which Jefferson built and lived in for more than forty years, contains many original furnishings and inventions, including a mirror that shows your reflection upside down and a seven-day clock built by Jefferson. Visitors can tour the home and vegetable gardens. Open daily. Admission is charged. Call 804-984-9822.

Historic Michie Tavern, located 3 miles from Charlottesville on VA 53, was built in 1780, making it one of Virginia's oldest existing homesteads. The tavern was disassembled and moved here in 1927. Rooms can be viewed, and fried chicken and other items are served for lunch. Employees wear eighteenth-century garb. The old gristmill is now a gift shop. Open daily. Admission is charged. Call 804-977-1234.

The University if Virginia is on the west end of Charlottesville and features several other architectural creations by Thomas Jefferson. Highlights include a building modeled after the Pantheon, the landscaped gardens, a statue of Jefferson, the bronze liberty bell, and the room where Edgar Allen Poe stayed as a student. Tours of the Rotunda and central grounds are given daily. Admission is free. 804-924-7969.

Ash Lawn-Highland, on C.R. 795 about 7 miles southeast of Charlottesville, is the circa 1799 home of President James Monroe. The house is built on a site selected by Monroe's friend Thomas Jefferson and contains many Monroe family furnishings. Open daily. Admission is charged. Call 804-293-9539.

CULTURAL OFFERINGS

A variety of fine wines are produced in central Virginia's vineyards. For a detailed guide on Virginia's wineries, call 800-828-4637, or stop by the Charlottesville/Albemarle County Convention and Visitors Bureau, housed in the Monticello Visitors Center building on VA 20, to pick up a copy.

McGuffy Art Center, at 201 Second Street NW, features works by local artists. Open daily except Monday. Admission is free. Call 804-295-7973.

Shenandoah Valley Art Center, at 600 West Main Street in nearby Waynesboro, has art galleries and studios displaying the works of resident artists. Open daily except Monday. Donation suggested. Call 540-949-7662.

The University of Virginia has a variety of dance, music, and theater performances by students and professionals. For current events, contact the Charlottesville/Albemarle County Convention and Visitors Bureau at 804-977-1783, or contact the university at 804-924-3777.

RECREATION

Shenandoah National Park is a 300-square-mile wooded park in a picturesque section of the state between the Blue Ridge and Allegheny Mountains. The park is a wildlife sanctuary, and local species include bobcat, fox, and deer. There are camping and cabin facilities here, though space is limited. Other attractions include a visitors center with exhibits and informational materials, a nature museum, waterfalls, picnic areas, nature trails, and fishing (license required). The nearest park entrances from Charlottesville are on U.S. 211 near Luray, on U.S. 33 near Lydia, and on U.S. 250 in Afton. Small charge for cars. For information and fees, call the superintendent's office at 540-999-3500.

Founder's Day takes place in Charlottesville on April 13, when ceremonies are observed in honor of Thomas Jefferson's birthday. Also in April in Charlottesville is the nine-day **Dogwood Festival**, which is celebrated with golf tournaments, lacrosse competitions, a carnival, and a parade. For the many happenings in the Shenandoah Valley, contact the Shenandoah Valley Travel Association at 540-740-3132.

ACCOMMODATIONS ....

For information on bed-and-breakfast inns, the **Guesthouse Bed and Breakfast Service** provides a brochure listing area choices for a fee of $1.00. Call 804-979-7264.

EXPENSIVE

Wintergreen Resort, 43 miles southwest of Charlottesville in Wintergreen, has two of Virginia's best golf courses (See Golf Information). Other activities include tennis, fishing, boating, and horseback riding. Families love the indoor and outdoor pools, wading pool, lake, playground, and supervised children's programs. Call 800-325-2200.

Keswick Hall, at 701 Club Drive in Keswick, 6 miles east of Charlottesville, is a 600-acre country resort dating back two hundred years. The exquisite decor of this resort, recently purchased and redecorated by Sir Bernard Ashley, the husband of the late Laura Ashley, features Laura Ashley fabrics, and the rooms, atmosphere, service, and food are exquisite. The 18-hole golf course, open only to resort guests, is one of Virginia's

finest. Call 804-979-3440 or 800-274-5391 (ASHLEY-1).

Omni Charlottesville, at 235 West Main Street, is located at the west end of Charlottesville's downtown mall. It has an atrium lobby, indoor and outdoor pools, exercise facilities, whirlpool, sauna, and large, comfortable rooms with refrigerators. Call 804-971-5500.

MODERATE

The Shenvalee, on U.S. 11 off of I-81 in New Market, has 27 holes of championship golf (See Golf Information). There's also an outdoor pool, tennis, fishing, putting green, driving range, and golf packages. Call 540-740-3181.

INEXPENSIVE

Best Western Cavalier Inn, at 105 Emmet Street (across from the University), has moderate to inexpensive rates and offers valet service and an outdoor pool. Call 804-296-8111 or 800-528-1234.

Luray Caverns Motel East, on Business U.S. 211, and **Luray Caverns Motel West**, on U.S. 211 Bypass, are located at respective ends of the Luray Caverns. Both have comfortable rooms in a convenient location near Shenandoah Park and caverns. For Luray Caverns Motel East, call 540-743-4531; for Luray Caverns Motel West, call 540-743-4536. For information on both, call 540-743-6551.

SHOPPING ....

Downtown Mall, located at the east end of Charlottesville, is a six-block, brick pedestrian mall, with specialty shops housed in buildings dating from the nineteenth and early twentieth centuries. There are also many restaurants and bars in the mall.

RESTAURANTS ....

FINE DINING

Metropolitain, at 214 West Water Street, is co-owned by two chefs—one American, one French—creating an interesting blend of European and continental American influences. Specialties include pork chops with black-bean chili, grilled tuna with ratatouille, sweet-potato salsa, and desserts like chocolate almond torte with mocha custard. Din-

ner served daily. Call 804-977-1043.

Keswick Hall, at 701 Club Drive in Keswick, is open daily for breakfast, lunch, dinner, tea, and Sundays for brunch. Entrées range from seafood to fine beef and local game such as venison and rabbit. The English chef uses fresh local ingredients. Call 804-979-3440 or 800-ASHLEY-1.

C & O, at 515 East Water Street, is a fine French restaurant that's a twenty-year tradition in Charlottesville. Meat dishes in French sauces predominate here, as do seafood selections, like Coquilles St. Jacques, and some vegetarian dishes. There's also a fine selection of local wines. Lunch is served

Museum of American Frontier Culture, Staunton
Photo courtesy of the Virginia Division of Tourism

Charlottesville and vicinity, VA

weekdays; dinner is served daily. Call 804-971-7044.

Martha's Cafe, at 11 Elliewood Avenue in Charlottesville, has indoor and outdoor dining. Located near the university, this restaurant is popular with students. Bestsellers are enchiladas and other vegetarian entrées. Adding to the experience is the offbeat decor, with potted plants and goldfish in a bathtub. Call 804-971-7530.

The Old Mill Room is in the Boar's Head Inn, on U.S. 250 about 1½ miles west of Charlottesville. Waiters wear colonial costumes, and the specialties are veal and prime rib. Call 804-296-2181.

Parkhurst Restaurant, on U.S. 211 about 2 miles west of Luray, serves steaks, seafood, chicken, and pasta from a variety of world cuisines, and the views are beautiful. Dinner is served daily. Call 540-743-6009.

JUST FOR KIDS ....

The Virginia Discovery Museum, at 524 East Main Street in Charlottesville, has interactive exhibits, like costumes in a dress-up area, a reconstructed log cabin kids can enter, and a giant kaleidoscope. Admission is charged. Call 804-977-1025. Additionally, the **Wintergreen Resort** offers special children's activities.

SIDE TRIPS ....

Luray, approximately 50 miles north of Charlottesville, has one of the state's best golf courses at Caverns Country Club (See Golf Information), and

several other attractions to occupy non-golfers. **Luray Caverns**, located on U.S. 211, are the largest caverns in the eastern United States. Hour-long tours of the caverns begin every twenty minutes, and include a look at the one-of-a-kind stalacpipe organ that plays real music. Remember to bring a sweater, as the underground caves stay cool year round. Also on the premises is a collection of over a hundred vintage cars and carriages. Call 540-743-6551. In an adjoining park, you'll find the **Luray Singing Tower** with an impressive bell carillon. Forty-five-minute recitals are given from March through October. Days and times of performances vary by season. Call 540-743-6551.

New Market is 12 miles west of Luray on U.S. 211. The city boasts the 27-hole golf club, **The Shenvalee**. Call 540-740-9930. Also of interest here are the **New Market Battlefield Historical Park**, located on George Collins Parkway, which has the Hall of Valor Civil War Museum on the premises. For the park, call 540-740-3102; for the museum, call 540-740-3103. **The Endless Caverns**, off U.S. 11, are just south of New Market. The caverns are open year round for tours. Again, bring a sweater, as the cave stays cool all year. Call 800-544-CAVE.

Staunton (pronounced Stanton) is about 35 miles west of Charlottesville. The city is the proud birthplace of President Woodrow Wilson, and the **Woodrow Wilson Birthplace**, at 18 North Coalter Street, was his birthplace home that has been turned into a museum about his life. Exhibits and memorabilia include his 1919 Pierce-Arrow limo. Open daily. Call 540-885-0897. History buffs will also enjoy the **Mu-**

seum of **American Frontier Culture**, at 1250 Richmond Road (off I-81). This facility is a living museum where eighteenth- and nineteenth-century American farm life (and the European influences that affected it) are demonstrated. Open daily. Call 540-332-7850. A small museum about Staunton native sons, the **Statler Brothers**, is at 501 Thornrose Avenue. Call 540-885-7297. Other notable attractions nearby are the **Grand Caverns Regional Park** in Grottoes (call 540-249-5705), and the **Natural Chimneys Regional Park** near Mount Solon, featuring limestone rock formations (call 540-350-2510).

Orange, located 25 miles northeast of Charlottesville, was the home of President James Madison. His home, **Montpelier**, was later owned by the DuPont family and is currently being restored to its state during Madison's lifetime. Visitors can take guided tours of the home, gardens, and the cemetery where James and Dolley Madison are buried. Montpelier is on VA 20, about 4 miles south of Orange. Open daily. Admission is charged. Call 540-672-2728.

GENERAL INFORMATION ....

For more information, contact the Charlottesville/Albemarle Convention and Visitors Bureau at 804-977-1783; or contact the Shenandoah Valley Travel Association at 540-740-3132, and ask them for a copy of the *Shenandoah Valley Travel Guide and Calendar of Events*.

Part Two

NORTH CAROLINA

Jockey's Ridge State Park, Nags Head
Photo by T&T, courtesy of NC Travel and Tourism Division

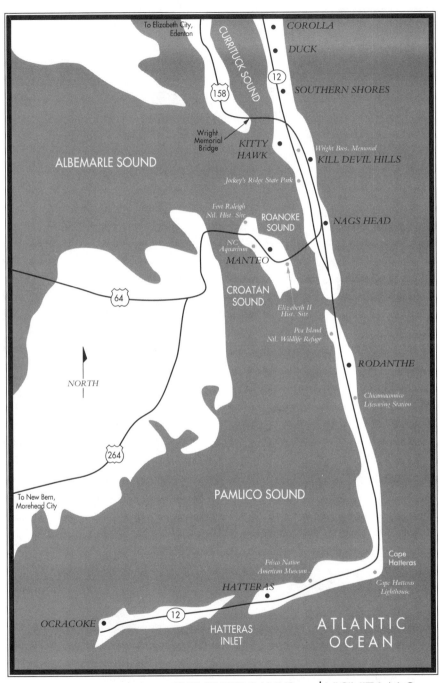

THE OUTER BANKS and VICINITY, N.C.

The Outer Banks and vicinity

INTRODUCTION

The Outer Banks are a series of spindly barrier islands that arch around the northern coastline of North Carolina. Their temperate climate, striking beauty, and fine golf courses make them a natural choice for golfers, beach lovers, and families.

Each part of the Outer Banks has different sites and characteristics, and visitors can choose where to stay depending on their interests. The largest towns include Manteo, Nags Head, Kill Devil Hills, and Kitty Hawk, all of which attract families in summer and outdoor enthusiasts in fall and spring. Newer, somewhat quieter, and more upscale developments are in Duck and Corolla. However, no matter where you head to on the Outer Banks, you'll find terrific beaches and plenty to do.

Aside from the beaches near area hotels, nature lovers may want to spend time at the Cape Hatteras and Cape Lookout National Seashores, which have miles of federally protected beaches.

While vacationers now flock to the shores of the Outer Banks, their lovely blue waters were once known as the "Graveyard of the Atlantic," due to the more than 2,000 shipwrecks that have occurred here since 1526 (the first year such records were kept). In fact, a new museum focusing on the treacherous nautical history of the Outer Banks will open in 1997. There were several reasons that ships found navigating the waters of the Outer Banks so difficult. The sandy Frying Pan Shoals, that produce a relaxing offshore sound like waves washing over rocks, once caused many a ship and crew to run aground. Also to blame was the occasional autumn "nor'easter," caused by a clash between the cold Labrador Current originating in Norway and the warm Gulf Stream that makes the seas so tepid and inviting for visitors in season. These storms not only were the cause of many shipwrecks, along with the waves and winds, they are responsible for the constant reshaping of the Outer Banks.

Aside from its beaches and golf courses, the Outer Banks have plenty of engaging historic sites. In 1903, the Wright Brothers made their famous first flight at Kill Devil Hills. Yet the Outer Banks' history goes earlier still, as this is where Sir Walter Raleigh's colonists set foot in the New World, and where Virginia Dare became the first English child born in the New World in 1587.

The normal monthly temperatures for the area, as measured at the Manteo airport, are: January, 43.1; February, 45; March, 51.7; April, 59.9; May, 67.9; June, 75.5; July, 79; August, 78.9; September, 73.9; October, 64.4; November, 55.9; December, 47.4. The tourist season runs roughly from late April through October.

GOLF INFORMATION ....

NAGS HEAD GOLF LINKS, NAGS HEAD (919) 441-8073

Like the other courses located on the Outer Banks, Nags Head Golf Links is a classic links-style course. Architect Bob Moore didn't move earth to create this course; he merely organized the land into a fine 18-hole, par 71 layout. The fairways roll gently among dunes, wetlands, and a few trees. The course's yardage of 6200 (yardage starts at 5800) is not really relevant when the wind is blowing off Roanoke Sound, which is fairly often. A player needs to play the ball low, dust off the bump-and-run shot, and avoid the deadly pot bunkers and lovegrass rough.

Carts: Mandatory. *Greens Fees:* $35-$75, depending on season/ 18 holes (less for resort guests through packages), including cart. *Tee Time Policy:* Can be reserved up to a year in advance.

SEA SCAPE GOLF COURSE, KITTY HAWK (919) 261-2158

This Art Wall designed course, opened in 1965, provides thrilling views of the Atlantic Ocean on one side and Albemarle Sound on the other. As described by head professional Bryan Sullivan, Sea Scape is a little bit of Scotland in North Carolina. The length of the course is of little relevance when the wind blows over these link-like holes (all right, for you number types: the black tees measure 6424 yards, while the white and red measure 6062 and 5536, respectively). The fairways and greens are firm, but watch out for the sea grass and gorse.

Carts: Mandatory. *Greens Fees:* $40-$65, depending on season/ 18 holes, including cart. *Tee Time Policy:* Can be reserved up to a year in advance through hotel packages. Non-guests can also request times.

THE SOUND GOLF LINKS, HERTFORD (919) 426-5555, (800) 535-0704

Located on the mainland just across from the Outer Banks, and on the edge of Albemarle Sound (hence its name), this course, designed by the talented and prolific Dan Maples, winds its way through wetlands, marshes, and groves of moss-draped oaks, pines, and birch trees. This natural environment attracts a wide cross section of wildlife on and around the course. The course, a par 72 reaching 6500 yards (yardage starts at 4665), requires accuracy and a game that can survive gusty winds. Regardless of whether you are on your game, the Sound Golf Links is a beautiful, exciting course not to be missed when traveling to the Outer Banks.

Carts: Mandatory. *Greens Fees:* $30 Monday-Thursday, $35 Friday-Sunday/ 18 holes, including cart. *Tee Time Policy:* Can be reserved well in advance for weekdays; for weekends, call the Wednesday before.

THE POINTE GOLF COURSE, POWELLS POINT (3½ MILES NORTH OF WRIGHT MEMORIAL BRIDGE) (919) 491-8388

The Pointe is a Russell Breeden designed course that opened July 1, 1995. Although at 6320 yards it is not very long by today's tortured standard, a player will do well to leave this course with a good score. Located on the Outer Banks, the Pointe offers spectacular views of Currituck Sound. Fairways are defined by lakes, wetlands, bunkers, waste areas, mounds, slopes, and trees. The greens provide a significant amount of excitement, as they are guarded by lakes (very closely in some cases), sand bunkers, grass bunkers, trees, slopes, etc. The greens are multi-shaped and small to medium in size, with a fair amount of tiering.

Carts: Mandatory (except 10/1-5/24). *Greens Fees:* $32 (1/2-3/31), $45 (10/1-1/1 and 4/1-5/24), $55 (5/25-9/30)/ 18 holes, including cart. *Tee Time Policy:* Should reserve one month ahead.

Elizabethan Gardens, Manteo
Photo by William Russ,
courtesy of NC Travel and Tourism Division

The Emerald Golf Club, New Bern (919-633-4440). (See Side Trips.)

ATTRACTIONS ....

TOURS

Motorized Tours

Historically Speaking Outer Banks Tours offers complete group tours and tours where visitors can step on and off; call 919-473-5783.

The **Beach Bus** is a new attraction. It features English-style double-decker buses that carry visitors along a route with stops at various points of interest. For information, contact David or Diane Hoare at 919-255-0550.

Boat Tours

For sunset cruises, try the **Crystal Dawn** at Pirate's Cove Yacht Club; call 919-473-5577. Or try the **Osprey** at Manteo's waterfront, which additionally offers dolphin-watching cruises; call 919-473-6644.

Air Tours

Kitty Hawk Aero Tours (call 919-441-4460) and **Southeast Air Tours** (call 919-473-3222) give aerial tours of the Outer Banks.

HISTORIC PLACES

Fort Raleigh National Historical Site, on U.S. 64 at the north end of Roanoke Island, was home to the famous "Lost Colony," a group of settlers who came to the island in 1587 and mysteriously disappeared. It's also

Surf fishing, NC Outer Banks
Photo courtesy of NC Travel and Tourism Division

Golf Vacations Even Non-Golfers Will Enjoy

the site of an earlier settlement that was abandoned. Visitors can watch an orientation film and tour the fort grounds. Call 919-473-5772. Admission is free.

The **Elizabethan Gardens** are also located at the Fort Raleigh National Historic site. The gardens contain several varieties of flowers and other plants, many species of animals and birds, fountains, statues, and courtyards. The history of this site and its Tudor-style buildings can be explored through video presentations and tours given by interpreters in colonial dress. Call 919-473-3234. Admission is charged.

The **Wright Brothers National Memorial**, on U.S. 158 at milepost 8.5 in Kill Devil Hills, is where the Wright Brothers' first flight occurred in 1903. The living quarters have been restored, and the visitors center houses a replica of their plane and additional exhibits. Call 919-441-7430. Admission is charged.

The **Chicamacomico Lifesaving Station**, in Rodanthe on N.C. 12, was originally built in 1874 to assist sailors in danger off the shores of the Outer Banks. Of the eleven Crosses of Honor awarded in the United States, six went to men working at this station. One notable exhibit here relates to the rescue by six Americans of forty-two British sailors from the British frigate *Mirlo*, which sank after a surprise attack from a German U-boat. On Thursdays in the summer, visitors can watch rescue drills. Limited hours between May and October. Call 919-987-1552 or 919-987-2401. Admission is free.

There are several historic lighthouses on the Outer Banks. Among the more distinctive ones are the **Cape Hatteras Lighthouse**, built in 1870, and the American coast's tallest at 208 feet (call 919-995-4474); **Bodie** (pronounced "body") **Island Lighthouse**, built in 1872 (call 919-441-5711); **Currituck Beach Lighthouse**, built in 1875 (call 919-453-4939); and **Ocracoke Lighthouse**, built in 1823, making it North Carolina's oldest operating lighthouse (928-4531). There is no admission charge at any of the lighthouses. All of the lighthouses have visitors centers, but the public can only enter and climb the Cape Hatteras Lighthouse and the Currituck Beach Lighthouse.

MUSEUMS/SCIENCE CENTERS

North Carolina Aquarium on Roanoke Island, on Airport Road off U.S. 64 in Manteo, features a variety of fish and marine life native to the Outer Banks. Aside from tanks, there are special hands-on exhibits and educational programs kids will enjoy. Call 919-473-3493. Admission is charged.

Elizabeth II State Historic Site, located at Ice Plant Island over the bridge from Manteo, is a reproduction of the sixteenth-century sailing ships used for the voyages to Roanoke Island organized by Sir Walter Raleigh. This ship museum demonstrates what daily life was like for these colonists. During the summer, the presentation is enhanced with live actors who dress, act, and even talk the part. There's a visitors center as well as picnic areas on the island. Next door is the Outer Banks History Center with historic displays. Call 919-473-1144. Admission is charged.

CULTURAL OFFERINGS

The Lost Colony is the longest-running outdoor drama in the country, having been continuously performed here since 1937. It's also where Andy Griffith and others got their first acting break. This drama, written by Pulitzer Prize–winner Paul Green, tells of the 117 men, women, and children who were sent here by Sir Walter Raleigh to create a settlement in the wilderness of Roanoke Island. Three years later, these people disappeared, and their fate is unknown to this day. The play is shown at the Waterside Theater in Manteo, on Roanoke Island next to the Elizabethan Gardens. Shows are held nightly except Sunday from mid-June to late August. Call 800-488-5012 for information. Admission is charged. A more recent production is the one-woman play *Elizabeth R*, in which British actress Barbara Hird portrays Queen Elizabeth I. The play is shown in the Pioneer Theater in downtown Manteo. Performances are Wednesdays in July only. Admission is charged. Call 919-473-1144.

There are several art galleries on the Outer Banks, with works to suit every taste. A good place to start is **Gallery Row** in Nags Head, but some other notable galleries include the **Seaside Art Gallery**, located in the TimBuck II shopping center in Corolla; **John de la Vega's Gallery** in downtown Corolla; and the **Morales Art Gallery**, which has two locations, one at 207 East Gallery Row in Nags Head, and the other at Scarborough Faire in Duck.

RECREATION

Jockey's Ridge State Park in Nags Head is named after the East Coast's highest active sand dune, which rises to 100 feet at its peak. This park has free admission and offers kite flying,

sand skiing, hiking, hang gliding (nearby is **Kitty Hawk Kites**, the largest hang-gliding school in the world; call 919-441-4127), or basking in the natural beauty of this mini-desert, where wildlife ranges from beetles to grey foxes. Hours vary by season. Call 919-441-7132.

Camping is available at **Cape Hatteras National Seashore** at five different sites. For fees, rules, camping arrangements, and other information, call 919-473-2111.

Pea Island National Wildlife Refuge is a 5,000-acre marshland that is home to many species of birds and waterfowl, such as snow geese and egrets. Call 919-473-1131. Admission is free.

Fishing is terrific in these waters. Because the Gulf Stream is just 12 miles offshore, there's an abundance of marlin, tuna, sailfish, and dolphin. On Roanoke Island, several marinas offer charter-boat fishing, crabbing, and dock fishing; and similar fishing and boating opportunities await at marinas on the Pamlico Sound off Cape Hatteras, in Silver Lake on Ocracoke Island, and at Oregon Inlet (where, for a small fee, several nearby restaurants will prepare and serve your fresh catch).

Other water sports, such as jetskiing, water-skiing, kayaking, and paddleboating are available on Roanoke Island. Various hotels along the Outer Banks (see Accommodations) also have great tennis facilities.

SEASONAL EVENTS

The **Rogallo Kite Festival** at Jockey's Ridge State Park is in June, and in mid-July, the **Wright Kite Festival** is at the Wright Brothers National Memorial.

The **Virginia Dare Day Celebration** takes place in August at the Fort Raleigh National Historic Site in Manteo. Call 919-473-5772. Also in August, in honor of Virginia Dare, is the annual casting of local infants to appear in *The Lost Colony*. Each Wednesday from mid-June to Labor Day from 4 P.M. until sunset there's a **Sunset Festival** at Pirate Cove Yacht Club in Nags Head. Call 919-473-1451 or 800-762-0245. The Fourth of July brings several family-oriented events, and in August, there's a **New World Festival of the Arts** in Manteo. Call 919-473-2838.

The **Annual Wacky Watermelon Weekend** is held in August on Cape Hatteras. This two-day celebration features a parade, crowning of the Watermelon Queen, a windsurfing regatta, and several humorous contests such as seed spitting and watermelon throwing. Call 919-441-6800.

For more information on these or other events, call the Dare County/Outer Banks Tourist Bureau at 919-473-2138 or 800-446-6262.

ACCOMMODATIONS ....

EXPENSIVE

The elegant **Sanderling Inn Resort** is on N.C. 12 in Duck (1461 Duck Road). A stay here includes breakfast, wine and hors d'oeuvres, a private beach, outdoor veranda with chairs, indoor and outdoor pools, tennis courts, and fitness facilities. There's a wonderful restaurant by the same name next door. Call 919-261-4111.

Tranquil House Inn, on the Manteo waterfront, is fashioned and named after a former Victorian inn.

There's a wrap-around porch; Victorian-themed rooms, many overlooking the water; and a library with a fireplace. The inn also has a great waterfront restaurant called 1587. Call 919-473-1404 or 800-458-7069 (for the restaurant, call 919-473-1587).

MODERATE

The **3 Seasons Guests House/Bed & Breakfast**, located at 4628 Sea Scape Drive in Kitty Hawk, overlooks the terrific Sea Scape Golf Course (See Golf Information). There's a cozy fireplace, outdoor jacuzzi, tennis court, pool, golf packages, and bicycles. Call 919-261-4791 or 800-847-3373.

Advice 5 Cents (though rooms cost a bit more) is a new bed-and-breakfast at Scarborough Lane in Duck. Guests are pampered with afternoon tea, beach chairs, and private sunning decks. There's also tennis and a pool. Call 800-ADVICE5.

Quality Inn-Sea Oatel, at Milepost 16.5 in Nags Head, has some oceanfront rooms, a pool, and wading pool. Call 919-441-7191 or 800-228-5151.

Quality Inn-John Yancey Motor Hotel, at Milepost 10 in Kill Devil Hills, is great for families as it has a pool, playground, patios and balconies, refrigerators, and special "family-size" rooms. Call 919-441-7727 or 800-228-5151.

MODERATE/INEXPENSIVE

Elizabethan Inn, on U.S. 64/264 in Manteo, is centrally located to area attractions. This Tudor-style motel features an impressive fitness complex with two pools, racquetball, aerobics classes, and massage. The Elizabethan Restaurant is also here. Call 919-473-2101 or 800-346-2466.

Nags Head Inn, located at 4701 South Virginia Dare Drive, is a five-story inn with a whirlpool and indoor and outdoor pools. Rooms have refrigerators and balconies. Rates are reasonable for this beachfront location. Call 919-441-0454 or 800-327-8881.

Budget Host Inn, located at Milepost 9 in Kill Devil Hills, has relatively spacious rooms and a covered heated pool. Call 919-441-2503 or 800-982-2503.

SHOPPING ....

For outlet shopping, try the **Nags Head Factory Outlet Center** with outlets like Polo/Ralph Lauren and London Fog. Call 919-441-7395.

Scarborough Faire, located on N.C. 12 in Duck, is a quaint village-like collection of twenty-three shops and restaurants under the natural drapery of oaks and pine trees. Also in Duck, at Milepost 9.5 on Beach Road, north of the water tower on the sound, are the **Waterfront Shops**.

In Kill Devil Hills, **Sea Holly Square** has several stores, from gift shops to a country store. In Corolla, across from Buck Island, is **TimBuck II**, a shopping center with over sixty shops.

RESTAURANTS ....

FINE DINING

The **Blue Point Bar and Grill**, at the Waterfront Shops in Duck, is a fine restaurant with a 1950s-style atmosphere. The cuisine is contemporary southern (e.g., crab cakes and jambalaya). Call 919-261-8090.

Kelly's Outer Banks Restaurant and Tavern, at Milepost 10.5 on U.S. 158 in Nags Head, has good food, and some of their recipes have been published by *Bon Appétit*. The emphasis is on fish here, with popular selections being crab fettucini, Roanoke crab cakes, and a raw bar. Non-fish selections include prime rib and chicken. The walls display local memorabilia. Call 919-441-4116.

CASUAL DINING

Awful Arthur's Oyster Bar, at Milepost 6 on U.S. 12 in Kill Devil Hills, is a casual place with a copper-topped oyster bar, plenty of fresh-steamed seafood and pitchers of beer, as well as sandwiches, steaks, and unique seafood "burgers." It's popular with locals and visitors. Call 919-441-5955.

The Weeping Radish Brewery and German Gardens, on U.S. 64 in Manteo, brews three types of beer at its on-site brewery, which visitors can tour. Families may enjoy the beer garden with its gingerbread house and playground. Cuisine includes sausages and other German dishes in a similarly themed dining room and pub. Waitresses wear Bavarian clothing. Call 919-473-1157.

Owens' Restaurant, at Milepost 17 on U.S. 158 in Nags Head, is a popular spot which has been run by the local Owens family for over fifty years. This casual place serves chicken, steaks, and seafood, as well as kids' meals. The restaurant has a nautical theme and local artifacts on the walls, while upstairs, the Station Keepers Lounge is where lifesaving crews used to hang out. Call 919-441-7309. Also owned by another member of this family is **Clara's Steam**

The Village of Ocracoke

Photo by William Russ, courtesy of NC Travel and Tourism Division

Bar and Seafood Grill, on Roanoke Island in Manteo. Call 919-473-1727.

The Channel Bass, on N.C. 12 in Hatteras, is another great seafood restaurant. The restaurant has a nautical decor and serves traditional fare, including Hatteras chowder and fresh regional fish dishes, as well as terrific pies. Call 919-986-2250.

JUST FOR KIDS ....

Kids ages five to thirteen who are interested in ecology and culture can become a Cape Hatteras Seashore Ranger (and earn a patch to prove it) by completing a checklist of requirements and worksheets. The checklist is available from either the Hatteras Island Visitors Center or the Pea Island National Wildlife Refuge and can take sev-

eral days to complete. Other programs for kids are sponsored at the North Carolina Aquarium on Roanoke Island and at Jockey's Ridge State Park. **Kitty Hawk Kites** (with shops in Kill Devil Hills and other locations) has a new children's program. Call 919-441-4127.

Sun-Sational Sitters offers babysitting services at your hotel room or cottage by mature adults (four-hour minimum required). Call 919-441-TOTS for fees and information.

SIDE TRIPS ....

Ocracoke is an old fishing village on Ocracoke Island, just south of Cape Hatteras. The island is reachable only by ferry. During the forty-minute ride, visitors often spot dolphins. The island is where the pirate Blackbeard was captured and beheaded in 1718 in response to a price placed on his larcenous head by the English Crown. It's also home to the mysterious Ocracoke ponies, whose presence baffles biologists and historians, as these animals are not native to the United States. The British Cemetery, officially British soil, is here. The small plot, where four unknown British soldiers are buried, was donated to England in 1942, though the grounds are tended by natives (properly referred to as "Outer Bankers"). For ferry schedule and information about Ocracoke, call 919-928-4531.

Elizabeth City is located on U.S. 17 about an hour inland from the Outer Banks. The city has a thirty-block historic district with the largest concentration of pre-Civil War commercial buildings in North Carolina. **The Museum of the Albemarle** documents the natural and cultural history of the region with exhibits on Native Americans, European settlers, wooden decoys, and other subjects. For more information, call the Elizabeth City Chamber of Commerce at 919-335-4365. Near Elizabeth City, on U.S. 17 North, there's a visitors center for the **Great Dismal Swamp**, the country's only living peat bog (swamp is a misnomer).

Edenton is a quaint town about an hour-and-a-half inland from the Outer Banks on U.S. 17. The women of Edenton had the first "tea party" in 1774 (in the political sense of the Boston Tea Party), and a bronze teapot commemorates their bravery. Many of the old homes and buildings, built and occupied by wealthy merchants and planters, are now open to the public. Admission charges to individual homes

are relatively small; however, package tours are available. Tours run daily; hours vary seasonally. Contact the Historic Edenton Visitors Center at 919-482-2637.

Morehead City, a resort town known for its beaches and fishing, is located south of the Outer Banks area. The **Morehead City Country Club** has a quality, semi-private golf course; call 919-726-4917 for information. However, the real attraction here is the fishing, which is terrific for blue marlin, mackerel, tarpon, and several other species. Onshore fishing, as well as offshore boat charters, is available. In the summer, there's an amateur fishing tournament, and the fall brings the Atlantic Beach fishing tournament in September and a seafood festival in October. For more information, call the Carteret County Tourism Development Bureau at 919-726-8148.

New Bern, located on the Neuse River, can make a nice side trip for both golfers and non-golfers, since the **Emerald Golf Club** is here. The Emerald Golf Club is a fine, Rees Jones designed course that opened in 1988. It hosts the Curtis Strange Shrine Classic (where professionals and celebrities play for charities) and has hosted the 1992 and '93 PGA Tour qualifying school. For information, call 919-633-4440. New Bern is a history buff's delight, as this was the former colonial state capital. One of the more outstanding sights here is the **Tryon Palace and Gardens**, which served as the former residence of the colonial royal governor. At the time, the palace understandably was considered the most beautiful home in America. There are also two other historic homes on the grounds. Call

919-638-1560 for information. Near Tryon Palace is the **New Bern Firemen's Museum**, which houses firefighting equipment from the 1800s, Civil War artifacts, and several objects from New Bern's namesake city in Switzerland. Call 919-636-4087. For visitor information, call 919-637-9400.

GENERAL INFORMATION ....

For more information, contact the Dare County Tourist Bureau at 919-473-2138 or 800-446-6262, or the Outer Banks Chamber of Commerce at 919-441-8144. For information on local shops, restaurants, hotels, and more, get a copy of the *Sunny Day* guide, published by Surfside East (800-SUNNY-DA). You can pick these up in local shops or at the Outer Banks Chamber of Commerce at the corner of Colington Road and Mustian Street in Kill Devil Hills. The Outer Banks Chamber of Commerce also distributes, in coordination with Dare County Tourist Bureau, an *Outer Banks Vacation Guide* that's updated annually. *The Restaurant Guide of the Outer Banks* is published by Three Dogs, Inc., P.O. Box 1442, Kill Devil Hills, North Carolina, 27948; or call 919-261-7529.

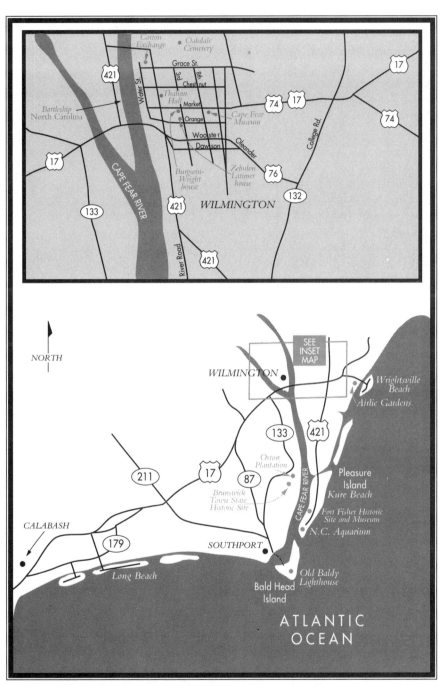

WILMINGTON and the CAPE FEAR COAST, N.C.

Wilmington and the Cape Fear Coast

INTRODUCTION ....

The Cape Fear Coast is the region that begins around Wilmington and Wrightsville Beach, North Carolina, and ends on the southernmost point of the North Carolina coast, just a short drive from Myrtle Beach, South Carolina. Wilmington, the region's largest city, is located inland from the cape and situated on the Cape Fear River. The shores of the Cape Fear Coast encompass Wrightsville Beach, Carolina Beach, and Kure Beach, all considered to be among the best beaches in the eastern United States. Of these, Wrightsville Beach and Kure Beach are especially family oriented, although Wrightsville Beach is considered by many to be more upscale. Incidentally, the state park at Carolina Beach, and the surrounding 100-mile radius, is the only area in the world where the Venus's-flytrap, the fly- and meat-eating marvel of the plant world, is indigenous.

The city of Southport and Bald Head Island are 35 miles south of

Wilmington, and another 35 miles south is the tiny fishing town of Calabash, as well as Ocean Isle Beach and Sunset Beach (whose golf courses are considered by some to be part of the Myrtle Beach/Grand Strand golf area). Although the entire area has public-access golf courses, you'll find many of the finest golf courses in North Carolina and the United States clustered around these locales south of Wilmington. However, Wilmington offers most of the area's historic sites, museums, and cultural events.

The city of Wilmington was incorporated in 1739 and named for the Earl of Wilmington. Throughout the city's history, Wilmington's port has been essential to United States trade. During the Civil War, it was the final Confederate port to be closed by the Union. Also during the Civil War, it was the site where many Confederate blockade runners risked their lives to smuggle munitions and other needed supplies from Europe and export cotton in turn.

Recent renovations to the Wilmington waterfront have made it a popular draw for tourists, with its many shops and restaurants. Additionally, the city has nearly 200 blocks of architecture listed on the National Register of Historic Places.

Bald Head Island, off the mainland city of Southport, is ideal for golfers, beach lovers, and nature enthusiasts, and it's one of North Carolina's best-kept secrets. The island gets its name from a large sand dune where the vegetation was worn bare from being used as a lookout during the Revolutionary and Civil Wars. Though small, the island is never crowded—even at the height of its season—and it boasts an 18-hole,

George Cobb golf course surrounded by acres of salt marshes, forest, and tidewater creeks. The island is reachable only by ferry from Southport, (call 910-457-5003 for transportation to the island; there is a charge for the ferry ride). Strictly enforced rules keep the number of visitors down, and island transportation is restricted to golf carts and bicycles. This serves to protect the island's abundant native plants and wildlife, including the endangered loggerhead turtle. Each year during the summer egg-laying season, the island's conservancy holds nightly "turtle watch" programs in which groups of twenty people, led by naturalists using special flashlights, watch turtles build their nests on the beach. Participants help guide mother turtles on shore, and later in the summer, groups help newly hatched baby turtles find their way to the Atlantic unharmed. Visitors can come to the island for the day to tour, enjoy the beaches, or play golf. For longer stays, the island has two bed-and-breakfasts and several homes for rent. Hourly ferries make getting on and off the island easy for overnight and day guests.

Normal monthly temperatures for the Cape Fear Coast area, as measured in Wilmington, are as follows: January, 43.8; February, 46.4; March, 54.1; April, 61.7; May, 69.4; June, 76; July, 79.4; August, 78.5; September, 73.5; October, 63.4; November, 55.6; December, 47.4. The most popular vacation months here are from April through November, with the peak season running roughly from May through September.

GOLF INFORMATION ....

MARSH HARBOUR, CALABASH (910) 579-3161 OR (800) 377-2315

Marsh Harbour, opened in 1980, is one of the finest courses in North Carolina. Along with Oyster Bay Golf Links (see below) and the Legends and the Heritage Club in Myrtle Beach, Marsh Harbour is part of the renowned Legends Group of courses owned by Larry Young. It is a beautiful, challenging course that is rated among the best public courses by *Golf Digest*. This 6690-yard (tees start at 4795 yards), Dan Maples layout features a par of 71 and is cut through marshes, wetlands, and trees. As with many of the courses in this area, wildlife is abundant, so even if you're not on top of your game, the activity around the course is captivating. Marsh Harbour has three exceptional par 5s: the ninth, fifteenth, and seventeenth. The ninth is a 540-yard dogleg left that is bordered on the left with water from tee to green. The second shot is the gamble, for the player can cut across a marsh to a narrow deep green. The 570-yard fifteenth, the number one handicap hole, offers many watery graves. The tee shot must skirt wetlands to the left; the second shot must find an island fairway protected with water on the right, front, and rear; and the approach plays over a marsh. The beautiful seventeenth is 510 yards, and it also plays along wetlands to a large green that is surrounded by marshes and trees. As is obvious from the brief description of these holes, patience should be your modus operandi for this lovely course.

Carts: Mandatory. *Greens Fees:* $82/ 18 holes in high season; cart: $17 per person in high season. *Tee Time Policy:* Can and should reserve several months in advance; must give deposit for advance times during high season.

OYSTER BAY GOLF LINKS, SUNSET BEACH (910) 579-3528 OR (800) 377-2315

This is another very fine Dan Maples layout, rated among the top public courses in the United States and North Carolina. Like Marsh Harbour, it's affiliated with the Legends Group, which also includes the Legends and the Heritage Club in Myrtle Beach. It is set among marshes, wetlands, lagoons, lakes, pines, oaks, and oyster shells (no kidding). Wildlife is abundant and fascinating, with egrets, herons, ducks, cormorants, ibises, gulls, terns, and gators (to name a few) visible from the course. Oyster Bay is a par 71, almost 6785-yard course with a high slope of 137 and a course rating of over 74. Nonetheless, as with many of Maples's courses, a great premium is placed on course management and patience. In a sense, a player needs to think about shooting for targets on each shot—a good thought even for wide-open courses. Fifteen holes involve water, and bunkers guard and define many fairway landing areas. The greens are surrounded by water, bunkers, trees, and on the picturesque seventeenth, by the course's trademark oyster shells.

Carts: Mandatory. *Greens Fees:* $45-$75/18 holes, depending on season; cart: $17 per person. *Tee Time Policy:* Can reserve up to a year ahead; must give deposit for advance times during high season. It's best to reserve well in advance.

SANDPIPER BAY GOLF AND COUNTRY CLUB, SUNSET BEACH (910) 579-9120 OR (800) 356-5827

Sandpiper is another lovely course designed by Dan Maples, and consistent with the property's purpose as a wildlife sanctuary, Maples has preserved the lay of the land. Sandpipers, herons, egrets, hawks, and eagles are abundant, as are deer and alligators. The course, winding through oaks, cypress pines, lakes, and marshes, is a fun, wide-open layout with six par 3s, seven par 4s, and five par 5s.

Carts: Mandatory. *Greens Fees:* $14–$46, depending on season and packages/18 holes. *Tee Time Policy:* Call for times (public course).

SEA TRAIL PLANTATION, SUNSET BEACH (800) 546-5748

Sea Trail Plantation features three courses, each designed by one of three top architects: Dan Maples, Rees Jones, and Willard Byrd. Each course is a par 72 and stretches out to approximately 6750 yards, with tees beginning at apporximately 5000 yards. The Maples Course, rated among the top new resort courses when it opened in 1986, is a picturesque layout set among mature oaks, cypress, pine forests, lakes, and wetlands. The small to medium greens are defined and protected by an assortment of obstacles and hazards, including ponds, lakes, bunkers, waste areas, and trees.

The Jones Course, opened in the spring of 1990, is well treed, but that is not to say there is any shortage of water to worry about. An interesting hole is the tenth: it's a 345-yard, sharp-right dogleg which hugs a lake from tee to

The North Carolina Coast
Photo courtesy of the NC Travel and Tourism Division

Golf Vacations Even Non-Golfers Will Enjoy

green. Depending on the wind, a player is tempted to play for the green—a 275-yard carry—or cut off as much of the lake as possible to leave a very short approach. Even if a player chooses the more prudent path, approaches to this green are pretty scary, as it's protected to the right, back, and left with water.

The Byrd Course, true to his form, requires accurate shotmaking and finesse. Errant shots lead to high numbers, so a successful player here will be patient, bring a couple of extra balls, and be careful in his or her club selection so as to keep the ball in play.

Carts: Mandatory. *Greens Fees:* $28-$62, depending on time of year/18 holes. *Tee Time Policy:* Call anytime to reserve tee time.

BALD HEAD ISLAND CLUB, BALD HEAD ISLAND (910) 457-7310 OR (800) 234-1666

This stunning, links-style, George Cobb layout is something to behold, as well as play. Bald Head, rated four stars by *Golf Digest's Places to Play*, is set near the ocean among salt marshes, lagoons, and maritime forests. Wildlife of all sorts are visible, including herons, ibis, egrets, alligators, raccoons, and squirrels. With the everpresent wind, the course, stretching to over 6800 yards (with a minimum of 4810 yards), is a real test (witness its unusually high slope of 143). Water is a factor on fifteen holes, and on a rough day, you might find yourself looking for the yellow balls with stripes in the bottom of your bag. The first six holes start nicely with a few short par 4s, a par 5, and a par 3. The fun starts on the seventh. It's a reachable par 5 (depending on the wind) with water from behind the tee to just

short of the green. The ninth is a long par 4 that is bordered by water going all the way up the left side, behind the green, and back down the right side. The sixteenth is a par 3 jewel, with an awesome view of the ocean. Finally, the eighteenth is a bear at 460 yards, with water on both sides of the fairway in the tee-shot landing area. The approach is to a long and narrow green, bunkered on both sides and very difficult to hit. All in all, this is a gem that must be played.

Carts: Mandatory from Memorial Day to Labor Day. *Greens Fees:* $43 for members and temporary members (guests on the island who purchase membership), $65-$78 for non-members/18 holes. *Tee Time Policy:* Can reserve up to a week in advance for members and temporary members; for non-members, reserve at least seven days ahead.

OTHER EXCELLENT AREA COURSES:

Lion's Paw Golf Links, Sunset Beach (800-233-1801), a Willard Byrd designed course that can stretch to 7003 yards, features water on each hole on the links-style back nine. **The Pearl Golf Links,** Sunset Beach (910-579-8132), is set against the backdrop of a 900-acre marsh preserve. The Pearl features two 1987 Dan Maples courses that were considered among the best new public courses in the United States by *Golf Digest* and have hosted the North Carolina Open and Amateur Championships. **Ocean Harbour Golf Links**, Calabash (910-579-3588), was considered by *Golf* to be among the best new public courses in the world when it opened in 1989. This 7004-yard, par 72, Clyde Johnston design is set between the

Calabash River and the Intracoastal Waterway and crosses the North and South Carolina border four times. **Brunswick Plantation Golf Links**, Calabash (910-287-7888), and **North Shore Country Club**, Sneads Ferry, located north of Wilmington (910-327-2410), are two other good area courses.

ATTRACTIONS ....

TOURS

Walking Tours
Wilmington Adventure Walking Tours depart daily at 10 A.M. and 2 P.M., April through October, from the bottom of Market Street near the waterfront. Call 910-763-1785. Maps for self-guided tours can be obtained from the Cape Fear Convention and Visitors Bureau, 24 North Third Street. Call 800-222-4757.

Guided tours of Bald Head Island via golf cart last about two hours. For information or reservations, call 910-457-5003.

Boat Tours
Black Water Tours conducts guided canoe and kayak wildlife tours by appointment. Joe Spitzer is an excellent tour guide whose personable demeanor and extensive work at the North Carolina Aquarium in Fort Fisher make him well qualified to give this tour. Call 910-791-8756.

Narrated cruises are also a good way to get oriented to the area. In Wilmington, you can board the *Captain J.N. Maffitt*, which schedules a stop for touring the Battleship *North Carolina*. Tours depart from Market Street,

Henrietta II, *Wilmington*
Photo by William Russ,
courtesy of NC Travel and Tourism Division

May through September. Call 910-343-1611 or 800-676-0162. The *Henrietta II* paddlewheel riverboat takes visitors on sightseeing, dinner, and holiday cruises between April and December. Call 910-343-1611 or 800-676-0162.

HISTORIC PLACES

If you enjoy historic buildings, you'll find several sites of interest in Wilmington. Two historic houses located two blocks apart are open to the public as museums. One, the white, Georgian-style colonial **Burgwin-Wright House** was built in 1770 on the same foundation as the former city jail, and it served as General Cornwallis's headquarters in 1781. Inside are closets (rare in those days), and outside, a separate kitchen building. Open Tuesdays through Saturdays. Closed in January. The house is located at 224 Market Street (at Third Street). Admission is charged. Call 910-762-0570. The other, the **Zebulon Latimer House**, is located at 126 South Third Street. It is a four-story, Italian Revival home built in 1852 by a wealthy merchant. This house was the first in Wilmington to have electricity. Tours run Tuesday through Saturday. Admission is charged. Call 910-762-0492.

Wilmington's **Oakdale Cemetery**, located at 520 North Fifteenth Street, is where Henry Bacon, the designer of the Lincoln Memorial, and other famous citizens are buried. There are segregated sections for Confederate veterans, yellow fever victims of 1862, Jews, and Masons. Admission is free.

In nearby Kure Beach is the **Fort Fisher State Historic Site**, located on U.S. 421. The fort, probably the most sophisticated one in the Confederacy, was designed to protect ships as they entered the city's port. The fort withstood two bombardments, but finally fell near the end of the war, paving the way for the South's defeat. Ironically, simple erosion has caused more damage to the fort than the Union artillery. The fort itself resembles huge ant hills, as its earthen mounds were created by constructing the bombproofs and covering them with sand and earth to absorb the shock from explosions. Inside the visitors center are an audiovisual presentation and displays of Civil War ammunition and other artifacts. Open Tuesday through Saturday year-round and Mondays April through October; hours vary seasonally. Admission is free. Call 910-458-5538.

The World War II–era Battleship *North Carolina*, moored on the coast of the Cape Fear River, is now a memorial to the war dead. The museum has a ten-minute orientation film as well as exhibits. From there, visitors can enter the ship's iron shell and view the rooms. Open daily 8 A.M. until dark. Located on Battleship Drive on Eagle Island. From the first Friday in June through Labor Day, there's a seventy-minute light-and-sound production, *The Immortal Showboat*, aboard the battleship in the evening. Admission is charged for entrance to the ship and the show. For information, call 910-251-5797.

MUSEUMS/SCIENCE CENTERS

The **North Carolina Aquarium at Fort Fisher**, on U.S. 421 within the Fort Fisher State Recreational Area, features marine species found within a five-mile radius of the museum. Because the Gulf Stream comes near Cape Fear's shoreline, the more than 200 species (encompassing about 200,000 specimens) of local fish, reptiles, and invertebrates tend toward tropical varieties, and many are quite colorful. Admission is charged. Call 910-458-8257.

The **Cape Fear Museum**, at 814 Market Street, houses exhibits on the natural and cultural history of the lower Cape Fear area. Of note are a nineteenth-century replica of the city, a jersey worn by Michael Jordan, and a sound-equipped model of Fort Fisher. Open Tuesday through Saturday from 9 A.M. to 5 P.M. and Sunday from noon to 4 P.M. Admission is charged. Call 910-341-7413.

Other notable museums (admission charged for each) include **St. John's Museum of Art**, at 114 Orange Street, which has prints by Mary Cassatt, Jugtown pottery pieces, and various paintings and sculptures, many by North Carolina artists. Open Tuesday through Sunday. Call 910-763-0281. The **Bellamy Mansion**, at Market

The Cotton Exchange, Wilmington
Photo by William Russ, courtesy of NC Travel and Tourism Division

Street and Fifth Avenue, houses exhibits on design arts and local history. The architecture and lore of this antebellum home are part of its charm. Open Wednesday through Saturday. Call 910-251-3700. The **Wilmington Railroad Museum**, at 501 Nutt Street, focuses on southeastern railroad lines such as the Atlantic Coast Line and the Wilmington & Weldon Railroad. Outside exhibits include an old caboose and a steam locomotive you can board; the inside features a working, scale-model railroad and a recreated waiting room with sound effects. Open daily March through October; limited hours other months. Call 910-763-2634.

In Southport, the **Maritime Museum**, at 116 North Howe Street, has artifacts from sunken ships, old naviga-

tional instruments, and more. Open Tuesday through Saturday from 10 A.M. to 4 P.M. Admission is charged. Call 910-457-0003.

CULTURAL OFFERINGS

Thalian Hall Center for the Performing Arts hosts a variety of quality arts groups and performers throughout the year. The ornate-columned white building, built in 1858 as a city hall, is where nineteenth-century luminaries like Buffalo Bill and Lillian Russell performed. For tickets and information, call 910-343-3664.

The **Opera House Theater Company**, at 2011 Carolina Beach Road, presents a variety of professional theater productions. For information, call 910-762-4234.

Airlie Gardens, on Airlie Road off U.S. 74, has picturesque grounds that once were a rice plantation. Visitors can tour by car or on foot. Open daily March through September. Admission is charged. Call 910-763-4646.

SEASONAL EVENTS

There are several local music festivals featuring top talent. In Wilmington, the **North Carolina Jazz Festival** occurs in February and the **Cape Fear Blues Festival** is in July. However, the biggest annual event is Wilmington's **North Carolina Azalea Festival** in April. The **Old Wilmington by Candlelight Home Tour** takes place over two weekends in early December, as do other Christmas season activities. For more information on these or other events in the Wilmington area, call the Cape Fear Coast Convention and Visitors Bureau at 800-222-4757.

Southport's annual **North Carolina Fourth of July Festival** is well attended, with plenty of family oriented activities. For information, call the Southport-Oak Island Chamber of Commerce at 910-457-6964.

ACCOMMODATIONS ....

EXPENSIVE

The **Blockade Runner Resort Hotel**, at 275 Waynick Boulevard in Wrightsville Beach, has rooms with beautiful ocean or sound views from private patios. Guests can enjoy a lifeguarded pool, golf and tennis packages, an exercise room that includes whirlpool and sauna, and a children's program in summer. Call 910-256-2251 or 800-541-1161.

Marsh Harbor Inn Bed and Breakfast, on Bald Head Island, is a quiet, elegant inn with fifteen individually decorated rooms. Rooms feature poster beds and bleached-wood floors. Some rooms have private porches equipped with rocking chairs, and there are more chairs on the expansive front porch. Gourmet breakfasts are included (with a complimentary *New York Times* that comes via fax service), as are afternoon wine and hors d'oeuvres, and a personal golf cart for getting around the island. In season, custom-tailored meal selections are created by the resident chef. Call 800-957-4972.

MODERATE

Catherine's Inn, at 410 South Front Street in Wilmington, is a lovely, two-story historic home with stately columns and ornate detailing. Guests enjoy beautifully appointed rooms, a waterfront setting, and complimentary breakfast and refreshments. Call 910-251-0863 or 800-476-0723.

The **Docksider Inn**, on U.S. 421 in Kure Beach, is an oceanfront inn with wood siding and comfortable rooms and efficiencies. Call 910-458-4200.

INEXPENSIVE

Ocean Isle Motel, at 16 Causeway Drive in Ocean Isle Beach, is on the ocean and has reasonably priced, comfortable rooms. It offers a jacuzzi, an indoor and an outdoor pool, and a free continental breakfast. Call 910-579-0750.

Admiral's Quarters Motel, at 113 South Fort Fisher Boulevard in Kure Beach, is an oceanfront motel with spacious, comfortable rooms that have private balconies. There are two ocean-front pools, and efficiencies are available. Call 910-458-5050.

SHOPPING ....

The **Cotton Exchange** building, on North Front Street across from Wilmington's riverfront, houses restaurants and specialty shops. Inside the old, red-brick building you can see hurricane rods and iron lanterns. Open Monday through Saturday from 10 A.M. to 5:30 P.M. (some shops open Sunday from 1 to 5 P.M.). For information, call 910-343-9896. Also on Wilmington's riverfront, where Ann and Water Streets meet, is **Chandler's Wharf**, whose old buildings are now restaurants and specialty shops. Open daily except Sundays.

RESTAURANTS ....

FINE DINING

The chef at **Gardenias**, at 7105 Wrightsville Avenue in Wrightsville Beach, uses local ingredients to create new dishes or rework classics. The wine list is impressive and the desserts are decadent. Open daily in season; closed Mondays in winter. Call 910-256-2421.

CASUAL DINING

The Pilot House, at 2 Ann Street on Wilmington's riverfront, is located in a restored 1870 home. This airy restaurant has a nautical feel and windows facing the river. House specialties include Cape Fear chowder, crab melt, several fish and meat dishes, and a brownie-like Caribbean fudge pie. Din-

ers receive pewter bread plates and water goblets. Call 910-343-0200.

The **Oceanic Restaurant and Grille**, at 703 South Lumina Avenue in Wrightsville Beach, is a good choice for beachfront dining. There, you'll find fresh, perfectly cooked seafood and shellfish. Specialties include the day's catch cooked one of six different ways, a seafood lasagna, and she-crab soup. Save room for key lime pie, cheesecake, or one of their other terrific desserts. Open daily for lunch and dinner. Call 910-256-5551.

Wally's, at 4 Marina Drive in Wrightsville Beach, is a lively place on the waterfront that features fresh seafood. It's popular with visitors and locals alike for meals, and in summer, for the music and cocktails on the outside deck. Call 910-256-2002.

The **River Pilot Cafe** on Bald Head Island is an intimate restaurant located at the marina. The menu emphasizes seafood with a regional creative flair. Popular items include the seafood and pasta combination, pepper-Parmesan salad dressing, and the coconut cake. Meat lovers have plenty of choices, as well. Open for lunch and dinner. Call 910-457-7390.

Located 35 miles south of Wilmington on U.S. 17, and just south of Sunset Beach and Ocean Isle Beach, **Calabash** is a seafood lover's delight. The town has some thirty restaurants, all vying for status as *the* place to go for authentic Calabash-style seafood, which is breaded and fried. Locals and visitors alike say you can't go wrong no matter which restaurant you choose, and in high season, you'll probably have to wait for a table. For a couple of recommendations, try **The Original Ella's of Calabash**, at 1148 River Road, between N.C. 179 and the waterfront on Beach Drive (call 910-579-6728), and **Larry's Calabash Seafood Barn**, on N.C. 179 (call 910-579-6976).

JUST FOR KIDS ....

Several local resorts offer children's programs, such as Wrightsville Beach's **Blockade Runner Resort's Sandcampers** program for ages five through twelve, and Bald Head Island's **Camp Baldy** for ages four through twelve. Camp Baldy is open to those with a temporary golf club membership, available to all who stay on the island. The program includes swimming, games, and much more. For Camp Baldy information, call 910-457-7500. In other areas, check with your hotel for the availability of such programs.

SIDE TRIPS ....

Orton Plantation and **Brunswick Town State Historic Site** are both about 18 miles south of Wilmington on N.C. 133. Orton Plantation Gardens is a twenty-acre tract overlooking the Cape Fear River that once was a bustling rice plantation. While the Orton House, built in 1730, can be viewed from the garden walkway, it's not open. However, visitors can enjoy gardens lined with stately moss-draped oaks and blooming magnolias, azaleas, and camellias. Open daily March through November; hours vary by season. Admission is charged. Call 910-371-6851. Brunswick Town State Historic Site is a museum of the first settlement on the Cape Fear Coast. Exhibits depict early settlement life, and visitors can view the original home foundations. Admission is free; hours vary seasonally. Call 910-371-6613.

Poplar Grove Plantation, on U.S. 17 about 14 miles northeast of Wilmington, features a Greek Revival–style mansion and demonstrations of blacksmithing, weaving, fabric making, and more. You can also tour the many restored buildings. Open Monday through Saturday from 9 A.M. to 5 P.M., and Sunday from 12 to 5 P.M.; closed in January. Admission is charged. Call 910-686-9989.

GENERAL INFORMATION ....

For more information on this area, contact the Cape Fear Coast Convention and Visitors Bureau at 910-341-4030 or 800-222-4757. For Bald Head Island, contact their information center at 800-234-1666. For publications listing current events, look for *Encore* and *This Week Magazine* in Wilmington. On Bald Head Island, there's the *Bald Head Island Gazette*, and the information center can send you their *Armchair Guide*.

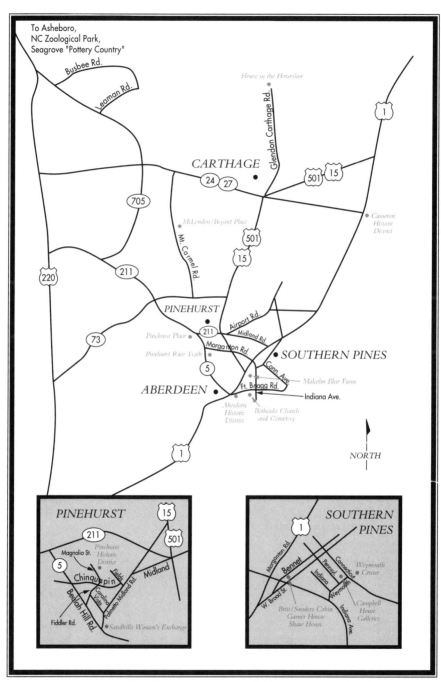

PINEHURST and the SANDHILLS REGION, N.C.

Pinehurst and the Sandhills Region

AREA CODE: 910

INTRODUCTION ....

For golfers, Pinehurst probably needs no introduction, given its world-class reputation for fine courses, including at least two of the world's top ten courses. Yet this decidedly civilized area, with clustered hillside villages, historic homes and farms, and beautiful lakes and mountain ranges, has plenty of offerings for non-golfers, which can make for an enjoyable and relaxing countryside jaunt (especially for shoppers and history buffs) while their companions are on the golf course.

Though the Pinehurst area's main tourist attractions are clustered within three neighboring towns—Pinehurst, Southern Pines, and Aberdeen—there are a few outstanding attractions outside these areas.

The village of Pinehurst, designed by Frederick Olmsted (whose other masterpieces include Asheville's Biltmore Estate and New York's Central Park), has an old-fashioned New England feel. Lovely Georgian-style homes add to its charm. Because pines surround the village, one can easily see where the name Pinehurst originated, and the soil here contains so much sand that the region is nicknamed the sandhills.

Normal monthly temperatures for the Pinehurst area, as measured in Fayetteville, are as follows: January, 40.3; February, 43.3; March, 51.7; April, 60.6; May, 68.5; June, 75.7; July, 79.4; August, 78.3; September, 72.5; October, 61.4; November, 52.7; December, 43.9. The golf season starts up in March and stays in full swing through October.

GOLF INFORMATION ....

PINEHURST RESORT AND COUNTRY CLUB, PINEHURST (910) 295-6811 OR (800) ITS GOLF

Throughout this book, one may notice the excitement and awe this author feels for courses designed by Donald Ross, Robert Trent Jones, Sr., Tom Fazio, Rees Jones, and Ellis Maples. At least one or more of Pinehurst Resort's eight courses are designed by each of these architects (the eighth course, designed by Tom Fazio and aptly named "The Centennial" to mark the 100-year anniversary of the resort, opened in March 1996). The resort dates back to 1895, and the first of four Donald Ross courses opened in 1899. Since that time, Pinehurst has deservedly been hailed as being among the finest golf resorts in the world, and Pinehurst's Number 2 course consistently has been considered among the top five courses in the world. The resort also has been the regular site of

several major tournaments, including the North and South Amateur for Men since 1901, for Women since 1903, for Senior Men since 1952, for Senior Women since 1958, and for Junior Boys and Girls since 1979. Additionally, the North and South Open Championship (considered a "major" on the PGA Tour in the first half of the century) was played here from 1902 to 1951. This tournament boasted Ben Hogan's first professional victory, as well as victories by Walter Hagen, Byron Nelson, Sam Snead, Cary Middlecoff, and Tommy Bolt. Other major tournaments played at the course include the 1936 PGA Championship; the 1951 Ryder Cup Matches; the 1962 United States Men's Amateur Championship; the 1989 United States Women's Amateur Championship; the 1994 United States Senior Open Championship; and the upcoming 1999 United States Men's Open Championship.

Although all of Pinehurst's courses are excellent, Number 2, as indicated above, is the crown jewel. First opened in 1907 and constantly fine-tuned by Ross, the 7020-yard (tees begin at 5,966 yards), par 72 course challenges every part of one's golf game. The tee shot must be accurate and often shaped with a draw or a fade to hold the sloping fairways. Approaches must be precise, well measured, and have the proper trajectory to hold the crowned greens that play even smaller than they appear because they fall off around the edges. The short game must be razor sharp to recover from the dips and swales around each green. As Ray Floyd described the course, it is "truly magnificent." If you must decide upon one place to travel to play golf, make it the Pinehurst Resort.

Carts: Required at some courses. *Greens Fees:* $180-$200 for Number 2 and Number 7 in high season; other courses are less and fees are lower in the offseason/18 holes. *Tee Time Policy:* Best to book well in advance; guests of the resort and those playing through golf packages at hotels and advance-tee-time agreements with Pinehurst will be able to get tee times. It is very difficult for non-guests to get tee times here unless staying at an area hotel that has an agreement with the resort, though non-guests can try to obtain same-day tee times in hopes of a rare cancellation or opening.

THE PINE NEEDLES GOLF COURSE, PINEHURST (910) 692-8611

Pine Needles is a 1927 Donald Ross course that, in a testament to the durability of his designs, was the site of the 1996 United States Women's Open. Additionally, the course was named by *Golf* as one of the "Top 100 You Can Play." This par 71 course offers tees that range from 5039 to 6708 yards and rating/slope ratio from 68.4/118 to 72.2/131. It also offers many classic characteristics of a Ross designed course. For example, Ross's method of walking a site to find the eighteen best settings for greens is evident at Pine Needles, since the greens seem to naturally fit the landscape. The fairways, although generous, reward a well-placed tee shot by providing the player with the best angle to approach the green. Additionally, the course is almost devoid of water, reflecting Ross's view that a two-shot penalty was, and still is, too severe. Ross did believe that every course should have long, tough par 4s (Pine Needles has five par 4s that are over

430 yards) because such holes, he said, are "the ultimate test of a golfer's skill." In addition to this very fine course, Pine Needles is the site of the "Golfari"—a five-day expedition for women to have fun while improving their game that has been conducted by Peggy Kirkland Bell since 1969.

Carts: Required during peak season. *Greens Fees:* $99/18 holes in the high season. *Tee Time Policy:* Must reserve a week in advance; for peak seasons (especially spring, but also fall), book well in advance.

THE PIT GOLF LINKS, PINEHURST (910) 944-1600

The Pit is a truly remarkable layout that has been carved out of what remains of a sand excavation. Thus, it offers some of the most unusual terrain a golfer will ever encounter. Designed by Dan Maples and opened in 1985, it quickly was recognized by *Golf Digest* to be among the top seventy-five public courses in the United States. The tees on this par 72 course range from 4759 to 6600 yards—not long by modern standards—but the rating/slope ranges from 68.4/121 to 72.3/139. This very high slope reflects the difficulty presented by the Pit's natural hazards. Most of the fairways are bordered by sandhills, grassy dunes, scrub oaks, Carolina pines, and an assortment of gnarled underbrush. Missed greens usually result in missing balls, because many of the greens are surrounded by woods, lovegrass, dunes, and ridges. This wide variety of natural hazards makes it necessary to play a patient, smart game of golf to score well at the Pit.

Carts: Required most of the time (mandatory in high season). *Greens Fees:*

$85 in season, $42 off season/ 18 holes, including cart. *Tee Time Policy:* Call for tee time (this is a public course); best to call well ahead for high season.

TALAMORE AT PINEHURST, PINEHURST (910) 692-5884

(Note: Talamore also has a golf and travel service specializing in the Pinehurst area; call (800) 552-6292.)

Talamore is another excellent course in the Pinehurst area designed by Rees Jones. Opened in 1991, this par 71 course reaches to just over 7020 yards from the back tees (4995 yards from the front tees), but it sports a remarkable slope of 142 (the slope begins at 125 while the rating is from 69 to almost 73). Like many of this younger Jones's courses, Talamore's obstacles are obvious, and they suggest the shots required by the player. Executing these shots, however, is the test, and you'll know you're in for a challenge on the first hole, a 607-yard par 5. What makes Talamore outstanding is its diversity: the par 3s range from 153 to 233 yards, the par 4s from 330 to 442 yards, the par 5s from 507 to 607 yards; there are six doglegs; a variety of water, wetland, and sand hazards; the fairways are lined with towering Carolina pines; and the greens come in all shapes, sizes, and rolls. Finally, although caddies are available to tote your golf bag, they are not much help on yardages and green-reads. But don't be too hard on them, as these caddies are llamas.

Carts: Mandatory. *Greens Fees:* $26-$70 ($38 for guests with golf packages)/ 18 holes, including cart. *Tee Time Policy:* Call a week in advance.

Llama caddies, Talamore Golf Club
Photo courtesy of NC Travel and Tourism Division

OTHER EXCELLENT AREA COURSES:

Pinehurst Plantation Golf Club, Pinehurst (910-695-3193), is a 4½-star course according to *Golf Digest's Places to Play* and was named one of the "Top 100 You Can Play" by *Golf* in 1996. It features an Arnold Palmer/Ed Seay design that can stretch to 7135 yards (the tees start at just over 5000 yards). The rating/slope from the back tees is 74.5/140. The **Legacy Golf Links**, Aberdeen (910-944-8825), is a 1991 course that was designed by the Jack Nicklaus Golden Bear team under the direction of Jack Nicklaus, Jr. It sports tees that range from 4948 to 6989 yards. **Mid Pines Resort**, Southern Pines (910-692-2114 or 800-323-2114), is a 6516-yard, classic Donald Ross design with elevated tees and greens; narrow, heavily wooded fairways; and over 100 bunkers. The **Pines Golf Resort**, Pinebluff (910-281-3165), is a rolling 6650-yard, par 72 track among towering loblolly and longleaf pines, dogwoods, and azaleas. **The Club at Longleaf**, Pinehurst (910-692-6100), features a 6600-yard, par 71, Dan Maples layout that was opened in 1988. The course is set on a former horse-training estate, and the links-like front nine moves through steeplechase hedges, while the back nine travels through dense forest with numerous elevation changes and lovely ponds.

ATTRACTIONS ....

TOURS

Kirk Limousine/Van Transportation and Tours offers guided tours of the area. Call 910-281-4369. Pinehurst Resort and Country Club also offers historical tours to guests.

HISTORIC PLACES

Both **Aberdeen** (a few miles south of Pinehurst on U.S. 15/501) and **Cameron** (about ten miles north of Southern Pines on U.S. 1), have historic districts where visitors can enjoy a self-guided walking tour, in addition to several antique dealers. Maps of Aberdeen are available at the Town Hall, 115 Poplar Street. Cameron hosts an annual Antique Street Fair in May and October. A pamphlet with Cameron's shops and historic places is available from the Pinehurst-Southern Pines-Aberdeen Area Convention and Visitors Bureau.

The **Shaw House**, located in Southern Pines at Morganton Road and S.W. Broad Street, was built around 1840 by Charles C. Shaw, whose son became Southern Pine's first mayor. Though not as elaborate as some other antebellum homes of the wealthy, this architecturally interesting house is headquarters to the Moore County Historical Society. Open Wednesday through Sunday 1 to 4 P.M. Call 910-692-2051. Also on the premises are the 1770 Britt-Sanders cabin (known as the Loom House, since it contains an antique loom—weaving demonstrations are scheduled throughout the year), and the 1770 Garner House, an early log cabin with hand-forged hinges, board doors, and period furnishings. Hours are seasonal. Admission is charged for all of the above.

The House in the Horseshoe State Historic Site is located 15 miles north of Pinehurst in Sanford. This clapboard home belonged to pre-Revolutionary politician Philip Alston. The name comes from the horseshoe river bend on which it sits. Guided tours are available. Open daily; hours vary. Admission is free. Call 910-947-2051.

The **Malcolm Blue Farm** (circa 1825) in Aberdeen is on the National Register of Historic Places. There's a farmhouse, barns, wooden water tower, and old gristmill. The farm hosts special events, such as the annual Historic Crafts and Skills Festival in late September, and December's Christmas Open House. Tours by appointment; a small fee is charged. Call 910-944-9483 or 910-944-7558.

CULTURAL OFFERINGS

The Performing Arts Center, at 250 Northwest Broad Street in Southern Pines, dates back to 1898. The center hosts performances in various arts, including music, theater, and dance, mainly by local and regional groups. Call 910-692-3799 or 910-692-4356.

Campbell House Galleries, on Connecticut Avenue N.W. in Southern Pines, showcases the works of regional artists, including several pieces that are for sale, within a quaint Georgian-style home. The gallery also has public tennis, basketball, and fitness courts. Open weekdays from 9 A.M. to 5 P.M. Call 910-692-4356.

Midland Crafters is located on N.C. 2, east of Pinehurst's traffic circle. Visitors can watch craft demonstrations and purchase locally made pottery, jewelry, leather goods, weavings, and other items. Open daily. Call 910-295-6156.

The Weymouth Center, on East Vermont Extension in Southern Pines, has a variety of lectures, concert series, and holiday events. Call 910-692-6261.

RECREATION

The 1915 **Pinehurst Harness Track** is on the National Register of Historic Places. For a schedule of spectator events such as harness racing, call 1-800-433-TROT. Among other events are polo competitions, which take place April through June and September through November. Call 910-949-2106 for polo information. For horseback riding instruction or carriage and pony rides, call **Pinehurst Livery Stable**, on N.C. 5 near the racetrack. 910-296-8456 or 910-295-1114.

Tennis is abundant in Pinehurst, with more than a hundred public courts. Contact the Moore County Parks and Recreation Department at 910-947-2504. Many hotels and resorts also have tennis facilities. Contact your hotel or the Pinehurst-Southern Pines-Aberdeen Area Convention and Visitors Bureau at 800-346-5362.

The Horticultural Gardens, at the Sandhills Community College on Airport Road in Pinehurst, boasts one of the largest collections of holly on the East Coast. There's also a special pine garden, as well as the elegant Tudor-style Sir Walter Raleigh Garden. Open daily. Call 910-692-6185. For more outdoor exploration, head to the 667-acre **Weymouth Nature Preserve and Museum**, located off U.S. 1. Open daily. Call 910-692-2167.

Car racing fans can head to Rockingham (at U.S. 1 and N.C. 177) for the Rockingham Dragway, which hosts the NHRA Winston Invitational and other races. Call 910-582-3400. The North Carolina Motor Speedway is also in Rockingham. This racetrack presents the AC-Delco 200/500 and other NASCAR races. Call 910-582-2861.

SEASONAL EVENTS

In April, the **Stoneybrook Steeplechase Races**, a prestigious event established in 1948, draws spectators from all over. Also in April is the 100-mile **Tour de Moore** bicycle race, which attracts international competitors. April also brings the **Pinehurst House and Gardens Tour**, sponsored by the Southern Pines Garden Club, during which you can view lovely private area homes.

In May, there's a popular **Carthage Buggy Festival**. **The Fine Arts Festival** is held in August at the Campbell House Galleries. For information, call 910-692-4356.

Many golf tournaments take place here, most notably the United States Senior Open, the Women's United States Open and the Men's United States Open. As golf tournaments are too numerous to list, contact the Pinehurst-Southern Pines-Aberdeen Area Convention and Visitors Bureau for more details at 910-692-3330 or 800-346-5362. For weekly updates on events taking place in this area, call the Events Line at 910-692-1600.

ACCOMMODATIONS ....

Accommodations in Pinehurst offer golf packages for particular courses, so check with your hotel for golf package availability at courses you want to play before making reservations.

EXPENSIVE

The Pinehurst Resort and Country Club, at Carolina Vista, is one of the Historic Hotels of America, and is the original resort hotel in Pinehurst. The resort recently celebrated its hundredth birthday, and during its illustrious past, has hosted Rockefellers, Roosevelts, Morgans, and DuPonts. The main building, known by some as "The Carolina" and "The Queen of the South," is a palatial, white, four-story hotel with a signature brass cupola at the top and columned, wrap-around porches with rocking chairs. The resort has seven magnificent golf courses, including two of the top ten courses in the world (see Golf Information). The service and exquisitely appointed rooms are topnotch. Amenities include five pools, twenty-four tennis courts, seasonal children's programs, lawn games, and a fitness center. Accommodations range from hotel rooms to condominiums and villas. Call 910-295-6811 or 800-487-4653 (ITS GOLF).

Pine Needles Resort, on N.C. 2 just off U.S. 1 in Southern Pines, is another prestigious resort with its own renowned golf course (see Golf Information), but with a more woodsy, rustic feel. The two-story hotel is aptly named, as it is surrounded by pines and pine needle carpeting. Rooms are wood-paneled and homey, and many have golf course views. Call 910-692-7111 or 800-747-7272.

MODERATE

Holly Inn, located on Cherokee Road, is an English-style inn with a hunt club decor. Aside from tennis and golf privileges, the antique-furnished rooms are attractive and cozy. Call 910-295-2300 or 800-682-6901.

Hampton Inn, 1675 U.S. 1 South in Pinehurst, has comfortable rooms in a central location, and guests can enjoy the pool and free breakfast. Call 910-692-9266 or 800-333-9266 or 800-HAMPTON.

INEXPENSIVE

The Pine Crest Inn, on Dogwood Road in Pinehurst, is an eighty-four-year-old, English country-style inn whose largely repeat business is attributed to its courteous staff, excellent service, and convenient walking distance from Pinehurst Village. The interior is homey and welcoming. Call 910-295-6121.

The Heritage, in Whispering Pines, 5 miles north of Pinehurst, offers camping facilities. This pretty, 200-acre campsite has a lake with sandy beach, canoeing, boating, fishing, a playground, hayrides, barnyard petting farm, and other family oriented activities. Partial and full hookups are available; some with flush toilets, laundry, and hot showers. Call 910-949-3433.

SHOPPING ....

At the **Sandhills Women's Exchange** you can find old-fashioned handcrafts and homemade baked goods. Light lunch is served weekdays. Open Monday through Friday; open Saturdays except in January and February. Call 910-295-4677.

Antique dealers can be found in Aberdeen and in Cameron, and Southern Pines has a historic district with several shops and restaurants. Pinehurst Village has a collection of shops, art galleries, and restaurants in turn-of-the-century-styled buildings. **Pinehurst Place** is an historic building containing eight specialty shops and a restaurant. Call 910-295-1761.

For an eye-popping selection of pottery, try the approximately sixty shops in nearby Seagrove (see Side Trips).

RESTAURANTS ....

DINNER THEATER

Mannie's Dinner Theater, at 210 West Pennsylvania Avenue in Southern Pines, has dinner and Broadway shows with professional casts. Dinner begins at 7:00 and the curtain goes up at 8:30. Reservations are required. Call 910-692-8400.

FINE DINING

The Carolina Dining Room, in the Pinehurst Resort and Country Club, has crystal chandeliers and views of the hotel's manicured grounds. The dinner menu offers entrées—mainly beef, chicken, and seafood—served American style or in rich European sauces, as well as a prix fixe meal. Open daily for breakfast, lunch, and dinner (served by candlelight, with entertainment in season). Reservations required. Call 910-295-6811.

CASUAL DINING

Holly Inn, on Cherokee Road in Pinehurst, is an upscale casual Victorian-style dining room consistent with the inn's quaint overall decor. Serves breakfast and dinner daily. Call 910-295-2300.

Pine Crest Inn, on Dogwood Road in Pinehurst, offers great food and southern hospitality. Favorites are the beef and fresh vegetable dishes, and homemade desserts. Reservations recommended. Serves breakfast and dinner daily. Call 910-295-6121.

Pinehurst Playhouse Restaurant, at 100 West Village Green in Pinehurst, is a casual lunch place located, along with several little shops, in an old theater. The restaurant serves light, quick fare such as sandwiches named after famous Broadway plays. Call 910-295-8873.

In Southern Pines, **Beefeaters**, at 672 S.W. Broad Street, is a casual, lively place serving juicy prime rib, seafood, pork, chicken, beef, and a huge salad bar. Open daily for dinner. Call 910-692-5550.

Nell Cole Graves of J. B. Cole Pottery, Seagrove

Photo by William Russ, courtesy of NC Travel and Tourism Division

JUST FOR KIDS ....

See the Pinehurst Livery Stable under outdoor recreation for pony rides. There are also several junior golf events scheduled during the year. Some resorts have children's programs in summer.

SIDE TRIPS ....

The Museum of North Carolina Traditional Pottery is located off N.C. 705 in Seagrove, about an hour north of Pinehurst. Seagrove has about sixty pottery shops, including the museum shop. Visitors can watch demonstrations at the museum and the shops. The museum is open Tuesday through Saturday 10 A.M. to 3 P.M. A map of pottery places is available through the Pinehurst-Southern Pines-Aberdeen Area Convention and Visitors Bureau.

The North Carolina Zoological Park is located off U.S. 220 on N.C. 159 near Asheboro. This well-respected and growing zoo has indoor and outdoor exhibits with natural or plexiglass barriers that make encounters as close

as possible. The more than 800 exotic animals come from many regions of the world. Tram rides are available. Open daily. Admission is charged. Call 910-879-7000 or 800-488-0444.

The **Town Creek Indian Mound**, off N.C. 73 near Mount Gilead, is a 300-year-old Pee Dee Indian burial mound that has been archaeologically restored. The museum has additional local artifacts. Open daily April through October; closed Mondays from November 1 through March 31. Hours vary seasonally. Call 910-439-6802.

GENERAL INFORMATION ....

For more information, contact the Pinehurst-Southern Pines-Aberdeen Area Convention and Visitors Bureau (located in Southern Pines) at 910-692-3330 or 800-346-5362. Of special interest to golfers and their companions is their free publication, the Pinehurst-Southern Pines-Aberdeen Area *Golf Vacation Planning Guide*.

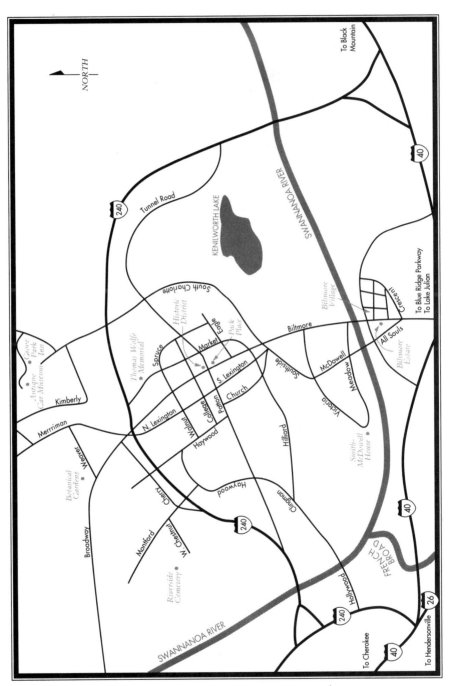

ASHEVILLE and VICINITY, N.C.

Asheville and vicinity

AREA CODE: 704

INTRODUCTION ....

Asheville is a lovely mountain resort, with a charming blend of old and new. While the city began as a humble trading post in the late eighteenth century, it has blossomed into a major southeastern resort. Settled about 1792, it was originally called Morristown, and later, Buncombe Courthouse. In 1797 the name of Asheville, to honor governor Samuel Ashe, was officially declared.

The city is surrounded by breathtaking views of the Blue Ridge Mountains, as well as excellent golf courses. The scenic drive into Asheville is spectacular, especially on the slower, more scenic Blue Ridge Parkway, but even the approach from the interstates is impressive.

Aside from great scenery and mountain golf courses, there are dozens of other activities in or near the city and a variety of special seasonal activities. Unlike many beach resorts that thrive in certain seasons but roll up their sidewalks in cooler months, Asheville is a

Whitewater rafting, near Asheville

Photo courtesy of Buncombe County,
NC Tourism Development Authority

year-round vacation spot, although its golf season is limited in winter. During summers, Asheville offers a relatively cool respite, with activities ranging from swimming in a natural waterslide to hot-air ballooning; in autumn, the renowned Culturefest and vivid displays of brilliant colors on cascading mountainsides attract visitors. During the holiday season, celebrations of a variety of cultural holidays, from Hanukkah to Christmas to Kwanzaa, take place. One of the highlights of the holiday season is the Victorian Christmas display at the Biltmore Estate, the former mansion of George W. Vanderbilt. The later winter months bring skiing and other cold-weather activities. Come spring, Asheville offers whitewater rafting and spectacular floral displays, including the Biltmore Estate's annual Festival of Flowers.

The normal monthly temperatures for Asheville are: January, 35.7; February, 38.9; March, 47.4; April, 55.6; May, 63.4; June, 70.3; July, 73.7; August, 72.8; September, 66.7; October, 56.2; November, 47.5; December, 39.4. The most popular seasons for visitors are summer and fall.

GOLF INFORMATION ....

REEMS CREEK GOLF CLUB, WEAVERVILLE (704) 645-4393

Western North Carolina's newest championship, par 72 course is located only minutes from Asheville. Set in a valley and completely surrounded by the scenic Blue Ridge Mountains, Reems Creek, designed by Hawtree & Son of Oxford, England, offers a Scottish-highland look with its rolling terrain, deep swales, and large knolls. The course measures less than 6500 yards (tees begin at 4605 yards), but this is demonstrative of the fact that length does not translate into difficulty—the course's slope is a strong 133. An additional plus here are efforts to maintain speed of play.

Carts: Mandatory. *Greens Fees:* $38 weekday, $42 weekend/18 holes, including cart; $22 weekday, $24 weekend/9 holes, including cart. *Tee Time Policy:* Can reserve up to thirty days in advance; groups of twenty or more should reserve six months ahead.

MOUNT MITCHELL GOLF CLUB, BURNSVILLE (704) 675-5454

Set in the shadow of Mount Mitchell (at 6684 feet, it is the highest mountain east of the Mississippi River), and surrounded by the 30,000-acre Pisgah National Forest, this course is truly breathtaking. The beautiful layout winds through hills and dales, into a lovely deciduous forest, and along and over the South Toe River. With tees measuring 5455 (red), 6125 (white), and 6495 (blue) yards, Mount Mitchell Golf Club provides a challenge to all levels of player. The number one handicap hole is the fourteenth, a 450-yard (420 from the white tees) par 4. The tee shot needs to be long and accurate, as the fairway is bordered by the South Toe River on the right and trees on the left. The approach then must be played over the river, which cuts across the fairway in front of the green.

Carts: Mandatory. *Greens Fees:* $40 Monday-Thursday, $46 Friday-Sunday and holidays/18 holes, including cart. *Tee Time Policy:* Can be reserved up to two weeks in advance.

ETOWAH VALLEY COUNTRY CLUB, ETOWAH (704) 891-7141, (800) 451-8174

This Edmund Ault design is rated four stars by *Golf Digest's Places to Play.* Surrounded by the Blue Ridge Mountains, Etowah offers panoramic scenery as well as 27 holes of splendid golf. The course rolls through hemlocks and hardwoods, and adding to the natural beauty are horticulturist Jean-Claude Linossi's lovely gardens of ornamental grasses, shrubs, and flowering plants situated behind each tee and green. The south nine can be played from 2822 to 3507 yards, the west from 2800 to 3601 yards, and the north from 2615 to 3404 yards. The greens are bent grass, and some are as large as 9000 square feet.

Carts: Required during certain times. *Greens Fees:* $20-$28/ 18 holes; cart: $15 per person. *Tee Time Policy:* Call forty-eight hours in advance.

OTHER EXCELLENT AREA COURSES:

The **Waynesville Country Club**, Waynesville (704-452-4617), is a Tom Jackson designed, 27-hole course on the edge of the Great Smoky Mountains National Park and Pisgah National For-est. **Colony Lake Lure Golf Resort**, Lake Lure (704-625-3000), is rated 3½ stars by *Golf Digest's Places to Play.* Colony Lake Lure's Apple Valley course is a beautiful mountain course that can stretch to 6726 yards, with a slope of 138. **Grove Park Inn**, Asheville (704-252-2711 or 800-438-5800), is an older, but classy, resort. The hotel is on the National Register of Historic Places and offers outstanding views.

ATTRACTIONS ....

TOURS

Walking tours of historic downtown Asheville are available. For information and times, call the **Buncombe County**

Blue Ridge Parkway, near Asheville
Photo courtesy of Buncombe County,
NC Tourism Development Authority

Preservation Society at 704-254-2343 or **Tour Services of Historic Asheville** at 704-255-1093. A self-guided "Urban Trail" map is available from the Asheville Visitors Center, 151 Haywood Street. Open daily. Call 704-258-6100.

HISTORIC PLACES

Biltmore Estate, on U.S. 25, is a magnificent 255-room French Renaissance mansion, and a must-see for all visitors. Built for George W. Vanderbilt, this palatial residence is the largest private home in the United States and was modeled after the chateaux of France's Loire Valley. The grounds alone encompass over 8,000 acres. Completed in 1895, it took some 1,000 men over five years to build this masterpiece; the home was then furnished with objects collected by Vanderbilt during his world travels. Pieces include artworks by John Singer Sargent, Pierre Auguste Renoir, and Albrecht Dürer; Minton china; antique tapestries; and oriental rugs. Outside you'll find remarkable gardens designed by Frederick Law Olmsted, whose other landmark designs include New York's Central Park and Pinehurst Village in North Carolina. A winery operates in what were once the dairy barns, and visitors can sample and take home award-winning Biltmore Wines. There are also three restaurants on the premises. The site hosts several special events, including a Victorian Christmas and the Festival of Flowers in Spring. Figure about six hours to properly tour the home, gardens, and winery. Open daily. There is a steep admission charge, but it's worth the cost. Call 704-255-1700 or 800-543-2961.

The Thomas Wolfe Memorial, at 48 Spruce Street (between Woodfin and Walnut Streets, next to the Radisson Hotel), is the childhood home of the famed author of *Look Homeward, Angel*. It also inspired the "Dixieland" boardinghouse from that novel (though Asheville was called "Altamont" in the book). The house, which locals call the "Old Kentucky Home," is furnished as it was in 1916. Open daily, spring through fall; closed Mondays in winter. Admission is charged. Call 704-253-8304. You can also visit **Riverside Cemetery**, on Birch Street off Pearson Drive, where Wolfe and author William Sydney Porter, or O. Henry, are buried. Call 704-258-8480.

MUSEUMS/SCIENCE CENTERS

Asheville has a large educational complex known as **Pack Place Education, Arts & Science Center**, which houses several museums. The complex is located in historic Pack Square on U.S. 25. Museums at Pack Place include the Asheville Art Museum, with a large collection of twentieth-century American art; and the Colburn Gem and Mineral Museum, with an impressive collection of shimmering crystals and gems, dinosaur footprints, mineral displays, and basically anything that comes out of the earth (even materials used to make contact lenses). One of the other two museums in the complex is The Health Adventure, a health and science museum with titled exhibit areas such as "Miracle of Life," "Brainstorm," "BodyWorks," as well as other hands-on exhibits that appeal to kids. In the exhibits, kids can hear their own heartbeat and try to jump as high as Michael Jordan, and special effects include a see-through talking woman and a skeleton pedaling a bicycle. Finally, the YMI Cultural Center, founded by George Vanderbilt in 1893, is a celebration of African-American history and culture. Admission charge to each museum; combination tickets are available. Visitor information can be obtained by calling 704-257-4500.

Smith-McDowell Museum of Western North Carolina History, at 283 Victorian Road, is Asheville's oldest brick house. Visitors can view antique furnishings, housewares, clothing, and jewelry. Some exhibits change periodically. Hours and days vary seasonally. Admission is charged. Call 704-253-9231.

CULTURAL OFFERINGS

The Asheville Symphony plays at the Thomas Wolfe Auditorium (in the Asheville Civic Center at 87 Haywood Street) and gives various performances throughout the year, often featuring guest artists. If you like symphonic music, you'll enjoy listening to this fine orchestra. For performance and ticket information, call 704-254-7046.

The Asheville Community Theater, at 35 East Walnut Street, has six productions annually, including comedies, dramas, and musical performances. Evening performances are on Friday and Saturday, and matinees are on Sundays. The theater is closed in July. Call 704-254-1320.

The Diana Wortham Theater, in Pack Place, has seating for 520, state-of-the-art acoustics and lighting, an orchestra pit, and beautiful detailed woodwork decor. The theater presents a wide variety of music, dance, and theater, and hosts companies and shows from all over the country. Call 704-257-4530.

The Asheville Civic Center, at 87 Haywood Street, hosts an array of performances, as it is the major entertainment facility for Western North Carolina. For information, call 704-259-5736.

For art galleries, see Biltmore Village under Shopping.

RECREATION

University Botanical Gardens, on Weaver Boulevard just off Broadway at the University of North Carolina at Asheville, is a ten-acre facility with a large array of plantlife native to the Southern Appalachian region. There's also a 125-year-old cabin on the grounds. Admission is free. Open daily. For hours, call 704-252-5190.

Whitewater rafting is available in kayaks, canoes, and rafts. You can find Class I through V rapids in the Asheville area, and there are several companies that offer full and half-day trips. For information, call the Asheville Visitors Center at 704-258-6100.

Fishing is excellent here, as there's an abundance of trout, bass, and bream. For lake fishing, some good choices are nearby Lake Julian, Lake Lure, and Lake Powhatan. For information on lake fishing, contact Franklin's at 704-253-7925. For fly fishing in local rivers, contact Hunter Banks Store at 704-252-3005.

This area has an abundance of gorgeous parks and preserves, many with camping and hiking. Some major parks include: **Great Smoky Mountains National Park**, with over 500,000 acres of forest (no admission fee, but call 615-436-1200 for information, or 800-365-CAMP for camping information); **The Blue Ridge Parkway**, which winds through mountain ridges from the Shenandoah National Park in Virginia to the Great Smoky Mountains National Park (call 704-298-0398 for information, or 704-259-0701 for Blue Ridge Parkway camping information); **Pisgah National Forest** (call 704-257-4200 for camping or 704-257-4203 for other information); **Chimney Rock Park**, near Lake Lure, features an elevator leading up to the Sky Lounge, where great views await (admission is charged, call 704-625-9611 or 800-277-9611); and the **Western North Carolina Nature Center**, where kids can enjoy a petting barnyard (admission is charged, call 704-298-5600).

The **Asheville Tourists** are a farm team of the Colorado Rockies. Games are played from April through August at McCormick Field, on U.S. 25. Call 704-258-0428.

For racing fans, the **New Asheville Speedway**, located at 219 Amboy Road, holds NASCAR-approved stock-car races on Friday nights from mid-April through mid-September. Call 704-254-4627.

Horseback riding, including trail rides and mountain pack trips, is available through several area stables. "Rock hounding" (searching for minerals and gemstones) is also popular here. A natural water park in the area, **Sliding Rock**, is nature's answer to man-made theme parks. This geological phenomenon features a waterfall and area for sliding and jumping into cool spring waters. There's a lifeguard on duty during designated hours. For information

The Grove Park Inn Resort, Asheville
Photo courtesy of Buncombe County, NC Tourism Development Authority

and directions to these attractions, contact the Asheville Visitors Center at 704-258-6100.

Biltmore Estate's famous **Festival of Flowers** is held during April and May. For information, call 704-255-1700 or 800-543-2961.

Southern Highlands Handicraft Fair takes place at the Civic Center on Haywood Street, just off I-240, with crafts exhibits from local artists and regional artists from nine southern states. Held the third weekend in July and October. Call 704-298-7928.

The **Gee Haw Whimmy Diddle Competition** is in August at the Folk Art Center (See Shopping). People come from all over to perform and compete in music, dance, and storytelling. Call 704-298-7928.

Mountain Dance and Folk Festival (started in 1927) is held the first weekend in August. The event takes place at the Asheville Civic Center, where the region's best players perform folksongs and ballads on banjos, fiddles, and other instruments. Other performances include clogging and other country dancing. For tickets, call 704-251-9999. For information, call the Asheville Chamber of Commerce at 704-258-6107.

From July until Labor Day (except the first weekend in August, when the Annual Mountain Dance and Folk Festival occurs), **Shindig-on-the-Green** takes place Saturday evenings in front of City Hall at College and Spruce Streets. Call 704-255-6111.

CultureFest is a series of events held between mid-August and September which celebrates the area's diverse cultures, from mountain arts and crafts to Native American arts and heritage. Call the Asheville Visitors Center for details at 704-258-6100.

Shakespeare in the Park takes place on weekends from early June until late August, with performances by the Montford Park Players. For performance information and tickets call 704-254-4540.

Belle Chere is North Carolina's largest street festival, attracting over 300,000 people each July. The festival features entertainment, sporting events, food, and arts and crafts. For information, call 704-253-1009.

ACCOMMODATIONS ....

EXPENSIVE

The Grove Park Inn Resort, at 290 Macon Avenue, was built in 1913 and is listed on the National Register of Historic Places. Over the course of the inn's history, it has hosted such famous guests as Woodrow Wilson, Franklin Roosevelt, Thomas Edison, and Henry Ford. The lobby has a massive fireplace and is comfortably furnished with sofas and couches, and guests enjoy views of lovely Sunset Mountain from their balconies. The hotel provides guests with a sports center, indoor and outdoor pools, nine tennis courts, shops, and a championship golf course. Next door is the Antique Car Museum and Grovewood Gallery. Call 704-252-2711 or 800-438-5800.

Haywood Park Hotel and Promenade is located at 1 Battery Park Avenue in downtown Asheville. The deluxe hotel has pretty rooms and suites with refrigerators (some with jacuzzis and computer hookups), free continental breakfast, an exercise room, sauna, and valet parking. Call 704-252-2522 or 800-228-2522.

MODERATE

Great Smokies Holiday Inn Sunspree Resort, on One Holiday Inn Drive, has a pool, sauna, children's program in season, tennis courts, and an 18-hole championship course. Call 704-254-3211.

Cedar Crest Victorian Inn, at 674 Biltmore Avenue, is a circa-1894, English-style inn with ten rooms and two cottage suites, all with authentically appointed interiors. This inn is across from Biltmore Estate and has a friendly staff that pampers guests throughout their stay. Amenities include turn-down service, evening coffee, chocolates in the parlor, and a free continental breakfast. Call 704-252-1389.

INEXPENSIVE

Comfort Inn, at 800 Fairview Road off I-240, has moderate to inexpensive rates and is a good choice for families, as it has a playground, pool, whirlpool, health club privileges, and continental breakfast provided for guests. Call 704-298-9141.

Days Inn, at 1500 Tunnel Road, is another good value, especially for families. This mountainside motel has pretty views, a playground, pool, and restaurant. Call 704-298-5140.

Howard Johnsons, at 190 Hendersonville Road, provides special events during autumn foliage season and certain holidays. Rooms have private patios and balconies with nice views. Call 704-274-2300.

SHOPPING ....

The Folk Art Center, located 5½ miles east of Asheville on the Blue Ridge Parkway at milepost 382, is sponsored by the Southern Highlands Handicraft Guild. There are art exhibits, craft demonstrations, museum galleries, and a craft shop. Open daily; hours vary by season. Admission is free. Call 704-298-7928.

Biltmore Village is a collection of shops and art galleries housed in restored English-style homes. Like the estate bearing his name, this model village was commissioned by George Vanderbilt.

Biltmore Homespun Shops, next to the Grove Park Inn, was founded in 1901 by Mrs. George Vanderbilt as a way to preserve the local home arts of hand-dyeing, spinning, and weaving originally brought here from England and Scotland. There's a museum with exhibits on weaving and textiles, and a crafts shop. Open daily. Admission is free. Call 704-253-7651.

RESTAURANTS ....

FINE DINING

Horizons Restaurant, in the Grove Park Inn, serves excellent food, but the mountain views steal a lot of the show. Specialties include medallions of venison and bouillabaisse. Dinner only. Call 704-252-2711.

Gabrielle's, in the Richmond Hill Inn at 87 Richmond Hill Drive, serves homemade pasta, beef, and fish dishes, with a wide selection of fine wines. This elegant restaurant is smoke free. Reservations and jacket are required. Diners

Biltmore Estate
Photo courtesy of Buncombe County, NC Tourism Development Authority

are serenaded by piano music Wednesday through Sunday evenings. Serves dinner daily and Sunday brunch. Call 704-252-7313.

CASUAL DINING

23 Page and The New French Bar, at the Haywood Park Hotel, specializes in seafood, pasta, and homemade desserts. This four-diamond, casual but elegant restaurant offers dishes from various regions of the United States. Serves dinner daily. 704-252-3685.

Blue Ridge Dining Room, at the Grove Park Inn, has spectacular mountain views and great food. They serve breakfast, lunch, and dinner, with special dinner buffets on Fridays (seafood) and Saturdays (prime rib), and a buffet at Sunday brunch. Call 704-252-2711.

The Mountain Smokehouse, 20 South Spruce Street, serves dinner daily. This fun, casual place serves up barbecued beef, pork, and chicken in hearty portions along with smoked turkey, catfish, ham, corn-on-the-cob, potato salad, and hush puppies. Six nights a week you'll also be treated to great foot-stomping bluegrass music. Reservations are recommended on weekends. Call 704-253-4871.

Try the lively **Barley's Taproom**, at 42 Biltmore Avenue, for what many call the best pizza in town. Consistent with its name, this restaurant has some eighteen beers on tap. Serving lunch and dinner daily. Call 704-255-0504.

Cafe on the Square, at One Biltmore Avenue, has been voted locally as the best downtown eatery in Asheville. The restaurant serves a variety of entrées, soups, and salads. Open for lunch and dinner Monday through Saturday. Call 704-251-5565.

JUST FOR KIDS ....

Kids will especially love Sliding Rock (See Non-Golf Outdoor/Indoor Recreation); The Health Adventure at Pack Place, with a special room for kids under eight (See Museums/Science Centers); and Ghost Town, a western theme park in Maggie Valley (see Side Trips).

SIDE TRIPS ....

Cherokee, 48 miles west of Asheville at the intersection of U.S. 19 and U.S. 441, is the home of a 56,000-acre Cherokee Indian Reservation. Most of the people on the reservation are the descendants of Cherokee who escaped being forced to move to Oklahoma on the tragic "Trail of Tears." Several museums and attractions that introduce visitors to the history, culture, and art of the Cherokee are located on the reservation. *Unto These Hills* is a popular outdoor drama that describes the Cherokee history, and the Qualla Arts and Crafts Cooperative is the best place to find authentic Cherokee art. For information, call the Cherokee

Travel and Promotion Office at 800-438-1601.

In **Maggie Valley**, between Cherokee and Lake Junaluska on U.S. 19, you'll find a theme park called **Ghost Town**, with family-style entertainment and rides. Open May through October, with varying hours. Admission is charged. Call 704-926-1140 or 800-446-7886.

Flat Rock, about 30 miles southeast of Asheville off I-26, is the site of **Connemara**, author Carl Sandburg's 264-acre farm. Sandburg lived here with his family from 1945 until his death in 1967. Visitors can tour the farm buildings and grounds. On cold mornings, they can watch the fog come on little cat feet (just kidding—a little Sandburg humor). Admission to grounds is free; small charge for tours. For more information, call 693-4178. Also here is the **Flat Rock Playhouse Theater**, North Carolina's oldest professional summer theater, with evening and matinee performances May through September. Call 704-693-0731.

Black Mountain, about 15 miles east of Asheville off I-40, is a quiet mountain community that offers great mountain music and shopping, including several antique dealers.

GENERAL INFORMATION ....

For more information, contact the Asheville Visitors Center at 704-258-6100, or the Asheville Travel and Tourism Office at 704-258-6109 or 800-257-1300. The visitors center can provide you with a Mountain Festivals and Events Calendar, and other current-events tabloids, such as *Fun Things to Do in the Mountains. Your*

Guide to Great Smoky Mountain Golf is also available from the Asheville Visitors Center. For information on Black Mountain, contact the Black Mountain/Swannanoa Valley Visitors Center at 800-669-2301.

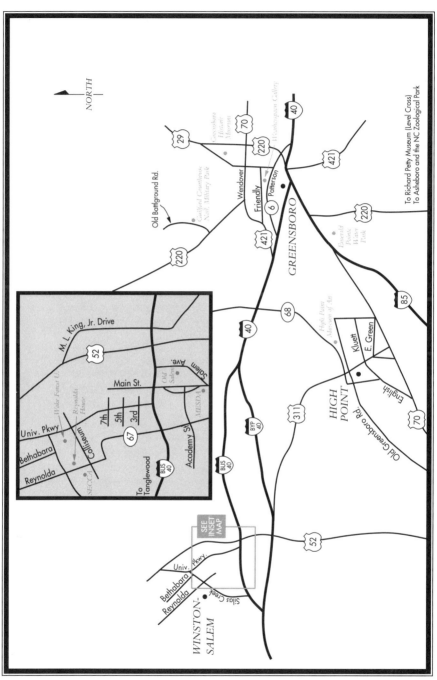

WINSTON-SALEM, GREENSBORO, HIGH POINT and VICINITY, N.C.

Winston-Salem, Greensboro, High Point, and vicinity

"THE TRIAD"

AREA CODE: 910

INTRODUCTION ....

Winston-Salem, Greensboro, and High Point make up the area of piedmont North Carolina known as "The Triad." Nestled in the northern foothills and surrounded by forests and farmland, the Triad is a friendly, relaxed place with an interesting blend of tradition and progress. Though bustling with manufacturing, and its attendant modern skyscrapers, as well as the culture, arts, and large universities of a sophisticated urban area, the Triad has a reassuring small-town feel to it—a welcome change from the urban blight some prosperous cities seem to breed. While the world-renowned golf may be an initial draw to the area, visitors will discover a variety of shopping, museums, historical sites, and arts.

Winston-Salem, an amalgam of two separate cities incorporated as one in 1913, forms an interesting marriage of old-world tradition and industry. The town of Salem was settled in the 1750s by Moravian clergy and laymen. The

Moravians were a small Protestant sect who originally emigrated from Moravia, now a part of Czechoslovakia. They were devout pacifists who lived a simple, quiet life and were known for their quality trades and handcrafts. Winston, on the other hand, began as a prosperous industrial and commercial city founded on the thriving tobacco company created in the late eighteenth century by R.J. Reynolds. Winston's industry grew so quickly, it eventually surrounded Salem, and finally merged with it. Aside from its rich history, the city is also known internationally for its prestigious North Carolina School of the Arts.

Greensboro, named after Revolutionary War General Nathanael Greene, is located 27 miles east of Winston-Salem. Like Winston-Salem, this city is a clean, yet prosperous, center of manufacture (including textiles, which makes Greensboro a natural choice for clothing, bedding, and towel outlets). During the Civil War, the city served as a supply depot for Confederate troops, and it was here that Jefferson Davis met with General Johnston to settle the terms of the South's surrender. However, Greensboro has made its mark on history many other times, as it is the birthplace of first lady Dolley Madison and author O. Henry, as well as the location of the Woolworth where black students from North Carolina A & T State University held the famous sit-ins that became a seminal moment in the Civil Rights Movement.

The other part of the Triad, High Point, received its name for being the highest point in the state along the North Carolina and Midland Railroad. High Point's location made it a pros-

perous center for trade, and the city continues to enjoy a firmly established niche as a manufacturing center for furniture and hosiery. Shoppers love this city, reputed to have the world's largest furniture stores, as well as retail furniture stores offering the best furniture prices in the United States.

Normal monthly temperatures, as measured in Greensboro, are: January, 36.7; February, 40; March, 48.8; April, 57.6; May, 65.9; June, 73.1; July, 76.9; August, 75.7; September, 69.7; October, 58.6; November, 49.5; December, 40.5. Most visitors come in summer. Golf is available all year, as weather permits, though some find the area too cold between November and March.

GOLF INFORMATION ....

BRYAN PARK COMPLEX AND GOLF CLUB, BROWNS SUMMIT (910) 375-2200

This club is the site of two outstanding courses: Champions and Players. The Champions course was considered among the best new public courses in 1990 by *Golf Digest,* and in 1992, *Golf World* declared it one of the few public courses worthy of hosting a United States Open. The course is a par 72, Rees Jones layout measuring 7135 yards from the tips (the whites are 6622, the gold is 5977, and forward tees are 5395). Champions meanders around Lake Townsend (the centerpiece of 1000-acre Bryan Park), has rolling fairways, and is lined with cedars, dogwoods, pines, oaks, and poplars. Champions features particularly strong par 3s, the fourteenth being the most difficult of the bunch. The hole can reach up to 230 yards, and the green is protected in front by a massive bunker and bordered on the right and back by the lake.

The Players course is a 1974 George Cobb design that Rees Jones renovated in 1988. Its tees range from 5260 to 7076 yards. Golfers can walk this wide-open course, which like the Champions, is lined with lovely stands of trees and bordered by Lake Townsend on a number of holes. All in all, this municipal facility, run by Greensboro Parks and Recreation, might be the finest golf available to the public in the country.

Carts: Required during certain times. *Greens Fees:* $20-$34/ 18 holes. *Tee Time Policy:* Can be reserved a month ahead for weekdays, three days ahead (preferably the Wednesday before) for weekends and holidays.

OAK HOLLOW GOLF COURSE, HIGH POINT (910) 883-3260

Oak Hollow, listed among the top 75 public courses in the United States by *Golf Digest*, is a 1972 Pete Dye design. This course, measuring almost 6500 yards from the back tees (the whites are 6022 and forward are 4796 yards), has many classic Dye features including: an island tee, a green on a narrow peninsula surrounded by water, grass bunkers, sand traps lined with pilings, railroad ties bordering fairways, and small- to medium-sized sloped greens that play very fast. Water is a factor on twelve holes, and the fourteenth, a 420-yard par 4, has a large oak on the left side of the fairway, creating problems for drives that wander behind it. Golfers can walk this course anytime and will have lots of funds left after paying greens fees to buy the yardage book.

(Pete Dye is a master of deception and players should follow yardages so that they do not fall prey to his many obstacles and hazards.)

Carts: Not required. *Greens Fees:* $13 weekday, $16 weekend/ 18 holes. *Tee Time Policy:* Can be reserved two days ahead (call Thursday for weekends).

TANGLEWOOD PARK, CLEMMONS (910) 766-5082

Tanglewood Park was once the 1200-acre country estate of W.N. Reynolds. The grounds are now a golf and recreation complex, and the Championship course located here is a vintage Robert Trent Jones, Sr., layout that opened in 1958. *Golf Digest* considers it one of the top seventy-five public courses in the United States and declared it one of the top courses in North Carolina. *Golf Digest's Places to Play* rated it 4½ stars. It was also named one of the "Top 100 You Can Play" by *Golf* in 1996. Tucked into the hills and valleys of red-clay tobacco country, the course is the annual host of the prestigious Vantage Senior Championship and the site of Lee Trevino's one-shot 1974 PGA Championship win over Jack Nicklaus. Having undergone some renovations and refurbishments, Tanglewood is now a well-conditioned modern course that will provide challenge and enjoyment to all levels of player. The course can stretch to over 7000 yards (tees start at 5119 yards), much of it over, around, and probably through the multiple and massive bunkers. The finishing holes on each side exemplify this distance and the sea of sand. The seventh is a 243-yard par 3, bordered on the left by a pond and a bunker, and flanked to the right with two deep bunkers. The eighth is a 440-yard par 4 dogleg to a large green totally surrounded by bunkers, and the ninth is a mere 439-yard par 4 that plays uphill to a steeply sloped green. The sixteenth is a 183-yard par 3 that plays like a large bunker spoiled by a green in the center. The seventeenth is a reachable par 5, but to do so, the golfer has to cross a huge cross bunker, then negotiate greenside bunkers. The eighteenth is a 439-yard par 4 that plays up a steep hill to a green protected on the right with a deep bunker and surrounded in the back with sand. Pars on all these holes would likely earn you a spot on the tour. The other course here, the Reynolds course, is a tight layout which, though not as challenging as the Championship course, is a fine and challenging golf course.

Carts: Required at certain times (cart optional at Reynolds course). *Greens Fees:* $30-$65, depending on the course and season/18 holes (Championship Course fees are higher than Reynolds Course). *Tee Time Policy:* Can be reserved seven days in advance; lodge guests can book tee times when making room reservation.

OTHER EXCELLENT AREA COURSES:

Oak Valley, Clemmons (910-940-2000), is an Arnold Palmer designed course that opened in December 1995. **Stoney Creek Golf Club**, Stoney Creek (910-449-5688), is located about 12 miles out of Greensboro. This 1992 par 72 course starts tough and can continue that way if you play from the back tees, which can reach 7063 yards with a rating/slope of 74.1/144; however, all players can enjoy this course because the other tees start at

4737 yards with a rating/slope of 69.8/123.

ATTRACTIONS ....

TOURS

In **Old Salem** (see Museums/Science Centers), visitors can take a ninety-minute guided walking tour that highlights the culture, architecture, and trade of this eighteenth-century Moravian community. Tours leave from the visitors center. For times and ticket fees, call 910-721-7300. Walking tour maps of downtown Winston-Salem's historic buildings and a brief orientation film are available at the Winston-Salem Visitors Center at 601 West Fourth Street. Call 910-725-2361 or 800-331-7018. Visitors who call ahead receive a reception with complimentary Moravian cookies and beverages. **Carolina Treasures,** 1031 Burke Street, provides guided tours of Winston-Salem for groups of two or more. Call 910-631-9144, in advance if possible.

HISTORIC PLACES

The Moravians who settled the Winston-Salem area created two settlements: Bethabara, intended to be temporary, and Salem, created as a permanent trade settlement. Both are now historic sites, with restored and original buildings from the eighteenth century. Both sites charge admission for tours, though the grounds can be walked free of charge. **Historic Bethabara Park**, located on 2147 Bethabara Road, was originally established in 1753. Visitors can see the original Gemeinhaus (the German colonial church), the community garden, a reconstructed fort, the Potter's House, and an archeological site. There's also God's Acre, a cemetery where the first Easter Sunrise service was held in 1758. Costumed guides bring visitors through the village. The park is open daily but the buildings are closed from December 1 through March 31. Call 910-924-8191. **Old Salem**, located on Salem Road south of Winston-Salem's business district, dates from 1766. Many of the eighteen restored buildings can be toured, while the others are private homes or part of Salem College (by founding date, the oldest women's college in the country). Interpreters wear the unique, yet practical, Moravian garb and take visitors through the largely unchanged streets. They also demonstrate and/or explain Moravian customs, from casting lots on marriage propos-

als to crafts and trades. Special times to visit Old Salem are at Christmas, Easter (there's still a sunrise service), and the Fourth of July. On the Fourth of July, Old Salem recreates the evening in 1783 when the entire Moravian village made the state's only known celebration of the end of the war. There's a grand procession by torchlight to the village square, where everyone raises their voice in song. Tours are available Monday through Saturday from 9 A.M. to 5 P.M. and Sunday from 12:30 to 5 P.M. You can get a ticket at Old Salem that includes MESDA (see below), as it is in the same area. Old Salem also has a new art and cultural museum which will have changing exhibits. For information, call 910-721-7300.

R.J. Reynolds Tobacco USA, at 1100 Reynolds Boulevard near Wake

Historic Bethabara Park
Photo courtesy of Winston-Salem Convention and Visitors Bureau

Winston-Salem, Greensboro, High Point, and vicinity, NC

Forest University, is where some 8,000 cigarettes are made every minute of production (up to 275 million in a day!). The plant offers free tours of their computerized factory and exhibits on the history, manufacture, and marketing of the tobacco industry. Call 910-741-5718.

Blandwood Mansion and Carriage House, at 447 West Washington Street in Greensboro, is a furnished nineteenth-century, Italian villa–style home that belonged to former governor John Motley Morehead. Open daily. Admission is charged. Call 910-272-5003.

The **Mendenhall Plantation**, at 603 West Main Street in Jamestown, just south of Greensboro, is a restored Quaker plantation settlement that features demonstrations of daily nineteenth-century Quaker life. Exhibits include a wagon with a false bottom that was used to transport slaves on the Underground Railroad. Open daily from April through December. Call 910-454-3819.

Guilford Courthouse National Military Park, on New Garden Road off U.S. 220 in Greensboro, was established in 1917 and commemorates the battle fought here between British troops led by General Cornwallis and General Nathanael Greene's American troops in March of 1781. Though the British won, they were weakened by the difficult victory, which contributed to their eventual defeat at Yorktown. Two signers of the Declaration of Independence, John Penn and William Hooper, are buried here. The visitors center has a twenty-minute orientation film and artifact displays. Battle sites can be toured on foot or by car. Open daily.

Admission is free. Call 910-288-1776.

The **World's Largest Bureau**, at 508 North Hamilton Street in High Point, is a 1926 building that looks like a chest of drawers—a symbol of the city's esteemed status in home furnishings.

MUSEUMS/SCIENCE CENTERS

Reynolda House Museum of American Art, on Reynolda Road in Winston-Salem, is located in the former home of the R.J. Reynolds' family. The rambling, 1917 home has a striking interior centered around a two-story living room with a cantilevered balcony and an ornate, handcrafted balustrade. The museum features over 2,500 pieces of fine American art, mainly paintings spanning from 1755 until the present, but also crystal and other furnishings. Upstairs is a display of antique clothing once belonging to the family, from wedding gowns to children's outfits. On Sundays, a musician serenades visitors on the Aeolian organ, whose strategic pipe locations make it possible to "move" the sound around the house. Admission is charged. Call 910-725-5325.

Museum of Early Southern Decorative Arts (MESDA), at 924 South Main Street next to Old Salem, is comprised of actual early southern interiors that have been transplanted from homes in Maryland, Virginia, the Carolinas, Georgia, and Tennessee. The exhibits, which date from the early eighteenth century through 1820, are spread over nineteen rooms and six galleries. Display cases also exhibit silver, guns, and other items. Guided tours only; visitors must place cameras and bags in lockers before touring. Visitors can purchase individual tickets or combination tickets for MESDA and Old Salem. Open daily. Call 910-721-7360.

Wake Forest University, off Reynolda Road in Winston-Salem, was established in 1834 and has several exhibits open to the public, including a small but interesting collection at the Museum of Anthropology (call 910-759-5282), as well as a Fine Arts Center with changing arts exhibits. For university information, call 910-759-5000.

SciWorks (The Science Center and Environmental Park of Forsyth County), at 400 Hanes Mill Road in Winston-Salem, has over 45,000 square feet of creative scientific exhibits. These include working volcanoes, gravity-defying objects, live animals in a 15-acre environmental park, nature trails, and a state-of-the-art planetarium. Admission is charged. Call 910-767-6730.

The Southeastern Center for Contemporary Art (SECCA), at 750 Marguerite Avenue in Winston-Salem, is a showcase museum of quality contemporary art, with some twenty-five exhibits each year. The museum is in a 1929, English-style, stonework building that once belonged to industrialist James G. Hanes. A gift shop is on the premises. Admission is charged. Call 910-725-1904.

Greensboro Historical Museum, at 130 Summit Avenue, is located within a nineteenth-century church. Exhibits include profiles of famous Greensboro natives like author O. Henry (William Sydney Porter) and first lady Dolley Madison, as well as information on significant local events such as the Revolutionary War Battle of Guilford Courthouse and the Civil Rights-era lunch counter sit-ins. There are also antique autos, colonial furnishings, artworks, and more. Open Tuesday through Sunday. Ad.mission is free. Call 910-373-2043.

Natural Science Center of Greensboro, Inc., at 4301 Lawndale Road, is a museum of natural sciences. Exhibits cover paleontology, geology, and science and technology. Kids seem to especially love the dinosaur exhibits, the zoo, and the planetarium. Open daily. Admission is charged. Call 910-288-3769.

The Furniture Discovery Center is located at 101 West Green Drive in High Point. The museum not only describes High Point's history as the furniture-making capital of the United States, but also includes exhibits on how different kinds of furniture are designed and assembled. The special-exhibit area has fully furnished rooms recreated in miniature (e.g., Queen Elizabeth I's bedroom). Open daily from April through October; closed Monday from November to March. Admission is charged. Call 910-887-3876.

The Angela Peterson Doll and Miniature Museum, located next to the Furniture Discovery Center in High Point, contains over 1400 dolls and miniatures from all over the world, both new and antique. Examples of exhibits include rare and valuable Shirley Temple and Barbie dolls, a nativity scene with some fifty crèche dolls (including one dating from the fifteenth century), and miniature shadow-box scenes (e.g., a bullfight and tea party). The museum hours are the same as those at the Furniture Discovery Center. Admission is charged. Call 910-885-3655.

High Point Museum/Historical Park, at 1805 East Lexington Avenue, is dedicated to the manufacturing, military, and cultural history of High Point. The 1786 John Haley House on the grounds has period furnishings from the colonial era. There's also a blacksmith shop and weaver's shop, with seasonal demonstrations. Closed Mondays. Admission is free. Call 910-885-6859.

CULTURAL OFFERINGS

The Delta Arts Center, on East Third Street in Winston-Salem, has exhibits and performances in the visual and folk arts, music, and drama. Open weekdays. Call 910-722-2625.

The prestigious **North Carolina School of the Arts** ("NCSA"), at 200 Waughtown Street, was founded in 1963, making it the first residential, state-supported school for the performing arts in the United States. Each year, the school produces musical performances (including classical, jazz, chamber ensembles, and more), classical and contemporary plays, and various dance productions including ballet, modern, and others. The school also produces the musical series "Something for Everyone." Most performances produced by NCSA take place at the Stevens Center, at 405 West Fourth Street in downtown Winston-Salem. The box office for NCSA productions can be reached at 910-721-1945.

Greensboro Cultural Center, at 200 North Davie Street, is home to several quality local performing arts groups, including the Greensboro Symphony Orchestra (call 910-333-7490); the Greensboro Ballet (call 910-333-7480); the musical-revue company Razz Ma Tazz, which performs new and nostalgic pieces (call 910-373-2506); and the Community Theater of Greensboro

(call 910-333-SHOW). Within the center are five art galleries, including the Green Hill Center for North Carolina Art, with quality works by regional artists. Call 910-373-2712.

Another outstanding art gallery is the University of North Carolina at Greensboro's **Weatherspoon Art Gallery**, at Spring Garden and Tate Streets. It contains six galleries exhibiting twentieth-century American art. Closed Monday. Call 910-334-5770.

Greensboro's **Carolina Theatre**, at 310 South Greene Street, was originally a vaudeville theater. It now hosts classic- and fine-film series, dance recitals, theatrical performances, and concerts. Call 910-333-2600.

The Greensboro Coliseum Complex, at 1921 West Lee Street, hosts a variety of popular entertainers, performing arts, and sports events. Call 910-373-7474.

RECREATION

Greensboro has several terrific gardens open to visitors. One of the most outstanding is the **Greensboro Arboretum in Lindley Park**, located off Wendover Avenue. This 17-acre park includes nine separate collections of trees and other native plants, many shaped and displayed in beautiful, interesting ways. Call 910-373-2199. Another is **The Bog Garden**, located on Hobbs Road north of Friendly Avenue. This lush, swampy area features an elevated, wooden walkway from which you can view the many wildflowers and exotic plants. Call 910-373-2199. Located near The Bog Garden are the popular **Bicentennial Gardens**, featuring seasonal flowers and shrubs, and the David Caldwell property. Call 910-373-2558.

Emerald Pointe Water Park, on South Holden Road (Exit 121 off I-85) in Greensboro, is the largest water park in the Carolinas. The park has thirty-two rides and attractions, from slides and pools to the Sky Coaster ride, which makes you feel like you're sky-diving. Open late May to September. Admission is charged. Call 910-852-9721 or 800-555-5900.

The 1200-acre **Tanglewood Park**, located in Clemmons, 12 miles south-west of Winston-Salem off I-40, is a golfer's dream (see Golf Information). However, there's an abundance of other outdoor activities in the park, includ-ing bicycle and hiking trails, swimming, tennis, a wedding chapel used since 1809, horseback riding, hay rides, paddle boats, and canoes. There's even a bed-and-breakfast (See Accommoda-tions). Admission is charged to the park. Call 910-766-0591.

For information on the dozens of other parks in the Winston-Salem area, contact the Forsyth County Parks and Recreation Department at 910-727-2946.

Spectator sports fans have several choices. The **Greensboro Bats** play Class A minor league baseball at the War Memorial Stadium, 510 Yanceyville Street. Call 910-333-BATS. The **Win-ston-Salem Warthogs** also play Class A minor league baseball. Their games are at Ernie Shore Field, at 401 West Thirtieth Street in Winston-Salem. For information, call 910-259-2233. The **Carolina Dynamo**, a professional soc-cer team and the winner of two na-tional championships, play at Simeon Stadium in High Point. Call 910-852-9969. The **Carolina Monarchs** are an ice hockey team affiliated with the Florida Panthers. The Monarchs play their home games at the Greensboro Coliseum, 1921 West Lee Street. Call 910-852-6170.

SEASONAL EVENTS

For golfers who enjoy watching tournaments, the PGA's annual **Greater Greensboro Chrysler Classic Golf Tournament** takes place in April at Forest Oaks Country Club, located on U.S. 421. For information and tickets, call 910-379-1570 or 800-999-5446. In addition, Tanglewood Park hosts the Senior PGA Tour's **Vantage Champi-onship** in October. Call 910-766-0591 or 910-766-5082.

The Triad is a great center for per-forming arts, and as such, is a natural for quality arts festivals such as the **Piedmont Crafts Fair,** featuring jury-selected artists, in October at the Benton Convention Center in Win-ston-Salem (call 910-725-1516). As for music festivals, there's the **Opera Day** at the North Carolina School of the Arts (call 910-725-2022), the **Music at Sunset** symphony concert series in summer at Tanglewood Park (call 910-725-1035), and the **Eastern Music Festival** from June through August (call 910-333-7450).

Other unique events in the Win-ston-Salem area include the **Old Sa-lem Spring Festival** in late April, where early American crafts and chores relating to spring are showcased (call 800-441-5305); a garden tour of Old Salem in late July; and military re-en-actments throughout the year at His-toric Bethabara Park (call 910-924-8191).

In High Point, the prestigious **North Carolina Shakespeare Festival** takes place from mid-August through early October. Call 910-841-2273. Also in High Point, early December brings an annual presentation of Charles Dickens's *A Christmas Carol*. 910-841-6273.

The Festival of Lights at Tanglewood Park is a spectacular display that uses more than 750,000 lights. Animated and holiday scenes such as ducks on a pond, windmills, Santa scenes, and steeplechasing make for a magical after-dark drive through the park. Admission fee per vehicle. Open nightly mid-November through early January. Call 910-766-0591.

ACCOMMODATIONS ....

EXPENSIVE

Radisson Marque, at 460 North Cherry Street in Winston-Salem, is a fine highrise hotel located downtown. There's a heated pool, sauna and exercise facilities, tennis and golf privileges, and other deluxe amenities. The interior features a nine-story atrium with glass elevators. Call 910-725-1234 or 800-527-2341.

Biltmore Hotel, at 111 West Washington Street in Greensboro, provides guests with free evening refreshments, continental breakfast, concierge service, and complimentary limousine service. This stately, 1895 hotel is furnished with antiques. Call 910-272-3474 or 800-332-0303.

Radisson Hotel High Point, at 135 South Main Street in High Point, is located downtown near the theater, museums, and furniture outlets. The hotel features a fitness room, indoor pool, and jacuzzi. Call 910-889-8888.

MODERATE

Manor House Bed and Breakfast at Tanglewood Park, in Clemmons, 12 miles southwest of Winston-Salem off I-40, is a terrific choice for golfers and their companions since it's located on the grounds of Tanglewood Park (See Recreation and Golf Information). The inn, once owned by R.J. Reynolds's brother, Will, has cozy rooms furnished with rich prints, wood paneling, and antiques. These rooms and the old trophy room downstairs give the inn an English hunt-club feel. At the dining room, be sure to ask Georgie, who serves a wonderful breakfast, about the ghost who reputedly haunts the manor. There's also a motel with eighteen rooms (perhaps a better choice for families with young children). Call 910-766-0591.

Park Lane Hotel/Four Seasons, at 3005 High Point Road in Greensboro, has amenities like free airport transfers, breakfast, an exercise room with sauna, and pool. Call 910-294-4565 or 800-942-6556.

Augustus T. Zevely Bed and Breakfast Inn, at 803 South Main Street in Winston-Salem, is a charming colonial inn located in the heart of Old Salem. The twelve rooms are furnished with pieces from Lexington Furniture's Old Salem collection, which adds to the sense of colonial authenticity. Call 910-748-9299 or 800-928-9299.

Premier Bed and Breakfast, at 1001 Johnson Street in High Point, is located a mile from downtown in the historic district. Guests here enjoy a fabulous breakfast spread, fireplaces, a swing on the front porch, and complimentary refreshments. Call 910-889-8349.

Old Salem, Winston-Salem
Photo courtesy of NC Travel and Tourism Division

Courtyard by Marriott, at 3111 University Parkway in Winston-Salem, offers guests reasonable rates, a pool, and a free continental breakfast in the lobby. Call 910-727-1277.

Days Inn, at South Elm Street off I-85 in Greensboro, has a pool, playground, and the rates include breakfast. This is a good place for families. Call 910-275-9571.

Howard Johnsons Lodge, 2000 Brentwood Street in High Point, is about 2 miles south of downtown, near the furniture outlets. The motel offers an outdoor pool and, for a small charge, will allow pets. Call 910-886-4141.

SHOPPING ....

In Winston-Salem, **Reynolda Village** is a collection of specialty shops located on Reynolda Road, next to Wake Forest University and Reynolda House. The shops are housed in what were farm sheds and cottages when the Reynolds family lived next door.

If you visit Old Salem, a stop in the old shops and taverns there is a must. Many have been in continuous business since the nineteenth century. The famous **Winkler Bakery**, where Moravian cookies are handmade in six flavors (the most famous being ginger), is located here. The bakery also offers pumpkin muffins, sugar cakes, and other goodies. Call 910-721-7302. **T. Bagge— Merchant** is still in its original 1755 building, though it now sells reproductions and crafts made in Old Salem. Call 910-721-7387. The **Furniture and Accessories Shop** sells reproductions of furniture, flatware, and other household items seen at MESDA and Old

Salem, including the Old Salem furniture collection manufactured by Lexington Furniture Industries.

Replacements, Ltd., on I-85/40 at the Mount Hope Church Road exit in Greensboro, specializes in discontinued and active china, as well as crystal, flatware, and collectibles. The showrooms have an outstanding inventory of replacement pieces as well as special buys from various manufacturers. Open daily. Call 800-REPLACE (910-737-5223).

The Gallery of Antiques, at 801 Merritt Drive in Greensboro, is the largest antique mall in North Carolina. Call 910-299-2426.

High Point is a furniture shopper's heaven, with some 60 retail furniture stores. Contact the High Point Convention and Visitors Bureau (910-884-5255) to obtain a current copy of *The Furniture Shopping Directory*. This publication lists galleries and their types of offerings; the back of the directory has tips on preparing for furniture shopping in High Point.

RESTAURANTS ....

DINNER THEATERS

Barn Dinner Theatre, 120 Stage Coach Trail in Greensboro, is among the oldest dinner theaters in the United States. Guests enjoy a buffet dinner of roast beef and fresh fish and a Broadway play. Open Wednesday through Sunday evenings (nightly in December). For information and reservations, call 910-292-2211.

FINE DINING

Zevely House, 901 West Fourth Street in Winston-Salem, is nestled in an old, cozy brick house with a fireplace and antique furnishings. The menu features creative haute cuisine, with selections like venison, potato cakes with salmon and caviar, and mixed grill with lamb chops. Open for brunch on Sunday and dinner daily; reservations suggested. Call 910-725-6666.

Madison Park, at 616 Dolley Madison Road in Greensboro, serves continental entrées such as lamb chops, Black Angus beef, and grilled salmon, as well as appetizers such as venison sausage and quail vinaigrette. Call 910-294-6505.

J. Basul Noble, at 114 South Main Street in High Point, has fabulous food in a cosmopolitan setting. Gourmet selections include grilled rack of lamb, loin of rabbit, and pork loin chops. The luscious desserts include a raisin-cognac bread pudding. Call 910-889-3354.

CASUAL DINING

Old Salem Tavern Dining Room, (built in 1816 as an annex to the original tavern, which dates to 1784), is in Old Salem at 736 South Main Street. The tavern serves lunch and dinner daily except Sundays, when it serves lunch only. Today's servers still don Moravian garb, and the menu features Moravian specialties like chicken pie, roast duck, and gingerbread with lemon ice cream. Call 910-748-8585.

Lucky 32, at 109 South Stratford Road in Winston-Salem, is an upscale casual restaurant that draws a local business crowd at lunch. To assure a wide variety, their menu changes by a third every month. Selections include seafood, chicken, pasta, pork, and plenty of "guilt free" dishes. The desserts are excellent.

Check out the mural at the entrance containing a myriad of local symbolism. Call 910-724-3232.

JUST FOR KIDS ....

In 1997 an interactive history museum will open in Old Salem with exhibits designed for children from ages four to twelve. Features will include a clock that runs backward and a sculpture for climbing. For information, call 910-721-7300.

In Greensboro, the **Natural Science Center of Greensboro, Inc.** has a Kids Alley, with special hands-on exhibits. (See Museums/Science Centers). Admission is charged. Call 910-288-3769. Also in Greensboro is **Celebration Station** at 4315 Big Tree Way. This indoor/outdoor recreation complex includes water rides, go-carts, miniature golf, and video arcades, which are certain to entertain kids of all ages. Call 910-316-0606.

SIDE TRIPS ....

NASCAR fans will love the **Richard Petty Museum**, located south of Greensboro in Level Cross, on Branson Mill Road off Old U.S. 220. The museum displays memorabilia celebrating the seven-time Winston Cup Series Champion. There's an orientation film, and exhibits like Petty's cars and racing suits. Open Monday through Saturday. Admission is charged. Call 910-495-1143.

The North Carolina Zoological Park is 25 miles south of Greensboro in Asheboro. The zoo has over 800 exotic animals and more than 35,000

tropical plants in indoor and outdoor display areas. Call 910-879-7000 or 800-488-0444. (For more information, see the Pinehurst chapter, under Side Trips.)

GOLFER'S SIDE TRIPS ....

(Note: These courses are a good distance from the Triad, all located over an hour's drive east of Greensboro. However, they are three of the state's best new courses, and thus, golfers may want to consider working them into travel to or from the area, or planning a special side trip to play them. After reading the reviews below, decide for yourself, but be sure to check mileage before heading there from the Triad.)

DEVILS RIDGE GOLF CLUB, HOLLY SPRINGS (919) 557-6100 (ABOUT 60 MILES SOUTHEAST OF GREENSBORO)

Devils Ridge, a John LaFoy layout, opened in 1991. The course, rated 4 stars by *Golf Digest's Places to Play*, is one of the most challenging and scenic courses in the area, with each hole offering the player a unique and different layout. This par 72 course has four sets of tees that stretch from 5244 to 7002 yards (the championship tees have a high slope of 138 and rating of 73.7). Greens fees are reasonable and carts are required only on weekends during the busy season.

Carts: Required weekends April-October. *Greens Fees:* $22 Monday-Thursday, $27 Friday, $33 weekends and holidays/18 holes. *Tee Time Policy:* Can be reserved one week in advance for individuals; groups can reserve earlier.

This 7045-yard (from the "Devil" tees; tees start at 5505 yards), par 72 layout was designed by Rees Jones and was recently ranked among the top ten new resort courses in the United States by *Golf Digest*. This, however, is only half the story. The course was designed originally by Robert Trent Jones, Sr., in the 1950s. It opened in 1957 on a location that typifies piedmont North Carolina: gently rolling hills, meandering streams and brooks, varieties of hardwoods, towering pines, and beautiful shrubbery. True to his tenet on golf architecture, the elder Jones created "the illusion that the great golf holes were on the ground just lying there, waiting to be grassed over." When the course needed an overhaul, the younger Jones was tabbed because of his high quality renovations of the renowned Brookline, Hazeltine, Baltusrol, and Congressional courses. The result is a great layout that has been brought into the modern era and is located in an ideal setting. Aside from the Devil tees, the blue's measure 6721 yards, the white's 6207 yards, and the red's 5505 yards. Although the entire course is a pleasure, the par 3s are outstanding. For example, the 159-yard fourth is remarkable. Two lakes are short of the green on the right and left. The smallish, two-tier green is fronted by a brook and flanked by grass and sand bunkers.

Carts: Required weekends and holidays before noon April-November. *Greens Fees:* $34 weekday, $49 weekend/ 18 holes; $17/9 holes. *Tee Time Policy:* Should reserve up to a week ahead.

Guilford Courthouse National Military Park, Greensboro
Photo by William Russ,
courtesy of NC Travel and Tourism Division

THE NEUSE GOLF CLUB, CLAYTON (919) 550-0550 (ABOUT 70 MILES SOUTHEAST OF GREENSBORO)

This John LaFoy course is considered by *Golf Digest* to be among the top ten new courses in 1995. LaFoy, who began his career as a protégé of George W. Cobb, has managed to create the feeling of a mature, seasoned course. This was accomplished not by moving a lot of dirt, but rather by using the natural lay and contours of a fine piece of land. The course, which runs along the winding Neuse River, has multiple tees, so it can be played from 6027 to 7010 yards (the course rating/slope of the black tees are hefty at 73.5/136). Although each hole at the Neuse has its own look, there are a couple that bear mentioning. The par 5 fourth, measuring 527 yards, is special because it runs alongside the Neuse River. The par 3 fourteenth, measuring anywhere from 125 to 192 yards, is a wonderful test. From the tee, a lake opens up all the way down to the right of the green. On the left and short of the green is a waste area containing a few trees and bushes; large mounds, swales, and grass bunkers are located around the green, which starts narrow and then opens up like a light bulb. All in all, the fourteenth is a fascinating hole that conjures up thoughts of a different "noose." Finally, the par 4 eighteenth will take the kick out of any player. It is 432 yards and requires a steep uphill approach. The green is 44 yards deep, with an unusual bowl-like depression squarely in the middle. If the pin is in the back right corner, be happy to get out alive with a bogey.

Carts: Required weekends and holidays before 2 P.M. April-October. *Greens Fees:* $20 Monday-Thursday, $23 Friday, $27 weekends and holidays/18 holes. *Tee Time Policy:* Can be reserved two weeks in advance; the course will honor special requests for advance tee times.

GENERAL INFORMATION ....

For information on Winston-Salem, contact the Winston-Salem Convention and Visitors Bureau at 910-725-2361 or 800-331-7018. For information on Greensboro, contact the Greensboro Area Convention and Visitors Bureau at 910-274-2282 or 800-344-2282. For information on High Point, contact the High Point Convention and Visitors Bureau at 910-884-5255. *Triad Style* is a free publication listing current events in the area. It is distributed at restaurants and major visitor sites.

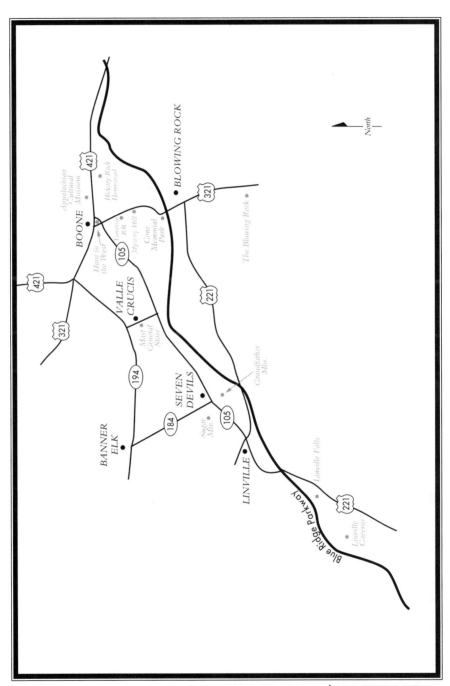

BOONE, BLOWING ROCK, BANNER ELK and LINVILLE, N.C.

Boone, Blowing Rock, Banner Elk, and Linville

"THE HIGH COUNTRY"

AREA CODE: 704

INTRODUCTION ....

North Carolina's "High Country"—the northern mountain region encompassing the towns of Boone, Blowing Rock, Banner Elk, and Linville—is as mountainous as its name implies. This largely unspoiled region was used as a hunting ground by Daniel Boone in the 1760s before he continued on to Kentucky, and some community names still reflect Daniel Boone's influence—for instance, there's a place still known as "Meat Camp" where Boone stored some of the meat he had hunted. Although the region has been a summer resort since the 1800s, it's still far from commercial or crowded.

The student population of Appalachian State University in Boone creates a college-town atmosphere there, and you'll find performing arts, museums, and historical sites throughout the region. But the greatest number of activities in the area are for those who enjoy nature and the outdoors in a beautiful mountain setting. Golfers, hikers, nature photographers, mountain climbers, gem seekers, spelunkers, hunters, fishermen, birdwatchers, whitewater rafters, campers, and horseback riders will all find plenty of opportunities to enjoy themselves in the High Country. Skiing is popular here in the winter, though golf season is over by then.

Aside from its beauty, the High Country is a place of mystery, where natural phenomena like caves and waterfalls continually amaze and delight visitors. Some must-see sites include Mystery Hill, with its crooked house and water that flows uphill, and the Blowing Rock (a different site than the town of Blowing Rock), where snow falls upside down and an invisible breath of air blows back light objects thrown over a mountain's edge. Blowing Rock's mysterious powers are explained only in a legend. The story tells of a Chickasaw maiden whose Cherokee lover, torn between returning to his tribe or staying with her, jumps over the Blowing Rock. The forlorn maiden prays for several days, until the Great Spirit creates a gust that blows her young brave back into her arms—a wind that still blows to this day.

The normal monthly temperatures here, as measured in Blowing Rock, are: January, 29.4; February, 31.7; March, 40; April, 48.5; May, 56.8; June, 63.4; July, 67; August, 66.1; September, 60.3; October, 50.5; November, 42.3; December, 33.4. The most popular tourist seasons for golfers and hikers are summer and fall (when leaves are in their fiery splendor).

Rural scenery, western North Carolina
Photo courtesy of NC Travel and Tourism Division

Golf Vacations Even Non-Golfers Will Enjoy

GOLF INFORMATION ....

BOONE GOLF CLUB, BOONE
(704) 264-8760

Located in the Watauga Valley, this par 71, Ellis Maples designed layout, opened in 1959, is a Blue Ridge Mountain beauty. The course is cut through a mature, deciduous forest and includes laurel thickets, ponds, the rambling New River, and magnificent views of surrounding mountains. The fairways are spacious and range from level to gently rolling; the greens are large and undulating. Holes come in all varieties, with par 3s ranging from 146 yards to over 200 yards, par 4s from 279 yards to over 420 yards, and par 5s that stretch to over 580 yards.

Carts: Mandatory before 2 P.M. *Greens Fees:* $30 weekdays, $35 weekends and holidays/18 holes. *Tee Time Policy:* Can be reserved a week in advance.

HAWKSNEST GOLF AND SKI RESORT, SEVEN DEVILS (704) 963-6561

If you enjoy mountain golf, then Hawksnest, at an elevation of 4800 feet, may be the ultimate. This par 72 course ranges in length from 4799 yards to 6244 yards. The signature hole is a 210-yard par 3 with an elevation drop of 125 feet. The tee is cut from the mountain's edge.

Carts: Mandatory. *Greens Fees:* $32 weekday, $36 weekend/18 holes; $20/9 holes, weekdays only. *Tee Time Policy:* Can be reserved seven days in advance; call earlier for groups/outings.

LINVILLE GOLF COURSE, LINVILLE
(704) 733-4311

(Note: Open to Eseola Lodge guests only)

Set in the Blue Ridge mountains, Linville is a Donald Ross gem that is consistently ranked among the top courses in North Carolina, and in 1996, it was included in *Golf's* "Top 100 You Can Play." Bordered by Lake Kawana, this links-style course has four sets of tees: the gold is 5086 yards, the red is 5437 yards, the white is 6279 yards, and the blue is 6780 yards. Par is 72, and the course slope from the blue tees is a formidable 135.

Carts: Mandatory. *Greens Fees:* $50/18 holes, including cart. *Tee Time Policy:* Lodge guests and members only; can be reserved four days in advance.

HOUND EARS LODGE AND CLUB, BLOWING ROCK (704) 963-5831

(Note: Open to Hound Ears Lodge and Club guests only)

Hound Ears is a par 72, George Cobb design that measures 6165 yards. The fairways are narrow, and the greens are small, fast, and sloping. Ponds and streams are a factor on seventeen holes. The layout is classic mountain, with frequent elevation changes. The par 3, 110-yard fifteenth is a lovely short hole that plays downhill, with a green that is surrounded by water and sand.

Carts: Required at certain times. *Greens Fees:* Approximately $40/18 holes; cart: $15. *Tee Time Policy:* Can be reserved two days in advance.

ATTRACTIONS ....

MUSEUMS/SCIENCE CENTERS

Two cultural museums depict the social and natural evolution of the area, including Native American artifacts: **The Appalachian Cultural Museum,** located in the University Hall in Boone off Blowing Rock Road (call 704-262-3117) and **Appalachian Heritage Museum**, at the Mystery Hill complex (see Recreation) on U.S. 321 near Blowing Rock (call 704-262-0399). Admission is charged for both museums.

The Museum of North Carolina Minerals, at Milepost 331 on the Blue Ridge Parkway at the junction with N.C. 226, has an extensive collection of minerals indigenous to the state, from the brilliant and beautiful to the dull yet practical. Open daily April through October, closed Monday and Tuesday from November through March. Admission is free. Call 704-765-2761.

Hickory Ridge Homestead, at 591 Horn in the West Drive in Boone, is a living museum depicting eighteenth-century life in the Appalachian Mountain region. This is where *Horn in the West* is performed (see Cultural Offerings). Open Tuesday through Sunday from May through October. Admission is charged. Call 704-264-2120.

CULTURAL OFFERINGS

Horn in the West, the nation's second-oldest outdoor theater production, depicts the lives of Daniel Boone and other eighteenth-century settlers. Performances are held nightly, except Mondays, from mid-June through mid-August at the Daniel Boone Amphitheater. Admission is charged. Call 704-264-2120. Located beside the theater are the **Daniel Boone Native Gardens**, filled with many local plants. Open daily from May through September. Call 704-264-6390.

Two galleries that display local artists' works are **The Jones House**, at 604 West King Street in Boone (call 704-262-4576), and the **Catherine Smith Gallery**, in the Farthing Auditorium at Appalachian State University in Boone (call 704-262-4046). There is no admission charge at either gallery.

Other cultural events at Appalachian State University include drama, dance, and children's productions presented by the Theater and Dance Department (call 704-262-3028), and a Festival of Music Theatre called "An Appalachian Summer" which takes place throughout the campus in both indoor and outdoor venues (call 704-262-4046 or 800-841-2787). For information about the university's **Dark Sky Observatory**, call 704-262-2000.

RECREATION

Blowing Rock (call 704-295-7111) and **Mystery Hill** (call 704-264-2792) are both fun and amazing, and are located about 5 miles apart on U.S. 321 southeast of the town of Blowing Rock. At Blowing Rock, visitors can witness natural phenomena such as snow that falls upside down and a mysterious wind that blows light objects back up over the cliff. At Mystery Hill, water flows uphill, and there's a crooked house, pioneer museum, mock grave, gardens, observation tower, and fabulous views. Admission is charged at both.

Tweetsie Railroad, off U.S. 321 between Boone and Blowing Rock, is a mountain/western theme park. The three-mile railroad trip around the park has a mock Indian raid and a railroad robbery. You'll also find other rides, shops, a railroad museum, and entertainment such as clogging, bluegrass music, and staged performances. Open mid-May through Halloween; hours vary seasonally. Admission is charged. Call 704-264-9061 or 800-526-5740.

Three major parks here are the **Moses H. Cone Memorial Park**, **Julian Price Memorial Park**, and **Grandfather Mountain** (the first two parks are free; admission is charged for Grandfather Mountain). Cone Memorial Park, at Milepost 294 on the Blue Ridge Parkway near Blowing Rock, is located on the former summer estate of the textile magnate Moses H. Cone. This park has lake fishing, 25 miles of trails, and the Moses Cone Estate and Crafts Center (see Shopping). Open daily May through October. Call 704-295-7591. Julian Price Memorial Park, at Milepost 295 on the Blue Ridge Parkway, has over 4,000 wooded acres with a 47-acre lake at its center. The park allows hiking, canoeing, fishing, and camping at designated sites. Grandfather Mountain, at Milepost 305 off the Blue Ridge Parkway, is a United Nations–designated biosphere reserve, and is located at the highest point of the Blue Ridge Mountains. If you dare, cross the famous Mile-High Swinging Bridge, suspended 1,000 feet over the gorge. There's also a museum here on local plants, wildlife, and natural history, as well as live bears and a new otter habitat. Call 704-733-4337.

Linville Caverns, on U.S. 221 four miles south of the Blue Ridge Parkway, are the only natural caverns in the Carolinas. They reach 2,000 feet underground, where the temperature is a constant fifty-one degrees (bring a sweater). Open weekends only December through February, and daily for the rest of the year. Call for hours. Admission is charged. Call 704-756-4171.

Linville Falls and Gorge has two awe-inspiring waterfalls, one 120 feet and the other 90 feet, which cascade into the gorge below. There are hiking trails for both experienced hikers and those who want an easy hike. The visitors center is equipped with restrooms. No admission is charged, but a special permit is required to enter some of the hiking trails.

For more waterfalls, head to **The Cascades** on the Parkway, which has a series of waterfalls along a ½-mile trail. This scenic trail, which most hikers can handle, is at Milepost 272 of the Blue Ridge Parkway just under 4 miles from the junction of the Blue Ridge Parkway and U.S. 421.

The abundant wildlife in the region makes hunting a popular sport in the High Country, though it is prohibited on the Blue Ridge Parkway and Grandfather Mountain. For information on how to obtain current licensing information, contact the Boone Convention and Visitors Bureau at 704-264-2225.

Other outdoor activities are rock climbing (there are several local outfitters) and gem hunting. The **Blue Ridge Gemstone Mine and Campground**, a short drive away in nearby Mitchell County, has more than fifty minerals you can dig for. Call 704-765-5264. Horseback riding is available at Smith's Quarter Horse Farm (call 704-898-4932), Blowing Rock Stables (call 704-295-7847), and Banner Elk Riding Stables (call 704-898-5424).

The fishing is great here, as waters brim with trout, bass, and other species. However, you'll need a permit or license to fish. The season is from April 1st until the end of February; March is restocking time.

In Boone, July brings the **Firefly Festival**, with crafts, entertainment, and children's events. The annual **Gospel Singing Jubilee** takes place in mid-August. In Blowing Rock, the **Annual Tour of Homes** takes place in July; visitors can tour several of the private homes in the town. Also in Blowing Rock, **Art in the Park** takes place on one Saturday a month from May through October. During this monthly festival, visitors can purchase local artists' works. During the second weekend of July, Grandfather Mountain has the annual **Highland Games and Gathering of the Clans**, a traditional Scottish celebration with lots of food, entertainment, and more. Grandfather Mountain also has two renowned **Nature Photography Weekends**, one in early June, the other in mid-October.

ACCOMMODATIONS ....

EXPENSIVE

Chetola Resort, on North Main Street in Blowing Rock adjacent to the Moses Cone Park, is a charming country resort with a canopied entrance; spectacular views; and nicely furnished rooms, suites, and condos, many with private balconies. Guests have use of facilities that include an indoor pool, fitness center, tennis courts, racquetball, and a 7-acre lake with canoes and paddle boats. There's a social director on the premises to coordinate activities available to guests, who would have to work hard at being bored here. Call 704-295-5500 or 800-CHETOLA.

Hound Ears Lodge and Club, off N.C. 105 outside of Blowing Rock, is named for the rock formation hanging over the club. Guests leave this four-star resort feeling relaxed and pampered. Among many perks here are a heated pool with lifeguard, children's activities in summer, a golf course open only to guests, tennis, exercise facilities, and winter sleigh rides. Call 704-963-4321.

MODERATE

Days Inn, on the U.S. 321 Bypass in Blowing Rock, has an indoor pool and a restaurant on the premises. The rooms are spacious and comfortable. Call 704-295-4422 or 800-325-2525.

INEXPENSIVE

Holiday Inn, at 1855 Blowing Rock Road in Boone, has an outdoor heated pool, fitness center, and free continental breakfast. Though the executive suites range toward moderate, the regular rooms are quite reasonable. Call 704-264-2451 or 800-HOLIDAY.

High Country Inn, at 1785 N.C. 105 in Boone, has an indoor and an outdoor pool, exercise room and sauna, hot tub, and reasonable rates. For a little more, suites with a fireplace or jacuzzi are available. Call 704-264-1000 or 800-334-5605.

SHOPPING ....

If you enjoy old-fashioned country stores, you'll want to stop by the **Mast General Store**, located on N.C. 194 in Valle Crucis. The original 1883 store is designated as a National Historic Landmark. Open daily. Call 704-963-6511. A second, newer store is located in the Old Boone Mercantile in downtown Boone. Call 704-262-0000. The **Todd General Store**, 10

Grandfather Mountain, near Linville
Photo by William Russ, courtesy of NC Travel and Tourism Division

miles north of Boone off N.C. 194, dates from 1914. Open daily; hours vary by weekday and season. Call 704-877-1067.

At the **Moses Cone Estate and Craft Center** you'll find quality handiworks from members of the Southern Highlands Craft Guild. Located in Moses H. Cone Memorial Park, at Milepost 294 of the Blue Ridge Parkway. Admission is free. Open daily from May 1 through October 31.

RESTAURANTS ....

FINE DINING

The Green Park Inn Restaurant on U.S. 321 in Blowing Rock. This American bistro-style restaurant serves filet mignon, pasta, rack of lamb, and other selections. They serve lunch Friday and Saturday, breakfast and dinner daily, and brunch Sunday. Fridays they have big band music ($10 without dinner; $5 with dinner). Reservations required for dinner, brunch, and big band music.

Hearthside Cafe, at Chetola Resort on North Main Street in Blowing Rock, features regional cuisine. Open for breakfast daily, lunch Monday through Saturday, dinner Tuesday through Saturday, and brunch on Sunday. Call 704-295-5505.

CASUAL DINING

Dan'l Boone Inn, at 105 Hardin Street in Boone, is a family-style restaurant serving southern favorites like fried chicken or ham and biscuits, all homemade and delicious. Each meal has three courses (soup, entrée with vegetable, and dessert), plus beverage and bread, at reasonable prices. Open seven days a week, though hours vary by season. Call 704-264-8657.

Cottonwood Grille and Brewery, at 473 Blowing Rock Road in Boone, serves mesquite-grilled steak and other southwestern American fare in a festive atmosphere. There's a micro-brewery on site, and live entertainment Sunday and Tuesday evenings. Call 704-264-7111.

JUST FOR KIDS ....

Several resorts, such as the Chetola Resort and the Hound Ears Lodge and Club, offer children's activities during the summer months. Contact the resort you plan to stay with regarding the availability of such programs.

SIDE TRIPS ....

In **Ashe County**, north of Boone on the Blue Ridge Parkway, award-winning **Blue Ridge Frescoes** painted by Ben Long can be seen at St. Mary's Church in Beaver Creek, and at Holy Trinity Church in Glendale Springs. Open daily; admission is free. Call 704-982-3076. In West Jefferson, the **Ashe County Cheese Factory** (the only one within the Carolinas) has free guided tours and a gift shop. Open Monday through Saturday. Call 704-246-2501.

GENERAL INFORMATION ....

For information on Boone, contact the Boone Convention and Visitors Bureau at 704-264-2225 or 800-852-9506. For information on Blowing Rock, contact the Blowing Rock Chamber of Commerce at 704-295-7851. For information on Banner Elk, contact the Banner Elk Chamber of Commerce at 704-898-5605. Information on the entire area can be provided by the High Country Host. Call 704-264-1299 or 800-438-7500. For a listing of current events, pick up a copy of *Mountain Times* or *North Carolina Mountains Insiders Guide*.

Part Three

SOUTH CAROLINA

South Battery residence, Charleston
Photo courtesy of Charleston Area Convention and Visitors Bureau

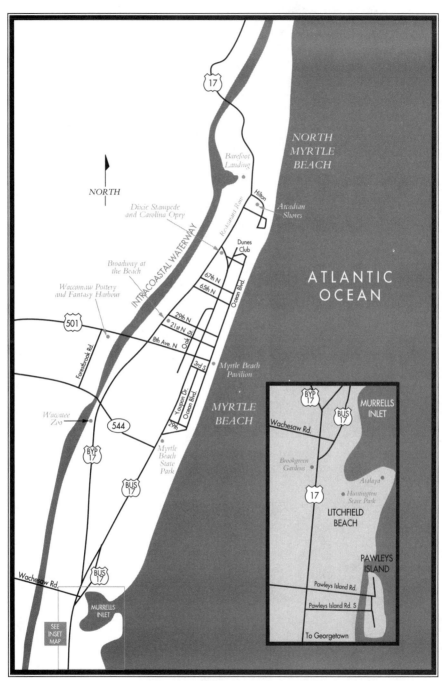

MYRTLE BEACH and PAWLEYS ISLAND, S.C.

Myrtle Beach and Pawleys Island

AREA CODE: 803

INTRODUCTION

Myrtle Beach is situated in the heart of the "Grand Strand," a 60-mile stretch of beautiful beaches from Little River to Georgetown, South Carolina. Although Myrtle Beach began booming in the 1960s, it has been a popular vacation spot since the turn of the century. The area's name, selected through a contest held in 1900, was derived from the abundance of wax myrtle growing in the area.

Myrtle Beach is heaven on earth for avid golfers, as well as those who love the beach, entertainment, and shopping. Golf has boomed in Myrtle Beach for several reasons: the climate permits year-round play, and the low water table allows the courses to contain a variety of water hazards. Also, the area has been actively promoting its golf courses for over thirty years. Not surprisingly, the golf package was invented in this area, which is often referred to as the "golf coast" because of the many excellent public courses that are available in an oceanside setting.

Myrtle Beach is definitely not a secluded resort. Yet, for those who enjoy communing with nature on the beach, fishing boat, or golf course, and then being able to find the hustle and bustle of civilization vis-à-vis shopping, amusement parks, night clubs, restaurants, and other activities—all in a family oriented setting—Myrtle Beach is an excellent choice. The combination appeals to many, as Myrtle Beach attracts some 11 million visitors each year.

Normal monthly temperatures are: January, 45.8; February, 48.6; March, 55.9; April, 62.9; May, 70.5; June, 76.6; July, 80; August, 79.1; September, 74.6; October, 65.1; November, 56.7; December, 49.3. The most popular season is summer, followed by school vacations. Golf season is year-round, but peaks in spring and fall.

GOLF INFORMATION ....

This choice of courses is tough to narrow, as to date, there are eighty-seven public golf courses, many of them championship caliber, and about a hundred courses will exist once current proposals are fulfilled. Among the proposed new courses will be a PGA Tournament Players Course, opening in 1997.

The following reviews cover several of the best courses in the area; however, you may want to contact **Myrtle Beach Golf Holiday**, a non-profit golf association offering marketing information on more than seventy local golf courses, as well as over ninety local hotels and other accommodations with golf packages at special rates. To contact Myrtle Beach Golf Holiday, call

803-448-5942 or 800-845-4653.

Additionally, golfers visiting Myrtle Beach may want to play some of the courses along North Carolina's Cape Fear Coast, just a few miles north (See the Wilmington and the Cape Fear Coast chapter for more information).

ARCADIAN SHORES GOLF CLUB, MYRTLE BEACH (803) 449-5217

Arcadian Shores Golf Club, which opened in 1974 and is affiliated with the Myrtle Beach Hilton Oceanfront Resort, was Rees Jones's first layout. Consistent with many of this younger Jones's designs, Arcadian Shores is traditional and quite challenging, though still playable by golfers of varying skill levels. The course's back tees stretch to almost 7000 yards, and have a slope of 136 and a rating of 73.2. The champion and white tees measure 6468 and 5974 yards, respectively. The course is relatively flat, with fairways lined by an assortment of mature oaks and pines. However, this doesn't make the course too tight, as the trees add scenery without affecting play. Water is a factor on almost half of the holes, and the course has as much sand as you would find down on the beach (there are sixty-four traps in all). Because it's well trapped, the course puts a premium on approach shots to the greens. The greens range from small to medium sized, and they are quick and well sloped in some places. A hole that typifies the course is the par 3 second, which is considered the best par 3 in the area. It is 205 yards, requires a carry over water, and is protected by a large bunker on the left. Because the green is very deep, club selection is difficult, and the player often finds him or herself with a fairly long putt. Par is not easy, but the beauty of the hole and the course make up for it. The lovely thirteenth is the signature hole and the number-one handicap hole on the course. It's a par 4 with a fairway that severely slopes to a lake-guarded green. A bunker protects the rear of the green, and if you hit your ball in the lake, it may be protected (or eaten) by an alligator.

Carts: Mandatory. *Greens Fees:* Approximately $80 in high season/18 holes, including cart. *Tee Time Policy:* Can be reserved up to a year in advance with a credit card. Singles are given advance tee times.

HEATHER GLEN GOLF LINKS, LITTLE RIVER (803) 249-9000 OR (800) 868-4536

Heather Glen is made up of three separate 9-hole layouts, and the player selects the 18-hole combination he or she wishes to play. From the back tees, each combination is about 6800 yards. Similarly, the white tees for each combination are in the 6300-yard range. The forward tees range from 5053 to 5146 yards. The course, designed by Willard Byrd and Clyde Johnston, was chosen as America's best new public course in 1987, and it is currently listed as one of the top public courses in the United States by *Golf Digest*. It winds through heather-covered dunes (hence its name), pines, oaks, dogwoods, hollies, streams, brooks, lakes, and lots of sand (which happens to reside in large bunkers). Many of the tees are elevated and require the player to negotiate some slim landing areas. The fairways are lined with everything from bunkers to mounds, lakes, trees, and dunes. The greens come in an assortment of sizes

and slopes (some forward and some undulating) and are guarded by the same intimidating factors that protect the fairways.

Carts: Mandatory. *Greens Fees:* Approximately $65-$80/18 holes, depending on course, season, golf package. *Tee Time Policy:* Can reserve up to eleven months in advance, but deposit required.

HERITAGE GOLF CLUB, PAWLEYS ISLAND (PART OF THE LEGENDS GOLF CLUB) (800) 377-2315

Heritage is another course ranked among the top public courses in the United States by *Golf Digest* and *Golfweek*. Not only does this course have very fine golf, it is set among some of the prettiest property and surroundings one can find in the area. The course is part of the Legends Group of courses, which includes The Legends Golf Club nearby (see below) and the Marsh Harbour and Oyster Bay Golf Links courses up the coast in North Carolina (See the Wilmington and the Cape Fear Coast chapter). Heritage Golf Club and The Legends are so closely affiliated that, though the courses are in different locations, tee times for Heritage are made at The Legends. The course is cut through magnificent oaks and magnolias and winds through lakes and marshes bordered by myrtles, azaleas, and camellias. A sea breeze from the Atlantic is everpresent, and the wildlife includes ospreys, egrets, herons, an assortment of gulls, quite a few alligators, and an occasional deer. You won't find any bears here, however, except perhaps the course itself, which can measure 7100 yards from the back tees with a course slope of 137 and rating of 74.2. The blue, white, and forward tees measure 6575, 6100, and 5325 yards, respectively. A hole representative of the course is the eighteenth—a 530-yard par 5. Water runs all the way down the right side of the hole, cutting into the fairway just beyond the tee, and then again just before the green. The tee shot not only has to avoid the water, but also two large bunkers. A lay-up needs to be well measured to avoid the water in front of the green, and it also needs to leave the player with a distance in which he or she can stop the ball quickly on the green, which is very shallow. Finally, the green is protected on all sides by bunkers and water.

Carts: Mandatory. *Greens Fees:* Approximately $65, depending on season and day/18 holes; cart: $20. *Tee Time Policy:* Can be reserved up to one year in advance; deposit required for peak-season times.

THE LEGENDS GOLF CLUB, MYRTLE BEACH (SEE ALSO HERITAGE GOLF CLUB)
(803) 236-9318
OR (800) 377-2315

The Legends is a 54-hole complex. All three courses—Heathland, designed by Tom Doak; Moorland, designed by P.B. Dye; and Parkland, designed by Larry Young—opened within the last five years. Heathland, considered among the top fifteen courses in South Carolina, spans from 5115 to 6785 yards. The fairways are lined by a variety of trees indigenous to South Carolina, including many pines and oaks, and the bermuda greens are well protected by sand, water, mounds, and other hazards. The green on the par 3 third hole, at 30 yards deep and 50 yards wide, is as big a green as you will find (it could prob-

ably double as a landing strip for local B-52s), and it slopes from front to back. The hole measures 210 to the center of the green, but that's only where the fun begins.

The Moorland course, considered by *Golf Digest* to be among the best new courses in the United States when it opened in 1990, has tees ranging from 4939 (forward) to 6832 yards (gold), with the whites measuring 5807 yards and the blues 6405 yards. Do not be fooled by the length, however—the course rating/slope from the gold tees is an unbelievable 76.8/140, and the blues are also tough at 74.8/135. Like most links courses, Moorland doesn't have trees to cause players any worry, but it does have plenty of other obstacles: long holes that play into the wind; lots of water, sand, natural vegetation, waste areas, mounds, hills, and bulkheads; fast, undulating (severely in some instances) greens; and anything else that can cause a golfer fits while playing (or surviving).

Parkland, the third course, opened in 1992, making it the newest addition to the Legends. The back tees stretch out to 7170 yards, while the middle and forward tees are 6425 and 5570 yards. Unlike Moorland, Parkland is more akin to United States–style courses, as long carries are required to reach the tree-lined, rolling fairways. The greens are large, moderately sloped, and well protected by bunkers that, in some cases, are cavernous. With its three outstanding courses, The Legends offers a great assortment of golf and is a must if you are in the Myrtle Beach area.

Carts: Mandatory. *Greens Fees:* Approximately $30-$75, depending on course and season/18 holes. *Tee Time*

Myrtle Beach
Photo courtesy of Myrtle Beach Area Chamber of Commerce

Policy: Can be reserved up to a year in advance. Guests at The Legends receive preferred tee times.

TIDEWATER GOLF CLUB, NORTH MYRTLE BEACH (803) 249-3829, (800) 446-5363

Tidewater is another must-play in the Myrtle Beach area. This course was named the best new public course by *Golf Digest* in 1990, and recently, the magazine named it the number-one course in the Grand Strand area. It was designed by Ken Tomlinson, or perhaps more accurately, one may conclude that, given the course's natural beauty, it was only found and organized by Mr. Tomlinson. Tidewater is set among forests, marshland, creeks, lakes, valleys, hills, and several rather large homes. The course has five sets of tees that measure from 4665 to 7150 yards. The landing areas are conducive to the shot required from the tee—the long holes have generous landing areas, while the short holes require accuracy. Similarly, the undulating, sloping, tiered greens range in size, depending on the length of the typical approach. However, the greens are generally quite large, some being more than 50 yards in length. As a result, a player can boast to friends that he or she reached many of the greens in regulation, but this would be only half of the story, because holing out putts is a challenge on this course.

Carts: Mandatory. *Greens Fees:* $42–$82, depending on day and season/18 holes. *Tee Time Policy:* This public course takes tee times a year in advance (with a credit-card guarantee); advance times are required.

WILD WING PLANTATION, CONWAY (800) 736-WING

If you enjoy high quality, one-stop shopping, Wild Wing is the place. It sports four 18-hole courses designed by renowned architects. The Avocet was designed by Larry Nelson, the 1983 United States Open champion and two-time PGA winner. It measures a monstrous 7127 yards from the dark teal tees—eight of ten par 4s are over 400 yards, and 4 are over 450 yards (which seems long for an accuracy-type player like Nelson)—although the magenta tees are a more civilized 6614 yards. The course features moguls and mounds, some large elevation changes for these parts, marshes, wetlands, lakes, and split fairways. Some interesting touches include a recreation of St. Andrews's "Valley of Sin" and North Berwick, Scotland's Redan, which is a grassy bank above the green that can be used to ricochet the ball onto the putting surface.

The Falcon course is a Rees Jones design that measures 7082 yards (tees start at 5190 yards) and was considered one of the best new courses in the Myrtle Beach area in 1994. Features on this course include: holes framed with pine forests, a par 3 with a 90-yard bunker, holes bordered from tee to green with lakes, a green perched on a peninsula, links-like dunes, a forgiving punch-bowl green, and Sahara-like bunkers extending over 500 yards.

The Hummingbird course, the first of two Willard Byrd designs at Wild Wing Plantation, is rated 4 stars by *Golf Digest's Places to Play*. The layout, with tees ranging from 5168 to 6853 yards, is links style, with strands of lovegrass and other native grasses forming the course's perimeter.

Finally, the Wood Stork course (named after the only stork native to the United States), is Willard Byrd's second offering at Wild Wing Plantation and is also rated 4 stars by *Golf Digest's Places to Play*. This course features water on every hole, some heavily wooded holes, and massive bunkers. Four sets of tees range from 5409 to 7044 yards.

Carts: Mandatory. *Greens Fees:* $17-$110, depending on season and course/18 holes, including cart. *Tee Time Policy:* Must guarantee with credit card or pre-pay.

CALEDONIA GOLF AND FISH CLUB, PAWLEYS ISLAND (800) 483-6800

Caledonia, on the site of a colonial rice plantation bordering the Waccamaw

Myrtle Beach Pavilion
Amusement Park
Photo courtesy of Myrtle Beach Area Chamber of Commerce

River, opened in 1994 and was considered among the best new courses in 1995 by *Golf*, and it is rated 4½ stars by *Golf Digest's Places to Play*. In his first independent design, Mike Strantz, a protégé of Tom Fazio, has created a compact, 6500-yard course (tees begin at 4968 yards) that plays to a par 70. The beauty of the course's surroundings, however, is what's special about Caledonia. Centuries-old live oaks, natural lakes, and abundant wildlife create a lush environment for a round of golf.

Carts: Mandatory. *Greens Fees:* $95/18 holes, including carts. *Tee Time Policy:* Call anytime, or book through hotel.

OTHER EXCELLENT AREA COURSES:

The Dunes Golf and Beach Club, Myrtle Beach (803-449-5914), is a 7015-yard, par 72 course designed by Robert Trent Jones, Sr. To get on this golfer's gem, rated by *Golf* as being one of the "Top 100 You Can Play," you must either arrange it through the pro at a local club, or participate in a golf package through the Caravelle Resort or Driftwood on the Oceanfront (See Accommodations), or one of four other area hotels. **Wicked Stick Golf Links**, Surfside Beach (800-548-9186), was designed by architect Clyde Johnston with the help of John Daly. This links-style course is set among expansive dune fields, large waste areas with gorse-like vegetation, and pot bunkers, and it features the "Daly" tees (in John's image—long with wide landing areas). **Myrtlewood Golf Club**, Myrtle Beach (800-283-3633), features the Palmetto course, a par 72, 6957-yard course by Ed Ault, and Pinehills, a par 72, 6640-yard course by Arthur Hills. **The Long**

Bay Club, 15 miles west of North Myrtle Beach (800-344-5590), is a 7021-yard, Jack Nicklaus signature course that is considered among the top courses in South Carolina. **Myrtle Beach National Golf Club**, between Myrtle Beach and Conway (800-344-5590), features three courses designed by Arnold Palmer and Francis Duane. **Litchfield Country Club**, Litchfield Beach (800-922-6348), is a 6752-yard, Willard Byrd layout that opened in 1966 and sports water on seventeen holes. **The River Club**, Pawleys Island (803-626-9069 or 800-344-5590), is a scenic, Tom Jackson design measuring 6677 yards with wide-open fairways, large undulating greens, and lots of water. **Willbrook Plantation at Litchfield Beach and Golf Resort**, Litchfield Beach (803-237-4900 or 800-344-5590), is a 6704-yard course that renowned architect Dan Maples considers one of his best. **The Witch**, 4 miles east of Conway (803-347-2706), is another excellent Dan Maples course. It is set in the low country wetlands and measures 6702 yards. **Blackmoor Golf Club**, Murrells Inlet (803-650-5555), is set on a former rice plantation. This 6614-yard, Gary Player course winds through hardwoods, pines, and wetlands. **Indigo Creek Golf Club**, Surfside Beach (803-650-0381), is a 6747-yard, par 72 course by architect Willard Byrd that winds through tall pines, lakes, marshlands, and wildflowers. **Pawleys Plantation**, Pawleys Island (803-237-1736), is considered among the top courses in South Carolina. This 7026-yard, Jack Nicklaus course winds through towering pines and wetlands, and features a double green and split fairway. **Surf**

Golf and Beach Club, North Myrtle Beach (803-249-1524), was recently redesigned by John LaFoy and features a fine, 6842-yard, par 72 and reasonably priced greens fees.

ATTRACTIONS ....

TOURS

Boat Tours

The Barefoot Princess offers sightseeing, dinner, and sunset cruises. Departures are from Barefoot Landing in North Myrtle Beach (see Shopping). Call 803-272-7743.

Motorized Tours

Two Myrtle Beach companies, **Palmetto Tour and Receptive Service** (call 803-626-2660) and **Leisure Time Unlimited** (call 803-448-9483) offer guided tours and tour packages.

HISTORIC PLACES

Though pop history, a notable music history spot is **The Bowery**, a small bar on Ocean Boulevard near the Pavilion in downtown Myrtle Beach, where the group "Alabama" got their start in the 1970s.

MUSEUMS/SCIENCE CENTERS

Museums here are in large part for entertainment purposes. **The Ripley's Believe It or Not! Museum**, 901 North Ocean Boulevard, has vivid exhibits on strange people and events, and an ornate replica of Cleopatra's barge constructed entirely of sugar. Call 803-448-2331. **The Myrtle Beach National Wax Museum**, 1000 North Ocean Boulevard, displays uncanny likenesses of famous people in wax. Call 803-448-9921. Both museums are located near the Myrtle Beach Pavilion and charge an admission fee.

CULTURAL OFFERINGS

While not your traditional cultural offering, listening to beach music and dancing the shag are firmly entrenched in Myrtle Beach culture—the shag has been the official dance of South Carolina since 1984. To experience these South Carolina institutions for yourself, try **Studebaker's**, 2000 North King's Highway (call 803-448-9747) and **Razzies Beach Club** (inside the "2001" nightclub complex), at 920 Lake Arrowhead Road, off of "Restaurant Row" on U.S. 17 (call 803-449-9434).

Live theater, dinner theater, and other family-style entertainment are major cultural attractions in Myrtle Beach. The following are some of the more popular ones: **The Carolina Opry**, at the intersection of Business U.S. 17 and the U.S. 17 Bypass, is world famous for its unique southern-style entertainment, and it is now said to rival Nashville's famous Grand Old Opry. Call 803-238-8888 or 800-THE OPRY. Right across the parking lot from the Carolina Opry is **Dixie Stampede**, a non-alcoholic dinner theater that offers a four-course dinner and entertainment that includes horse stunts, wagon races, music, and comedy. Guests are seated in the northern or southern section, depending on their home state. During the evening's competition, contestants in various events ride for the North or the South while the audience encourages their home side. Call 803-497-9700 or 800-433-4401. **The Carolina Palace Theater**, at Broadway at the Beach (See Shopping), is a showcase theater which attracts well-known entertainers. Call 800-426-6667. At Barefoot Landing (See Shopping), you'll find the **Alabama Theatre**, featuring live country-and-western music and the **American Pride Show**, a blend of comedy and music with a western theme. Call 803-272-1111 or 800-342-2262. **Fantasy Harbour**, behind the Outlet Park at Waccamaw, has several theaters that give the complex a theme-park feel. These include: the Gatlin Brothers Theatre, Magic on Ice, the Ronnie Milsap Theater, the Medieval Times Dinner and Tournament, and the Cercle Theater. For tickets and information for all shows except Medieval Times, call 803-236-8500 or 800-681-5209; for the Medieval Times Dinner and Tournament, call 803-236-8080. All charge admission fees.

RECREATION

Brookgreen Gardens, on U.S. 17 in Murrells Inlet, is the largest sculpture garden in the world. The grounds feature a lovely layout of water, fountains, flowers, sculptures, and poetry and prose etched in stone. The more than 500 sculptures were created by 241 American artists over the past 130 years. The sculptures include several pieces by Anna Huntington (who, with her railroad magnate husband, Archer Huntington, designed and built the gardens in the 1930s). There's also a sizeable wildlife sanctuary. Admission is charged. Call 803-237-4218.

For tennis fans, Myrtle Beach has more than 200 courts to choose from. For details, contact the Myrtle Beach Area Chamber of Commerce at 803-626-7444.

Captain Dick's Marina, on U.S. 17 in Murrells Inlet, offers fishing trips, sightseeing trips, pirate tours (narrated by a "real" pirate), parasailing, and jetskiing. Call 803-651-3676.

Amusement parks are abundant here. One popular choice is the **Myrtle Beach Pavilion Amusement Park**, located in the heart of Myrtle Beach on Ocean Boulevard. This must-see landmark combines family fun with old-time nostalgia. Built more than fifty years ago, the park retains some of the original rides, including a wooden carousel, plus several newer rides, such as the spinning and tilting Wipe-Out, for a total of thirty-seven rides in all. Visitors can walk right in from the beach. Admission is charged by the ride. Open 1 P.M. to midnight from May to early October; limited hours March and April. Call 803-448-6456. Nearby is another amusement park, **Family Kingdom**, at Third Avenue South and Ocean Boulevard, with kiddie and regular rides, costumed characters, and entertainment. Admission is charged. Call 803-626-3447.

Also abundant are water parks. **The Myrtle Waves Water Park** is on U.S. 17 Bypass at 3000 Tenth Avenue North (near Broadway at the Beach). This park has over thirty rides, which are covered by one admission price. Call 803-448-1026. At **Wild Water and Wheels Water Park**, guests can enjoy grand-prix racing, miniature golf, and more than 33 rides (mostly water rides). This park has three area locations in North Myrtle Beach, Myrtle Beach, and Surfside Beach. Admission is charged. Call 800-833-9453, extension 555. Another themed attraction here is **Mayhem Manor**, a house of horrors at 204 Ninth Avenue North, near the Pavilion. Admission is charged. Call 803-626-4413.

Myrtle Beach State Park, on U.S. 17 just south of Myrtle Beach, has surf fishing, a beach, swimming pool, nature trails, covered picnic areas, and grills. Camping facilities and cabins just off the beach have full hookups, hot showers, twenty-four-hour security, and stores on the grounds selling food, supplies, and gifts. In summer, the park offers a children's nature program. This is the best accommodations buy in Myrtle Beach, and from Sundays through Wednesdays in summer, except for the major-holiday weekends, the park is rarely crowded. For camping fees (admission is free), call 803-238-5325.

Another state park is **Huntington Beach State Park**, on U.S. 17 in Murrells Inlet. Of note here is the Moorish-style Atalaya mansion (circa 1933), the former residence of Archer Huntington (who built Brookgreen Gardens, which is also open to the public, with his wife). At the state park, there's also fishing, camping, nature trails, and a snack stand. Open daily until dusk. For fees and other information, call 803-237-4440.

SEASONAL EVENTS

The biggest annual event in Myrtle Beach is the **SunFun Festival** in June, with parades, contests, celebrity appearances, and plenty of family-style fun. Also popular is September's **Atalaya Arts and Crafts Festival** in the courtyard of the late Archer Huntington's moorish-style mansion, Atalaya (See Recreation). Murrells Inlet is a natural choice for the April **Seafood Festival**, and in May, the community of Little River hosts a **Blue Crab Festival**. October brings the **Surfside Family Beach Festival** in Surfside Beach, **Brookgreenfest** at Brookgreen Gardens in Murrells Inlet, and **Octoberfest** at Chapin Park in Myrtle Beach. November brings the state **Bluegrass Festival** at the Myrtle Beach Convention Center. December features special candlelight tours and other seasonal celebrations. Golfers and fishers will enjoy the many amateur and professional golf and fishing events, including the PGA Senior Tour Championship in November. For information on these and other events, including fees, call the Myrtle Beach Area Chamber of Commerce at 803-626-7444.

ACCOMMODATIONS ....

EXPENSIVE

The Myrtle Beach Hilton Oceanfront Golf Resort, at 10,000 Beach Club Drive, is perfect for golfers and their families. This modern, oceanfront high-rise hotel is centered around an atrium, and all rooms have balconies overlooking the ocean. Aside from its decor, beachfront location, restaurants, shops, pool with poolside service, and live entertainment, this resort also has on its premises one of the finest golf courses in the area—Arcadian Shores (See Golf Information). Even the menu at the Arcadian Restaurant revolves around a golf theme. Call 803-449-5000.

Radisson Resort Hotel at Kingston Plantation, at 9800 Lake Drive, next to the Hilton, is a pretty, oceanfront resort with gardens and lakes where wildlife such as snowy egrets, sea turtles, and ducks make their home. Accommodations range from hotel rooms overlooking the ocean to lakeside villas and townhomes. The resort has a pool and a health spa with tennis facilities. Call 803-449-0006 or 800-876-0010.

The Isle of America Resort, to be built on the former site of the Myrtle Beach Air Force Base, will open in 1998 or later. Plans include a luxury hotel; golf villas; a 27-hole championship public golf course, designed and managed by Hale Irwin; and for non-golfers, an on-site theme park called Isle of America, with rides and attractions based on the folklore, legends, and history of the United States. For information on how to make reservations, contact the Myrtle Beach Area Chamber of Commerce at 803-626-7444 or 800-356-3016.

MODERATE

The Caravelle Resort and Villas, at 6900 North Ocean Boulevard, is a beachside resort offering hotel rooms and villas. For golfers, it offers golf privileges at the Dunes Golf and Beach Club. Swimmers can enjoy indoor and outdoor pools, and a lazy-river ride. Other amenities include a whirlpool, sauna, game room, and cocktail party for arriving guests. Call 803-449-3331 or 800-845-0893.

Crown Reef Resort, at 2913 South Ocean Boulevard, has indoor and outdoor pools (including one with a bridge leading over the pool to the beach), as well as spas, kiddie pools, a 275-foot lazy-river ride, and exercise room. Call 800-405-7333.

INEXPENSIVE

Driftwood on the Oceanfront, at 1600 North Ocean Boulevard, is a good choice for families who would rather forego glitzy surroundings for comfortable, reasonably priced rooms in a beachfront location (with two pools to boot). Guests here also enjoy golf privileges at the Dunes Golf and Beach Club. Call 803-448-1544 or 800-942-3456.

Ocean Dunes/Ocean Sands Resort and Villas is a complex of beachfront hotels, villas, apartments, and townhouses that cater to families at a reasonable cost. Amenities include game rooms, kiddie pools, a spa, on-site restaurants and grocery stores, tennis facilities, and a children's program in summer. Call 803-449-7441 or 800-845-6701.

For a budget vacation, you may want to camp at the **Myrtle Beach State Park**. Staying here Sundays through Wednesdays (except holiday weekends) is also a good way to avoid the crowds (See Recreation).

SHOPPING

Broadway at the Beach, located on U.S. 17 Bypass between Twenty-first Avenue North and Twenty-ninth Avenue North, is a new, village-like complex centered around a small lake located inland near the beach areas. The complex combines shopping, dining, and entertainment, and the over seventy-five specialty stores include a Sam Snead signature store. Call 800-FUN-IN-MB.

Another shopping center with dining and entertainment is **Barefoot Landing**, on U.S. 17 in North Myrtle Beach. The complex is spread around the Intracoastal Waterway on one side and a freshwater lake on the other. Stores are mainly specialty shops, with about a dozen outlet stores. Non-shoppers can enjoy Alligator Adventure (a live reptile museum), the wooden carousel, a riverboat ride on the intracoastal waterway aboard the *Barefoot Princess*, the "Barefoot Simulator" ride (a realistic video ride taking you down a roller coaster, ski run, and more). There are also several entertainment theaters here (See Cultural Offerings). Call 803-272-8349.

The place to purchase famous Pawleys Island hammocks, or simply watch island craftsmen make them (as they've done since 1880), is at **The Hammock Shops**, located on U.S. 17 in Pawleys Island. Other local items are also available. Call 803-237-8448. Additionally, there are several other shops on Pawleys Island that are worth investigating.

There are currently two outlet centers for discount shoppers. **Outlet Park at Waccamaw**, located next to Waccamaw Pottery on U.S. 501, is the largest outlet center on the East Coast, with over 125 factory outlet stores and free tram rides from store to store. Call 803-236-1303 or 800-444-VALU. **Myrtle Beach Factory Stores Outlet Center** is also on U.S. 501. It includes Off Fifth (a Saks Fifth Avenue outlet) and similar names.

RESTAURANTS ....

There are approximately 1800 restaurants in the greater Myrtle Beach area. If you like driving a main drag to find a place that grabs you, try cruising "Restaurant Row" on U.S. 17 between Myrtle Beach and North Myrtle Beach, where you'll surely find something for everyone. Seafood lovers, take note: Murrells Inlet, about 12 miles south of Myrtle Beach, is known for its quality seafood restaurants.

FINE DINING

Thoroughbred's, at 9706 North King's Highway, features fine continental selections, including steak and seafood, and has a great wine menu. Reservations are recommended; serves lunch and dinner daily. Call 803-497-2636.

The Library, at 1212 North King's Highway, caters to the unusual, featuring creative sauces and dishes with a Southern flair. The menu features a wide selection of steak, seafood, and poultry dishes. The quaint decor is both eclectic and cozy. Serves dinner only. Call 803-448-4527.

CASUAL DINING

Golfers will enjoy **Sam Snead's Tavern**, at 9708 North Kings Highway. This wood-paneled, pub-like restaurant features ribs, steaks, chicken, and more with (what else?) a golf theme. Call 803-497-0580.

A new addition to the **Hard Rock Cafe** restaurant family is in Myrtle Beach at Broadway on the Beach. This Hard Rock is distinguished from its counterparts by its pyramid shape, with a glass tip weighing 2,500 pounds. Inside, memorabilia includes guitars played by Pete Townshend, Tina Weymouth of Talking Heads, and the late greats, Jerry Garcia and Jimi Hendrix. Continental selections include burgers and sandwiches, salads, ribs, and vegetarian selections. The restaurant features music videos on large screens, and there's a raised center stage for live entertainment. You may have to wait for a table, as this restaurant is quite popular. Call 803-946-0007.

Dockside Restaurant and Gazebo Bar, on Business U.S. 17 in Murrells Inlet, specializes in regional low country cuisine, mainly seafood dishes, as well as steaks for the landlubbers. The interior has a nautical decor. Serves dinner only. Call 803-651-5850.

Sea Captain's House, at 3002 North Ocean Boulevard, is a circa 1930, family-owned restaurant that's a Myrtle Beach institution. Seafood and steaks are served in a powder blue, wooden captain's house overlooking the ocean. Call 803-448-8082.

Cagney's Old Place, at 9911 North King's Highway, has a more interesting decor than food, but you may enjoy the turn-of-the-century feel. The menu features seafood, steaks, chicken, and a popular chocolate-fudge pie. There's also a bar and dancing. Call 803-449-3824.

JUST FOR KIDS ....

(For amusement and water parks, see Recreation.)

For the under-twenty-one crowd, there's a non-alcoholic nightclub, the **Attic**, with concert performances by nationally known artists, a live d.j. nightly, great sound and lighting equipment, and a large dance floor. Open 7 P.M. to midnight. Located at the Myrtle Beach Pavilion, 812 North Ocean Boulevard. Call 803-448-6456.

Several area hotels have kids' programs, and many also offer babysitting services. Contact your hotel for programs.

SIDE TRIPS ....

Pawleys Island, a resort area south of Myrtle Beach, is a nice day trip, most notably for its Hammock Shops (See Shopping), or playing golf (See Golf Information).

Georgetown is about 32 miles south of Myrtle Beach off U.S. 17. The historic downtown is lined with charming old buildings. One building that's open for tours is the **Harold Kaminski House**, 1003 Front Street, a pre-Revolutionary war structure furnished with antiques from the eighteenth and nineteenth centuries. Open Monday through Friday. Admission is charged. Call 803-546-7706. **The Rice Museum**, at 633 Front Street, focuses on the history of rice cultivation, once the foundation of Georgetown's economy. Admission is charged. Call 803-546-7423. For narrated boat tours on varying themes (ghost stories, natural history, etc.) contact **Captain Sandy's Tours** at 803-527-4106. For information about Georgetown, call the Georgetown Chamber of Commerce at 803-546-8436.

Twelve miles south of Georgetown on U.S. 17 is **Hopsewee Plantation** (circa 1740), the birthplace of Thomas Lynch, Jr. This elegant rice plantation features a Georgian staircase where Lynch and other signers of the Declaration of Independence once gathered. Open Tuesday to Friday from March through October. Admission is charged. Call 803-546-7891.

GENERAL INFORMATION ....

For more information, contact the Myrtle Beach Area Chamber of Commerce at 803-626-7444 or 800-356-3016. Free publications that include information and a calendar of events are *Strand* magazine, available from merchants, and *Stay & Play*, available from the chamber of commerce.

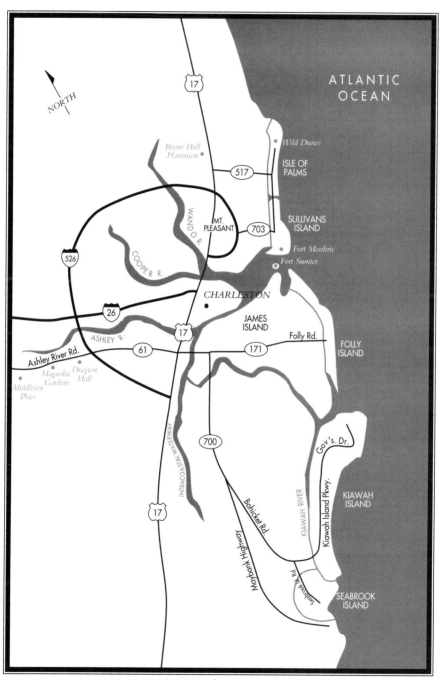

CHARLESTON and SURROUNDING ISLANDS, S.C.

Charleston and surrounding islands

INCLUDING ISLE OF PALMS,

KIAWAH ISLAND, AND

MOUNT PLEASANT

AREA CODE: 803

INTRODUCTION ....

The Charleston area is a golfer's dream, boasting several of the greatest golf courses in the country, and probably the world. Non-golfers, however, cherish this area as well. Historic Charleston was once a port city at the center of United States commerce, due to its prime location between the Cooper and Ashley Rivers. It is a charming and fascinating city, and as one of the oldest English settlements and the birthplace of the Civil War, it has played a crucial role in the history of our nation.

Charleston's people are fiercely proud, yet friendly, toward the many tourists they receive each year. The city itself, much of which can be savored on foot, has an unhurried feel and an old European air, with streets lined by beautifully preserved antebellum mansions (including the famous "Rainbow Row" seen in countless artists' renderings of the city) and churches.

Many of the golf courses covered in

this book are in the surrounding areas of Charleston. However, they are all within easy reach of Charleston, ranging from approximately a fifteen- to thirty-minute drive from downtown. Mount Pleasant is a suburb of Charleston with a public golf course; Isle of Palms and Kiawah Island are beach resort areas with courses accessible to both resort guests and outsiders. Both resort areas are family oriented, though Isle of Palms is somewhat more built up and has more shopping, hotels, and restaurants than Kiawah Island (which has one resort hotel and, at present, only a few restaurants, all but two being within the resort hotel).

From Charleston and the mainland, the Isle of Palms is easily accessed via a new highway extension, the Isle of Palms (IOP) connector (S.C. 517). The connector leads onto the island, once accessible only by boat and railroad bridge. Isle of Palms is on a barrier island with the Intracoastal Waterway on one side and the Atlantic Ocean on the other. The island's natural setting, with its rolling sand dunes and subtropical trees (such as magnolias, palms, palmettos, myrtles, and oaks), features more than a hundred species of birds (including egrets, herons, ospreys, pelicans, and terns), and more than twenty species of land mammals (aside from its human population). It's a great spot for golfers, and for nature and beach lovers, as well.

Kiawah Island is quiet and relatively unspoiled. The entrance to the resort area is surrounded by marshlands, but visitors who are allowed past the security gate at the front are soon rewarded by abundant wildlife, miles of bicycle and jogging paths, hiking trails, twenty-eight tennis courts, boating, canoeing,

fishing, playgrounds, bird–watching, 10 miles of relatively uncrowded beaches, and four of the finest golf courses and practice facilities you can find anywhere.

The normal monthly temperatures for the Charleston area as follows: January, 48.4; February, 51; March, 57.9; April, 65.4; May, 72.8; June, 78.8; July, 81.8; August, 81; September, 76.8; October, 67.9; November, 59.7; December, 52.2. High season runs mid-March through October.

GOLF INFORMATION ....

WILD DUNES RESORT, ISLE OF PALMS (803) 886-2301 OR (800) 845-8880

Wild Dunes boasts two, 18–hole championship courses: the Wild Dunes Links Golf Course (1979) and the Harbor Golf Course (1985), both designed by Tom Fazio.

The Links course, rated in the top one hundred courses in the United States by *Golf Digest*, *Golf*, and others, and among the top five courses in South Carolina by *Golf Digest*, is an excellent layout. When the wind is blowing, as it usually is, the course is more than challenging from the back tees, which stretch this course to more than 6700 yards. The Links requires a player to keep the ball low and in play, since balls that get up into the wind usually end up in the sandy dunes. The fairways roll, so a player often finds him or herself with an unusual stance or lie. The greens are medium in size, fairly quick, and well protected by the dunes. Because the greens are somewhat elevated, running the ball close to the hole is tricky. The ninth and last three holes on the inward half are the most challenging. The par 4 ninth, which always seems to play into the wind, is a long 451 yards. With a fairway wood or long iron in hand for your second shot, and a smallish green with a bunker on the right and water on the left, a player will do well to escape with par. The sixteenth hole is a par 3,175-yard hole that plays entirely over a marsh and usually into the wind. The seventeenth is a lovely par 4 bordered by ocean and beach dunes on one side and island dunes on the other. The final hole is a 500-yard, downwind par 5 that tempts the player to go for the green in two. The green, however, is bounded by beach and sea oats, so often the best shot is a safe lay-up.

The Harbor Course plays to more than 6400 yards (tees start at 4774 yards), with nine of its holes right on the Intracoastal Waterway and two holes that play across Morgan Creek from Sullivan's Island to Wild Dunes. Thus, the course tests your target golf skills and takes you island-hopping in the process.

Carts: Mandatory. *Greens Fees:* Approximately $29-$110, depending on course and season (lower for resort guests)/18 holes. *Tee Time Policy:* Guests can reserve times when they book rooms. Non-guests should contact the pro shop; outside players can confirm tee times up to thirty days in advance with a credit-card guarantee.

KIAWAH ISLAND'S RESORT COURSES, KIAWAH ISLAND

Kiawah Island's four resort courses are all excellent, and packages for all are available through the resort. The Ocean Course (803-768-2121, extension 5300) is probably the best-known course on Kiawah. This 1991, par 72 course, which hosted the Ryder Cup the year it opened, measures between 5327 and almost 7400 yards. Designed by Pete Dye, the course is exciting, terrifying, challenging, overwhelming, and confounding—and probably will make for one of the most unforgettable rounds of golf you'll ever play. Wind is almost always a factor on this course, since it is set along the ocean. Most of the tees are atop sand dunes, while the gently rolling fairways are large, yet require carries over marshes, lakes, dunes, and other hazards. The greens are protected by a barrage of natural barriers—lakes, marshes, dunes, sand and grass bunkers, wastelands, and trees. The second hole is a par 5 that Colin Montgomerie somehow reached in two strokes during the 1991 Ryder Cup. The trouble is not so much the distance, but the fact that the green looks like it's propped up in the middle of a marsh. The fourth hole is a short, devilish par 4 with a small green atop a dune. Often playing downwind, the green is difficult to hit and/or hold. The thirteenth is a great par 4, bordered from tee to green by water on the right and dunes on the left. The green is a bit out in the water, so most players bail out left into the safety of a dune—often not a great trade. The par 3 seventeenth spans 197 yards. A lake in front of the green runs diagonally from left to right, and the green runs the same direction. Surrounding dunes leave a player little option but to go for the pin. If you are lucky enough to play the Ocean Course, remember to bring a couple of extra balls, your patience, and a camera with lots of film to capture the breathtaking ocean views.

Marsh Point (803-768-2121, extension 1717) is a 6472-yard (tees begin at 4933 yards), par 71, links-style course designed by Gary Player in 1976. Don't be fooled by the length of this course—it demands accurate drives to narrow fairways, most bordered by water on one side and trees on the other, as well as precision approach shots to the small and undulating greens. You'll most likely need every club in your bag, as this course offers great variety. The ninth and tenth holes border and work around one of Kiawah's many beautiful lakes. The ninth is a winding-right par 5, with the lake to your right and woods to your left. The tee shot can shorten the hole to the extent the player wishes to flirt with the water. The second shot should be placed as far left as possible, since the green is long and narrow and most accessible by shots from this position. The green slopes sharply to the middle, and the player can be faced with a putt with a break of 6 feet or more. The par 4 tenth is a dogleg right, once again bordering the lake on the right. If you keep your ball in play from the tee, you're faced with a two-tier green that is guarded by the lake and a host of bunkers. Pars on both of these holes is an accomplishment. (Note: Though currently closed for renovations and redesign, the course will reopen in the fall of 1996.)

Turtle Point (803-768-2121, extension 4050) is a 6919-yard (tees start at 5285 yards), par 72 course designed by Jack Nicklaus in 1981. The layout at Turtle Point has many trees, and half the holes are bordered by water. Three holes run along the ocean, making the constant sea breeze a factor in your shots. The 168-yard, par 3 fourteenth is lined with beach dunes on the right. The green is very deep, with bunkers on the left and front-right, and dunes everywhere else. The fifteenth, a 438-yard par 4, has dunes on the left. The green is protected by a large trap on the right and dunes behind and to the left. Your third shot always seems to be out of one of these sandy locales. The sixteenth is another par 3, measuring 173 yards. This hole faces the opposite direction from the fourteenth, and even though the sixteenth is only 5 yards longer than that hole, the wind often dictates a four or five club difference.

Osprey Point (803-768-2121, extension 4071), designed by Tom Fazio in 1988, is a par 72, 6678-yard course. Osprey Point is the favorite of many visitors to Kiawah, and it harbors an amazing assortment of birds, including eagles and hawks, as well as more exotic breeds such as egrets, terns, and herons. The course has a variety of tees that make play enjoyable for every caliber of golfer. The fairways are basically flat, and fifteen of the holes are bordered by water. Mounds, moguls, and sand and grass bunkers surround most of the greens, which vary in size from relatively small to quite large. Most, if not all, of the holes are memorable, so when on Kiawah, don't miss playing this course.

Carts: Mandatory at Turtle Point, Ocean Course, and Osprey Point. *Greens Fees:* $85-$131 Ocean, $40-$75 Marsh Point (prior to renovations), $50-$90 Osprey Point, and $70-$110 Turtle Point. *Tee Time Policy:* Non-resort guests should reserve seven days in advance at Turtle Point, and twenty-four hours in advance for Osprey Point; varies for Ocean Course, depending on accommodations

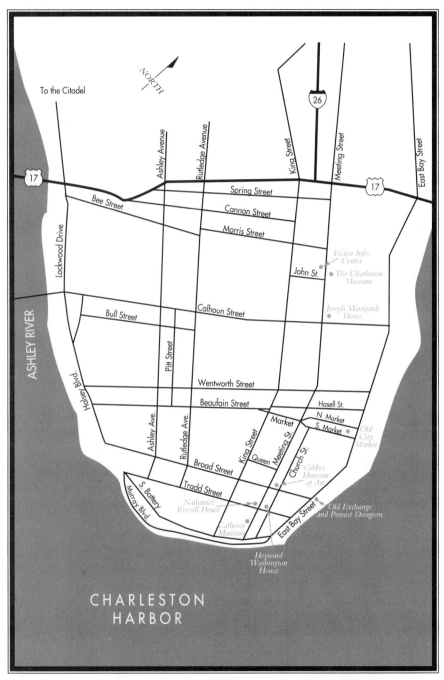

CHARLESTON, S.C.

(call course for details); for Marsh Point, call when the course reopens in fall of 1996.

DUNES WEST GOLF COURSE, MOUNT PLEASANT (803) 856-9000

This course was designed by Arthur Hills and ranked among the best new courses in 1992. Located in Mount Pleasant, Dunes West stands at the site of the former Wando Plantation, which was named after the local Indians and was once a center for the production of bricks, rice, and cotton.

The course plays to almost 6900 yards from the back tees. It is quite open with rolling fairways, large fast undulating greens, and water on six of its holes. You'd better do your scoring on the front nine, especially since the last five holes are very demanding. For example, the fourteenth is a 474-yard, par 4 dogleg right that plays to a green protected by a huge trap on the right. The fifteenth is another dogleg right, but is a 560-yard par 5. If you successfully avoid the series of bunkers to the right with your drive, the hole can be played in a number of ways, as the fairway splits for your second shot with another set of large bunkers. If you make it this far, the sixteenth is a 404-yard, par 4 dogleg left, with a lake to the right and traps to the left. Thus, the green requires an accurate approach. The seventeenth provides little relief. It's a 207-yard par 3. The green is protected with a bunker on the left and back, and water on the right. The eighteenth, while also difficult, is a lovely finishing hole, with a row of oaks lining the fairway through the green.

Carts: Mandatory. *Greens Fees:* $32-$75, depending on season/18 holes. *Tee*

Time Policy: No limits; first come, first served.

OTHER EXCELLENT AREA COURSES:

Seabrook Island Resort, Seabrook Island (803-768-2529), which has a terrific championship 18-hole course, is open to resort and non-resort guests.

ATTRACTIONS ....

TOURS

Walking Tours

Charleston offers several guided walking tours of its historic district. **The Civil War Walking Tour** given by licensed guide Jack Thomson leaves Monday through Wednesday at 9 A.M. from Mills House Hotel. Tours include a look at old photographs and standing sites. Call 803-722-7033.

Another novel tour is the **Charleston Tea Party Walking Tour**, an architectural and history tour in which guests view the courtyards, gardens, and interiors of homes, and enjoy tea afterwards in a private garden. Tours depart Monday through Saturday at 9:30 A.M. and 2:00 P.M. from King's Courtyard Inn. Call 803-722-1779.

For a less specialized tour, contact **Charleston Strolls**, which is recommended by the AAA as the best way to see Charleston. Tours depart Monday through Saturday at 9:30 A.M. and 1:30 P.M. from the Charleston Place Hotel, and 10:00 A.M. and 2:00 P.M. from the Mills House Hotel. Call 803-766-2080 or 803-884-9505.

Horse and Carriage Tours

Horse-drawn carriage tours of the city leave from the Old City Market, at Anson and Church Streets. There are a few companies offering these tours, the most easily recognized being the **Old South Carriage Company**, whose drivers wear confederate uniforms. Call 803-723-9712. Other companies include **Charleston Carriage Company** (call 803-577-0042), **Olde Towne Carriage Company** (call 803-722-1315), and **Palmetto Carriage Works, Ltd.** (call 803-723-8145).

Motorized Tours

Charlie Town Tours offers tours in air-conditioned buses that include video presentations and a scheduled stop to stroll along the waterfront overlooking Charleston Harbor. Call 803-849-6343. **Colonial Coach and Trolley Company** offers bus and trolley tours. Call 803-795-3000. **"Doin' the Charleston" Tours, Inc.** combines a bus tour with a laser-image show, with images of famous places destroyed long ago. Call 803-763-1233.

Boat Tours of Charleston's Harbor

The Charles Towne Princess, a Gray Line tour, offers breakfast, lunch, and dinner cruises, and covers eighty-five points of interest along the harbor. Reservations needed for dinner cruises only. Call 803-722-1112 or 800-344-4483. **The Schooner Pride** is a topsail schooner offering afternoon and sunset cruises. If you want, you can even help with the sailing. Call 803-795-1180.

HISTORIC PLACES

Historic Homes

There are a number of well-preserved antebellum homes open for tours year round. The Charleston Metro Chamber of Commerce can furnish visitors with a walking tour map of the historic district, which is rich in varied architectural styles and legends. Combination tickets can be purchased for certain homes. For information, call 803-577-2510.

The **Heyward-Washington House**, at 87 Church Street, was built in 1772 and owned by Thomas Heyward, a signer to the Declaration of Independence (and yes, Washington did in fact sleep here in 1791). The interior is beautifully detailed and furnished with period pieces. Tours run Monday through Saturday from 10 A.M. to 5 P.M., and Sunday from 1 to 5 P.M. Admission is charged. Call 803-722-0354. Also

Magnolia Gardens, Charleston
Photo courtesy of Charleston Area Convention and Visitors Bureau

open for tours is the **Calhoun Mansion**, at 16 Meeting Street, once owned by John C. Calhoun. Calhoun was a former vice-president of the United States who later was an instrumental leader in the South's secession from the United States. Later, during the Civil War, he served as a Confederate general. Built in 1876, the mansion has a marvelously elegant interior and high ceilings, a stairwell with a 75-foot domed ceiling, and a ballroom with a 45-foot glass skylight. Tours run Thursday through Sunday from 10 A.M. to 4 P.M. Closed in January. Admission is charged. Call 803-722-8205.

Other houses which offer tours (all charge admission) include: the nineteenth-century **Aiken-Rhett House**, at 48 Elizabeth Street, which was owned by Governor William Aiken (call 723-1159); the Greek Revival **Edmondston-Alston House**, at 21 East Battery, built in 1825 (call 803-722-7171); the neoclassical **Nathaniel Russell House**, at 51 Meeting Street, which was built in 1808 with an unsupported flying staircase—an architectural marvel which spirals from floor to floor (call 803-724-8481); and the New Adam–style **Joseph Manigault House**, at 87 Church Street, built in 1803 (call 803-723-2926).

Other homes to view (from outside and across the street *only*, as they are privately owned) are the colorful bevy of homes along East Bay Street, known as Rainbow Row, as well as the homes along East Battery Street overlooking Charleston Harbor. As you wander the streets of the historic district, you'll notice that many of the homes have piazzas, or porches, on the side of the house. You'll also notice that many of these homes face the street sideways, with the wider front (where the front door is located) on what would normally be the side of the house. This peculiar design resulted from old property tax laws that charged according to the footage of the house facing the street.

Historic Buildings and Churches

The Old Exchange and Provost Dungeon, at 122 East Bay Street, was built between 1667 and 1771 and was once used as a customs house. Downstairs is a grisly exhibit depicting the old dungeon, where the British held political prisoners during the Revolutionary War. It's also where captured pirates were imprisoned, including the "Gentleman Pirate" Stede Bonnet, who during his trial blamed his piracy on a nagging wife, but was nevertheless hanged at what is now White Point Gardens. Open daily. Admission is charged. Call 803-727-2165.

St. Philip's Church, at 146 Church Street, dates from 1838. The most interesting site is the graveyard, where John C. Calhoun reposes. Ironically, Calhoun's wife is buried on the church side, and although he became a notable South Carolina and United States politician, he is buried in the graveyard annex across the street, along with other "foreigners" (i.e., those not born and raised in Charleston!).

St. Michael's Church, at the intersection of Meeting and Broad Streets, was built in 1761. It is one of America's oldest churches and stands at the "four corners of law"—where it is joined by the post office, the state courthouse, and the city hall.

Military History

The first shot of the Civil War was fired on **Fort Sumter**, in Charleston Harbor. The fort still remains and can be reached by boat. The tour of the fort lasts just over two hours; National Park Rangers give a presentation and are available for questions. For tour boat information, call 803-722-1691. To contact the park superintendent's office, call 803-883-3123 or 803-883-3124.

A statue of **John C. Calhoun**, a famous South Carolina politician and a major proponent of secession from the Union is located at a park at the intersection of Meeting and Calhoun Streets. Calhoun's statue stands with his back to the North, of course.

Patriots Point, in the nearby suburb of Mount Pleasant, is interesting for those who enjoy exploring Charleston's military history or witnessing such traditions as the annual Blessing of the Fleet in April. You can tour the aircraft carrier *Yorktown*, a submarine, a destroyer, a Coast Guard cutter, and various models of military aircraft, including the famous "Fighting Lady" from World War II. Admission is charged. Call 803-884-2727.

MUSEUMS/SCIENCE CENTERS

The Charleston Museum, at 360 Meeting Street, is the country's oldest museum, dating to 1773. The museum showcases the natural and cultural history of South Carolina's low country. There's a large "Discover Me" room with special hands-on exhibits for kids. Admission is charged. Call 803-722-2996.

The Civil War Museum, at 54 Broad Street, houses a large collection of Civil War artifacts such as weapons, uniforms, flags, and saddles, and has a gallery where Civil War collectibles are sold. Admission is charged. Call 803-577-7766. Works displayed at the **Gibbes Museum of Art**, at 135 Meeting Street, are by various American painters, mostly Southerners, and span from the eighteenth century to the twentieth century. The collection includes several portraits of notable figures from United States history. Admission is charged. Call 803-722-2706.

CULTURAL OFFERINGS

Dock Street Theater, on Church Street across from St. Philip's Church, is one of America's oldest theaters. The old seats and stage are interesting, and there are various live stage productions offered throughout the year. Call 803-720-3968.

SEASONAL EVENTS

In March and April, the annual **Charleston Festival of Houses and Gardens**, offering tours of homes normally closed to the public, takes place. For information, call the Historic Charleston Foundation at 803-723-1623.

From late May through early June, Charleston hosts a world-class arts festival, **Spoleto Festival USA**. The festival includes a rich combination of traditional and experimental cultural arts including: ballet, choral music, paintings, symphonies, operas, and plays. Many participating artists are well known, while others are the rising stars of tomorrow. Many events require tickets. For more information, call 803-722-2764. **Piccolo Spoleto** is a smaller, less-formal festival within Spoleto

Charleston waterfront
Photo courtesy of Charleston Area Convention and Visitors Bureau

Festival USA (although it is run separately). Piccolo Spoleto showcases local and regional arts of various traditional and experimental forms. It also stages fun events around the city, including a children's parade. Some events charge admission, while others are free. For more information, contact the Charleston Office of Cultural Affairs at 803-724-7305.

ACCOMMODATIONS ....

If you need help finding accommodations, you can call the Low Country Reservation Service at 800-774-8000. For historic bed-and-breakfasts, call 803-722-6606 or 800-743-3583.

EXPENSIVE

Two Meeting Street Inn, at 2 Meeting Street, is a beautiful, old inn featuring a wood-paneled dining room with a crystal chandelier, and antique-furnished rooms. Call 803-723-7322.

King's Courtyard Inn, at 198 King Street, is a Historic Hotel of America built in 1853. In the evenings, guests receive wine and sherry in the lobby, and turn-down service is available. Call 803-723-7000.

Wild Dunes Resort, on Isle of Palms, is among the finest golf resorts in the United States. It offers sports and recreation programs for adults and children, pools, and great beaches. Call 800-845-8880.

Kiawah Island Resort, on Kiawah Island, is a family- and golf-oriented, beachfront resort with four restaurants, an outdoor pool and many other amenities. During summer and holidays, they offer a kids' program (Kamp Kiawah), a teen program, and special holiday and nature programs. Call 800-845-2471 in South Carolina; outside of South Carolina, call 800-654-2924.

The Charleston Place Hotel, at 130 Market Street, is a deluxe hotel with an upscale shopping arcade located in the historic district. Call 803-722-4900.

MODERATE TO INEXPENSIVE

Best Western King Charles Inn, at 237 Market Street, has an outdoor pool and is located one block from the Market. Call 803-723-7451.

Days Inn, at 155 Meeting Street, is located in the center of the historic district and has an outdoor pool. Call 803-722-8411.

Quality Inn Heart of Charleston, at 125 Calhoun Street, is conveniently located next to the historic district. The hotel isn't deluxe, but the rooms are nice and there's an outdoor pool. Call 803-722-3391.

SHOPPING ....

The flea-market shopper will love the **Old City Market** at the beginning of Charleston's historic district. The open-air buildings are packed with booths offering local wares, including spices, cloth dolls, Civil War memorabilia, t-shirts, and sweetgrass baskets woven by sea island women (who can be seen weaving and often chatting amongst themselves in their native Gullah dialect).

For small specialty shops, check out the shops in Shed A of the Market, as well as the **Rainbow Market**, just across the street from the Market. King and Church Streets also have clusters of small shops.

For those in search of large, prestigious franchises, **Charleston Place** (located near the Market in the Charleston Place Hotel), contains Polo by Ralph Lauren, Banana Republic, Laura Ashley, and others.

RESTAURANTS ....

Though Charleston has a surprisingly wide variety of cuisine, visitors will undoubtedly enjoy low country cuisine, which includes items like she-crab soup, veal, quail, fish, and shellfish, as well other local specialties such as fried gator tail.

FINE DINING

82 Queen (the name is the address) is considered by many to be the best restaurant in town. The interior of this converted house, decorated with eighteenth-century period furniture and paintings, makes a cozy place for a meal, and the outstanding food (from seafood, veal, fowl, lamb, beef, and other low country favorites to exquisite desserts) creates a pleasurable dining experience. Outside dining is available on the patio. Call 803-723-7591.

Louis' Charleston Grill, at 224 King Street, is named after its famous chef, Louis Osteen, and has received national praise for its excellent local seafood, fowl, steaks, and other dishes prepared in a unique interpretation of low country cuisine. The restaurant features live jazz nightly. Call 803-577-4522.

Poogan's Porch is located at 72 Queen Street in a lovely old home and is well known for such local favorites as fried-chicken salad, creole, jambalaya, quail, alligator, peanut-butter pie, and other southern-style dishes. Call 803-577-2337.

CASUAL DINING

TBonz, at 80 North Market Street, is a fun steak and brew place connected to **Kaminsky's**, a bakery offering scrumptious cakes and pastries. The menu features "pub grub," such as chicken wings, a fried giant onion, nachos, fajitas, and of course, steaks. Their international beer list is spectacular and includes local brews like Palmetto Beer. Call 803-577-2511.

For Irish pubs serving good food and beer, try **Tommy Condon's**, at 160 Church Street (call 803-577-3818), or **Mike Calder's Pub**, at 288 King Street (call 803-577-0123).

Across from the Market is a fast-food court with pizza, burgers, Chinese food, etc., and indoor seating.

JUST FOR KIDS ....

Several island resorts in the areas surrounding Charleston (See Golf Information) have children's programs, especially during high seasons. Many also offer babysitting services.

Piccolo Spoleto has events of special interest to children, such as parades and puppets. (See Seasonal Events).

SIDE TRIPS ....

Boone Hall Plantation, off U.S. 17, 6 miles north of Charleston, is the most photographed plantation in America. The grounds of this Georgian-style mansion include slave cabins from the 1700s, gin houses where cotton was processed after harvest, and a live-oak walkway planted in 1743 by Captain Thomas Boone. Call 803-884-4371.

Charles Towne Landing, off S.C. 171, just south of downtown Charleston, is located at the original settlement site of Charleston. The site is a state park offering tram tours of the original fortification (circa 1670) aboard replicas of trading ketches from the seventeenth century. The park also has extensive English gardens, an animal forest, and a Settlers' Life Area containing herbs and plants widely grown and used in the seventeenth century. Call 803-852-4200.

Cypress Gardens, at 3030 Cypress Garden Road, is 24 miles north of Charleston. Tours of this 163-acre swamp garden are available by foot and glass-bottomed boat. The swamp, whose dark waters reflect the flowers that grace its edges, was once used as a reservoir to water the surrounding rice fields. Call 803-553-0515.

Drayton Hall, on Ashley River Road (or S.C. 61), is 9 miles northwest of Charleston. The home is a unrestored mansion dating from the early eighteenth century that is a National Historic Landmark. The Georgian-Palladian home contains a sculpted ceiling, hand-carved woodwork, and original paint from the eighteenth and nineteeth centuries. Call 803-766-0188.

Magnolia Plantation and Gardens, on Ashley River Road (or S.C. 61) is the home of America's oldest major garden, planted in 1680. The plantation is best known for its azaleas and camellias. There's also a petting zoo, herb garden, biblical garden, tropical garden, maze, and observation tower. The grounds can be seen on foot or by tram ride. The original house was destroyed during the Civil War, but its replacement represents post-war plantation life. Call 803-571-1266.

Middleton Place, on Ashley River

Road (or S.C. 61) is located 14 miles northwest of Charleston. The plantation's trademarks are its "butterfly-shaped" sculptured lakes and gardens. The plantation was the home of Arthur Middleton, who represented South Carolina at the signing the Declaration of Independence. The mansion reflects the lives of this influential Southern family, and in the plantation stableyards, visitors can see demonstrations of daily plantation chores. Call 803-556-6020.

GENERAL INFORMATION ....

Contact the Charleston Area Convention and Visitors Bureau at 803-853-8000, or the Charleston Metro Chamber of Commerce at 803-577-2510. The Visitors Information Center is located on the corner of Meeting and John Streets, two blocks north of Calhoun Street.

Helpful publications that give more information and a calendar of events include the *Official Tours and Attractions Guide* and *A Guide to Charleston's Islands*, available from local stores, hotels, and the chamber of commerce.

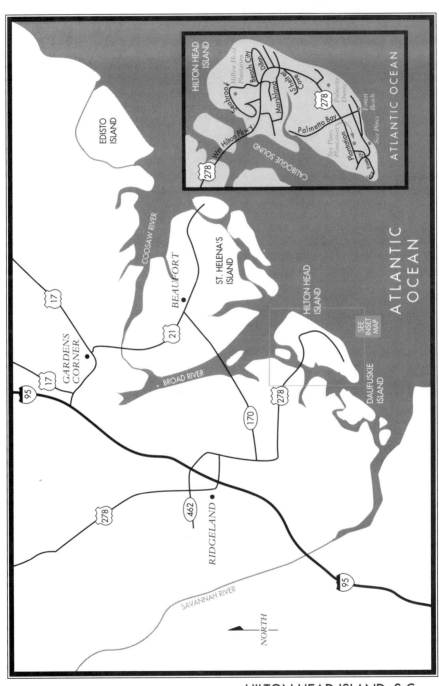

HILTON HEAD ISLAND, S.C.

Hilton Head Island

INTRODUCTION ....

Hilton Head Island is a 12-mile-long, 5-mile-wide island at the southernmost end of South Carolina. The island has a relaxed, but sophisticated, feel, and although highly developed with golf courses, restaurants, and shopping centers, it retains many beautifully preserved areas.

Almost all of the 1.5 million visitors who come to enjoy the picturesque beaches, lagoons, sea marshes, and wooded areas on the island also partake in activities ranging from golf and tennis to shopping, nightlife, and historic tours.

Though Hilton Head Island's first inhabitants, the Ewascus Indians, lived here at least 4,000 years earlier, the island was named after William Hilton, who "discovered" it in 1663. Hilton was an English sea captain commissioned by Barbados planters to find new lands for growing indigo and sugar. "Head" refers to the fact the island is at the headlands of Port Royal Sound. After finding the island satisfactory, Hilton began advertising for settlers in London newspapers, touting, among other things, the island's "pleasant ayr." By the eighteenth century, the island's robust soils had led to the evolution of a rich farming community for indigo, rice, and cotton. However, this all changed during the Civil War, when the plantations were left in ruins. Despite the destruction wrought on the island during this period, a legacy of its historic past remains, as reflected in present-day foods, culture, and historic sites found here.

Normal monthly temperatures for Hilton Head are: January, 49; February, 51.5; March, 58.5; April, 65.1; May, 72.2; June, 78; July, 80.8; August, 80; September, 76.3; October, 67.7; November, 59.4; December, 52.1. Although Hilton Head is a year-round vacation destination, the busy season runs roughly mid-March through late October.

GOLF INFORMATION ....

While eight of the island's most spectacular golf courses— found mainly at two prestigious island resorts—are covered in detail below, and other recommendations are listed, the island has a total of twenty-two public golf courses, many designed by today's greatest golf architects (e.g., Pete Dye, Tom Fazio, Jack Nicklaus, and others), and the surrounding areas have another seventeen courses. For information on all the Hilton Head courses, contact the Hilton Head Convention and Visitors Bureau at 803-785-3673.

PALMETTO DUNES AT PALMETTO DUNES RESORT (800) 827-3006

Palmetto Dunes is a 2,000-acre re-sort with five quality golf courses designed by a virtual who's who of golf architects. Each course has its own personality and provides a challenge for players of all levels of skill.

The Jones Course, a Robert Trent Jones, Sr., layout, was opened in 1969. Like many of his designs, the course features large sloping and undulating greens. Some of the greens are slightly elevated, and all are protected by some sort of hazard, mostly sand traps. Water comes into play on eleven of the holes, and many of the fairway landing areas are also protected by bunkers. The blue tees stretch to 6710 yards, the white to 6148 yards, and the forward to 5425 yards. Par from all tees is 72, and the course slope ranges from 123 to 117. A very fine three-hole stretch starts on the 198-yard, par 3 eighth. The hole plays over water to a wide, shallow green protected front, left, and back by deep bunkers. The ninth, a 510-yard par 5, is rated the course's number-one handicap hole. Water runs along the right side from the tee to the back of the green. The lay of the land and the wind seem to lead many players into this lateral hazard. The tenth hole, another par 5, is 540 yards and heads straight out towards the ocean—hence, into the wind. This time, the player needs to protect against going to the left to stay in bounds. The green is very deep, and as always, protected with bunkers to the left and right.

The Fazio Course is another excellent design by George Fazio. Since its opening in 1974, it has been highly rated, and is ranked by *Golf Digest* as one of the top one hundred courses in the nation. Like most of George Fazio's courses, this one provides great enjoyment and challenge to all calibers of golfer. For example, the back tees play to a par 70, with a slope of 132 and a rating over 74—tough for any player. The blue and white tees play to a par 72, while still maintaining a good challenge (as evidenced by ratings/slopes of 72.6/126 and 71.2/123). As with other George Fazio courses, it's fun to play from different tees from time to time— the perspective and angles make it feel like you're playing an entirely different course. This course features small, tough greens that are well guarded by bunkers and water. The fairway landing areas on many holes have massive bunkers that a player will eventually need to escape from (or romp through, as you like).

The first of two Arthur Hills courses is the Hills Course. This course opened in 1986 and was built on a series of sand dunes. As a result, there are many interesting and fun elevation changes from shot to shot and hole to hole. The greens provide a wide variety of shapes, sizes, and contours and are protected with traps, water, and even trees. A great stretch on this course starts on the 434-yard seventh, the number-one handicap hole. The hole often plays into the wind, and the fairway has dolomites (mounds) on the right and is lined by trees on the left. In addition, the green is quite deep and has bunkers on each side. The eighth, a 156-yard par 3, plays over water to a shallow green. Because this hole also plays into the prevailing wind, club selection is difficult. The ninth is a lovely par 5 measuring 518 yards. The tree-lined fairway rolls down to a small green guarded by water in front and on the left, discouraging many attempts to reach it in two.

Palmetto Halls Plantation, which is affiliated with the Palmetto Dunes Resort, has a second Arthur Hills course of the same name, opened in 1991. Rated 4 stars by *Golf Digest's Places to Play*, it can stretch to almost 7000 yards (tees start at 4956 yards) and is a par 72. The course was built on rolling terrain and is lined with oaks and pines. Water again is a factor, but this time, wetlands also come into play. As with many newly designed courses, there are several mounds and shaped bunkers on a majority of the holes.

The Cupp Course, designed by Robert Cupp, opened in 1993. The back tees measure to almost 7100 yards (the front tees measure 5220 yards), and it has an amazing slope of 141 and a rating of 74.8.

Carts: Mandatory, although walking is allowed on the Fazio Course after 2 P.M. *Greens Fees:* Approximately $50-$100, depending on course, season, and golf package/18 holes. *Tee Time Policy:* Guests can reserve sixty days in advance; non-guests, thirty days in advance. Non-guests must call at least a day in advance.

SEA PINES RESORT (800) 845-6131

Harbour Town Golf Links at the Sea Pines Resort has it all. The course, opened in 1969, was designed by Pete Dye and Jack Nicklaus. It is cut through more than 300 acres of Spanish moss–draped oaks, pines, and magnolias. Wildlife is at every turn in the surrounding marsh, lakes, and trees, and the landmark red-and-white lighthouse is majestically placed behind the eighteenth hole. Adding to the scenery are the yachts in Calibogue Sound. The course is ranked as one of the best in South Carolina, the United States, and the world. It has hosted the PGA Heritage

Classic since its opening in 1969, and the winners of this tournament have included most of the hall-of-famers from the last half of the century—from Arnold Palmer, Jack Nicklaus, Hale Irwin, and Johnny Miller, to Fuzzy Zoeller, Nick Faldo, Bernhard Langer, and Greg Norman. The course requires a player to properly execute most, if not all, of the shots in his or her bag. It measures just over 5000 yards from the front tees to 6912 from the back tees (the white markers measure 6119 yards). Length is helpful but not necessarily required—it is more important to hit fairways and, on some holes, particular sides of fairways. For example, the ninth hole is only 337 yards, but the green is blocked by tall pines if the player doesn't find the right side of the fairway. The greens are not elevated or overly undulating, but they are small (Kenny Knox, playing in the 1991 MCI Classic, holds the record for least putts in a regulation tournament at Harbour Town). As a result, a player needs to bring a strong short game with him or her to have a shot at par. All in all, the surroundings, the atmosphere, and the golf at Harbour Town Golf Links is as good as it gets. Don't miss it.

Also at Sea Pines Resort are the Ocean Course (Hilton Head's first course, a 1960 George Cobb design recently redesigned and rebuilt by golf architect/PGA Tour Player Mark McCumber), and the Sea Marsh Course. Call 803-842-1894 or 800-SEA-PINES for these courses.

Carts: Can request to walk after 1 P.M. *Greens Fees:* Harbour Town, $177.45 (lower rates for play after 1 P.M. are available from 5/13-9/8); Ocean Course and Sea Marsh Course, approximately $85/18 holes, including cart. *Tee Time Policy:* Members have priority. Guests of the resort can reserve times up to ninety days in advance; non-guests can reserve fourteen days in advance. A credit-card guarantee is required to hold times.

HILTON HEAD NATIONAL GOLF CLUB (803) 842-5900

Hilton Head National, a marvelous course designed by Gary Player, opened in 1989. The course, which hosts the Amoco Centel Golf Tournament, winds its way through lovely forests, lakes, and ponds. Gary doesn't place much of a premium on distance, evidenced by the fact that, from the back tees, the course does not reach 6800 yards (with tees starting at 5589 yards). He does, however, put a premium on a smart, imaginative player with a solid short game. The slope of 132 attests to the fact that length is not what golf is, or should be, about. Interestingly, the management of the course guarantees that it will be one of the best-conditioned courses in the area—a tall order on Hilton Head Island. See for yourself.

Carts: Mandatory. *Greens Fees:* $75 in high season, but golf packages are available/18 holes. *Tee Time Policy:* Can be reserved up to a year in advance.

INDIGO RUN GOLF CLUB (803) 689-2200

From the opening hole, players begin to sense the special charm of the Golden Bear Golf Course at Indigo Run. The course's lovely, low-country setting is enhanced by mature oaks, cypress, meandering lagoons, and freshwater wetlands. The course has four sets of tees that stretch from 4974 to 7014 yards. As is clear from the gold tees' slope of

Hilton Head Island
Photo courtesy of Hilton Head Island Chamber of Commerce

132 and rating of 73.7, this course is a challenge. However, you will find few gimmicks and little moved earth. Rather, the Golden Bear is a traditional, straightforward layout that presents an honest, thoroughly enjoyable test of golf.

Carts: Mandatory. *Greens Fees:* $65–$80 in high season/18 holes, including carts. *Tee Time Policy:* Can be reserved up to six months in advance.

OTHER EXCELLENT
AREA COURSES:

Oyster Reef Golf Club (803-681-7717) is a 7027-yard (tees start at 5288 yards), Rees Jones course cut through thick Carolina pines and live oaks. This 1982 course offers lovely views of Port Royal Sound. **Port Royal Golf Club** (803-686-8801) offers three 18-hole courses, one by Willard Byrd and the other two by George Cobb. The club is located on the site of Civil War battlegrounds. **Shipyard Golf Club** (803-686-8802) features 27 holes set among oaks, pines, magnolias, wildflowers, and lagoons. **Callawassie Island Club**, Beaufort (See Side Trips) (803-521-1533/800-221-8431), is a very fine Fazio course with 27 holes.

ATTRACTIONS ....

TOURS
(for tours of nearby islands, see Side Trips)

Water Tours

For a cruise around the island, the ***Spirit of Harbour Town*** offers local sightseeing, day trips to Savannah, and dinner cruises every month but January. Call 803-842-7179. *Adventure Cruises, Inc.* also offers sightseeing and dinner cruises around the island. Call 803-785-4558. Reservations are required for cruises.

Land Tours

On Hilton Head, sightseeing tours are given by **Low Country Adventures, Ltd.** (call 803-681-8212), **Camelot Limousine and Tours** (call 803-842-7777), and **Discover Hilton Head** (call 803-842-9217).

HISTORIC PLACES

In the **Sea Pines Forest Preserve** on Hilton Head you can catch a rare glimpse of an ancient Indian shell ring, a large structure of seashells, animal bones, and nuts (although getting there and back requires about a 2-mile walk). The ring is believed to have been made around the time the Egyptian pyramids were built. There is admission fee per vehicle to enter Sea Pines unless you are lodging there.

Another landmark within Sea Pines is the **Harbour Town Lighthouse** located at Harbour Town Marina, in an elegant section of the island. To golfers, the red-and-white stripes may seem familiar, since the PGA Tour frequently stops at the resort's golf course.

MUSEUMS/SCIENCE CENTERS

The Hilton Head Island Museum offers beach walks, history tours, and more. Call 803-689-6767 for a schedule of events and fees.

CULTURAL OFFERINGS

For dates, times, and programs of performances by the **Hilton Head**

Orchestra, call 803-842-2055. For dance performances, contact the **Hilton Head Island Dance Theater** at 803-785-5477.

Various quality theatrical performances are given by the **Hilton Head Playhouse** at the new Self Family Arts Center. Call 803-785-4878.

RECREATION

A recent Robb Report survey voted Hilton Head Island "best in the world for tennis." And with little wonder—there are over 300 tennis courts here, more than any other resort in the United States. Many of the tennis facilities are located at resorts, including the Sea Pines Resort (where the *Family Circle* Magazine Cup Tennis Tournament is held in early April), among others. More great tennis courts are available at seven public clubs, such as the Port Royal Racquet Club and the Van de Meer Shipyard Racquet Club.

WaterFun Park is a popular water-slide park on Hilton Head Island that is great fun for kids and adults. For information and park hours, call 803-842-8108 or 803-842-6662. Admission is charged.

The Harbour Town area has miles of bike paths and bicycle rental stores. Other outdoor sports for which you can rent equipment include scuba diving, windsurfing, jetskiing, water-skiing, parasailing, boating, swimming, and in-line skating. Horseback riding, including guided trail rides, is available at Lawton Stables. Call 803-671-2586.

SEASONAL EVENTS

March brings the month-long **Springfest**, which involves a Wine

Fest, seafood festival, tours of island homes, entertainment, sports events, and other activities. Call 803-686-4944. The **St. Patrick's Day Parade** is also a popular March event (though not necessarily on the 17th, so call 803-837-4956 for information). The *Family Circle* **Magazine Cup Tennis Tournament**, which is at the Sea Pines Racquet Club, begins late March and ends in April. Call 800-677-2293. April also brings the annual **MCI Classic Golf Tournament** at the Harbour Town Golf Links. Call 803-671-2448. Special events are planned every Easter, and many sporting events, including fishing, tennis, golf, and other sports, are held annually. For a current calendar, contact the Hilton Head Convention and Visitors Bureau at 803-785-3673.

ACCOMMODATIONS ....

While Hilton Head is a relatively expensive vacation spot, you'll not only find top luxury, but more moderately priced accommodations and rentals, as well. The Hilton Head Central Reservation Service (call 800-845-7018) is a free reservation service that can provide you with a range of options.

EXPENSIVE

Hyatt Regency Hilton Head at the Palmetto Dunes Resort, located mid-island on U.S. 278, is a deluxe, oceanfront hotel offering comprehensive resort facilities, golf and tennis packages, and rooms with balconies. (Also see the listing for the Hilton at Palmetto Dunes, below, and Golf Information for additional information.) Call 803-785-1234. **Palmetto Dunes Resort**, part of the same complex, has

luxury villas. Call 800-845-6130.

The Westin Resort, at 2 Grasslawn Avenue, is a top-rated oceanfront hotel against which all other hotels on the island are compared. At the entrance, visitors are greeted by an abundance of flower gardens. The rest of the hotel likewise has an air of grace and beauty, and lots of amenities. Call 803-681-4000 or 800-228-3000.

Disney's Hilton Head Island Resort, at 16 Shelter Cove Lane, opened in March 1996 and consists of quaint, old-fashioned cottages surrounding a main lodge, as well as a private beach, restaurants, entertainment, and other resort amenities. Call 803-341-4100 or 800-859-8644.

MODERATE/EXPENSIVE

The Hilton at Palmetto Dunes Resort, at 23 Ocean Lane, is modern and luxurious, as you might expect. Call 803-842-8000.

Sea Pines, at 32 Greenwood Drive, was Hilton Head's first resort and is located on 5,000 acres encompassing the lovely Harbour Town Yacht Basin. This golfer's dream boasts the Harbour Town Golf Links, Ocean, and Sea Marsh courses, as well as world-class tennis, three pools, horseback riding, nature tours, special children's activities, and the annual MCI Classic Golf Tournament. Accommodations are luxury waterfront or golf course villas. Call 803-785-3333 or 800-925-4653.

INEXPENSIVE

Holiday Inn has more than one hotel on the island. Call 800-HOLIDAY for information, locations, and rates.

Comfort Inn and Suites, at 2 Tanglewood Drive, is one of the few places (except some rentals) that allow pets. It also offers children's programs, a pool, beachfront location, and the WaterFun Park, making this a great choice for families. Call 803-842-6662 or 800-228-5150.

Fairfield Inn by Marriott, at 9 Marina Side Drive, is a comfortable and economical efficiency inn, with easy access to amenities such as beach and pool. Call 803-842-4800 or 800-228-2800.

SHOPPING ....

The island has about thirty-six shopping centers and more than 300 stores, ranging from large retail outlet centers to quaint specialty shops. For discount shoppers, the **Low Country Factory Outlet Village**, on U.S. 278 near the entrance to the island, has about forty stores. Open daily; hours vary seasonally. For information, call 803-837-4339. Additionally, **Shoppes on the Parkway**, on U.S. 278, has thirty outlet stores. Call 803-686-6233.

Two major shopping areas are **Coligny Plaza**, located in Coligny Circle, with over thirty stores, and **Pineland Mill Shops**, at the intersection of William Hilton Parkway and Matthews Drive, with about thirty high-end stores (e.g., Royal Daulton, Bass, etc.).

RESTAURANTS ....

Hilton Head Island's 12-mile stretch has more than a hundred restaurants, and most resort hotels offer several. Many restaurants on the island offer early-bird or happy-hour dinner specials. In the summer high season, reservations are a good idea whenever possible. Being a sea island, Hilton Head offers plenty of great seafood—look for local specialties such as Frogmore stew, roasted oysters, and Daufuskie deviled crab.

FINE DINING

Barony Grill, at the Westin Resort, has the elegant look and feel of an old European hunt club. It offers prime rib and beef dishes as well as terrific seafood, lamb, veal, and magnificent desserts. Call 803-681-4000.

Harbourmaster's, at Shelter Cove Harbor, has beautiful views of Yacht Harbor and many fine seafood dishes. Some house specialties include dishes like grilled tuna, snapper with almonds, and rack of lamb. Jacket required. Call 803-785-3030.

CASUAL DINING

Hudson's Seafood House on the Docks, at 1 Hudson Road, is huge, serves fresh seafood, and has a terrific mud pie. During the summer months, there's live entertainment the kids will probably enjoy. Call 803-681-2772.

For homestyle southern food, try the **Old Fort Pub**, at Hilton Head Plantation, serving chicken-fried steak in gravy, oyster pie, shrimp and grits, and spicy Hoppin' John. Call 803-681-2386. **The Harbour Town Grill**, at 11 Lighthouse Lane, is located within the Harbour Town Golf Links clubhouse at Sea Pines. The decor includes paintings of former Heritage Tournament champions and views of the golf course. Open daily for breakfast, lunch, and dinner. (There is an admission charge for non-guests to come into Sea Pines resort.) Call 803-671-3119.

The Little Venice Ristorante, at Harbourside II in Shelter Cove, serves Italian specialties like shrimp fra diavolo, veal in marsala wine, and linguine with clam sauce. Pasta is fresh and homemade. A "nice little Italian place" with outdoor dining in clement weather. Call 803-785-3300.

JUST FOR KIDS ....

There are many children's programs, mostly at the island hotels and resorts. **Camp Comfort** is offered at the Comfort Inn and Suites, which has its own supervised water park on the premises. Children's programs usually require children to be a resort guest. For information on resort programs, contact the Hilton Head Convention and Visitors Bureau, or your hotel. Some non-resort children's programs are: **Island Recreation Center,** which offers day camps, and educational and athletic programs (call 803-681-7273); **Kreation Station,** providing art classes for all ages (call 803-842-5738); and the **Museum of Hilton Head Island** which offers the "Island Explorers Program" for grades K-5 (call 803-689-6767).

Babysitting services are available from **Companions, Nurses and Nannies** (call 803-785-3600) and **Cradle 'N' All** (call 803-686-5055).

SIDE TRIPS ....

St. Helena's Island is to the north of Hilton Head Island. Here, you'll find the **Penn Center Historic District,** the site of a post–Civil War experiment in the education and self-sufficiency of freed blacks. Other unique spots on St. Helena's include the striking white-clapboard **Coffin Point Plantation** with its red tin roof, the eighteenth century **Chapel of Ease,** and the 1855 **Old Brick Church.** The town of **Frogmore** is the home of Dr. Buzzard, a renowned witch doctor, and Frogmore stew. For guided tours, contact **Gullah-n-Geechie Mahn Tours** at 803-838-7516.

Golfers and non-golfers will enjoy a side trip to **Beaufort,** which has the four-star-rated, 27-hole **Callawassie Island Club,** a Fazio gem. For tee times and other information, call 803-521-1533 or 800-221-8431. For non-golfers, the entire downtown district of Beaufort (pronounced "Bewfort") is on the National Historic Register and has been chosen as the filming location for several movies, including *Forrest Gump* and the *Prince of Tides.* There's an Italian Renaissance mansion, nicknamed "the castle" by locals, whose bricks appear to change color with the weather (from tan to gray to pink). Two museum houses are the **George Parsons Elliott House Museum,** used by Union troops as a hospital during the Civil War, and the **John Mark Verdier House Museum,** utilized by Union troops as their headquarters (there's an admission charge for both). There's also an 1863 National Cemetery for Civil War dead in the city. The annual **Gullah Festival** takes place here on Memorial Day weekend. The Chamber of Commerce (1006 Bay Street) has self-guided tour maps. For escorted tours, contact **The Point Historic Tours** for motorized tours (call 803-522-3576), **The Spirit of Old Beaufort** for walking tours (call 803-525-0459), and **Carriage Tours of Beaufort** for horse-drawn buggy tours (call 803-524-3163).

GENERAL INFORMATION ....

Contact the Hilton Head Convention and Visitors Bureau at 803-785-3673, or stop at the Hilton Head Island Visitor Information Center located on U.S. 278. For information on Beaufort, contact the Beaufort Chamber of Commerce at 803-524-3163.

For publications with helpful information and a calendar of events, get a copy of *Hilton Head Island Vacation Planner*, available from the Hilton Head Convention and Visitors Bureau.

Part Four

GEORGIA

Stone Mountain Park
Photo courtesy of the Georgia Department
of Industry, Trade & Tourism

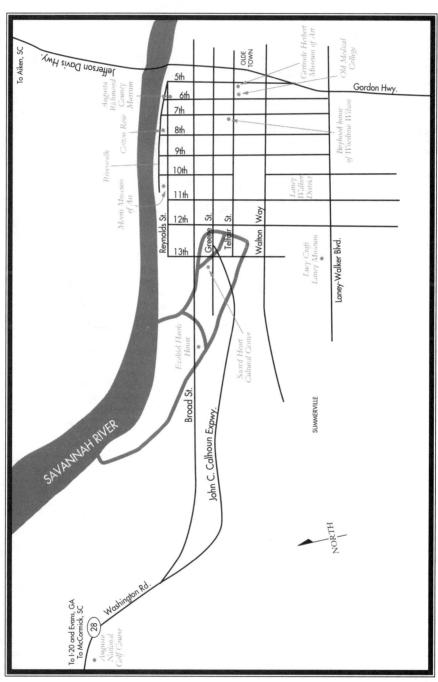

AUGUSTA, GA.

Augusta

AREA CODE: 706

INTRODUCTION

Like Pinehurst in North Carolina, Augusta is well-known to golfers. The area's most famous golf course is the Augusta National Golf Course, which hosts the prestigious Masters® golf tournament, drawing hundreds of thousands of spectators and visitors. Most golfers will have to settle for watching the Masters®, though, because Augusta National is closed to the public. However, there are several excellent daily fee public courses here that golfers can play.

While golf is the current focus of Augusta's tourism, the area has been a popular winter resort since just after the Civil War, when ruined fortunes forced wealthy families to take paying guests into their homes. Today's Augusta still emanates hospitality and southern pride, and the city itself is immaculate and well kept. Augusta has more to keep non-golfers happy than one might expect, such as historic sites, museums, arts and architecture, along with outdoor sports like fishing, boating, and waterskiing.

The Masters® golf tournament
Photo courtesy of Augusta Convention and Visitors Bureau

Aside from being a golf mecca, Augusta has a rich history. The second-oldest city in the state, it was founded in 1736 by James Oglethorpe and named after Princess Augusta. Over the course of its history, it has served many important uses, having been a military outpost during the American Revolution, a former state capital, a center of the cotton and tobacco industries, a testing site for a prototype of the cotton gin, and home to the South's first continuously published newspaper. It is also the birthplace of singer James Brown and the former home of President Woodrow Wilson, as well as the home of three colleges: Paine College, Augusta College, and the Medical College of Georgia.

The normal monthly temperatures are: January, 43.9; February, 47.4; March, 55.5; April, 62.7; May, 70.7; June, 77.5; July, 80.8; August, 79.7; September, 74.5; October, 63.8; November, 55; December, 47.2. Though Augusta's climate is generally ideal for golf and other outdoor activities year-round, most tourists come during Masters® week (the first full week in April).

GOLF INFORMATION ....

Within the surrounding area, there are some eleven public courses. For a complete list of these courses, contact the Augusta-Richmond County Convention and Visitors Bureau and request a copy of their pamphlet, *Augusta Georgia Golf Planner.*

JONES CREEK GOLF CLUB, EVANS
(706) 860-4228

Jones Creek, designed by Rees Jones and opened in 1986, is already considered among the best courses in the United States by *Golf Digest.* The PGA also appears to recognize this as one of the best courses in the country—Jones Creek has hosted the tour qualifying school on several occasions. The course ranges in length from 5430 to over 7000 yards, and it boasts an incredible 139 slope from the back tees. The course winds through dense woodlands of pines, maples, oaks, and dogwoods, as well as lakes and creeks. Jones Creek features some bearish par 4s, such as the 456-yard, dogleg left seventh; the 460-yard, dogleg left seventeenth; and the 452-yard, dogleg right eighteenth. Each of these holes requires long, accurate drives to tree-lined fairways followed by well-measured approaches to the deep greens on seven and sixteen, and to a shallow green on eighteen. The par 3s come in a variety of distances, and the par 5s are reachable. As head pro Greg Hemann says, "Jones Creek is a very fine course that everyone should have a chance to play."

Carts: Mandatory. *Greens Fees:* (packages offered through Radisson Riverfront Hotel), $33 Monday-Thursday, $40 Friday, $43 Saturday-Sunday/18 holes, including cart. *Tee Time Policy:* Can be reserved six days in advance.

CEDAR CREEK GOLF CLUB, AIKEN,
SOUTH CAROLINA (ABOUT 25 MILES
FROM AUGUSTA) (803) 648-4206

Cedar Creek, opened in the spring of 1991, was designed by Arthur Hills. The prolific Hills is one of the top active architects in the country, with two of his Florida courses, Eagle Trace and Bonita Bay, considered among the top one hundred courses in the country by *Golf Digest.* Cedar Creek, which is cut through towering South Carolina pines, winds its way over and around a variety of lakes, ponds, and streams. This par 72 layout ranges from 5231 to over 7200 yards, with a number of gentle elevation changes throughout the course. The rating/slope ranges from 69.1/115 to 73.3/125. The number-one handicap hole is the 404-yard, par 4 sixth. About 250 yards from the tee, the player is confronted with a cypress that splits the right side of the fairway. A well-placed tee shot on the left side of the fairway not only avoids the cypress, but also leaves an easier approach to the green. The green is fairly narrow, very deep, and falls away on all sides.

Carts: Walking permitted during week and after 1 P.M. on weekends. *Greens Fees:* $25 weekdays, $35 weekends/18 holes, including cart. *Tee Time Policy:* non-members can reserve a week in advance.

OTHER EXCELLENT
AREA COURSES:

Hickory Knob State Park Golf Course, McCormick, South Carolina (864-391-2450), a lovely 6500-yard, par 72 course designed by Tom Jackson, is set on Thurmond Lake (also known as Clarks Hill Lake). **Forest Hills Golf Club**, Augusta (706-733-0001), is a 6800-yard, par 72 course designed by Donald Ross in 1926. It has a rating/slope ranging from 69.8/117 to 72.8/124. **Reynold's Plantation**, Eatonton (706-485-0235), is about an hour-and-a-half's drive from Augusta, but golfers should make every effort to play their Great Waters Course while they're in the area (though there's not a lot for non-golfers there). This excellent, Jack Nicklaus course, opened in 1992, is rated 4½ stars by *Golf Digest's Places to Play*. It also was recently named as one of *Golf's* "Top 100 You Can Play." It has tees that range from 5057 to 7058 yards and a rating/slope ranging from 69.2/114 to 73.8/135. Also at Reynold's Plantation is the Plantation Course, a 6656-yard, par 72 course that opened in 1987 and has a rating/slope ranging from 69.1/117 to 71.2/125. The resort hotel here, Reynold's Plantation (706-467-3151), offers discount packages for guests, although outside play is permitted on both courses.

Historic Cotton Exchange Welcome Center and Museum, Augusta

ATTRACTIONS ....

TOURS

Motorized Tours

Historic Augusta Tours conducts tours on Saturday from 10:30 A.M. to noon. Reservations are required by noon the day before. Tours depart from the Cotton Exchange Building at 32 Eighth Street. Call 706-724-4067. **Discover Augusta Tours** gives two-and-a-half hour van tours for up to six passengers at a time. Call 706-736-7577.

Boat Tours

You can get pontoon rentals at the marina and either self-tour or have Captain Bates accompany you. Call 706-722-1388.

HISTORIC PLACES

The Old Towne Historic District of Augusta has elegant Georgian and other style buildings. **The Cotton Exchange** and the **Riverwalk** are at its center. The Cotton Exchange building, at 32 Eighth Street, houses the visitors center, but also can be toured (there's even an old chalkboard that still displays turn-of-the-century cotton prices). Admission is free. Call 706-724-4067. The Riverwalk is dotted with shops, hotels, malls, cafés, and an amphitheater. Under the entrance plaza at Reynolds and Eighth Streets, you can see watermarks left from the many floods that have sieged the city during the past 250 years. For information on special events taking place at the Riverwalk, call 706-821-1754.

Meadow Garden, at 1320 Independence Drive, is an eighteenth-century home on the National Register of Historic Places, with distinctive double stairs leading up to the front porch. It belonged to George Walton, a Georgia governor and a signer of the Declaration of Independence. Open weekdays. Admission is charged. Call 706-724-4174.

Woodrow Wilson lived in Augusta as a boy from 1860 through 1870, when his father was pastor of the First Presbyterian Church. His home, at 419 Seventh Street, will soon be opened for tours. Call 706-724-0436.

The 1797 **Ezekiel Harris House**, at 1822 Broad Street, was a tobacco merchant's home and now contains authentic colonial furnishings. Open Tuesday through Saturday 1 to 4 P.M. Admission is charged. Call 706-724-0436.

The Confederate Powderworks is at 1717 Goodrich Street at the Augusta Canal. All that remains of the original building is a 168-foot chimney that is now a war memorial. Modern mills now stand where the powderworks once were located. Admission is free. For more information, call the Historic Augusta Office at 706-724-0436.

For those who enjoy architecture, a walk or drive through the old Summerville area (known as "The Hill") is a must.

MUSEUMS/SCIENCE CENTERS

The Georgia Golf Hall of Fame Golf and Garden Attraction is scheduled to open in the spring of 1998 at the Riverwalk, between Tenth and Thirteenth Streets. This 24-acre attraction will include gardens, waterways, exhibits on the history of the game, and an interactive holographic theater. For information, call 706-724-4443.

The Augusta-Richmond County Museum, at 540 Telfair Street, has regional art, history, and science exhibits. Call 706-722-8454. For more art, especially regional works, head for the **Morris Museum of Art** at One Tenth Street. Open daily except Monday. Admission is charged; on Sunday admission is free. Call 706-724-7501. **The Gertrude Herbert Institute of Art**, at 560 Reynolds Street, also featuring regional art, is located in an ornate, federal-style mansion built in 1818 for Mayor Nicholas Ware. Open daily except Monday. Admission is charged. Call 706-722-5495.

Fort Discovery will open in late 1996 in the Port Royal Building at Riverwalk and Seventh Street. Interactive exhibits for adults and children will focus on various sciences and technology, including current and future applications. Call 706-791-7621.

CULTURAL OFFERINGS

The Augusta Symphony gives concerts from autumn through spring (call 706-826-4705), as does the **Augusta Opera Association** (call 706-826-4710). **The Augusta Ballet** performs October through March (call 706-826-4721), and the Chorale Society performs pop and classical music September through May (call 706-826-4713). The **Augusta Players, Inc.** produce plays throughout the year. Call 706-826-4707.

The Augusta-Richmond County Civic Center at 601 Seventh Street hosts well-known acts, from rock bands to ballet to children's shows. Call 706-724-7545.

A variety of new art galleries can be found in six buildings known as

Artists Row, in the 1000 block of Broad Street downtown. For more information, contact the Greater Augusta Arts Council at 706-826-4704 or 706-826-4702. The arts council is housed in the ornate, 1898 Sacred Heart Cathedral, at 1301 Greene Street, which can be self-toured (pamphlet costs $1).

Augusta is known for its water sports, from fishing to water-skiing. Two great places to enjoy the water are the **Riverfront Marina** at Prep Phillips Drive (call 706-821-1754), and the **Savannah Lock and Dam,** northwest of Augusta. At the Savannah Lock and Dam you can picnic, hike, paddleboat, and see the historic mills lining the river. Twenty-two miles north of the city, on the South Carolina border, is **Thurmond Lake** (also known as Clarks Hill Lake), which is among the largest inland bodies of water in the United States with over 1200 miles of shoreline. For information, call 706-722-3770. For kayaking, canoeing, and camping equipment, go to **American Wilderness Outfitters Ltd.** (AWOL for short) at 522 Shartom Drive. Call 706-738-8500.

The biggest event of the year is, of course, the **Masters**® in April, and spectators need to make reservations far in advance. For information, call 706-667-6000.

The Augusta Invitational Rowing Regatta, which brings rowing teams from the United States and Europe, is held in late March or early April. Call 706-722-1071.

Festivals with music, food, entertainment, and crafts are held the first Saturday of each month on the Riverwalk. Call 706-821-1754. September brings the famous **Horse Barrel Racing** event. Call 706-724-0851.

For more information on these events and others, contact the Augusta-Richmond County Convention and Visitors Bureau at 706-823-6600 or 800-726-0243.

ACCOMMODATIONS ....

The Masters Housing Bureau can assist you with travel arrangements during the tournament. Call 706-855-8898 or 800-244-4709. For numerous chain motels offering terrific rates, your best bet is away from town off I-20, or out by the airport, located south of Augusta on the Bobby Jones Expressway (I-520).

Radisson Riverfront, at 2 Tenth Street, is a lovely high-rise hotel. Deluxe rooms have balconies, and there's an exercise facility, concierge service, and golf packages for Jones Creek Golf Club (See Golf Information). Call 706-722-8900.

The Partridge Inn, at 2110 Walton Way, has rooms with balconies and Victorian antiques, outdoor verandas and porticos, golf, and a lovely breakfast buffet. Call 706-737-8888.

Sheraton, at 2651 Perimeter Parkway (about twenty minutes from downtown), is close to Augusta National and has exercise facilities and indoor/outdoor pools. Room rates include breakfast for two. Call 706-855-8100.

Days Inn Wheeler Road, at 3654 Wheeler Road, is a clean and comfortable motel offering free continental breakfast and local calls. Call 706-868-8610.

Holiday Inn Augusta, at I-20 and Washington Road, has an exercise room and an outdoor pool. Guests can book tee times with any local course through this hotel and receive a discount on the room. Call 706-738-8811.

SHOPPING

Shoppers can browse several stores along the Riverwalk. Antique dealers can be found along Broad Street downtown. For art galleries, try Artists Row (see Cultural Offerings).

Outlet shoppers may want to try **Burlington Coat Factory Warehouse** at 1329 Augusta West Parkway. Call 706-650-0544.

RESTAURANTS

FINE DINING

La Maison on Telfair, on 404 Telfair, is nestled in an old mansion and serves gourmet cuisine, with popular selections being rack of lamb and fresh-game dishes. Jackets required; reservations recommended. Serves dinner Monday through Saturday and lunch Thursday and Friday. Call 706-722-4805.

Calvert's, 475 Highland Avenue (in Surrey Center), was voted Augusta's "Best Elegant Dining" a few years ago. Specialties include veal picatta, roast duck montmorenci, and escargots calvert. Call 706-738-4514.

The Riverwalk, Augusta
Photo courtesy of Augusta Convention and Visitors Bureau

Augusta, GA

CASUAL DINING

Word of Mouth Café, at 724 Broad Street, is a combination restaurant and great nightspot, with a constant love affair between food and music. They serve appetizers like coconut shrimp and buffalo wings, and entrées like Satchmo's Sesame Shrimp and Louis Prima PastaVera. Call 706-722-3477.

The King George Restaurant and Pub, on the Riverwalk at 2 Eighth Street, is a casual English-style pub serving hearty fare like burgers, shepherd's pie, and steaks, as well as lighter selections like seafood and sandwiches. Call 706-724-4755.

JUST FOR KIDS ....

During the annual Augusta Invitational Rowing Regatta there are several special children's activities (See Seasonal Events). In summer, kids enjoy **Krystal River Water Park** in nearby Evans, Georgia (where Jones Creek Golf Club is located; see Golf Information). The park features refreshing water pools, slides, and rides, along with miniature golf and an arcade. It is located at 799 Industrial Park Drive in Evans. Call 706-855-0061.

GOLFER'S SIDE TRIP ....

(Note: This course is about 80 miles away from Augusta, located approximately between Augusta and Atlanta, but it is worth the drive.)

PORT ARMOR COURSE, GREENS-BORO (706) 453-4564

Considered to be among the top courses in Georgia (according to *The Golf Reporter*, it ranks second to Augusta), Port Armor is a Robert Cupp course that opened in 1986. The course is set among towering Georgia pines and gently rolling terrain on the shores of the lovely Lake Oconee, the second-largest lake in Georgia with almost 400 miles of wooded shoreline. The length of the course ranges from 5177 to 6926 yards, and it has a strong slope of 136 from the back tees. A solid iron game is required at Port Armor, for the greens are on the small side and are well protected with water, bunkers, and mounds.

Carts: Walking allowed at certain times. *Greens Fees:* $35 weekdays, $63.60 weekends/18 holes. *Tee Time Policy:* Call in advance for tee times; can reserve up to a week in advance.

GENERAL INFORMATION ....

Contact the Augusta-Richmond County Convention and Visitors Bureau at 706-823-6600 or 800-726-0243. For listings of attractions and current events, pick up a copy of *Au-*

Meadow Garden, Augusta
Photo courtesy of Augusta Convention and Visitors Bureau

gusta: The Magazine of Metropolitan Augusta at local stores or newsstands, or call 706-722-5833 to receive a copy.

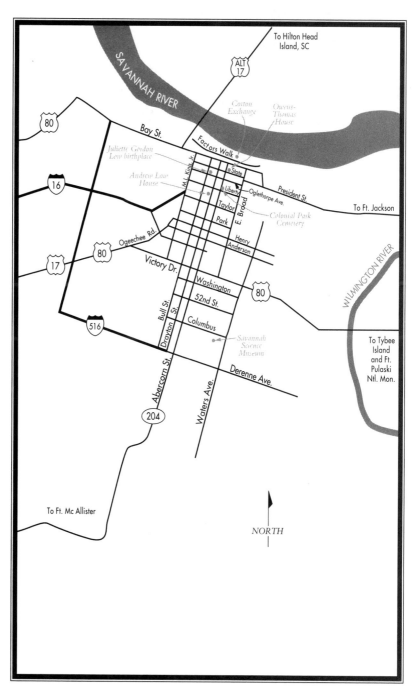

SAVANNAH and VICINITY, GA.

Savannah and vicinity

INTRODUCTION

Savannah is a city of antebellum beauty and southern charm. It was settled by General James Oglethorpe in 1733, when he landed at Yamacraw Bluff with some 120 other settlers. Just as Oglethorpe's original city-center plan intended, Savannah is spacious and beautifully laid out. The well-manicured parks, twenty-two city squares, and the Savannah River flowing through the downtown area combine to lend a feeling of carefully planned aesthetics to the city. The more than 1,000 restored historic district buildings are of various architectural styles, giving Savannah an old-world feel unmatched by other American cities (save perhaps Charleston, South Carolina, and Colonial Williamsburg).

Over the course of its history, Savannah has been a major colonial settlement, a port city at the center of the once-powerful cotton industry, and a fighting giant during the Civil War. Today's Savannah is still a significant manufacturing and port city, yet it offers visitors an abundance of remnants from its historic past, including Civil War and Revolutionary War sites, homes, churches, plantations, and museums. Savannah is also home to the nation's first golf course, built in 1794. But history is not the city's only attraction; there are also plenty of restaurants, festivals, and unique shops for non-golfers to explore. Savannah is listed among the top ten walking cities in the United States, and it has been called the "most beautiful city in North America" by *LeMonde*.

The city's attractions should be enough to satisfy any non-golfer, yet just fifteen minutes east of Savannah's lovely streets lie the sprawling white beaches of Tybee Island (a relatively uncrowded, family-friendly resort area). Golfers, in turn, will delight in Savannah's two excellent golf courses, both of which allow daily fee play. Additionally, Savannah is a mere 30 miles from Hilton Head Island, South Carolina (and the abundance of golfing opportunities offered there), thus making Savannah and Tybee Island a pleasant side trip or home base for golf travelers.

Harbor tour, Savannah
Photo courtesy of the Savannah Area
Convention and Visitors Bureau

The normal monthly temperatures for Savannah are: January, 48.9; February, 51.8; March, 59.2; April, 66; May, 73.5; June, 79.1; July, 81.8; August, 81; September, 76.6; October, 67.3; November, 59.1; December, 51.7. The most popular times for golfers are spring months, beginning in March (including St. Patrick's Day, a big holiday here) through May, and September through late October. There's a steady flow to Tybee Island's beaches during the summer.

GOLF INFORMATION ....

SOUTHBRIDGE GOLF CLUB, SAVANNAH (912) 651-5455

Southbridge is a Rees Jones layout that opened in 1988. In its short period of existence, it already has hosted the Georgia Open, and it annually hosts the Oglethorpe Invitational in July. This beautiful course winds through tall pines, dogwoods, and hardwoods, as well as an assortment of lakes, ponds, and brooks. In addition, consistent with Rees Jones's theory of design, the course clearly presents how it should be played to the player—in Jones's words, giving "definition in design." The hazards are visible and the bunkering directs the best approach to the target, be it the fairway or the green. If you do stray off the fairway, mounding often brings your ball back into play. The course can be played from four sets of tees: the reds play to 5181 yards, the whites to 6002 yards, the blues to 6458 yards, and the golds to 6990 yards. Many of these yards, almost 800, are on the course's par 3s. The second hole is 209 yards to a shallow green fronted by a giant bunker. The 194-yard fourth hole plays over water to a triple-tiered green. The twelfth is a mere 172 yards over water to a well-protected shallow green. Finally, the sixteenth is a 216-yarder playing to a long green protected by bunkers on the left and right. Twelve strokes on these four par 3s is quite an achievement.

Carts: Only required before 1 P.M. on Saturday and Sunday. *Greens Fees:* Approximately $35/18 holes, including cart. *Tee Time Policy:* Can be reserved one week in advance (can call earlier for groups of forty or more).

SAVANNAH INN AND COUNTRY CLUB GOLF COURSE, SAVANNAH (912) 897-1615

Savannah Inn, designed by Donald Ross in 1927, was rebuilt and improved by Willard Byrd in 1966. Over its history, Savannah Inn has hosted many tournaments, including the Georgia Open. The combined works of these two men create a lovely layout that is surrounded by pine trees, live oaks draped with Spanish moss, and palm trees. Additionally, the course is set among four lakes and several winding streams that come into play on ten holes. This par 72 course can reach almost 6900 yards and can be a handful, as attested to by its course rating of 73.5 and slope of 137 (the white tees are 6528 yards, while the reds are 5328 yards). The fairways are contoured, and as always with Ross designs, the greens are elevated and well bunkered, placing a premium on short shots. The fifteenth hole has been rated as one of the best holes in Georgia by the *Atlanta Constitution.* Although only 395 yards long, the drive needs to be accurate to avoid a stream on the left and a row of fairway bunkers on the right (another

stream is waiting if you miss the fairway to the far right). The approach is no easier, requiring a well-measured shot to a deep, elevated green sided by bunkers.

Carts: Mandatory. *Greens Fees:* $32 weekdays, $48 weekends before noon, $37 weekends after noon/18 holes. *Tee Time Policy:* Advance reservations required during peak season; suggested at other times.

OTHER EXCELLENT AREA COURSES:

See the chapter on Hilton Head Island, South Carolina, for additional courses in the area. The Hilton Head Island courses are located only about 30 miles north of Savannah.

ATTRACTIONS ....

TOURS

Motorized Tours

Gray Line Tours of Savannah run varying lengths and cover different sites (including a brief overview tour for time-strapped visitors). They have been endorsed by the Historic Savannah Foundation. For tour descriptions and reservations, call 912-234-8687. **Old Savannah Tours** has a similar selection of guided tours of varying lengths. They depart from the Savannah Visitors Center and also pick up from several hotels. Call 912-234-8128. Luxury bus tours are given by **Hospitality Tours of Savannah**, including themed tours, such as a Regency Antebellum Tour based on Eugenia Price's novels, which are set in Savannah, and tours focusing on the best-selling book

Midnight in the Garden of Good and Evil. The company also offers a twilight tour of Savannah that includes dinner. For information, call 912-233-0119.

Trolley Tours

Three companies give daily narrated tours aboard trolleys that stop at various points throughout the city's main historic areas. For information, contact **Old Town Trolleys** (call 912-233-0083), **Touring Savannah** (call 912-234-8128), or **Gray Line Tours** (call 912-234-8687).

Walking Tours

The Ghost Talk Ghost Walk tour is a fascinating narrated stroll through the colonial historic district aimed at believers and non-believers alike. The experienced guide will tell ghost stories based on the book *Savannah Specters and Strange Tales,* in addition to lore drawn from long-time city natives and studies conducted at Duke University. Departures are in the afternoon from Reynold's Square, at the monument of John Wesley. For times, call 912-233-3896. Other companies offering walking tours include **Tales of the South** (call 912-786-5101) and **Tours by BJ** (call 912-233-2335).

Carriage Tours

Carriage Tours of Savannah has horse-drawn surreys that transport visitors through the historic district. Narrated tours include historic and ghost tours. Departures are from the Savannah Visitors Center and the City Market; certain evening departures leave from the Hyatt Regency Hotel and the City Market. For a schedule and information, call 912-236-6756.

Savannah River Cruises

Savannah River Queen takes visitors on narrated sightseeing cruises, evening cruises (such as a gospel-entertainment dinner cruise with a southern-style buffet and a moonlight cruise with music and dancing), and Sunday brunch cruises. The boat departs from River Street behind City Hall. For reservations and information, call 912-232-6404 or 800-786-6404.

HISTORIC PLACES

The Savannah Historic District contains many buildings of historical and/or architectural significance. Some of the most interesting buildings and sites in the area include: The 1850 **United States Customs House** is located at the intersection of Bull and Bay Streets and features carved columns with capitals modeled from tobacco leaves. The 1905 **City Hall**, at Bull and Bay Streets, replaced the original that was built in 1799. The building is easily recognized by its gold-domed top and neoclassic architecture, and the inside has plaques and exhibits relating to the city's history. **Factors Walk** consists of a section of Bay Street nestled between Bay and River Streets with nineteenth-century cotton factories that have been turned into shops and restaurants. The highlight of the historic district is the restored **Riverfront Plaza**. This collection of historic buildings runs along the river and is dotted with museums, restaurants, pubs, parks, and shops.

Several historic homes are open for tours; all charge admission. The more outstanding house museums include: The Victorian **Juliette Gordon Low**

House, at 142 Bull Street, which was the birthplace of the founder of Girls Scouts USA (call 912-233-4501). **The Green-Meldrim House**, 14 West Macon Street, is an antebellum mansion (now a parish house) once used by General Sherman during his occupation of Savannah (call 912-233-3845). **The Owens-Thomas House**, at 124 Abercorn Street, is a Regency-style house with an 1820s-style garden and furnishings (call 912-233-9743). **The Davenport House**, at 324 East State Street, is a Federal-style house built circa 1820 and designed by the master builder for whom it's named (call 912-236-8097). The Victorian **Hamilton-Turner House**, at 330 Abercorn Street, was built in 1873 by a former city mayor and is reputedly haunted (call 912-233-4800).

The deceased buried in **Colonial Park Cemetery**, at East Oglethorpe and Abercorn Streets, read like a who's who of Georgia's early history. A signer of the Declaration of Independence and other prominent Georgians are interred here.

Laurel Grove Cemetery, at Thirty-seventh Street and Ogeechee Road, is believed to be the oldest black cemetery still being used. It contains the graves of both slaves and freedmen.

Old Fort Jackson, at 1 Fort Jackson Road, overlooking the Savannah River, is Georgia's oldest standing fort. The fort, begun in 1808, survived the War of 1812 and the Civil War. Open daily. Admission is charged. Call 912-232-3945.

Fort Pulaski National Monument, on U.S. 80 about 15 miles east of Savannah (near Tybee Island), is named after Casimir Pulaski, a Revolutionary War hero. It was occupied by Confederate, and later, Union forces during the Civil War. Restoration began in the 1930s, and it now appears as it did in the mid-1800s. Visitors can get an overview of the fort's history at the visitors center. Inside the fort, visitors can see officers' and enlisted men's quarters, a mess hall, and an infirmary. The fort took about 25 million bricks to complete, and its walls are about 7½-feet thick. Grounds have nature trails and a picnic area. Open daily. Admission is charged. For information, contact the superintendent at 912-786-5787.

Fort McAllister, on Fort McAllister Road outside of Richmond Hill (about 25 miles south of Savannah), was built to defend Savannah during the Civil War. Sherman's March to the Sea ended here, and his capture of the fort made the further defense of Savannah impossible. Though the capture took only about 15 minutes, Sherman called the assault "the handsomest thing I have seen in this war." Open Tuesday through Sunday. Admission is charged. Camping and boating facilities are available. Call 912-727-2339.

MUSEUMS/SCIENCE CENTERS

The Telfair Mansion and Art Museum is located at 121 Bernard Street. The 1818, Regency-style mansion was the royal governor's residence until his position evaporated after the Revolutionary War. The interior features an unusual octagon room, and the house is furnished with period antiques and family treasures, such as silver and porcelain pieces. The adjoining art museum has a large collection of American and European paintings, furniture, and decorative arts from the eighteenth through the twentieth centuries. Open daily except Monday. Admission is charged. Call 912-232-1177.

Ships of the Sea Museum, at 503 East River Street, has models of many ships that made marine history. The models range from hand-held size to huge, and the collection also includes ships in bottles, figureheads, anchors, scrimshaw, and other artifacts. Open daily. Admission is charged. Call 912-232-1511.

The Savannah History Museum, at 303 Martin Luther King, Jr., Boulevard, is housed in a historic landmark building that once was a train station. An old Central of Georgia Railway locomotive sits on the tracks at the center of the museum. Exhibits trace Savannah's history from its founding to the present, including displays on Eli Whitney's invention of the cotton gin, Savannah's cotton industry, war history, and more. An orientation film provides a good overview. Open daily. Admission is charged. Call 912-238-1779.

The River Street Train Museum, at 315 West River Street, has a fine collection of old and new model trains, and an intricate miniature village. Open daily. Admission is charged. Call 912-233-6175.

Two new museums are the **Civil Rights Museum** (contact the Savannah Area Convention and Visitors Bureau regarding exhibits and other information), and the **Mighty Eighth Air Force Heritage Museum**, at 175 Bourne Avenue in Pooler. Call 912-748-8888.

CULTURAL OFFERINGS

The Savannah Symphony Orchestra gives performances throughout the year. Their box office at 225 Abercorn Street is open weekdays. Call 912-236-9536 or 800-537-7894.

The Savannah Theater, at Chippewa Square, hosts a variety of dramatic productions and comedies. Call 912-233-7764.

The City Market Art Center, at 232 West St. Julian Street, has galleries and studios where several regional artists display and sell their works. Admission is free. Call 912-234-2327.

RECREATION

Fishing and hunting are plentiful in the area; for licensing requirements and information, call the Georgia Wildlife Resources Division at 912-651-2221. There are also many public fishing piers and boating ramps. For pier and boat-ramp locations, contact the Savannah Area Convention and Visitors Bureau at 800-444-CHARM.

Tennis facilities are abundant here. For a sampling of public courts (other than those in area resorts and hotels), try Daffin Park at 1500 East Victory Drive (call 912-351-3851), Forsyth Park at Drayton and Gaston Streets downtown (call 912-351-3852), Lake Mayer, at Montgomery Crossroad and Sallie Mood Drive (call 912-652-6780), and Louis Scott Stell Park, off Bush Road (call 912-925-8694).

The Savannah Sand Gnats are the local minor-league baseball team. They play home games at Grayson Stadium, 1401 East Victory Drive. For a schedule, call 912-351-9150.

Oglethorpe Speedway Park, at 665 Jesup Road in Pooler, has car races and other racing events on Friday and Saturday. For a schedule, call 912-964-8200 or 800-964-7069.

The city's public parks include **Ba-**

Fort Pulaski, Savannah
Photo courtesy of the Savannah Area Convention and Visitors Bureau

con Park, at Skidaway Road and Bacon Park Drive. The park has over 1,000 acres and features a 27-hole golf course, driving range, putting greens, a clubhouse, Memorial Stadium, tennis, archery, and more. **Forsyth Park,** at Gaston and Whitaker Streets (next to the historic district), has playing fields, a scenic fountain, scented gardens for the visually impaired, a playground, and tennis courts.

SEASONAL EVENTS

St. Patrick's Day is very big in Savannah. The annual parade rivals New York's in size and merriment—and the Savannah River is even dyed green for the occasion!

Aside from St. Paddy's, April is a big festival month. There's the **Seafood Festival** at the waterfront, with tasty samples from local restaurants and live

entertainment (call 912-234-8054). Also in early April (or sometimes late March) is the **Walking Tours of Old Savannah Gardens**, in which participants tour gardens and take tea at the Green-Meldrim House (call 912-238-0248). April's highlight, however, is the **Night in Old Savannah**, which takes place at the Savannah Visitors Center and features festive food, live music, kids' activities, and more. In May, the **Savannah Scottish Games and Highland Gathering** are held at Old Fort Jackson. Traditional Scottish foods, dress, and music can all be enjoyed at the festival. Call 912-964-4951 or 912-897-5781.

Christmas in Savannah is an enchanting, month-long celebration, with candlelight tours of city homes, musical presentations, plays, parades, caroling, and cultural events (including Kwanzaa activities) throughout the city, which is dressed in her finest for the season. For information on these and other festivities, contact the Savannah Area Convention and Visitors Bureau at 800-444-CHARM (2427).

ACCOMMODATIONS

EXPENSIVE

Savannah Marriott Riverfront, at 100 General McIntosh Boulevard, is a new and glitzy hotel with magnificent river views. Amenities include indoor and outdoor pools, concierge, poolside service, exercise facilities, a game room, shops, and a deluxe Club Level. Call 912-233-7722.

The Gastonian, at 220 East Gaston Street, consists of two quaint, four-story homes that were built in 1868 and are connected by an elevated walkway. Guest rooms have working fireplaces, balconies, fourposter beds, and other antiques. A pretty courtyard with a raised sun deck and a hot tub is nestled between the buildings. Rates include breakfast and afternoon refreshments. Call 912-232-2869.

MODERATE

Holiday Inn Midtown, at 7100 Abercorn Street, offers golf packages with the Savannah Inn and Country Club. Call 912-352-7100.

INEXPENSIVE

Fairfield Inn by Marriott, 2 Lee Boulevard at the intersection of Abercorn Street. Call 912-353-7100.

Budgetel Inn, at 8484 Abercorn Street, is a no-frills comfortable motel offering valet service, a pool, free breakfast. It will accept some pets. Call 912-927-7660.

SHOPPING

The Riverfront Plaza has a variety of shops and restaurants, all located in historic waterfront buildings. **Factor's Walk** (named after the cotton factors, or merchants, whose businesses once occupied the area) is an area that includes the Riverfront Plaza and about ten other blocks between River and Bay Streets. The area features many shops selling local items and more.

The City Market is on West St. Julian Street, between Ellis and Franklin Squares. This artsy complex has a variety of specialty shops, art galleries, restaurants, and cafés.

The Low Country Factory Outlet Village, 30 miles from the Savannah River Bridge on U.S. 278, has over forty-five outlet stores, such as Laura Ashley and J. Crew. Call 803-837-4339.

RESTAURANTS

FINE DINING

45 South, at 20 East Broad Street, is an upscale restaurant in an antebellum building on the same grounds as the Pirate's House Restaurant (See below). Popular dishes are rack of lamb, salmon, and breast of duck. Dinner served Fridays and Saturdays. Jacket required; reservations recommended. Call 912-233-1881.

Johnny Harris, at 1651 East Victory Drive, is Savannah's oldest continuously operating eating establishment. House specialties are prime rib, seafood, and barbecued pork and lamb. Jacket required in the main dining room on Saturday. Open Monday through Saturday for lunch and dinner. Live entertainment is offered on weekends. Call 912-354-7810.

CASUAL DINING

Huey's, at 115 River Street, is a waterfront Italian café serving breakfast, lunch, and dinner daily. The cuisine here is fresh, casual fare with a southern twist (e.g., blackened chicken sandwich with red beans and rice). Call 912-234-7385.

The Pirate's House, at 20 East Broad Street, is located in a 1754 inn. It's a bit of a tourist attraction, but still a fun place to eat. The award-winning menu features seafood specialties like oysters, shrimp, and crab. Other fine menu items include chicken cordon bleu, duck à l'orange, and a staggering selection of over thirty desserts. The restaurant is somewhat of a museum, as pirates and sailors once patronized the place, and it is said to have inspired the inn described by Robert Louis Stevenson in *Treasure Island*. Call 912-233-5757.

Mrs. Wilkes' Boarding House, at 107 W. Jones Street, serves homemade Southern favorites like fried chicken, biscuits, and pies in a family-style setting. Located in an 1870 house, it's an official city landmark restaurant, having hosted famous people and received much attention from the press over the years. Be prepared to wait in line at this popular spot. Serves breakfast and lunch weekdays. Call 912-232-5997.

JUST FOR KIDS ....

Massie Heritage Interpretation Center, at 207 East Gordon Steet, is a museum designed for children. Exhibits detail the city's history and architecture in a way that children can relate to, such as displaying a schoolroom from the 1800s. Open weekdays. Call 912-651-7022.

SIDE TRIPS ....

Tybee Island (from a Euchee Indian word meaning "salt") is located on U.S. 80 (or Victory Drive), about 18 miles east of Savannah. This quiet, family-oriented beach area has a playground, park, amusement park, waterslide, marina, and swimming areas. It is a nice respite from the bustling city. You'd never know by looking at this area now that it was once a hideout for pirates. Savannah gentlemen were also known to conduct duels here to settle their differences. The old, 1773 lighthouse (built to replace the one built by General James Oglethorpe in 1736, which later burned), contains historic artifacts. If they're so inclined, visitors can even make the steep trip up to the top of the lighthouse. Admission is charged. The science museum at Tybee Island has marine exhibits and several aquariums, including a touch tank. In summer, the museum conducts beach walks and seinings where visitors help pull up the net. Admission is charged. For information on Tybee Island, call Tybee Visitor Information at 800-868-2322.

GENERAL INFORMATION ....

Contact the Savannah Area Convention and Visitors Bureau at 800-444-CHARM (2427). They can provide you with a copy of the *Historic Savannah Visitors Guide*.

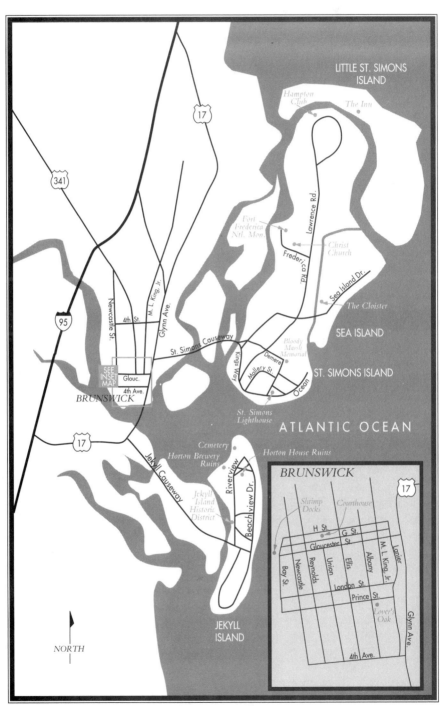

LITTLE ST. SIMONS
ISLAND

Hampton
Club

The Inn

Lawrence Rd.

Fort
Frederica
Ntl. Mon.

Christ
Church

Frederica Rd.

Sea Island Dr.

The Cloister

SEA ISLAND

17

341

Newcastle St.

4th St.

M. L. King, Jr.

Glynn Ave.

95

St. Simons Causeway

King's Way

Bloody
Marsh
Memorial

Demere

ST. SIMONS ISLAND

SEE
INSET
MAP

Glouc.

4th Ave.

BRUNSWICK

Mallery St.

Ocean

St. Simons
Lighthouse

ATLANTIC OCEAN

17

Cemetery

Horton Brewery
Ruins

Horton House Ruins

Jekyll Causeway

Jekyll
Island
Historic
District

Riverview

Beachview Dr.

BRUNSWICK

17

Shrimp
Docks

Courthouse

H St.

G St.

Gloucester St.

Bay St.

Newcastle

Reynolds

Union

Ellis

Albany

M. L. King, Jr.

Lanier

London St.

Prince St.

Lover's
Oak

Glynn Ave.

4th Ave.

NORTH

JEKYLL
ISLAND

BRUNSWICK and the GOLDEN ISLES, GA.

Brunswick and the Golden Isles

Little St. Simons Island
Photo courtesy of Brunswick and the Golden Isles
of GA Visitors Bureau

INTRODUCTION ....

The "Golden Isles," named by the Spanish explorers who settled and built missions here, are barrier islands on the coast of Georgia. They consist of St. Simons Island, the largest and most commercial of the four; Little St. Simons Island, the smallest; Jekyll Island, once a private retreat for the wealthy, and now an upscale resort island; and the likewise upscale Sea Island, which is a favorite of many of the well-to-do, including former presidents Dwight

Eisenhower, Jimmy Carter, George Bush, and Richard Nixon. All four islands have beautiful beaches and historic attractions, and three have terrific golf courses.

Though now bustling with seaside resorts, these islands have long been considered strategically desirable and were fought over by the English, Spanish, and French. The Battle of the Bloody Marsh, in which the English defeated the Spanish in 1742, was a decisive culmination of these disputes. The Golden Isles retain several remnants of these colonial occupations, and there's a rich legacy of ghost stories and other lore from this period. But the historical significance of the islands is not their most prominent feature. Instead, what strikes visitors most is the stunning natural beauty of their shores and golf courses.

Brunswick, located a short distance across the Marshes of Glynn and the Intracoastal Waterway, is the gateway to the Golden Isles. Though people heading for the beach areas may not realize it, as the main view of the city along U.S. 17 is of a developed shopping strip, Brunswick has a charming historic district, worth taking time to enjoy.

The normal monthly temperatures for the area, as measured in Brunswick, are: January, 50.8; February, 53.1; March, 60; April, 67; May, 73.6; June, 79.5; July, 81.9; August, 81.4; September, 77.9; October, 69.6; November, 61.3; December, 54. The peak golf season is April through late October, and spring and summer bring many beach visitors.

GOLF INFORMATION ....

THE SEA ISLAND GOLF CLUB, ST. SIMONS ISLAND (912) 638-5118

History just emanates from Sea Island Golf Club, from the avenue of giant live oaks at the entrance to the ruins of the Retreat Plantation adjacent to the clubhouse. The original nine holes are appropriately named "Plantation" and were built in 1927 by Walter Travis, the Australian-born winner of the British and United States Amateurs. In 1929, H.S. Colt and Charles Alison added the "Seaside" nine and reworked the Plantation nine, creating a 6900-yard (with tees starting at 5178 yards), par 72 layout. Recently, both Seaside and Plantation were named by *Golf* to be among the "Top 100 You Can Play." Like Walter Travis's Ewanok and Equinox courses in Manchester, Vermont, the greens at Plantation provide a fair amount of excitement. For example, the second hole is a short par 4 that plays to a elevated green surrounded by sand. The fourth is a 534-yard par 5 with a small green surrounded by trees and guarded by lots of sand. The green on the seventh, a 155-yard par 3, is on a V-shaped peninsula surrounded by water. On the Seaside nine, the classic hole is the 414-yard, par 4 seventh, a dogleg left that requires a drive of at least 220 yards over a marsh to a fairway that runs diagonally from right to left. The approach is then to a small, elevated green protected by a large bunker on the right front. It's an excellent hole that requires good thinking and execution.

Also on Sea Island is the "Retreat" nine built by Dick Wilson in 1960 and the "Marshside" nine built by Joe Lee. Retreat winds around two large lakes, while the Lee course is cut through marshes, as the name indicates. These two nines tally 6518 yards, and given their settings, they require extreme accuracy.

Carts: Mandatory. *Greens Fees:* Approximately $75-$90/18 holes; cart: $15 per person. *Tee Time Policy:* Call in advance for times.

JEKYLL ISLAND GOLF CLUB,
JEKYLL ISLAND (912) 635-2170
FOR OCEANSIDE OR (912) 635-2368
FOR OLEANDER, INDIAN MOUND,
AND PINE LAKES

Jekyll Island's golf history dates back to 1898, when club members built the island's first course. This nine-hole course, now known as Oceanside, was renovated by Walter Travis in 1926. From the back tees, the par 36 Oceanside measures almost 3300 yards, but with the wind, the elevated tees, small greens, and links-style layout, you may as well throw out your yardage book. Jekyll Island also features three challenging 18-hole, par 72 courses: the 6679-yard Oleander, designed by Dick Wilson (the twelfth hole is considered the most demanding par 4 in the state according to the *Atlanta Journal-Constitution*); the 6802-yard Pine Lakes, also designed by Dick Wilson, which features tree-lined fairways that wind through the island's interior; and the 6596-yard Indian Mound, designed by Joe Lee, which offers wide fairways and huge sloping greens.

Carts: Mandatory. *Greens Fees:* $26 weekdays, $30 weekends/18 holes. *Tee Time Policy:* Advance times required; guests can book when making room reservations, but course is open to public. The earlier in advance the better for high season.

Horseback riding on the Golden Isles
Photo courtesy of Brunswick and the Golden Isles of GA Visitors Bureau

Brunswick and the Golden Isles, GA

Hampton Club, St. Simons Island (912-634-0300), is a 6490-yard, par 72 layout designed by Joe Lee that winds through woods, marshland, and numerous lakes. **St. Simons Island Club**, St. Simons Island (912-638-5130), also is a 1974 Joe Lee design. This 6500-yard, par 72 course features narrow fairways and big, fast greens. For golfers who just can't quit when the sun goes down, **Golden Isles Golf Center**, Brunswick (912-264-1666), has a 9-hole, par 3 course and practice facility that stays open until 10 P.M.

ATTRACTIONS ....

TOURS

Driving Tours

The Brunswick Visitors Center, at 4 Glynn Avenue, has maps of island driving tours. Call 912-265-0620.

Motorized Tours

On St. Simons Island, **Island Tours** offers sea and land tours daily. They are located at 107 Marina Drive, Golden Isles Marina Village. Call 912-638-6882 or 800-940-3483. **Golden Isles Shuttle and Excursion** offers sightseeing tours and transportation to the airport. Call 912-634-1447. **The St. Simons Trolley**, located at the pier on Mallery Street, gives historic tours. Call 912-638-8954. Tram tours of Jekyll Island Club's striking historic district depart from the island's Historic District Orientation Center. Call 912-635-2762.

Fort Frederica,
Little St. Simons Island
Photo courtesy of Brunswick and the Golden Isles
of GA Visitors Bureau

Boat Tours

In Brunswick, **Coastal Expeditions**, at 3202 Third Street, offers tours given by local native Captain Vernon Reynolds. They also charter boats. Call 912-265-0392. Captain Reynolds' partner, Peter West, conducts dolphin and sightseeing cruises. Call 912-270-0082. Also in Brunswick is the *Emerald Princess* **Casino/Cruise Ship**, which offers five- and six-hour cruises with dining, entertainment, and a casino. Reservations required. Tours depart from the Brunswick Landing Marina. Call 800-842-0115. On St. Simons Island, **Coastal Charter Fishing**, at 110 Bracewell Court, has cruises and alligator-, bird-, and dolphin-watching tours. Call 912-638-8228. On Jekyll Island, **Island Tours, Inc.**, at 1 Pier Road, offers sightseeing, sunset dinner, and moonlight cocktail cruises, as well as dolphin-watching and marsh tours. Call 912-635-2891.

Bird-Watching Tours

Three tours specializing in watching the abundant local bird species are

Kennedy Charters on St. Simons Island (call 912-638-3214), **Marsh Hen Boat Tours** on Sea Island (call 912-638-3611 extension 5202, or 912-638-9354), and **Southeast Adventure Outfitters** on St. Simons Island (call 912-638-6732).

Nature Walks

At Brunswick's **Earth Day Nature Trails** (run by the Georgia Department of Natural Resources), paths traverse salt marshes, ponds, and coastal hammock high ground. There's also a wading-bird habitat, nesting platform, and an observation tower and decks on the premises. It is located at One Conservation Way off U.S. 17 at Sidney Lanier Ridge. Call 912-264-7218. On Jekyll Island, **Nature Walks**, at 1 Beachview Drive, is run by the island's recreation department and gives guided tours of the salt marsh and beach ecosystems. Call 912-635-2232.

HISTORIC PLACES

Brunswick is known as a shrimp capital of the world, and you can see the Brunswick shrimp fleet from U.S. 341 (which is called Bay Street in that section) between Prince and Gloucester Streets. On the same road, between Gloucester and Third Streets, you'll find several shrimp processing plants.

Lover's Oak sits at the corner of Prince and Albany Streets in Brunswick. Legend has it that this magnificent, 900-year-old tree is where Indian braves and their young loves would secretly meet. From Lover's Oak, cross over to London Street and you're in **Old Town**, where the old English street names remain intact. Notable buildings in Old Town are the historic **Mahoney-**

McGarvey House, at 1709 Reynolds, and the elegant **Old Courthouse Building** (built in 1907) at Union Street. On Newcastle Street, in Queen's Square, is a monument to Georgia's founder, James Oglethorpe.

On U.S. 17, a half mile south of Brunswick, is the **Lanier Oak**, where poet Sidney Lanier composed the *Marshes of Glynn* in the 1870s. On your way to St. Simons Island, you may want to get a glimpse of those marshes at **Marshes of Glynn Overlook Park**, which has picnic facilities.

Fort Frederica National Monument, on Frederica Road on the north end of St. Simons Island, was built by James Oglethorpe in 1736. The museum has a film about the area's tumultuous history, and park rangers conduct tours. In summer, there are special colonial-life programs. Open daily. Admission is charged. Call 912-638-8639.

Bloody Marsh Memorial, along Demere Road on St. Simons Island, about 6 miles south of Fort Frederica, is the site of the 1742 battle between the Spanish and English. The Spanish were advancing to attack Fort Frederica from the south when the English troops ambushed them, halting their plan and, ultimately, the Spanish invasion of Georgia. Open daily.

The 1883 **Christ Church,** at 6329 Frederica Road on St. Simons Island, stands where outdoor services were first held in 1736, and where an 1820 church was destroyed by Union troops. Open daily from 2 to 5 P.M. April through October, and from 1 to 4 P.M. November through March. Donation suggested.

Remnants of the plantation era are located throughout St. Simons Island. A few of the more popular plantations open for viewing are: **Hampton Plantation**, located next to the Hampton Club on the north end of the island, is where Aaron Burr stayed for a time after his duel with Alexander Hamilton. In the south, **Retreat Plantation**, now the Sea Island Golf Club, has ruins of a slave hospital and cemetery on the grounds that are available for viewing. And in the west, visitors can tour **Hamilton Plantation**, which is located on the river and has the remains of two slave cabins. For more information on these plantations, and others, contact the Brunswick and Golden Isles Visitors Bureau at 912-265-0620 or 800-933-COAST.

On Jekyll Island, the **Historic District Orientation Center,** located on Stable Road, features a video on the region's history. Tickets can be purchased for a half-hour tram ride through the island's historic district (or you can get maps for self-guided walking tours). Aside from the **Jekyll Island Club Historic District** (which was once a private playground of the wealthy), the tour takes visitors to see the **Millionaire's Village** cottages, which will knock your socks off. Among the sights there are a cottage owned by William Rockefeller and a 1904, Tiffany stained-glass church window. Admission is charged. Call 912-635-2762.

On Riverview Drive on the northwest end of Jekyll Island, you'll find the ruins of the **Old Horton Brewery**. Built by James Oglethorpe's aid, William Horton, this was the first brewery in Georgia; it supplied ales to the troops and other settlers. The ruins of Horton's 1742 house also are visible here. His was one of the oldest tabby (a building

material made primarily from crushed oyster shells) homes in Georgia. Nearby is an old family plot known as the du Bignon cemetery.

MUSEUMS/SCIENCE CENTERS

Mary Miller Doll Museum, at 1523 Glynn Avenue in Brunswick, has a large collection of handmade dolls. Admission is charged. Call 912-267-7569.

The Museum of Coastal History, at 101 Twelfth Street, is in the restored 1872 lighthouse keeper's home, next to the 104-foot St. Simons Lighthouse (now the home of the Coastal Georgia Historical Society). Fort St. Simons (captured from the English by the Spanish in 1742, although the Spanish were defeated later that same year), once stood at this site. Open daily. Admission is charged. Call 912-638-4666.

The Coastal Center for the Arts, at 2012 Demere Road on St. Simons Island, has changing exhibits featuring works by regional artists. Admission is free. Call 912-634-0404.

CULTURAL OFFERINGS

The Island Players present dramas at the Casino Theater in Neptune Park on St. Simons Island. Call 912-638-3031.

In the summer months, musical shows are performed at the **Nightly Musical Theater Festival** at the Jekyll Island Amphitheater on Stable Road. Call 912-635-3636.

RECREATION

Boats are available from several area marinas for sailing, diving, and fishing. For a detailed list of public fishing areas, public-access boat ramps, and companies that provide boating and fishing rentals, contact the Brunswick and Golden Isles Visitors Bureau at 912-265-0620 or 800-933-COAST.

Horseback riding is available at **Sea Island Stables**, 301 Frederica Road on St. Simons Island. Call 912-638-5170.

Aside from courts at area hotels, the following parks have public tennis facilities: in Brunswick, there's Ballard Park, Blythe Island, Howard Coffin Park, Northwood Estates, and Selden Park; on St. Simons Island, there's Epworth Park and Mallery Park.

For bicycle rentals on St. Simons Island, try **Eddie Collins Island Bike Shop** at 204 Sylvan Drive (call 912-638-0705), **Ocean Motion Beach Service** at 1300 Ocean Boulevard (call 912-638-8053), **Benjy's Bike Shop** at 130 Retreat Plaza (call 912-638-6766), and **St. Simons Beachwear** at 401 Mallery Street (call 912-638-5029). On Jekyll Island, try **Jekyll Island Bicycle Rental** on Beachview Drive (call 912-635-2648).

For water sports (parasailing, jetskiing, water-skiing, and scuba diving), try **Barry's Beach Service** (call 912-638-8053), **Golden Isles Water Sports** (call 912-638-SAIL), or the **Island Dive Center** (912-638-6590 or 800-940-3483), all on St. Simons Island.

Jekyll Island's **Summer Waves Water Park**, at 210 South Riverview Drive, has a wave pool, slides, kiddie rides, children's pool, and several heart-pounding waterslides and rides. Open Memorial Day through Labor Day. Admission is charged. Call 912-635-2074.

In March, there's a tour of island homes on Jekyll Island, as well as another tour which combines homes on St. Simons Island and Sea Island. For more information, call 912-638-8683. March also brings an arts festival to Jekyll Island and the **Spring Craft Show** to St. Simons Island.

In April, Brunswick presents its **Old Town Homes Tour**. April on Jekyll Island features an Easter-egg hunt, an antique and collectibles show, a boat show, and the Easter sunrise services.

May brings the annual blessing of the shrimp fleet on Mother's Day, and the **Tillandsia Festival**, which occurs throughout the area.

In July, the **Sunshine Festival** takes place on St. Simons Island, featuring crafts exhibits. In late August on St. Simons Island is the **Georgia Sea Island Festival**, a cultural heritage celebration with traditional island crafts, foods, and music.

In mid-October, there's the **Golden Isle Arts Festival** on St. Simons Island, with entertainment and juried arts and crafts exhibits. From November through February, **Golfer's Heaven** takes place on Jekyll Island. During this period, lodgers at participating accommodations receive discounted greens fees at the island courses. For information, call 800-841-6586. December brings a host of events in the area, from a bluegrass festival and a madrigal feast to special Christmas tours and celebrations.

ACCOMMODATIONS ....

EXPENSIVE

The Cloister, on Sea Island Drive, is Sea Island's five-star resort, with deluxe rooms in a luxurious tropical setting. Rates include three meals daily. Guests can use the private beach, beach club with spa, tennis courts, and the great golf course. Fishing, trap and skeet shooting, and other facilities are also available. The palm-dotted, landscaped grounds boast lovely flower gardens. Call 912-638-3611 or 800-732-4752.

The King and Prince Beach and Golf Resort, at 201 Arnold Road on St. Simons Island, is a beachfront resort with rooms and villas. It offers golf packages, free shuttle to the golf course, two pools, tennis, and a jacuzzi. It is located on the north end of the Hampton Club (See Golf Information), which is affiliated with the hotel. Call 912-638-3631 or 800-342-0212.

Sea Palms Golf and Tennis Resort, at 5445 Frederica Road on St. Simons Island, is an 800-acre resort that offers two pools, tennis, and packages for its 27 holes of golf. Call 912-638-3351 or 800-841-6268.

Jekyll Island Club Hotel, at 371 Riverview Drive, is on the National Register of Historic Places. The hotel offers a private beach club, children's activities in summer, horse and carriage rides, VCRs in all rooms, a Victorian afternoon tea, concierge, pool, tennis facilities, and golf packages (See Golf Information). Call 912-635-2600 or 800-333-3333.

Little St. Simons Island is a private resort that has eleven rooms. Package rates include meals, snacks, and all amenities except horseback riding. Activities include canoeing, bird-watching, fishing, boating, and guided nature walks. An unspoiled 7-mile beach graces the shores of this private barrier island.

A great choice for a quiet island getaway. Call 912-638-7472.

MODERATE

Brunswick Manor, at 825 Egmont Street in Old Town Brunswick, has four beautifully furnished rooms. Rates include full breakfast and afternoon refreshments. Call 912-265-6889

INEXPENSIVE

The Ramada Limited, 3241 Glynn Avenue in Brunswick (off U.S. 17 near the St. Simons/Sea Island Causeway and the Jekyll Island Causeway), offers golf packages and allows pets. They also have a pool, playground, tennis, and free breakfast. Call 912-264-8611.

The Quality Inn and Suites, 3302 Glynn Avenue (just across the street from the Ramada Limited), has a pool, free breakfast, and allows pets. Call 912-264-9111.

Days Inn Oceanfront, at 60 South Beachview Drive on Jekyll Island, is a beachfront motel that allows pets and has a pool, bike rentals, golf packages, and honeymoon packages. Call 912-635-3319.

SHOPPING ....

In Brunswick, recent downtown renovations have turned several Victorian-era buildings into a quaint shopping area.

On Jekyll Island, head to the Beachview Drive and Fortson Parkway intersection for gift-and-souvenir shops, drug stores, etc. More shops are in the **Jekyll Island Club Historic District**.

St. Simons Island has lots of shopping. Some popular places are the Village, Hanover Square, Demere Village, Frederica Walk North, Retreat Village, and the area on or near Frederica Road. At **Golden Isles Marina Village**, overlooking the St. Simons Causeway, there are several shops and restaurants.

Outlet shoppers may want to head over to **Darien's Magnolia Bluff Factory Shops**, which has over eighty outlets. To reach it, take Exit 10 off I-95.

RESTAURANTS ....

Don't forget to try the famous Brunswick Stew, which originated here. And, since Brunswick is a shrimp capital of the world, it's a great place to order fresh shrimp.

FINE DINING

The Cloister Hotel's Main Dining Room, on Sea Island Drive on Sea Island, is a five-star restaurant offering a six-course prix fixe dinner. The restaurant serves breakfast, lunch during the high season, and dinner. Jacket and tie required; reservations recommended. Call 912-638-5111.

The Grand Dining Room, at the Jekyll Island Club Hotel on 371 Riverview Drive, has a continental menu with fresh steaks, seafood, and pasta. Serves breakfast, lunch, dinner, and Sunday brunch. Reservations recommended. Call 912-635-2600 extension 1002.

CASUAL DINING

Allegro, at 2465 Demere Road on St. Simons Island, falls somewhere between fine and casual dining. The continental selections consist mainly of seafood, lamb, beef, pasta, and veal. The interior has a modern black-and-white

motif, and modern art decks the walls. Reservations recommended. Call 912-638-7097. **Allegro Café**, at the same address, serves seafood and pasta. Call 912-638-6097.

The Georgia Pig, at the intersection of I-95 and U.S. 17 in Brunswick, serves authentic barbecue. Head here for plates piled high with delicious barbecued pork and chicken. Call 912-264-6664.

For great Brunswick Stew (and other casual selections like sandwiches), try **SeaJay's Waterfront Cafe and Pub** (with waterside outdoor dining), at the Jekyll Harbor Marina (call 912-635-3200); **Frannie's Place Restaurant**, at 318 Mallery Street on St. Simons Island (call 912-638-1001); and **Spanky's**, 1200 Glynn Avenue in Brunswick (call 912-267-6100).

JUST FOR KIDS ....

Some area hotels and resorts have children's activities in the summer. Contact your hotel or the Brunswick and Golden Isles Visitors Bureau regarding the availability of such programs.

The Coastal Boating Academy, at 106 Airport Street on St. Simons Island, offers a kid's marine summer camp, though the rest of the year it's an adult boating school. Call 912-638-5678.

GENERAL INFORMATION ....

For more information on the area, contact the Brunswick and Golden Isles Visitors Bureau at 912-265-0620 or 800-933-COAST. They'll send you a free copy of their *Visitors Guide*, and their *Golf and Area Attractions Guide*.

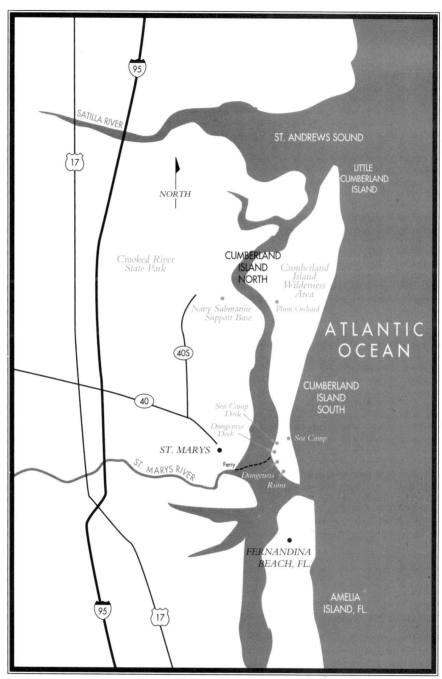

ST. MARYS and CUMBERLAND ISLAND, GA.

St. Marys and Cumberland Island

AREA CODE: 912

INTRODUCTION

St. Marys and Cumberland Island make a unique combination for golfers and non-golfers. St. Marys is in the southernmost area of Georgia's coast, about a stone's throw from Florida. The city enjoys a fine reputation—in its April 1996 issue, *Money* magazine named it the number-one small town in the United States. Additionally, the city boasts the excellent Osprey Cove golf course. And aside from having a terrific championship golf course, it's the gateway to Cumberland Island, Georgia's largest barrier island. (The city is also known for its naval submarine base and large paper mill.)

Cumberland Island National Seashore, run by the National Park Service, is one of the nation's most pristine beach areas, and its quota of daily visitors is limited. Wild horses roam the island's forests, marshes, and occasionally, its beaches—a reminder of the Spanish explorers who once inhabited the island. The island is a delight for naturalists, campers, and those needing an escape from civilization.

No stores exist on the island, and vehicles (even bicycles) and pets aren't allowed. If you're day-tripping or camping, you'll need to bring food, water, and other supplies. For less-rustic types, there's one deluxe hotel here, the Greyfield Inn, which has a fine restaurant patronized mainly by guests.

Non-golfers can enjoy the natural beauty of Cumberland Island while golfers stay on the mainland to play, making for a pleasant day trip or overnight stop to the area. In fact, there's a tour ferry to Cumberland from Fernandina Beach on Amelia Island. (See the Jacksonville, Amelia Island, and vicinity chapter.) It's also a pleasant side trip from Brunswick and the Golden Isles, which are located just 30 miles from St. Marys. (See the Brunswick and the Golden Isles chapter.)

St. Marys' and Cumberland Island's normal monthly temperatures, as measured in Folkston, Georgia, are: January, 52.9; February, 55.4; March, 62.2; April, 68; May, 73.9; June, 79.3; July, 81.4; August, 81.1; September, 77.9; October, 69.7; November, 61.7; December, 55.2. The tourist season runs from April through October, though the summer months are busiest for camping on the island. Peak golf seasons are March through May and September through November.

1990, winds through pine forests, marshes, and along the St. Marys River. Wildlife on and around the course includes deer, armadillos, alligators, hawks, herons, egrets, and ibises. The landing area for tee shots on this 6800-yard, par 72 course is generous, while green approaches require accuracy for low scoring. Demonstrative of the wide variety of holes on this course are the par 4 ninth and the par 5 eighteenth—two holes that share the same green. The 371-yard ninth is a dogleg right that requires an accurate approach to avoid sand traps on the front right of the green and a waste bunker on the left. The eighteenth is a reachable 500 yards, so long as the tee shot negotiates bunkers on the left side of the fairway. The approach needs to be well measured, because the green is shallow, and accurate, to avoid sand on the front right and left and mounds to the rear.

Carts: Mandatory. *Greens Fees:* $50 weekdays, $58 weekends/18 holes, including carts. *Tee Time Policy:* Call a week in advance.

OTHER EXCELLENT AREA COURSES:

See the chapter on Brunswick and the Golden Isles, Georgia, for additional courses in the area. The Brunswick and Golden Isles courses are located only about 30 miles north of St. Marys.

GOLF INFORMATION ....

OSPREY COVE, ST. MARYS
(912) 882-5575 OR (800) 352-5575

This links-style layout, designed by PGA touring pro Mark McCumber in

ATTRACTIONS ....

TOURS

Nature tours and other programs are given by park rangers on Cumberland Island during the summer. For infor-

mation, call the Park Service Superintendent at 912-882-4335.

HISTORIC PLACES

St. Marys has a historic district that
encompasses about twenty blocks. The
city was founded in 1788, and the district has well-preserved homes dating
back as early as 1787. Thirty-eight sites
are marked with braille and raised let-
ters (the "Braille Trail") for the visually
impaired.

On Cumberland Island, you can see
the ruins of **Dungeness**, a mansion
built by Lucy and Thomas Carnegie (a
home of the same name belonging to
Revolutionary War General Nathanael
Greene also once stood here). Another
Carnegie mansion on the island, **Plum
Orchard**, is currently under restoration
and is open for tours during limited
hours. For information and fees, call
912-882-4335.

MUSEUMS/SCIENCE CENTERS

The Dungeness Historical Site,
near the ferry stop on Cumberland Island, has a small icehouse museum covering the island's history, from its early
occupants, namely the Timulac Indians,
followed by English and Spanish settlers; to its later sale to a succession of
Revolutionary War–era officers; and its
still later sale to the Carnegie family.
Free tours are offered by park rangers.

A submarine museum will soon
open in St. Marys (a logical location,
given the naval base here). For information, call 882-4000 or 800-868-
8687.

RECREATION

**Cumberland Island National
Seashore** can be reached via a ferry

(the *Cumberland Queen*) which departs
daily between March 15 and September 30 from St. Marys, and Thursday
through Monday between October 1
and March 14. Advance reservations are
recommended, as the number of island
visitors is limited; reservations can be
made eleven months in advance. Also,
arrive at least thirty minutes before departure, since standby seating is available from no-shows. There are two ferry
stops on the island: Dungeness (better
for day visitors, as it's closer to the historic sites, beaches, and trails) and Sea
Camp (where campers depart). Ferry
passengers receive a quick orientation
and island map before departure. Remember, there are no stores or restaurants on the island, and pets, bicycles,
and other vehicles are prohibited on the
ferry. There is a fee for the ferry. For
information, call 912-882-4335.

While there are no lifeguards, swimming is permitted in designated areas
on the island. The beaches are unusually wide and long and are some of the
most beautiful beaches on the Atlantic
Ocean.

Light tackle fishing is allowed in the
surf or sound areas, and there's an abundance of bluefish, croaker, drum trout,
and red bass. Deer hunting is permitted on the island's north end on speci-
fied dates between late October and
February.

An entrance to **Okefenokee Swamp
Park** is on U.S. 1 and S.R. 177, about
30 miles west of St. Marys and 12 miles
southeast of Waycross. The largest existing freshwater swamp in the United
States, Okefenokee Swamp has mysterious dark waters, a jungle-like landscape, and lots of outdoor recreation
(though no camping). The admission

charge to the park includes a 1½-mile boat ride on Indian waterways. For an additional charge, you can take an extended tour (when guides are available). There's also a serpentarium, swamp ecology exhibits, wildlife shows, and a restored pioneer homestead. For information, call 912-283-0583.

SEASONAL EVENTS

St. Marys celebrates Mardis Gras in February. Another big celebration in St. Marys is the Fourth of July celebration, which features one of the largest fireworks displays in the Southeast, along with a variety of food and activities. **Native American Heritage Day** is held in August, and a rock-shrimp (a local culinary specialty served with coleslaw and beans) festival takes place in October. In nearby Kingsland, there's

A church in St. Marys

Photo courtesy of the GA Department of Industry, Trade and Tourism

a Labor Day weekend catfish festival, which includes a classic golf tournament, parade, beauty pageant, crafts, entertainment, and loads of catfish trimmed with coleslaw, hush puppies, and hominy grits. At Christmas, visitors can take candlelight tours of lovely homes in St. Marys, or enjoy a medieval-style madrigal feast in Kingsland.

For a current calendar of events in St. Marys, contact the St. Marys Tourism Authority at 912-882-6200; for Kingsland, contact the Kingsland Tourism Authority at 912-729-5999 or 800-433-0225. For the entire county, call the Camden County Chamber of Commerce at 912-729-5840.

ACCOMMODATIONS ....

EXPENSIVE

The Greyfield Inn is Cumberland Island's only hotel. This luxurious, Victorian-era home is still owned by the Carnegie family and is furnished with many antiques, including family china. While rates are steep, they include breakfast, a picnic lunch, and dinner (but no air conditioning). Jackets and dresses are required at dinner, which is signaled by a nightly chime. Call 904-261-6408.

MODERATE

Goodbread House, at 209 Osborne Street in St. Marys' historic district, is a quaint bed-and-breakfast, complete with white picket fence. This inn has high ceilings and pine floors that recall the Victorian era when it was built. Each room contains Victorian antiques and a fireplace. Call 912-882-7490.

St. Marys Family Hotel, at 2710 Osborne Road in St. Marys, offers free breakfast, some kitchenettes, and golf packages. Call 912-882-6250 or 800-768-6250.

Free camping is available on Cumberland Island by reservation. Bring all the supplies you need (again, there are no stores), but don't over pack, as there's a half-mile hike from the ferry to Sea Camp. For information, call the National Park Service Superintendent at 912-882-4335.

SHOPPING ....

In St. Marys, you'll find quaint shops in turn-of-the-century buildings along Osborne Road and on Bryant Street.

There's also a large shopping mall at the Kings Bay Village Shopping Center on the GA 40 spur.

Antique shoppers should head to Kingsland, west of St. Marys on GA 40. The town has several roadside antique shops. For information, contact the Kingsland Tourism Authority at 912-729-5999 or 800-433-0225.

RESTAURANTS ....

On Cumberland Island, the only restaurant is at the **Greyfield Inn** (See Accommodations). As it has a strict dress code, campers and day-trippers generally opt to pack sandwiches.

A local delicacy is rock shrimp, which tastes like a cross between shrimp and lobster and is usually served blackened, grilled, or fried. The rock shrimp at **Seagle's Restaurant and Lounge**, on the first floor of the Riverview Hotel in St. Marys, was featured in the October 1994 issue of *Southern Living*. The restaurant serves the delicacy fried, broiled, or blackened. Other fare includes seafood, steaks, and southern favorites like eggs-and-grits. They even sell boxed lunches for Cumberland Island day-trippers. Open daily for breakfast and dinner; open weekdays for lunch. Call 912-882-3242.

GENERAL INFORMATION ....

For Cumberland Island, call the National Park Service Superintendent at 912-882-4335 (ferry and information) or 912-882-4336 (camping and information), or call the Kingsland Tourism Authority at 800-433-0225 (for information only; they can not make reservations). For information on St. Marys, call the St. Marys Welcome Center at 912-882-4000 or 800-868-8687. For surrounding areas, call the Camden County Chamber of Commerce at 912-729-5840.

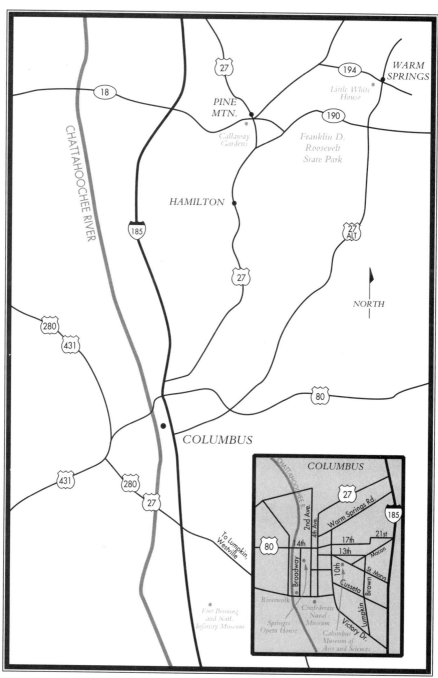

CALLAWAY GARDENS and COLUMBUS, GA.

Callaway Gardens and Columbus

INTRODUCTION ....

Callaway Gardens in Pine Mountain is a beautiful resort with three spectacular courses to keep golfers happy. But even non-golfers love its breathtaking scenery and many outdoor and indoor activities. Columbus, about 30 miles south of Pine Mountain, makes a pleasant side trip or home base for a visit to this region.

The founding of Columbus, Georgia's second-largest city, dates back to the early 1800s. Until recently, it has been a center of production for the textile industry. A mere stone's throw from Alabama, Columbus is home to Fort Benning, the largest infantry training center in the world, as well as to Columbus College, part of the University of Georgia. Although until now, it has drawn relatively few tourists on its own, Columbus's revitalization, along with the increased recognition from hosting the 1996 Olympic softball competition, may increase tourism in the near future.

As for golfers, Columbus offers Bull

Creek, a quality public course that ranks as one of the seventy-five best public courses in the United States. Other interesting places to visit in the region include Warm Springs (where Franklin D. Roosevelt spent much time during his last years—the springs eased his suffering from polio) and the quaint historic town of Lumpkin. Both of these cities make great side trips from the Callaway Gardens/Columbus area.

Normal monthly temperatures are: January, 45.7; February, 49.3; March, 57.2; April, 64.8; May, 72.3; June, 79.5; July, 81.9; August, 81.4; September, 76.4; October, 66; November, 56.7; December, 48.6. There's a steady stream of visitors to Callaway Gardens and Columbus year-round.

GOLF INFORMATION ....

CALLAWAY GARDENS RESORT, PINE MOUNTAIN (706) 663-2281 OR (800) 282-8181

With 63 holes of golf, Callaway Gardens is a prime golf destination. The flagship course is the Mountain View Course, which hosts the Buick Southern Open and is considered one of the best courses in the United States by *Golf Digest* and *Golf Magazine*. Set among lakes, pines, dogwoods, hollies, chrysanthemums, and azaleas (with over 700 variations), Mountain View was designed by Dick Wilson and remodeled by Joe Lee. Its length ranges from 5900 yards to over 7000 yards, with the back tees offering a stern challenge (as evidenced by the 138 course slope and a rating over 74). The tree- and water-lined fairways are narrow, and the greens

are large, elevated, undulating, and heavily bunkered. The signature hole is the 550-yard, par 5 fifteenth, which is bordered from tee to green by water with an inlet in front of the green.

The Garden View Course, also a Joe Lee design, is a 6392-yard (tees start at 5848 yards), par 72 course that is more wide open and forgiving than Mountain View. This course follows a trail of beautiful orchards and vineyards. Callaway's original course, Lake View, is a 6000-yard (tees start at 5452 yards), par 70 course designed by J.B. McGovern and Dick Wilson. It has flowering landscapes, and its signature hole is the 152-yard, par 3 fifth, which plays from an island tee. The last course at Callaway is Sky View. Also designed by Joe Lee, it is a par 31 executive course that reaches almost 2100 yards.

Carts: Mandatory. *Greens Fees:* $70 guests, $90 non-guests in high season (fees are lower in offseason)/18 holes, including cart. *Tee Time Policy:* Resort guests can book at time of confirmed room reservation. Others can call two days in advance.

BULL CREEK, COLUMBUS (706) 561-1614

Though Bull Creek offers two terrific championship courses, the East Course and the West Course, the 1972 West Course is a Joe Lee design that is ranked among the top twenty-five public courses in the United States by *Golf Digest*. Cut through a forested, rolling terrain that runs along Bull Creek, this 6921-yard (tees start at 5385 yards), par 72 municipal course can be played for less than $20, making it a terrific value. As with most Joe Lee courses, the fairways are tightly bordered by trees and

Callaway Gardens Resort, Pine Mountain
Photo courtesy of Tourist Division, GA Department of Industry and Trade

water. An excellent stretch of holes is the 188-yard, par 3 fourteenth; the 400-yard, par 4 fifteenth; and the 420-yard, par 4 sixteenth. The fourteenth plays over a lake to a green that is flanked by bunkers and trees. The fifteenth, the signature hole, is a dogleg right that winds around Bull Creek Lake, while the sixteenth is a tree-lined dogleg left. The sixteenth plays downhill from the tee and then uphill to the green, which is protected front and back by sand traps.

Carts: Not required. *Greens Fees:* $15/18 holes; carts: $10 per person. *Tee Time Policy:* Call in advance. For weekends and holidays, call the Wednesday before; weekdays can be booked further in advance.

ATTRACTIONS ....

TOURS

Heritage Corner Tours, at 700 Broadway, is run by the Historic Columbus Foundation and offers guided tours of Columbus. Tours depart 11 A.M. and 3 P.M. on weekdays, and at 2 P.M. on weekends. Call 706-322-0756. The foundation also has maps for self-guided walking tours.

The Chattahoochee Princess offers river rides, and dinner and late-night cruises on weekends. Call 706-324-4499.

HISTORIC PLACES

Ever since the Olympic crowd was scheduled to head this way, downtown restoration and construction began in earnest.

Sibley Horticulture Center,
Pine Mountain
Photo courtesy of Tourist Division, GA Department of
Industry and Trade

Columbus's historic district is spread over about thirty city blocks, and it encompasses the home of Coca-Cola's creator Dr. Robert F. Pemberton (11 West Seventh Street), a historic log cabin, and a farmhouse museum. In addition to the restored nineteenth-century buildings, the district also contains newer commercial areas.

Also of historic significance is the **Springer Opera House**, at 103 Tenth Street, which is an 1871 Victorian theater. The theater features gilt- and red-plush curtains and carpeting, and it still hosts performances. Call 706-327-3688. **The Old Train Depot**, at 1200 Sixth Avenue, is now an office building, but it retains signs designating separate areas for "white" and "colored" people—

haunting reminders of the recent past.

The picturesque, red-brick and iron-work area along the **Riverwalk** makes for a nice stroll. Highlights include the former **Confederate Ironworks**, at 801 Front Avenue, and the **Chattahoochee Promenade**, with fountains, gazebos, and monuments. From the Riverwalk, you can spot old mills and a waterfall.

MUSEUMS/SCIENCE CENTERS

The Columbus Museum, at 1251 Wynnton Road, features exhibits on the culture, history, and art of this region. Kids enjoy hands-on exhibits and Transformations, a large room with art projects. Open daily. Admission is free. Call 706-649-0713.

Columbus has two military museums. **The Confederate Naval Museum**, at 202 Fourth Street, contains artifacts and souvenirs of the Confederate navy, from uniforms, documents, utensils, and paintings, to the remains of the Confederate gunboats *Chattahoochee* and *Jackson*. Open daily except Monday. A donation is suggested. Call 706-327-9798. **The National Infantry Museum**, in the main post area of Fort Benning, is considered by some to be the best military museum in the United States. The artifacts cover military history spanning from the French and Indian War up through the recent Gulf War. Open daily. Admission is free. Call 706-545-2958.

The **Patterson Planetarium,** at 2900 Woodruff Farm Road, presents astronomy shows. Admission is charged. Call 706-568-2459.

CULTURAL OFFERINGS

Springer Opera House (See Historic Places), at 103 Tenth Street, has regular performances throughout the year. Call 706-327-3688. **Three Arts Theater**, at 1029 Talbotton Road, is home to the Columbus Symphony. Call 706-571-5893. To reach a recording that gives a listing of events at the Three Arts Theater and all other city-owned theaters, cal 706-571-5889.

RECREATION

Callaway Gardens, on U.S. 27 in Pine Mountain, contains over 14,000 acres. Though it is a resort, many of the facilities and grounds are open to the public (with some fees and admission charges). The grounds include lakes, beaches, gardens, woods, wildlife (including over 200 varieties of birds and 50 species of butterflies), a butterfly center, a horticultural center, a vegetable garden, an eighteenth-century pioneer cabin with period exhibits, dining facilities, and a memorial woodland chapel (built in honor of Ida Cason Callaway). Recreational activities include tennis, racquetball, deer and quail hunting, trap and skeet shooting, and a golf resort (See Golf Information and Accommodations). Call 800-282-8181.

Pine Mountain Wild Animal Park, at 1300 Oak Grove Road in Pine Mountain, has an extensive petting zoo and some exotic animals, such as lions and giraffes. Admission is charged. Call 706-663-8744 or 800-367-2751.

Golden Park, between Victory Drive and Lumpkin Boulevard in Columbus, is where the 1996 Olympic Women's Fast Pitch Softball competition was held. It's also home to the Columbus Redstixx minor-league baseball team. For a game schedule, call 706-571-8866.

There's a natural water park called **Flat Rock Park** on Flat Rock Road, near the Columbus Airport. Visitors slip down the natural rock slide into the large water hole.

SEASONAL EVENTS

The last weekend in April brings the **Riverfest Weekend** to the Riverwalk in Columbus. The event is a huge fair with a children's carnival, arts and crafts, food, music, and entertainment. In March or April, Callaway Gardens holds its annual **Azalea Festival**. Call 706-663-2281. Over Fourth of July weekend, Fort Benning holds a huge military pageant that includes paratrooper skydiving, parades, military bands, and a fireworks show that'll knock your socks off.

October is when the **Indian Cultural Festival** comes to Columbus College, with regional Native American dance and craft demonstrations, foods, storytelling, and music. There's also a fall festival at Callaway Gardens. Call 706-663-2281. Over Columbus Day weekend, the **Uptown Music Jam Festival,** which takes place in Columbus near the Riverwalk, features a wide variety of music styles, from jazz to big band to rock.

Thanksgiving and Christmas bring special events to the Little White House in Warm Springs (See Side Trips). Call 706-655-5870. Callaway Gardens also has special Thanksgiving and Christmas celebrations. Call 706-663-2281. If you're in the area during the holiday season (especially with kids), don't miss the **Fantasy in Lights Show** at Callaway Gardens, which runs from Thanksgiving week through New Year's Eve. Call 800-282-8181.

ACCOMMODATIONS ....

EXPENSIVE

Callaway Gardens Resort Hotel, on U.S. 27 in Pine Mountain, offers top-notch accommodations in a beautiful country setting. The resort has lakes, gardens, forests, and plenty of fine facilities, including seven dining rooms, tennis, racquetball, a fitness center, swimming pools, hunting and skeet shooting, and of course, fine golf. Accommodations run from suites and rooms to villas and cottages. Call 706-663-2281 or 800-282-8181.

The Columbus Hilton, at 800 Front Avenue in Columbus, is housed in the shell of an old gristmill. This deluxe hotel has a pool, golf privileges, and a luxury level. Call 706-324-1800.

MODERATE

Davis Inn is next door to Callaway Gardens at U.S. 27 and State Park Road in Pine Mountain. Guests here enjoy golf, tennis, health club, and swimming privileges at Callaway Gardens Resort Hotel. No credit cards accepted. Call 706-663-2522.

Courtyard by Marriott, at 3501 Courtyard Way next to the Peachtree Mall in Columbus, has a pool, exercise room, and a valet service. Some rooms have refrigerators, patios, and balconies. Call 706-323-2323.

INEXPENSIVE

A **Howard Johnsons Motel** with a pool, which opened in mid-1996, is at 1011 Fourth Avenue in Columbus. For more information, call 706-322-6641.

SHOPPING ....

Downtown Columbus has several unique shops, such as a voodoo shop (located on Ninth Street), as well as a smattering of nice antique shops worth browsing.

RESTAURANTS ....

FINE DINING

Bon Cuisine, at 113 Main Street in Pine Mountain, serves gourmet southern cuisine that has earned an honor from the Governor's Council on Tourism. Dinner served by reservation only Monday through Saturday. Call 706-663-2019.

The Georgia Room, at Callaway Gardens, is a wonderful restaurant that serves fine continental cuisine in a gracious setting. Reservations recommended. Call 706-663-2281 or 800-282-8181.

Bludau's Goetchius House, at 405 Broadway in Columbus, is in a restored antebellum home. It serves fine fare such as fresh swordfish, frog legs bourguignonne, and veal. A speakeasy is downstairs, and a riverfront patio is outside. Dinner served Monday through Saturday. Call 706-324-4863.

CASUAL DINING

Buckhead Grill, at 5010 Armour Road in Columbus, serves lunch weekdays and dinner daily. There's live acoustic-guitar music Sunday through Thursday. Popular items are ribs, steaks, fish, pasta, and sandwiches. Outdoor dining is available. Call 706-571-9995.

For a popular, off-beat place, try **Hogan's Heroes**, located in a converted gas station at 235 U.S. 29 in the town of Hogansville, about 35 miles from Pine Mountain. People have been known to come from all over, including Atlanta and Alabama, to enjoy the food. The changing menu features northern Italian cuisine, with specials like all-you-can-eat spaghetti night. Rumor has it the chef was transplanted from a New York restaurant. The floors are buckled, and the bathroom is ancient—a classic dive with food to die for. Cash only. Call 706-637-4953.

JUST FOR KIDS ....

The **Springer Opera House**, at 103 Tenth Street, has children's shows during the year. Call 706-327-3688.

SIDE TRIPS ....

Lumpkin is about 25 miles south of Columbus on U.S. 27. There, visitors should see **Westville Village**, which has been restored to look like 1850 and features exhibits, buildings, and demonstrations by costumed interpreters showing skills of that time (e.g., candlemaking, pottery, blacksmithing). Open Tuesday through Sunday; closed early January. Admission is charged. Call 912-838-6310. There's also a driving tour of the city, marked with stagecoach signs, featuring twenty-three houses built before 1850 (brochures are distributed at the Bedingfield Inn in the town square). In the square on Main Street is **Dr. Hatchett's Drug Store Museum**, with artifacts and a working soda fountain/ice cream parlor.

Seven miles west of Lumpkin on GA 39C, you'll find Georgia's smaller answer to the Grand Canyon, the 150-acre **Providence Canyon State Conser-**

vation Park. Check out the beautiful wildflowers there. Camping is permitted in designated areas. For hours and fees, call 912-838-6310.

Warm Springs, located 10 miles from Pine Mountain, is another quaint town in the region. A popular tourist site here is the **Little White House** where Franklin D. Roosevelt died in 1945 (the only house he ever owned), and the **FDR Museum and Theater**. The sites are located on Alternate GA 85 in Warm Springs and are open daily. Admission is charged. Call 706-655-5870. **Warm Springs Village** has over 60 shops and restaurants in restored nineteenth-century buildings. **The Antiques and Crafts Unlimited Mall**, 2 miles north of Warm Springs on Alt. GA 27, hosts two annual festivals in April and November. Call 706-655-2468. **The Victorian Tea Room** on Broad Street serves a lovely southern-style luncheon buffet and à la carte items. Open daily. Call 706-655-2319.

GENERAL INFORMATION ....

For more information on this area, contact the Columbus Convention and Visitors Bureau at 706-322-1613 or 800-999-1613. They'll send you a copy of their visitors guide and a brochure on Callaway Gardens. There's a twenty-four-hour visitors hotline at 706-322-3181 (accessible locally via 1610 AM radio). For information on Warm Springs, contact the Warm Springs Welcome Center at 800-FDR-1927.

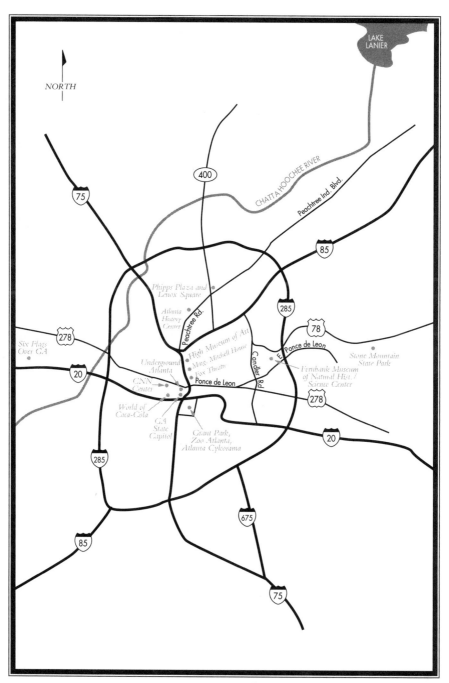

ATLANTA and STONE MOUNTAIN, GA.

Atlanta and Stone Mountain

AREA CODES:

404 (ATLANTA)

770 (STONE MOUNTAIN)

INTRODUCTION ....

Atlanta is a sleek, skyscraper-filled metropolis that bustles with traffic and an interesting mix of people. Though her citizens are from varying backgrounds, the city is united in civic pride, as evidenced during festivals, Atlanta Braves baseball games, and the preparations and festivities that surrounded the 1996 summer Olympics. The city's citizens are also renowned for their southern hospitality, which endures today throughout its streets, restaurants, shops, and elsewhere. Unlike other urban areas, Atlantans are usually friendly, even toward strangers. The city has a modern feel, but there are still many preserved historic sites scattered throughout the city.

The beginnings of this sprawling urban center were surprisingly humble. The city's original 1837 name was simply "Terminus," referring to its location at the end of a railroad line linking Georgia with Tennessee. Atlanta was still a young city when it was nearly destroyed by General Sherman's Union army during the Civil War (much like the depiction in *Gone With the Wind*), which explains why an early nineteenth-century city has mostly twentieth-century architecture.

Aside from its railroad and wartime history, Atlanta is a city of invention, both social and commercial. It was where Dr. Martin Luther King, Jr., leader of the non-violent Civil Rights Movement, was born, raised and buried; and it is where the first Coca-Cola was served (for medicinal purposes) in a city pharmacy.

Atlanta has a rich golf heritage with a wide array of spectacular courses, from older courses to some of the best new courses in the United States (although playing golf naturally requires some travel south or north of the downtown area). Atlanta is also the birthplace and burial place of one of golf's greatest heros: Bobby Jones. Aside from Atlanta's spectacular daily fee courses, nearby Stone Mountain also has great golf, as well as other recreational facilities that attract over 6 million visitors annually (See Side Trips and Golf Information). Thus, while the city is exciting and dynamic, the golf courses in the rural and suburban locations offer refreshing scenery and a quiet respite. In addition, Atlanta is a convenient distance from more golf and recreational opportunities at Lake Lanier Islands and at Callaway Gardens, near Columbus. (See the Callaway Gardens and Columbus chapter and the Lake Lanier Islands chapter.)

Atlanta's normal monthly temperatures are: January, 41; February, 44.8; March, 53.5; April, 61.5; May, 69.2; June, 76; July, 78.8; August, 78.1; September,

72.7; October, 62.3; November, 53.1; December, 44.5. The city draws visitors steadily throughout the year, but perhaps more so during spring and the Christmas season.

GOLF INFORMATION ....

ST. MARLO GOLF CLUB, DULUTH (770) 495-7725

Completed in 1995, St. Marlo was ranked as one of the top ten best new public courses by *Golf Digest*. Possessing a fair amount of landscaping, the course, which winds through 800 rolling, forested acres, features lovely ponds, brooks, and waterfalls. Designed by Denis Griffiths, this par 72 course is 6908 yards from the tips (6620 from the white tees, 6109 from the gold tees, and 5071 from the red tees). Griffiths, who lives close to St. Marlo, has designed and renovated, either by himself or with his mentor, Ron Kirby, many courses in the United States (mostly in Georgia) and throughout the world (including courses in Japan and Africa). His Pole Creek Golf Club in Winter Park, Colorado, was selected by *Golf Digest* as the best new public course of 1994.

Carts: Not required. *Greens Fees:* $58 weekday, $70 weekends/18 holes. *Tee Time Policy:* Can be reserved four days in advance.

WHITE COLUMNS GOLF CLUB, ALPHARETTA (770) 343-9021

Completed at the end of 1994, White Columns is Tom Fazio's first daily-fee course in Georgia. Like his other recently opened layouts, White Columns has been praised by the major golf publications. In its December

1995 issue, *Golf Digest* rated White Columns among the best new public courses in America, while *Golf* concurred in its February 1995 issue, calling White Columns one of the "Top Ten You Can Play." The course, set in the Crabapple area of North Fulton County, gently winds over 250 rolling acres, through towering pines and dogwoods, and around and over shimmering lakes and babbling brooks. The tees are rectangular, the Bermuda fairways are wide open, and the massive greens feature Crenshaw grass (the cutting edge in grass). As is true for all Fazio designs, there is great variety from hole to hole (the par 3s range from 169 to 230 yards, the par 4s from 350 to 460 yards, and the par 5s from just over 500 to almost 600 yards), and everyone can play and enjoy the course without feeling overwhelmed or roughed up. Good scoring, however, requires accurate, well-measured approaches and solid putting.

Carts: Not required. *Greens Fees:* $75 weekday, $90 weekend/ 18 holes. *Tee Time Policy:* Requested, not required; can be reserved five days in advance.

STONE MOUNTAIN PARK GOLF COURSE, STONE MOUNTAIN (770) 498-5715

In the shadows of the magnificent Stone Mountain lie two courses featuring a combination of designs by Robert Trent Jones, Sr., and John LaFoy. Stonemont is a 6683-yard, par 72 course, with holes one through five and fifteen through eighteen designed by Jones. It's not hard to spot the Jones holes, as the par 4s are all over 400 yards, with the exception being the devilish second, a 289-yard dogleg. The par 3 fifteenth, which reaches 230 yards, plays

to a classic Jones green—a narrow opening with all of the trouble around the front, while the smart shot is to the wide-open back of the green. The Lakemont-Woodmont course is a par 72 course that ranges from 5200 to almost 6600 yards. The front nine was designed by LaFoy, the back nine by Jones. Once again, it's easy to tell the Jones nine. It's a stern test, with all the par 4s over 400 yards except one, while the par 5s are shortish and invite low scores. A great hole is the 188-yard, par 3 sixteenth. It plays to a wide shallow green with Stone Mountain providing a spectacular backdrop.

Carts: Mandatory. *Greens Fees:* $40/ 18 holes, including cart. *Tee Time Policy:* Required in peak seasons. Guests in Stone Mountain get preferred tee times. Call one week ahead for weekdays; on weekends, call the Tuesday before at 7:30 A.M. Prepayment may be required.

COBBLESTONE GOLF COURSE (FORMERLY THE BOULDERS COURSE AT LAKE ACWORTH), ABOUT 25 MILES NORTH OF ATLANTA (770) 917-5151

On the banks of Lake Acworth, this Ken Dye (not related to Pete Dye) design combines lovely surroundings with a challenging layout. Considered among the top ten courses in Georgia by *Golf Digest*, this course offers tees that range from 5345 to 6830 yards and a rating/slope ranging from 68.7/123 to 73.1/140. Water comes into play on more than half the holes and makes things really interesting (scary) on four of Cobblestone's five par 3s. The 210-yard third plays along a lake that wraps around the right and back sides of the

Downtown Atlanta
Photo courtesy of Atlanta Convention and Visitors Bureau

green. The green on the 155-yard fifth sits right on the shore of another lake, while the 215-yard thirteenth requires traversing yet another lake. Finally, the 140-yard sixteenth has water running from behind the tee, along the left, and then behind the green.

Carts: Required Friday-Sunday and holidays. *Greens Fees:* Monday-Thursday $52, Friday-Sunday $59/18 holes, including cart. *Tee Time Policy:* Can be reserved four days in advance.

ATTRACTIONS ....

TOURS

Antiquity Tours of the Old South, at 30 Temple Avenue in Newnan, offers themed, personally guided tours that emphasize historic sites like homes, Civil War sites, or plantations. Call 770-251-6343. For guided, half-day, motorized tours of popular sites, try **Capital City Coach Lines, Inc.**, at 933-F Lee Street. Call 404-765-0500. For sightseeing half- and full-day trips within and around Atlanta, try **Capital City Excursions**, at 37 West Wieuca Road (call 770-954-7106), or **Gray Line Tours of Atlanta**, at 3745 Zip Industrial Boulevard (call 404-767-0594).

HISTORIC PLACES

The State Capitol, on Capitol Hill at Washington Street, with its gold-topped dome looming 237 feet above the street, features a hall of flags and hall of fame with busts of eminent

Georgians. The capitol also contains the **Georgia State Museum of Science and Industry**, whose collection includes Civil War and state flags, minerals, Indian relics, wildlife exhibits, and exhibits on famous Georgia sites. Open weekdays. Admission is free. Call 404-656-2844.

The Greek Revival–style **Governor's Mansion**, at 391 West Paces Ferry Road, is open to visitors Tuesday through Thursday from 10 to 11:30 A.M. Admission is free. Call 404-261-1776.

Wren's Nest, at 1050 Ralph D. Abernathy Boulevard SW, is the Victorian home of journalist and author Joel Chandler Harris, who wrote the popular "Uncle Remus" stories. Aside from its interesting memorabilia, the house itself has an eccentric feel and features guided tours and special storytelling programs. Admission is charged. Call 404-753-8535.

The World of Coca-Cola, at 55 Martin Luther King, Jr., Drive, is a fun tour on the world's most popular soft drink, featuring its past, present, and future. Exhibits tell about the famous drink's invention and manufacturing. There are also displays on the famous radio, television, and poster ads through the years. Incredible soda fountains are on display, and you can sample foreign beverages not for sale in the United States. Allow at least an hour for a self-guided tour. Open daily. Admission is charged. Call 404-676-5151.

The Fox Theater (the "Fabulous Fox"), at 660 Peachtree Street NE, is named after movie-mogul William Fox, who turned this Shriners Temple into a theater in 1929. Within its ornate walls are art deco, Moorish, and Egyptian detailing, as well as ballrooms and the world's largest Moller organ console. The theater still has shows and events. Tours run Monday, Thursday, and Saturday; call for hours. Charge for tours. Call 404-881-2100.

Oakland Cemetery, at 248 Oakland Avenue SE, was established in 1850 and is the burial place of Confederate and Union soldiers, politicians, golfer Bobby Jones, and the Pulitzer Prize–winning author of *Gone with the Wind*, Margaret Mitchell. A visitors center provides information. Open daily. Admission is free. Call 404-658-6019.

Kennesaw Mountain National Battlefield Park, 3 miles west of Marietta off I-75 or U.S. 41, is the site of a major battle fought during Union General Sherman's march toward Atlanta in 1864. There's a visitors center with an orientation film and exhibits. Open daily. Donation suggested. Call 770-427-4686.

Fort McPherson, located 3 miles southwest of Atlanta on Lee Street (off I-75), features guided tours of this 1889 fort. Admission is free. For information, call 404-752-3113.

MUSEUMS/SCIENCE CENTERS

Atlanta Heritage Row, at 55 Upper Alabama Street in Underground Atlanta, is a modern museum where visitors can interact with history via walk-through exhibits and audio and video recordings. There's also a collection of photographs and memorabilia. Admission is charged. Call 404-584-7879.

High Museum of Art, in the Woodruff Arts Center at 1280 Peachtree Street NE, has a large collection of European and American works of art dating from the fourteenth century to the nineteenth century. There are also decorative arts, photos, and prints on display, and a children's gallery. Admission is charged. Call 404-733-4400.

Cyclorama, at 800 Cherokee Avenue (in Grant Park) next to Zoo Atlanta off I-20, is a 42-foot-tall, 356-foot-circumference painting with lighting and sound effects creating a realistic portrayal of the Battle of Atlanta—one of only three such works in the United States. The painting is over a hundred years old. Open daily. Admission is charged. Call 404-624-1071.

The CNN Studio, at One CNN Center, offers tours of the worldwide cable news channel, including the CNN, Headline News, and CNN International news-networks studios. As the channel's owner, Ted Turner, also owns the Atlanta Braves, so it's not surprising to see souvenir shops here for both the Braves and CNN. Other shops, restaurants, an Omni hotel, and six theaters (including one that shows *Gone With the Wind* twice daily) are also located in the complex. Studio tours run daily. Admission is charged. Call 404-827-2491 or 404-827-2300.

Atlanta History Center, at 130 West Paces Ferry Road, has changing displays covering the many facets of Atlanta's past, including the Civil War, the life of Dr. Martin Luther King, Jr., the history of *Gone with the Wind*, and the creation of Coca-Cola. Aside from the history center, you can tour two historic houses (the 1840s plantation house, known as Tullie Smith Farm, and the lovely 1928 Swan House). Open weekends only. Admission is charged. Call 404-814-4000.

Jimmy Carter Presidential Library and Museum, at 1 Copenhill Road, explores the professional and personal life of the former United States president. Among the exhibits are a replica of the Oval Office and an interactive video display in which you can choose how to respond to certain crises. There are also gifts received from admirers during his presidency. Open weekdays and Sunday. Admission is charged. Call 404-331-0296.

Fernbank, at 767 Clifton Road, is an educational and environmental complex containing a museum of natural history, which shows theories of how life evolved on earth and offers light and sound exhibits. Call 404-370-0960. There's also a museum on the five senses and an IMAX virtual-reality video theater. The science center at the complex has a spectacular planetarium, a 65-acre forest with walking trails, and an observatory. Call 404-378-4311. Admission

The Fox Theatre, Atlanta
Photo by Kevin C. Rose,
courtesy of Atlanta Convention and Visitors Bureau

charged for certain attractions; call for fees. Open daily. The main number for the complex is 404-378-0127.

SciTrek, the Science and Technology Museum of Atlanta, at 395 Piedmont Avenue, has over a hundred interactive exhibits designed for all ages and has been called one of the best science museums in the United States. Open daily. Admission is charged. Call 404-522-5500.

Michael C. Carlos Museum, at 571 South Kilgo Street on the grounds of Emory University, is a collection of ancient arts from the Mediterranean, North America, and South America. Highlights include an Egyptian mummy, Greek statues, and pre-Columbian pottery. Open daily. Donation suggested. Call 404-727-4282.

CULTURAL OFFERINGS

The Woodruff Arts Center, at 1280 Peachtree Street NE, is comprised of several quality fine arts companies: the Alliance Theater Company (call 404-733-5000); the Atlanta College of Art; the Atlanta Opera, which performs from spring through autumn at Symphony Hall (call 404-355-3311); and the Atlanta City Ballet, which performs at the Civic Center Auditorium at 395 Piedmont Avenue. For information on the Woodruff Arts Center, call 404-873-2414. Also affiliated with the Woodruff Arts Center is the Grammy award–winning **Atlanta Symphony**, at 1292 Peachtree Street Northeast, which has a champagne-and-coffee series, the Master Season series, a family series, and a summer series. Call 404-892-2414 for ticket information.

A variety of professional performances and concerts take place at the

Rialto Theater, at 80 Forsyth Street (call 404-651-1234), the **Atlanta Civic Center** (call 404-523-6275), and the **Fox Theater** (including the annual Theater of the Stars at the Fox, which presents Broadway musicals between June and August. For information on Theater of the Stars, call 404-252-8960; for general information call 404-881-2100).

RECREATION

Atlanta Botanical Garden, on Piedmont Avenue at the Prado, offers a great chance to view some rare plants from exotic habitats like deserts and tropical forests. There are also plenty of plants native to Georgia and the United States. Open Tuesday through Sunday. Admission is charged. Call 404-876-5859.

Zoo Atlanta, at 800 Cherokee Avenue at Grant Park, is one of the finest zoos in the United States. It has natural habitat exhibits with animals from the Americas, Africa, Asia, and other areas, including lions, giraffes, elephants, and more. Open daily. Admission is charged. Call 404-624-5678 or 404-624-5600.

Six Flags Over Georgia, at 7561 Six Flags Road off I-20 in Mableton, is a 331-acre theme park built in 1967 as part of the Six Flags franchise, with entertainment, games, and over a hundred rides. Open daily in summer, weekends spring and fall. Admission is charged. Call 770-948-9290.

White Water Park, at 250 North Marietta Parkway in Marietta, has more than 40 acres of water rides and attractions for all ages and levels of courage. Rides have themes like the Bahama Bobslide and the Atlanta Ocean. Open daily Memorial Day through Labor Day. Admission is charged. Call 770-424-WAVE.

Chattahoochee Nature Center, at 9135 Willeo Road in Roswell, is a nature preserve encompassing more than 100 acres, with wildlife, ponds, and salt marshes that can be viewed from nature trails and raised wooden boardwalks. Admission is charged. Open daily. Call 770-992-2055.

Yellow River Wildlife Game Ranch, at 4525 U.S. 78 in Lilburn, is a 24-acre preserve for native creatures of Georgia, from the ordinary to the rare. Visitors can pet and feed the animals, and photos are permitted. Open daily. Admission is charged. Call 770-972-6643.

Atlanta is a professional sports fan's dream city, with pro football, baseball, and basketball teams. **Atlanta Braves** baseball (an especially hot team now that they won the 1995 World Series and were National League winners in 1991 and '92) is played at the Olympic Stadium. For tickets, call Ticketmaster at 404-249-6400 or 800-326-4000; for information, call 404-522-7630. The **Atlanta Falcons'** football games are played in the Georgia Dome, where the 1994 Super Bowl was played and the 1996 Olympic gymnastics competitions took place. For ticket information, call 404-223-8000. The **Atlanta Hawks** play basketball at the Omni Coliseum. For ticket information, call 404-827-3800.

Atlanta Motor Speedway is located 20 miles south of Atlanta in Hampton; take Exit 77 off I-75. Guided tours are conducted daily. Call 770-946-4211 for tickets; call 770-707-7970 for tours.

SEASONAL EVENTS

The Atlanta Flower Show takes place over four days in February, around Valentine's Day. In March, there's the annual **St. Patrick's Day parade**, which rivals New York's. April brings an **Antebellum Jubilee** to Stone Mountain Park. In Atlanta, April brings the annual, week-long **Dogwood Festival** and the world-famous **Atlanta Steeplechase** at Seven Branches Farm in nearby Cumming. In May, **Springfest** takes place at Stone Mountain Park, and the BellSouth Golf Classic takes place in nearby Marietta; in June, the **Atlanta Jazz Series** and the **Arts and Crafts Festival** are held at Stone Mountain Park. A plethora of special events are held throughout the Atlanta area during Fourth of July weekend. In September is the **Georgia Music Festival**, the **Atlanta Arts Festival** (one of the oldest and largest in the United States), and the **Folklife Festival** (which showcases nineteenth century daily life). November brings the **Veteran's Day Parade** and the **Lighting of the Great Tree** at Underground Atlanta. In December, numerous Christmas and Kwanzaa events are held throughout the city.

The Georgia Renaissance Festival takes place in Fairburn, about 15 miles south of Atlanta. The festival includes demonstrations, entertainment, foods, crafts, and games from sixteenth-century England. It runs weekends from late April through mid-June. Call 404-964-8575.

For more information about these and the many other events throughout the area, including admission fees, call the Atlanta Convention and Visitors Bureau at 404-222-6688.

World of Coca-Cola museum, Atlanta
Photo by Kevin C. Rose, courtesy of Atlanta Convention and Visitors Bureau

ACCOMMODATIONS ....

EXPENSIVE

Atlanta Hilton and Towers, located downtown at 255 Courtland Street NE, is centered around a brass-and-glass atrium with glass-enclosed elevators. There's a pool with poolside service, extensive exercise facilities, and an executive level. Call 404-659-2000.

There are two Ritz-Carltons in the city; the **Ritz-Carlton Atlanta Downtown** (call 404-659-6400), at 181 Peachtree Street NE, and the **Ritz-Carlton Buckhead** (call 404-237-2700), at 3434 Peachtree Road NE. Both offer four-star accommodations, fine dining facilities, concierge and va-let services, tennis, health club and golf privileges, refrigerators, mini-bars, and a luxury level.

MODERATE TO EXPENSIVE

Evergreen Conference Center, at 1 Lakeview Drive in Stone Mountain Park (See Side Trips), is an all-inclusive resort with some of the country's best golf and tennis facilities, pools, horse stables, boating, hiking, and health spa, all in a beautifully scenic rural setting. Call 404-879-9900 or 800-722-1000.

Westin Peachtree Plaza, at 210 Peachtree Street, is a deluxe hotel located downtown. The rooms are centered around an eight-story atrium, and the hotel has four restaurants, a revolving rooftop bar, concierge service, shopping arcade, health facilities, pool, and a luxury level. Call 404-659-1400.

Holiday Inn Express/Downtown Stadium, at 795 Washington Street NW, has eighty-four comfortable, though modestly furnished, rooms at reasonable rates for downtown. Call 404-658-1610 or 800-341-4343.

Biltmore Inn and Suites, at 30 Fifth Street NE, is located midtown. This elegant Georgian-style hotel features high ceilings and skylights. Guests enjoy free breakfast, a health club, and in-room wet bars and whirlpools. Call 404-874-0824.

MODERATE/INEXPENSIVE

Travelodge/Midtown, at 1641 Peachtree Street NE, is a good choice for families. This three-story motel has a pool. Call 404-873-5731 or 800-225-3050.

The Quality Inn Northeast, located at 2960 Northeast Expressway, north of Atlanta's dowtown area along I-85, has inexpensive rates, including special family rates. Guests enjoy free breakfast and a pool. Call 404-451-5231.

Comfort Inn has a motel in the Buckhead section at 2115 Piedmont Road NE (call 404-876-4444 or 800-876-4444), and in the downtown section at 101 International Boulevard (call 404-524-5555). Each offers moderate to inexpensive rates and has pools and whirlpools, health club privileges, and restaurants.

SHOPPING ....

Specialized tours of the city, which is a shopper's paradise, are available from

A through Z Transportation. Call 404-559-8405.

Buckhead Village, where Peachtree, Roswell, and Paces Ferry Roads meet, with its collection of unique specialty shops, clubs, restaurants, is a center for nightlife and shopping.

Underground Atlanta is where the original milepost (zero) of the Western & Atlantic Railroad was placed in 1837, marking the beginning of the city. The area (bounded by Wall, Central, and Peachtree Streets and Martin Luther King, Jr. Drive) had fallen into disrepair when a group of entrepreneurs decided to restore it. Today, it's a not-to-be-missed dining-and-entertainment complex, much of it actually underground, encompassing four blocks in the heart of downtown.

Two upscale malls in the city are the enclosed **Lenox Square Mall** in Buckhead, at 3393 Peachtree Road NE at Lenox Road, with well over a hundred stores (call 404-233-6767); and **Phipps Plaza**, diagonally across from Lenox Square, with stores like Saks Fifth Avenue and Tiffany & Company.

The state-operated **Atlanta State Farmers' Market** is among the largest produce markets in the southeastern United States. Located 10 miles south of Atlanta on I-75. Open twenty-four hours, seven days a week. Call 404-366-6910.

RESTAURANTS ....

Atlanta is a gourmand's delight, with a number of world-class restaurants and top chefs. The following is a mere sampling of what the city has to offer.

DINNER THEATER

Mystery fans will enjoy the dinner theater shows at **Agatha's**, 693 Peachtree Street NE. Call 404-875-1610.

FINE DINING

For authentic southern food, head to **The Horseradish Grill** (whose chef once cooked for the governor), at 4320 Powers Ferry Road. You can order such satisfying delights as tender, southern fried chicken with a crackling skin, as well as pork chops, fried catfish, shrimp paste with grits, melt-in-your-mouth biscuits, lemon chess pie, and apple-cider ice cream. Call 404-255-7277.

The Abbey, at 163 Ponce de Leon Avenue at Piedmont Road in midtown Atlanta, is a converted church with stained-glass windows and a 50-foot arched ceiling. The award-winning cuisine is served in candlelight by waiters dressed as monks. Special dishes are veal, venison, chicken, and seafood (especially the mahimahi). Open for dinner. Reservations recommended. Call 404-876-8831.

Hsu's, at 192 Peachtree Center Avenue in downtown Atlanta, is a terrific Chinese restaurant with Peking Duck and other gourmet Chinese specialties. Open Monday through Saturday for lunch and dinner, and Sunday for dinner only. Call 404-659-2788.

Nikolai's Roof, at 255 Courtland Street in the Hilton and Towers Hotel, offers a prix fixe dinner selected from a changing menu with Russian- and French-influenced continental selections. Reservations recommended. Open daily for dinner. Jacket and tie required. Call 404-659-2000.

CASUAL DINING

Mick's, at 557 Peachtree Street (although there are five other Mick's in Atlanta), is a 1950s-style restaurant with high stools at a counter, leather booths, and a bright tile floor. The all-American menu has basics like meatloaf, chicken pot pie, cherry coke, strawberry shortcake, and several ice cream desserts. There are also some cosmopolitan offerings like linguine and grilled pork chops. Open daily for lunch and dinner. Call 404-875-6425.

Winfield's, located north of downtown at 1 Galleria Parkway, has delicious hickory-grilled meat, poultry, and seafood dishes. There's live piano music Tuesday through Saturdays during dinner. Open daily for lunch and dinner; brunch is served on Sunday. Call 404-955-5300.

The Pleasant Peasant, at 555 Peachtree Street NW, has a quaint decor, as it was once a Victorian ice cream parlor. This popular, cozy restaurant, decked with antiques and plants, has impeccable service and a creative menu that includes dishes like Oriental plum pork and Calypso grouper. Serves dinner daily; lunch weekdays. Call 404-874-3223.

Mary Mac's Tea Room, 224 Ponce de Leone Avenue, is a family-owned restaurant with efficient service and southern hospitality, including southern-style dishes like fried chicken and ham. Open weekdays for lunch and dinner. Call 404-876-1800.

JUST FOR KIDS ....

American Adventures, at 250 North Cobb Parkway in Marietta, is a children's amusement park with rides, miniature-golf, indoor playground, carousel, imagination station, entertainment, arcades, and go-carts. Call 770-424-9283.

Center for Puppetry Arts, at 1404 Spring Street, gives children's performances throughout the year. There's also a museum about puppets. Call 404-873-3089.

Other attractions with kid-appeal are Zoo Atlanta, the Yellow River Game Ranch (where kids can feed and pet animals), White Water Park, and the High Museum's gallery for kids.

SIDE TRIPS ....

Located 20 miles east of downtown Atlanta off U.S. 78, **Stone Mountain Park** features Stone Mountain, a magnificent, 825-foot granite formation protruding out of the piedmont. Aside from the mountain itself, the park also offers over 3200 scenic acres with a 383-acre lake. The Confederate war figures (Robert E. Lee, Stonewall Jackson, and Jefferson Davis) carved in stone on the side of the mountain are an awesome artistic feat, and they can be viewed up close via a skyride. The park attracts the third largest number of tourists per year in the United States (about 6 million), after Disney World and Disneyland, respectively. There's also a terrific golf course here (See Golf Information). Other park attractions in-

Atlanta Botanical Gardens
Photo courtesy of Atlanta Convention and Visitors Bureau

clude a bell tower, riverboat cruises, nature trails, an antique car and music museum, a lakefront beach, and a Civil War museum and memorial hall with exhibits on the mountain's history. From summer to mid-autumn, there's an amazing laser-light show projected onto the mountain. Fees charged for various attractions. There's also a hotel (See Accommodations) and camping facilities are available by reservation. Open daily. For information, call 770-498-5702.

GENERAL INFORMATION ....

Contact the Atlanta Convention and Visitors Bureau at 404-222-6688. Ask them for a copy of *Reserve Atlanta Now* and a current seasonal guide and calendar of events. Welcome Centers are located at Underground Atlanta, Peachtree Center Mall, and Lenox Square Mall.

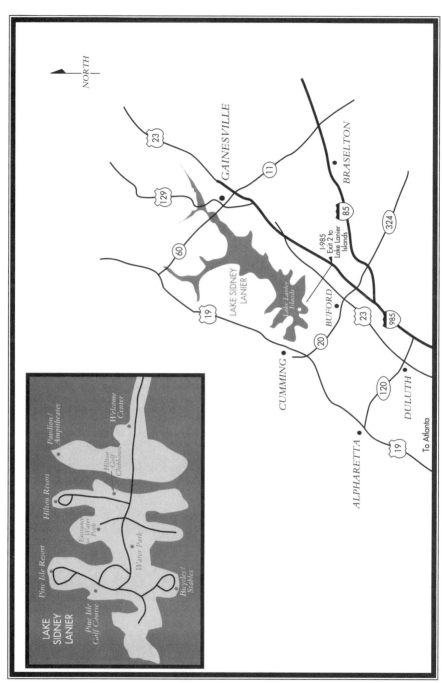

LAKE LANIER ISLANDS and VICINITY, GA.

Lake Lanier Islands and vicinity

INTRODUCTION ....

The Lake Lanier Islands Resort is a fortunate accident. In 1957, when the Army Corps of Engineers built Buford Dam to hold back the Chattahoochee River, the resulting lake, Lake Lanier, did not engulf the hills as expected, and the remaining islands became a perfect vacation spot. Actually, the mainland shores of the lake have additional beaches and campsites, but the islands covered in detail here are the home of two excellent championship golf courses. Both courses are affiliated with a deluxe resort hotel, and thus draw more of a golf crowd than do the lake's shores to the north, which attract an RV/outdoorsman crowd interested mainly in fishing, camping, and the like.

Lake Lanier was named after Georgia poet Sidney Lanier, who wrote the famous "Song of the Chattahoochee." This area, only about 45 miles northeast of Atlanta's city limits (reachable from I-85, or from the west by GA 400), is nicknamed "Atlanta's Beach." Since the lake hosted the 1996 Olympic rowing and sprint-canoe kayak competitions (and thousands of spectators camped here), it's now known internationally. Visitors to the islands should note there's a daily parking fee at the resort entrance.

For golfers traveling with kids, a trip to the Bavarian fantasy town of Helen is a must (See Side Trips and Golf Information). Couples should consider a side trip or overnight stay at Braselton's Chateau Elan, a gorgeous resort hotel with a famous winery, fine French restaurant, spa, and world-class golf (See Golf Information). And those who appreciate nineteenth-century architecture will enjoy a trip to the historic district of Gainesville, located on the northeastern edge of Lake Lanier.

The normal monthly temperatures for this area, as measured in Gainesville are: January, 38.9; February, 42.5; March, 50.7; April, 59.2; May, 66.1; June, 73; July, 76.5; August, 75.8; September, 70; October, 59.5; November, 51.2; December, 42.5. The most popular months are summer through autumn, since the lake offers a cool respite for city dwellers in summer, and during autumn, the leaves change colors.

GOLF INFORMATION ....

LAKE LANIER ISLANDS HILTON, LAKE LANIER (770) 945-8787

Lake Lanier Islands Hilton Golf Club, opened in 1988 and designed by architect Joe Lee, masterfully incorporates the beautiful lake into the course. Short by modern standards at 6341 yards (tees begin at 4935 yards), this course requires patient, accurate

shotmaking to score well and to not end up using your fifteenth club (the ball retriever). Starting out immediately on the first hole, a 519-yard par 5, the player needs to avoid the lake, which runs down the entire right side of the fairway and then behind the green. The par 4 second is a sharp dogleg right that stretches to 368 yards. Again, the lake borders the entire right side, and the temptation is to shorten the hole by attempting to carry as much of the lake as possible. On the straight-away, 436-yard, par 4 fifth, the number-one handicap hole, the player must carry the lake from the tee as well as on the approach, because the lake cuts into the fairway in front of the tee and again in front of the green. Measuring only 350 yards, the dogleg left twelfth hole is an interesting little par 4. The lake runs from the tee, down the dogleg, and all the way behind the green. If the player tries to cut off too much of the fairway, the landing area is very narrow and unforgiving. With some patience, the player can use two irons to get a shot at his or her birdie on this hole.

Carts: Mandatory. *Greens Fees:* $39 (1/1-3/31), $50-$55 (4/1-10/31), $45 (11/1-12/31)/18 holes, including cart. *Tee Time Policy:* Call one week in advance; hotel guests can reserve tee times earlier.

RENAISSANCE PINE ISLE RESORT, LAKE LANIER (770) 945-8921

Pine Isle has hosted the Nestle World Championships and is considered one of the best resorts in the United States by *Golf Digest.* Designed in 1974 by Gary Player and Ron Kirby and Associates, Pine Isle is not only challenging (at only 6596 yards from the back tees, its slope is a difficult 132), it is one of the most beautiful and scenic courses you will ever play. With the Blue Ridge Mountains as a backdrop, the course winds through towering Georgia pines and includes eight holes that skirt the hilly shores of Lake Lanier. As is the case with most Gary Player courses, yardage is not the key (the blue tees are only 6214 yards while the whites and reds are 5848 and 5297 yards, respectively). What is important is a player's control of the ball, an ability to hit each club in the bag and to adjust to various lies, and possession of a solid short game. A good example of all these requirements is Pine Isle's signature hole, the 489-yard, par 5 fifth, a dogleg left set along the shores of the lake, which

Chateau Elan Hotel and Winery, Braselton

Photo by Diane Kirkland, courtesy of the GA Department of Industry, Trade and Tourism

runs from the tee to behind the green. The tee shot is played over the lake to a fairway that narrows at 250-300 yards. A drive with a slight draw is the best shot and will leave the golfer with a reasonable shot at the green in two— an approach, however, that must be played over water. If the golfer wishes to lay-up, he or she must check their yardage, because three huge bunkers await any lay-up within 50 yards of the green. The green is deep and double-tiered, so once you're there, two putts is not guaranteed. All in all, the fifth is a classic Player hole.

Carts: Mandatory. *Greens Fees:* $60 weekdays, $65 weekends/18 holes. *Tee Time Policy:* Guests of the resort can make tee times when they make room reservations. Non-guests can call seven days in advance for weekdays, and the Monday before for weekend tee times.

CHICOPEE WOODS GOLF COURSE, GAINESVILLE (770) 536-5779

Chicopee Woods, opened in 1991, is another excellent Georgia course by architect Denis Griffiths. The gently rolling layout ranges in yardage from 5001 to 7040 yards (with a rating/slope ranging from 69/117 to 74/135). The fairways and greens are well bunkered, and water is a factor on three holes. The greens are elevated and covered with state-of-the-art Crenshaw grass. The signature hole, the par 5 eighteenth, plays from an elevated fairway to a green backed by the stately clubhouse. The course record of 66 is shared by former Masters champion and Senior PGA Tour player Tommy Aaron and ex-Nike Tour Player Jason Griffith. The combination of a good layout, consistently quick greens, and great value for your dollar should make your visit to Chicopee Woods quite enjoyable.

Carts: Not required. *Greens Fees:* Approximately $40/18 holes, including cart. *Tee Time Policy:* Call three days in advance at 9 A.M.

CHATEAU ELAN GOLF CLUB, BRASELTON (770) 271-6050

This Denis Griffiths design opened in 1989. Having already hosted local and state PGA events, the course is quickly becoming one of the more popular courses in both the Atlanta area and the state of Georgia. Winding through three lakes and two creeks, set among flower beds, azaleas and dogwoods, and located near the resort's famed French chateau and winery, the course could be described as a poor man's Augusta National. There is a wide assortment of distances one can play from hole to hole (on the par 3 sixteenth there are an amazing eight tee boxes, which range from 115 to 176 yards) on this par 71 course. The yardage ranges from the burgundy tee's 5092 yards to the gold tee's 7030 yards (with a slope that ranges from 119 to a bearish 136). Each hole is named after a type of wine, such as Muscat, Zinfandel, and Riesling. Chambourcin, the 547-yard, par 5 third, is the number-one handicap hole. A stream crosses in front of the tee and then meanders all the way up the left side of the fairway to the green. The hole doglegs left near the green, so the player is tempted to give it a go on the second shot. But watch out, the cloverleaf-shaped, bentgrass green is small and protected by no fewer than six bunkers. Whether or not you go for the green, go for this course while in the area. (Also on the grounds is the private Legends course designed by Gene Sarazen, Sam Snead, and Kathy Whitworth. A third course, the Woodlands, is expected to open in the summer of 1996.)

Carts: Mandatory on weekends. *Greens Fees:* $40-65, depending on season and day of week/18 holes. *Tee Time Policy:* Can be reserved seven days in advance.

OTHER EXCELLENT AREA COURSES:

Innsbruck Resort Golf Club, Helen (706-878-2100), is a 6748-yard par 72, including the par 3 fifteenth, which drops 190 feet from the tee to a green fronted by water. **Cobblestone Golf Course**, Lake Acworth (770-917-5151), is located 35 miles from Lake Lanier (see review in Atlanta chapter).

ATTRACTIONS ....

MUSEUMS/SCIENCE CENTERS

In Duluth, south of Lake Lanier off I-85, is the **Southeastern Railway Museum**, with antique cars and railroad memorabilia. The museum is located at 3699 Buford Highway. Open Saturdays only. Admission is charged. Call 770-476-2013.

CULTURAL OFFERINGS

Wine production in Georgia dates back to the early eighteenth century, and the **Foothill Wineries** near Lake Lanier have revived the old wine making traditions. Golfers should visit the winery at the **Chateau Elan Hotel and Winery**, at 100 Rue Charlemagne in Braselton, since the resort also has world-class golf (See Golf Information

Bavarian alpine village, Helen
Photo courtesy of Tourist Division, GA Department of
Industry and Trade

and Accommodations). Admission to the winery is free. Call 800-233-WINE (9463). Also in Braselton is the **Chestnut Mountain Winery**, off Exit 48 on I-85, which is located on 30 acres that include hiking trails and an observation tower. Call 770-867-6914. In Baldwin, the **Habersham Winery** on GA 365 produces a popular muscadine wine and sells other local food products. Admission is free. Call 706-778-9463.

From April through November, **Lanierland Country Music Park** presents country music concerts. The park is located on Jot 'Em Down Road, off GA 400 near Cumming. For information, call 770-887-7464.

RECREATION

The Lake Lanier Islands Resort has tennis courts, beaches, boat rentals, fishing, camping, and Georgia's largest water park. The resort has been run by the state, but is in the process of being taken over by a private company (the lake itself is maintained by the Army Corps of Engineers). You don't need to stay at one of the resort's hotels to take advantage of its recreational facilities,

but there is an entry fee to the islands. For more information, call 770-932-7200.

For boat rental information (including houseboats), call 770-932-7255. Boat owners have easy access to the lake through its eleven marinas and fifty-five boat launching lanes with parking areas. **Lake Lanier Islands Beach and Water Park**, inside the Lake Lanier Islands Resort, has water rides for all ages and levels of bravery, from calmer activities such as a kiddie lagoon, a beach, miniature golf, and wave pool, to those like the Intimidator (a slide that takes you up to thirty mph) and Blackout (where you shoot on a raft into total darkness). Open daily Memorial Day through Labor Day; weekends in September and May. Admission is charged, in addition to a parking fee at entrance gate to the islands. If you have questions on recreation in or around the water park, call Lake Lanier Islands at 770-932-7200.

For trail rides or pony rides, contact the **Lake Lanier Islands Stables** at 770-932-7233. For bicycle rentals, call 770-932-7233.

For those who want to venture north to Lake Lanier (as opposed to the Lake Lanier Islands Resort), the resource manager's office will give you a listing of fees and a map, which designates where fishing, boating, water-skiing, camping, and other activities are permitted. Advance reservations are recommended for camping and boating or other equipment rentals. For camping information and reservations, call the United States Army Corps of Engineers Resource Management Office at 770-945-9531.

Car races are held at **Road Atlanta**,

at 5300 Winder Highway off GA 53. Call 770-967-6143. A NASCAR-sanctioned Winston racing series takes place at **Lanier Raceway** on GA 53 East. Admission is charged. Call 770-967-2131.

In April, the **Atlanta Steeplechase** brings throngs of spectators to Cumming, located off GA 400 between Lake Lanier Islands and Atlanta. Admission is charged. For dates and information, call 770-887-6461.

Fourth of July weekend brings special events and fireworks over the water at the Lake Lanier Islands Resort. For information on this and other special events, contact the resort at 770-932-7200.

From November through December, the Lake Lanier Islands Resort is aglow with its spectacular holiday light display, **Magical Nights of Lights**. For more information, call the resort at 770-932-7200.

ACCOMMODATIONS ....

EXPENSIVE

Renaissance Pine Isle Resort, at 9000 Holiday Road, is a four-star lakefront resort hotel inside the Lake Lanier Islands Resort. Deluxe rooms have beautiful views, and guests enjoy golf, an outdoor hot tub, a private beach, an exercise room, seven tennis courts, a concierge, and an activities department for adults and children. Call 770-945-8921.

The Lake Lanier Islands Hilton

Lake Lanier Islands
Photo coutesy of Atlanta Convention and Visitors Bureau

Resort, at 7000 Holiday Road, is Lake Lanier Islands Resort's other luxury hotel and has rooms with either a lake or forest view. The hotel provides guests with a golf course, tennis courts, a health club equipped with a whirlpool and sauna, a pool, concierge, hot tub, and other amenities. Call 770-945-8787.

Chateau Elan, at 100 Rue Charlemagne in Braselton, is a French-style chateau hotel with a winery, world-class golf, spa, and beautiful scenery, which makes for a perfect romantic getaway or day-trip. Call 800-233-9463.

MODERATE/EXPENSIVE

The Dunlap House, at 635 Green Street in Gainesville, is a restored 1910 inn located in the city's historic district. Guests enjoy a leisurely breakfast and evening refreshments on the inn's veranda, and the rooms are decorated with reproduced period furnishings. Call 770-536-0200.

INEXPENSIVE

Holiday Inn, at 726 Jesse Jewel Parkway in Gainesville, has reasonable rates and allows pets in the rooms. Tennis courts, a pool, and a babysitting service are available. Call 770-536-4451.

SHOPPING ....

At the beach and water park, there's a souvenir and beachwear shop called **Breakers**.

RESTAURANTS ....

FINE DINING

Le Clos at Chateau Elan, at 100 Rue Charlemagne in Braselton, serves a gourmet prix fixe menu which includes fine wines made on the premises. Call 770-932-0900.

Sylvan's on Lake Lanier Islands at the Hilton, 7000 Holiday Road, is a romantic restaurant overlooking the lake that serves continental-style seafood, steaks, and more. Reservations recommended. Call 770-945-8787.

The Grille Room at the Renaissance Pine Isle Resort, 9000 Holiday Road, is an intimate dining experience, probably best enjoyed without the kids. Reservations suggested. Call 770-945-8921.

CASUAL DINING

At the Renaissance Pine Isle Resort, breakfast, lunch, and dinner are served daily at the **Gazebo** and the **Clubhouse**. Both have a wide variety of American continental selections. Call 770-945-8921.

The Lake Lanier Islands Hilton Resort has a poolside bar-and-deli serving sandwiches and other quick fare.

At the beach and water park, there are two restaurants and a snack shop: **The Island Grill** serves fare like hickory-smoked barbecued pork, chicken, hamburgers, and hot dogs. **The Beachside Cafe,** which serves hot dogs, hamburgers, pizza, and chicken sandwiches, has an arcade for the kids. Finally, **WILDWAVES Refresher** serves cool snacks for hot people, like ice cream, frozen yogurt, and frozen drinks.

JUST FOR KIDS ....

Organized children's activities are available at the **Lake Lanier Islands Hilton Resort** and the **Renaissance Pine Isle Resort** from May through August. For details, contact the hotels (See Accommodations). In addition, both hotels have babysitting services. During the busy season, try to make arrangements early (when you arrive, if possible).

There's an **Islands Birthday Club**, where you can purchase a package that includes admission to the beach and water park, a meal, plus a birthday cake for each guest. Call 770-932-7277.

SIDE TRIPS ....

Helen, a German alpine village north of Lake Lanier, is a fantasy land that exists mainly to entertain tourists. Once a fledgling lumber town, the town was revamped in 1969 to become a Tyrolean wannabe. Today's Helen has German bakeries, Alpine-style hotels, and an Alpine Amusement Park with rides and miniature golf in an old world German motif. Visitors can take a guided tour of Helen, which departs from Central Plaza at Main and Chattahoochee Streets. Golfers will enjoy the fine course at **Innsbruck Resort and Golf Club** (See Golf Information), which also has hotel accommodations (call 706-878-2100). Moreover, Helen has a fun museum— the **Museum of the Hills and Fantasy Kingdom of Fairytales**. At the museum, an animated host known as Barney O. Feller traces the town's history from its lumber days to its present state as a make-believe old world village. The museum's reconstructed vil-lage exhibit shows daily life in turn-of-the-century rural northern Georgia. The other half of the museum, Fantasy Kingdom of Fairytales, displays scenes from nursery rhymes and fairy tales. For information, call 706-878-3140.

You're in luck if you're in town for one of Helen's annual festivals. Special celebrations include **Oktoberfest** (which draws some 300,000 people). In December, the city features an old world **Alstadt Christmas Market**, with a tree-lighting ceremony, handmade crafts and decoration sales, and German-style seasonal goodies like Lebkucchen. February brings the Mardi Gras–like **Fashing Karnival**. For more information, call the Helen Convention and Visitors Bureau at 706-878-2181.

One mile southeast of Helen on GA 17, in what was once the center of the Cherokee Nation, is an ancient Indian mound known as the **Nanoochee Indian Mound**. Seven miles east of Helen, on GA 255, is the state's smallest covered bridge, **Stovall Covered Bridge**, which lies over the Chickamauga Creek. **Babyland General Hospital** is 9 miles southwest of Helen in Cleveland. This recreated turn-of-the-century "hospital" has soft-sculptured dolls by Xavier Roberts, creator of the well-known Cabbage Patch Dolls. Call 706-865-2171.

Gainesville is located on the northeastern shore of Lake Lanier. The city is most famous as a poultry-producing capital, but it also has other prosperous industries. Visitors, however, come to enjoy the lovely **Green Street Historic District**, with its renovated Victorian and classical-revival homes. Green Street Station here is home to the **Georgia Mountain Historical and**

Cultural Trust, where visitors can view mountain arts and crafts and historic exhibits. For more information, call the Gainesville Convention and Visitors Bureau at 770-536-5209.

GENERAL INFORMATION ....

For information on island recreation, contact the Lake Lanier Islands Resort at 770-932-7200 (for special events, call 770-932-7275). For camping and recreation on Lake Lanier (as opposed to Lake Lanier Islands), contact the United States Army Corps of Engineers Resource Management Office at 770-945-1467, or 770-945-9531. For information about Lake Lanier and surrounding areas, contact the Gainesville Chamber of Commerce at 770-536-5209.

Part Five

FLORIDA

Gasparilla Festival, Tampa
Photo courtesy of the FL Division of Tourism

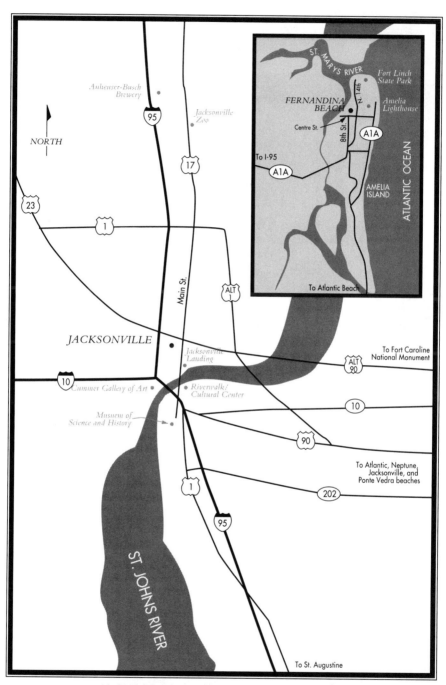

JACKSONVILLE, AMELIA ISLAND, and VICINITY, FL.

Jacksonville, Amelia Island and vicinity

AREA CODE: 904

INTRODUCTION

Jacksonville and Amelia Island are located at the northeast tip of Florida's Atlantic coast. Jacksonville, a port city built around the St. Johns River (the longest river in the state), has long been an important commercial and industrial hub. The city is an urban center and may appear at first glance to be the hospital and industrial capital of the world, yet it has a number of museums, theaters, historic sites, and more for visitors who can tear themselves off the beaches and links long enough to take a tour. Within Jacksonville's financial district are its lovely north and south river banks, and many of the city's cultural attractions are by the water as well. However, the area's major attraction *is* its beaches. Beaches in and around Jacksonville include Atlantic Beach, Neptune Beach, Jacksonville Beach, and Ponte Vedra Beach.

Amelia Island is about thirty minutes north of Jacksonville, and both areas boast some of the best golf courses in the country to go along with their world-class beaches. The 13.5-mile-long island was named by General James Oglethorpe after Princess Amelia, King George II's daughter. It has been ruled under eight different flags, and as such, has a colorful and rich history. Amelia Island has only one city, Fernandina Beach. Fernandina Beach's beginnings as a favored spot for smugglers and pirates earned it a reputation as a "festering fleshpot" (as phrased by President James Monroe). However, after the Civil War, the area grew rapidly in popularity among vacationers, earning it the reputation in the late nineteenth century as the "Queen City of American Resorts." And while one might argue that this area, with its fine beaches, is still a fleshpot of sorts, it's now a very glamorous one. Incidentally, because the island is close to the St. Marys and Cumberland Island area of Georgia (See St. Marys and Cumberland Island chapter), golfers and nature enthusiasts may want to stop there on the way to or from this area, or as a side trip. Ferries are available from St. Marys in Georgia or from Fernandina Beach as part of a naturalist tour of Cumberland Island. (See Boat Tours).

Ponte Vedra Beach is south of Jacksonville and has fabulous beaches and golf as well. Also south of Jacksonville is St. Augustine (See Side Trips). St. Augustine is the nation's oldest city, settled in 1513 by the Spanish, who came in search of gold but instead found what would centuries later become one of the United State's finest resort areas. Today, the city retains many of the buildings from its lengthy history (in

Dowtown Jacksonville
Photo courtesy of Jacksonville and the Beaches Convention and Visitors Bureau

Golf Vacations Even Non-Golfers Will Enjoy

addition to great beaches and golf courses of its own).

An additional draw to the area for golfers will be the World Golf Village complex, scheduled to open in 1998. This resort village, located just south of Jacksonville in St. Johns County, will house the International Golf Museum and Hall of Fame, a resort hotel, upscale dining and shopping facilities, and more (See Museums/Science Centers and Accommodations). The facility is expected to attract over a million visitors annually.

The normal monthly temperatures for Jacksonville are: January, 52.4; February, 55.2; March, 61.1; April, 67; May, 73.4; June, 79.1; July, 81.6; August, 81.2; September, 78.1; October, 69.8; November, 61.9; December, 55.1. The tourist season begins in February, but takes off from March through late October.

GOLF INFORMATION ....

AMELIA ISLAND PLANTATION, AMELIA ISLAND (904) 277-5907

(Note: Open to resort guests only)

Amelia Island is a 1250-acre resort featuring 27 holes designed by Pete Dye: the Oakmarsh (3263 yards, par 36), Oysterbay (3153 yards, par 35), and Oceanside (2832 yards, par 35) courses. Additionally there are 18 holes designed by Tom Fazio: the Long Point Course (reaching 6775 yards, with tees starting at 4927 yards, and a par 72). The resort and its courses have consistently received high rankings and praise from *Golf Digest, Golf, GolfWeek,* and *Golf Reporter.* The island and the courses are enveloped by live oaks, red maples, cedars, pines, magnolias, and palmettos,

and the courses are situated among sand dunes, sea oats, and marshes. Views of the ocean and the Intracoastal Waterway are plentiful from each course. For example, on Oceanside, holes four, five, and six wind along a dune ridge that overlooks the beach and the Atlantic Ocean. Oysterbay travels along salt marshes, and its eighth hole, recognized as one of the most difficult in Florida, features a tee on an island in the middle of a marsh. Long Point provides exciting back-to-back par 3s that play along the coastline. The 166-yard sixth plays from an elevated tee to a sharply undulating green. The 158-yard seventh plays through a narrow valley of dunes, with the ocean on the right and heavy vegetation on the left. Wind, as would be expected, is a major factor on these holes and most of the others on Amelia Island.

Carts: Mandatory. *Greens Fees:* Approximately $50-$60 weekdays, $85-$100 weekends/18 holes, depending on course played. *Tee Time Policy:* Can be made at time room reservations are made; open only to resort guests.

MARRIOTT AT SAWGRASS RESORT, PONTE VEDRA BEACH (904) 273-3720 OR (800) 457-4653

Providing some of the best golf in the country, the Sawgrass Resort offers 99 holes to resort guests and members on its Tournament Players Club (TPC) Stadium, TPC Valley, East, West, South, Marsh Landing, and Oak Bridge courses. Obviously, the most famous of the group is Pete Dye's TPC Stadium. Since it opened in 1980, that course has been the site of The Player's Championship. Judging the TPC Stadium by a few of such Player's Championship winners, Jerry Pate, Fred Couples, Davis

Amelia Island golf course
Photo courtesy of St. John and Partners Advertising and Public Relations

Love, Greg Norman, and Lee Janzen, it is safe to say that this Dye creation has matured into a wonderful test of golf (*Golf Digest* and *Golf* both consider the TPC Stadium to be among the top courses in the United States, and *Golf's* January 1996 issue ranks the TPC Stadium as the number-one course in Florida). One of Dye's design tenets— that a golf course should appear tougher than it actually is—might not hold true here. With mounding, knolls, swales, sand and grass bunkers, pot bunkers, waste bunkers, lakes and creeks, railroad ties, wind, and a variety of trees to go along with the fast, elevated, sloping, and undulating greens, the TPC Stadium course can have no mercy. The course plays to a par of 72, ranges in yardage from 5034 to 6857 yards, and has a course rating ranging from 68.7 to 74. As with most Dye finishing holes, the last three on the TPC Stadium are as exciting as it gets. The 497-yard, par 5

sixteenth is a reachable par 5, but its green sits on an angle in a lake, bringing water into play to the right and behind the green. If you lay-up, you must contend with an old oak sitting on the left side of the fairway about 70 yards from the green. The seventeenth hole, with its island green, is clearly one of the most recognized and exciting holes in golf. Finally, the 440-yard, par 4 eighteenth bends slightly to the left, with water down the entire left side, requiring two courageous shots to make par.

Carts: Required most times. *Greens Fees:* $50-$120, sometimes less, depending on season course is played and whether you are a member, guest, or non-guest/18 holes; carts: $16-$22. *Tee Time Policy:* Call in advance for times.

OTHER EXCELLENT
AREA COURSES:

Windsor Parke Golf Club, Jacksonville (904-223-4653), is a 1990,

Arthur Hills layout set among stately oaks and pines that was considered among the best new courses in the Southeast in 1991 by *Golf Digest*. **Golf Club of Jacksonville**, Jacksonville (904-779-0800), is a 6620-yard, par 71 course that is a Bobby Weed/Mark McCumber layout. This course is located within a mature setting of pine trees and classic Florida wetlands and has very reasonable greens fees. **St. Johns County Golf Club**, Eckton (904-825-4900), is a par 72, Robert Walker layout stretching to 6926 yards with a rating/slope of 72.9/130. The course winds over and around several lovely lagoons. **Ravines Golf and Country Club**, Middleburg (904-282-7888), has mountain-like features, including steep hills, sharp drops, and ravines. This Ron Garl/Mark McCumber layout, which stretches to 6784 yards with a par 72 layout, runs along Black Creek. **The Golf Club of Amelia Island**, Amelia Island (904-277-8015), is open only to guests of the Ritz-Carlton Hotel and the Summer Beach Resort. PGA Tour players Gene Littler and Mark McCumber combined to design this 6681-yard, par 72 course that features wetlands, marshes, ponds, dense forest, many flowers, elevated greens, and some very deep bunkers. **Sawgrass Country Club**, Ponte Vedra (904-273-3720), is an Ed Seay design that is often considered among the top courses in the United States by *Golf Digest*. The club offers 27 holes that travel along the ocean and through marshes and mature forests. **Ponte Vedra Inn and Club**, Ponte Vedra Beach (904-285-1111), features the 6573-yard, par 72 Ocean Course, which dates back to 1929. It has hills, ravines, and an everpresent ocean breeze. **Eagle Harbor Golf Club**, Orange Park (904-269-9300), is carved through a mature forest of towering pines with numerous lakes and ponds. This par 72, Clyde Johnston layout has tees that range from 5915 to 6838 yards. **The Champions Club at Julington Creek**, Jacksonville (904-287-4653), was designed by former PGA Tour player turned announcer Steve Melnik. This par 72 course is built among scenic wetlands of northeast Florida. **Cimarrone Golf and Country Club**, Jacksonville (904-287-2000), is a 6891-yard, par 72, David Postlethwait course with water on every hole. *Golf* considers this a "must play" course. **Hyde Park Golf Club**, Jacksonville (904- 786-5410), was built in 1925 by Donald Ross and is the site of Mickey Wright's first official LPGA win. The course offers small and elevated greens (a Ross trademark), rolling hills, ancient Spanish oaks, and huge Southern pines. **Ponce De Leon Golf and Conference Resort**, St. Augustine (904-829-5314), was one of the first courses in Florida. This 1916 Donald Ross design, located along the Intracoastal Waterway, winds through moss-laden oaks and magnolias. Also promising are the resort courses to open in 1998 at the **World Golf Village** just south of Jacksonville in St. Johns County. For information, contact the Florida's First Coast of Golf, Inc., at 800-877-PUTT, or contact the St. Johns County Convention and Visitors Bureau at 800-653-2489.

ATTRACTIONS ....

TOURS

The Jacksonville Historical Society offers guided tours of the city by prior appointment. Call 904-396-6307. For tours of Fernandina Beach's historic district, make an appointment at least 24 hours in advance with the **Amelia Island Museum of History**, at 233 South Third Street. At least four people are required for the tour. Call 904-261-7378.

Bus Tours

Sideline Tours offers sightseeing tours of Jacksonville for groups of all sizes. Call 904-278-9409.

Boat Tours

Riverwalk Cruise Lines give lunch and dinner sightseeing cruises and party cruises aboard the *First Lady*, docked along the St. Johns River. For a schedule, call 904-398-0797.

La Cruise Casino has day and evening cruises, which include a floating Vegas-style casino on board, as well as meals and entertainment. Located next to the Mayport Ferry. Call 904-241-7200 or 800-752-1778.

Greyfield Inn of Cumberland Island, Georgia (See St. Marys and Cumberland Island chapter), takes visitors via ferry from Fernandina Beach to Cumberland Island for naturalist tours. Call 904-261-6408.

Water Taxi

The Bass Marine Taxi takes passengers to downtown Jacksonville points along the St. Johns River (e.g., the Landing, the Southbank Riverwalk, and the River City Brewing Company) for $2. Call 904-730-8685.

HISTORIC PLACES

The Amelia Island Historic District is a fifty-block area with several buildings and homes that are registered as historic places. A tour here makes a nice drive or stroll, as there is a wide range of gracious and well-kept buildings of Victorian architecture, including examples of Queen Anne, Italianate, Chinese Chippendale, and Mississippi Steamboat styles. First, stop at the old rail depot, 102 Centre Street, where the Chamber of Commerce is located (call 904-261-3248) to pick up maps and other helpful information.

The 1878 **Palace Saloon**, at 117 Centre Street on Amelia Island, still in operation as a bar and restaurant, was once frequented by Rockefellers and their ilk. You can stop in for refreshment or simply to check out the pressed-tin ceiling, 40-foot mahogany bar, and frescoes of Charles Dickens and William Shakespeare. No admission charge. Call 904-261-6320.

MUSEUMS/SCIENCE CENTERS

The Museum of Science and History, at 1025 Museum Circle in Jacksonville, has exhibits on state history and ecology, which cover local wildlife, Indian history, and Civil War history. Don't miss the planetarium show. Open daily except Mondays. Admission is charged. Call 904-396-7062.

The Cummer Museum of Art, at 829 Riverside Avenue, is tucked within a fourteen-room mansion, making a beautiful setting for equally lovely works of art. The collection contains artworks ranging from the early Egyptian periods through the twentieth century, with a notable collection of antique porcelains, American paintings, and several paintings by the European masters. Open daily except Mondays. Admission is charged. Call 904-356-6857.

The Jacksonville Museum of Contemporary Art, at 4160 Boulevard Center Drive, has a sizeable Picasso collection, as well as several porcelains, pre-Columbian artifacts, and other classical and modern artworks. Open daily except Mondays. Admission is charged. Call 904-398-8336.

The Alexander Brest Museum at Jacksonville University, located at 2800 University Boulevard North, houses a large collection of pre-Columbian artifacts, Steuben glass, ivories, porcelains, and other items. Open daily except Sundays (closed Saturdays during school vacations). Admission is free. Call 904-744-3950. On campus you'll also find the former home of British composer Frederick Delius, which is open for tours by request. Call 904-744-3950.

The Amelia Island Museum of History, at 233 South Third Street on Amelia Island, is Florida's only oral history museum. While visitors can enter anytime during their hours, special tours are given at 11 A.M. and 2 P.M. Open daily except Sundays. Donation suggested. Call 904-261-7378.

The International Golf Museum and Hall of Fame, scheduled to open in 1998, will have special exhibit halls coordinated by the PGA Tour, the Ladies Professional Golf Association (LPGA), and the PGA of America. The museum will have interactive exhibits using the latest technology, as well as historical and traditional golf exhibits, and annual induction ceremonies. The Iwerks Theater will feature golf, and other, films. Also at the complex will be the International Golf Library, a golf academy, a 300-room resort hotel, time-share condominiums, and at least two 18-hole golf courses (one to be designed by hall of famer Sam Snead), with more golf courses planned in the future. Located at the intersection of I-95 and International Golf Parkway, 22 miles south of Jacksonville in St. Johns County. For information, call Florida's First Coast of Golf, Inc. (a local non-profit golf promotion organization) at 800-877-PUTT, or call the St. Johns County Convention and Visitors Bureau at 800-653-2489.

CULTURAL OFFERINGS

The Jacksonville Symphony Orchestra gives performances throughout the year. For information, call 904-354-5479.

Florida Theater Performing Arts Center, at 128 East Forsyth Street in Jacksonville, hosts popular concerts, Broadway shows, and other entertainment year-round. Call 904-355-5661.

RECREATION

Jacksonville Zoologic Park, at 8605 Zoo Road, has recently completed a $15 million expansion and renovation, with 73 acres of new exhibits, animals, and shows. There's a safari train ride and petting zoo. Notable attractions include rare water birds and white rhinos. Open daily. Admission is charged. Call 904-757-4462.

Anheuser-Busch Brewery, at 111 Busch Drive in Northside, offers free tours, either escorted or self-guided, to see how their beer is brewed and processed before shipment. Open Monday through Saturday. Admission is charged. Call 904-751-8117.

Fort Clinch, at 2601 Atlantic Avenue on Amelia Island, is a restored, oceanfront, Civil War–era brick fort. The site is in a state park with a large public beach and campsites. The fort schedules Civil War re-enactments throughout the year. Admission is charged. Call 904-277-7274.

The 2,500-acre **Little Talbot Island State Park**, about 17 miles northeast of Jacksonville, has unspoiled beaches, salt marshes, woods, and a playground. Swimming, fishing, surfing, and camping are allowed (call for fees). Call 904-251-2320.

For great tennis facilities, it's hard to beat Amelia Island Plantation, where the **Women's Tennis Championships** are held. Call 904-277-5145. Also, the Ponce de Leon Golf and Conference Resort (call 904-824-2821) and Marriott at Sawgrass Resort (call 904-285-7777) have quality tennis facilities.

As for spectator sports, Jacksonville has a new NFL football team called the **Jaguars**; for ticket information, call 904-633-6000. The minor-league hockey team is the **Jacksonville Bullets**, which plays at the Jacksonville Coliseum, at 1145 East Adams Street. Call 904-630-3900. Dog races are run at three places: from March through April at **St. Johns Greyhound Park**, on U.S. 1, a half-mile south of I-95; from May through September at the **Jacksonville Kennel Club**, 1440 North McDuff Avenue; and from November through April at the **Orange Park Kennel Club**, on U.S. 17 about a half-mile from I-295. For information, call 904-646-0001.

Fishing and boating are popular sports here. For pier fishing, head to the 1200-foot-long **Jacksonville Beach Pier**, or any other local beaches, piers, and canals. To charter a boat for deep-sea fishing, try the **Sea Love II** in St. Augustine (see Side Trips). Call 904-824-3328. For diving and scuba instruction, try **Dive Tour, Inc.,** in DeLand at 1403 East New York Avenue. Call 904-736-0571.

SEASONAL EVENTS

For golfers, the biggest event is **The Players Championship** held in March at the Tournament Players Club in Ponte Vedra Beach. Call 904-273-3382 or 800-404-7887. Also in March is the festival in honor of British composer and Jacksonville resident Frederick Delius, with musical performances, lectures, and exhibits. Call 904-744-3950.

In mid- to late April, visitors can tour lovely historic homes in the Riverside/Avondale section of Jacksonville which are otherwise not open to the public. Call 904-389-2449. Around the second full week of April, the **Women's Tennis Championships** are held at Amelia Island Plantation. The event is part of the women's professional tour. The first weekend in May, Amelia Island celebrates its **Shrimp Festival**.

In mid- to late September, the **Riverside Art Festival**, in Jacksonville's Riverside Park, has juried artists' exhibits, entertainment, and food. Call 904-389-4866.

In November, there's the **Great American Piano Competition** with jazz superstars, food, arts, and crafts. The event takes place in the Florida Theater in downtown Jacksonville. Call 904-353-7770. Also in November is the week-long **Jacksonville Jazz Festival**, held at Metropolitan Park along the St. Johns River. In November on

Amelia Island, there's the **Heritage Festival** celebrating the island's diverse culture.

Football fans flock to Jacksonville for the **Gator Bowl Festival**, which begins with a variety of parades, shows, and special events throughout December, leading up to the Gator Bowl, usually held on New Year's Day.

ACCOMMODATIONS ....

EXPENSIVE

Jacksonville Omni Hotel, at 245 Water Street, has marble floors, lots of glass and brass, and stands sixteen-stories high. There's a lounge, pool, fine restaurant, exercise room, and a luxury level. Located on the riverfront. Call 904-355-6664.

Marriott at Sawgrass, at 1000 TPC Boulevard in Ponte Vedra Beach, is a golfer's paradise, as it's one of the finest golf resorts in the country (See Golf Information). The elegant hotel has green glass windows, waterfalls indoors and out, and an atrium lobby with a skylight. Accommodations include rooms, suites, and villas with private balconies and patios. A partial list of perks includes children's programs, tennis, a private beach, boating, bikes, spa, pools, fishing, and golf packages. Call 904-285-7777 or 800-457-4653.

The 1300-acre **Amelia Island Plantation**, at 1501 Lewis Street, is another paradise for golfers, as its golf courses, open only to guests, are among the area's best (See Golf Information). There's a children's program, a social director for activities, a sports director for their extensive sports program, twenty-five tennis courts, paddleboats,

a private beach, pools, a sunken forest and marshland with boardwalk trails, and a spa. The rooms have balconies, patios, and washers and dryers. Call 904-261-6161 or 800-874-6878.

Another terrific luxury choice on Amelia Island, and one which allows access to the Golf Club of Amelia Island (which is located in the Summer Beach Resort and Country Club; see Golf Information) is the **Ritz-Carlton**, at 4750 Amelia Island Parkway. Call 904-277-1100.

World Golf Village Resort Hotel, to open in 1998, will be located at the intersection of I-95 and International Golf Parkway, 22 miles south of downtown Jacksonville. This 240-acre complex which will feature a resort hotel with golf courses (two opening initially, and at least one other to open later), and other major golf attractions (See Museums/Science Centers), as well as shopping and dining facilities.

MODERATE

Sea Turtle Inn, at 1 Ocean Boulevard in Jacksonville Beach, has a free cocktail reception in the evenings, an airport shuttle, coffee and newspapers in the morning, a pool, and a restaurant. Call 904-249-7402.

The Comfort Inn Oceanfront, at 1515 North First Street in Jacksonville Beach, has a heated pool, restaurants, lounges, and rooms that overlook the ocean. Call 904-241-2311.

INEXPENSIVE

Shoney's Inn, at 2702 Sadler Road in Fernandina Beach on Amelia Island, is a half-block from the beach and offers clean, comfortable, no-frills accommodations. Call 904-277-2300.

Golfers staying here will need to travel south to Jacksonville, Ponte Vedra, and elsewhere to play, as Amelia Island's best golf courses are open only to resort guests (See Golf Information).

SHOPPING ....

Jacksonville Landing is a main shopping district in the city on the north side of the St. Johns River. Here you'll find specialty shops, cafés, and restaurants. Also in Jacksonville, **San Marco Shopping Center** on San Marco Boulevard offers similar shopping, but in lovely, old, Mediterranean-style buildings. For more boutique and arts shopping, try **Avondale Shopping Center** on Riverside Avenue in nearby Avondale.

Amelia Island's **Centre Street** in Fernandina Beach's historic district has several shops worth browsing, and some fifteen other shops can be found at nearby **Palmetto Walk**. Upscale shopping can be found at the **Village Shops** next to Amelia Island Plantation, and in the seven shops within the Ritz-Carlton hotel.

RESTAURANTS ....

Amelia Island is a shrimping capital of the world, and a local specialty here is the Atlantic white shrimp, known for its distinctive sweet taste.

DINNER THEATER

The Alhambra Dinner Theater, at 12000 Beach Boulevard in Jacksonville Beach, has arched, Moorish styling (though it's not as ornate as its namesake Spanish landmark). Evening performances are Tuesdays through Sun-

days at 6 P.M.; call for matinée schedule. Guests can opt for the show only. Call 904-641-1212.

FINE DINING

Wine Cellar, at 314 Prudential Drive in Jacksonville, has classic continental cuisine, with dishes like Grecian shrimp, grilled salmon with dill-mustard sauce, and veal chops. Jacket required. Dinner served Monday through Saturday. Call 904-398-8989.

Dolphin Depot, at 704 North First Street in Jacksonville Beach, 12 miles east of the city, has Florida cuisine with an emphasis on seafood, but includes a variety of selections. Examples of offerings are she-crab soup, plantation pork tenders, Ocean County crab cakes, and chicken Daniel. Dinner served daily. Call 904-270-1424.

The Grill, at the Ritz-Carlton on Amelia Island, offers wonderful food and impeccable service. Specialties include the mahimahi filet with spring onion, lobster ragout, and swordfish; other selections include beef, chicken, and pasta. Dinner served daily. Jacket and reservations required. Call 904-277-1100.

Another fine restaurant on Amelia Island is the **Beech Street Grill**, at 801 Beech Street, which is located on a nineteenth-century sea captain's estate. The restaurant offers almost 200 wines, in addition to fine seafood specialties like cold poached seafood sausages. Call 904-277-3662.

CASUAL DINING

Johnny Rockets, at 2 Independent Drive in Jacksonville, is a 1950s-style diner serving classics like burgers, fries, BLTs, malts, and milk shakes (you get the idea), complete with old ads on the walls and neon. Open Monday through Saturday for lunch and dinner. Call 904-355-8718.

River City Brewing Company, at 835 Museum Circle at Southbank in Jacksonville, is a favorite with locals and visitors. They serve homemade beer specials and offer sampler-size mugs. The food, from seafood jambalaya and warm goat-cheese salad, to chicken, fish, and sandwiches, is tasty and goes well with the brew. There's live jazz at Sunday brunch and on Friday and Saturday evenings. Serving lunch and dinner daily, and Sunday brunch. Call 904-398-2299.

Island Grille, at 981 North First Street in Jacksonville Beach, serves seafood specialties like conch fritters, blackened snapper, and grilled tuna, but also offers beef, pork, and lamb entrées. Lunch and dinner served daily. Call 904-241-1881.

The Southern Tip, at 4802 First Coast Highway on Amelia Island, serves up southern specialties like black-eyed-pea cakes, crab cakes, steak Diane, pasta, and chicken. Lunch and dinner served daily. Call 904-261-6184.

JUST FOR KIDS ....

Several area resorts and hotels have children's programs. Check with your hotel regarding program availability. Also of special interest is the Jacksonville Zoo (See Recreation).

SIDE TRIPS ....

St. Augustine (about a 30-minute drive south of Jacksonville) is the oldest city in the United States. It is a wonderful city with many sixteenth-

and seventeenth-century buildings that, much like Toledo, Spain, give it the feel of a living, centuries-old city. It's a vacation spot in its own right, as it has 43 miles of beaches, but it also makes a wonderful day or overnight trip from the Jacksonville area. The rich history of the city dates chiefly to the days of Spanish exploration. The best way to start your exploration of St. Augustine is at the visitors center, at 10 Castillo Drive, which offers a fifty-two minute orientation film on the area's history titled *The Dream of Empire*. Call 904-825-1000. Although there are many more attractions in the city (all of those listed below charge admission except the Mission and the Cathedral), the following are some highlights: **The Castillo de San Marcos National Monument**, at 1 Castillo Drive, is a 300-year-old fort with 16-foot-thick walls, and garrison rooms and artillery that are still intact. Call 904-829-6506. The **Basilica Cathedral of St. Augustine** is a beautiful church dating to the sixteenth century. **The Spanish Quarter** (the entrance is at 29 St. George Street) is a colonial, living-history museum with several historic buildings and demonstration areas where you can see candlemaking, blacksmithing, basketry, open-hearth cooking, and more. Open daily. One admission charge gets you into all buildings at the Spanish Quarter. Call 904-825-6830. Being the oldest city, St. Augustine has several "oldest" attractions here, such as the **Oldest Store Museum** at 4 Artillery Lane. The museum store is a re-creation, but it carries genuine old-fashioned items like corsets and penny candies. Open daily. Call 904-829-9729. **The Mission of Nombre de Dios**, north

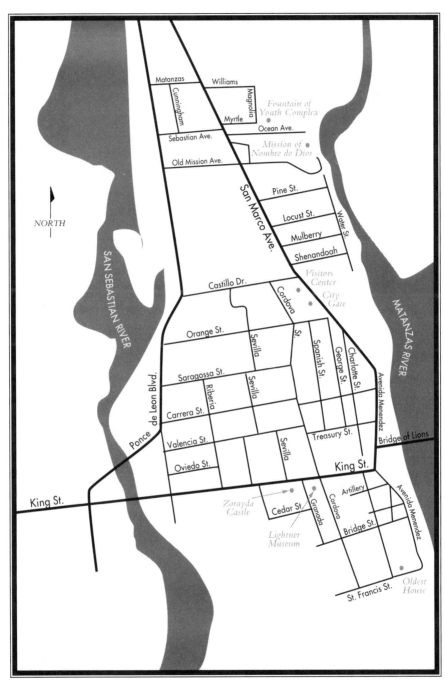

ST. AUGUSTINE, FL.

of the historic district at San Marco Avenue and Old Mission Road, is where the first Christian mass was celebrated in the United States. **Zorayda Castle**, at 83 King Street, is a gorgeous, 1883 building inspired by Spain's Alhambra. Call 904-824-3097.

There's also plenty of (fun) shlock in St. Augustine. **The Fountain of Youth Complex**, at 155 Magnolia Avenue, was built in honor of Ponce de Leon, who spent his youth exploring much of Florida. This touristy complex has an Indian village, planetarium, a two-story globe with an exhibition on Spanish history in the western hemisphere, and more. Open daily. Admission is charged. Call 904-829-3168. Other satellite attractions are an alligator farm (call 904-824-3337), a **Ripley's Believe It or Not! Museum** (call 904-824-1606), **Potter's Wax Museum** (call 904-829-9056), as well as many other similar attractions (all charge admission). Visitors can also take horse and carriage tours of the city. For more information, contact the St. Augustine Visitor Information Center at 904-825-1000.

Fort Caroline National Monument, at 12713 Fort Caroline Road, is about 15 miles from Jacksonville. The fort was built in the mid-sixteenth century by French Huguenots (who were overrun by the Spanish), creating the first Protestant colony on the continent. A small museum here tells the site's history. Open daily. Admission is free. Call 904-641-7155.

Kingsley Plantation is on Fort George Island, which can be reached from Fort Caroline by heading west to FL 9A, then taking FL 105 northeast for approximately 10 miles. The plantation and slave cabins here were built by a slave trader in 1792. The home is small, considering their wealth. Tours run Thursdays through Mondays, though the grounds are open daily. Admission is free. Call 904-251-3537.

GENERAL INFORMATION ....

Contact the Jacksonville and the Beaches Chamber of Commerce at 904-366-6600. They'll send a free guide, the *Jacksonville and the Beaches Visitors Guide*. For Amelia Island, contact Amelia Island Tourism Information at 904-277-0717 or 800-226-3542. A local nonprofit organization, Florida's First Coast of Golf, Inc., can send detailed golf information on this area. Call 904-798-9142 or 800-877-PUTT.

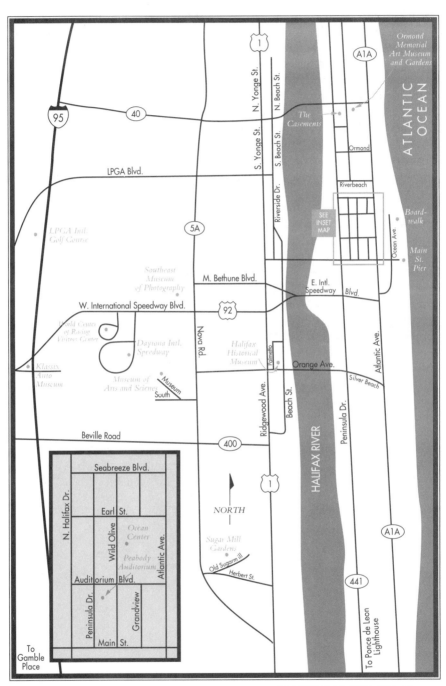

DAYTONA BEACH, FL.

Daytona Beach

INTRODUCTION

Daytona Beach, on the Atlantic coast, is one of Florida's oldest resort areas, and it still maintains the cars-and-beach theme of its past. Because the city is bordered by the Atlantic Ocean on one side and the Halifax River on the other side, it's made up of two main communities, one on both sides of the river. The beachside is the strip between the Atlantic Ocean and the Halifax River, and the mainland is the area on the west bank of the Halifax River that spreads inland. Within the beachside and mainland areas are smaller communities. The oldest beachside communities are those in the north, such as Ormond-by-the-Sea and Ormond Beach. These were popularized as vacation spots as far back as the early 1900s, when wealthy people would race their cars down the beach (cars are still permitted on the beach during the day in certain designated areas). The middle section, Daytona Beach, is internationally known as a beach resort and as the United States' mecca of stock-car racing (NASCAR is centered here). Newer sections are located to the south of Daytona Beach.

Daytona Beach has several great golf courses, and the weather and landscape here are ideal for the sport, as evidenced by the fact the LPGA's home course, designed by Rees Jones, is here. For non-golfers, the 23-mile-long, 500-foot-wide beaches and the great weather alone are worth the trip, but the area offers lots of activities, attractions, and culture as well, especially for museum and history lovers. Additionally, Daytona Beach is about an hour-and-fifteen-minute drive from Orlando and all the attractions there.

The area gets a steady stream of visitors from late March through October. However, most families and college students come here in the spring and summer, which makes sense given the school-year calendar and the normal monthly temperatures, which are: January, 57.5; February, 59; March, 64.3; April, 69.3; May, 74.7; June, 79.4; July, 81.2; August, 81; September, 79.4; October, 73.4; November, 65.9; December, 60.1.

GOLF INFORMATION ....

Of particular interest to golfers is Daytona's **Free Golf Program**. If you stay in certain accommodations for two or more nights between June 3 and October 10, you pay non-golf-package rates and receive a free round of golf daily at designated courses, provided you tee off after 1 P.M. For information, call 800-881-7065.

Also, a non-profit organization here called **Golf Daytona Beach** promotes local golf and represents nine golf

courses and over thirty hotels in the area. They can send you a color brochure detailing accommodations, courses, and golf packages available. You can then contact your chosen accommodation to arrange reservations and tee times. For information, call 800-881-7065.

LPGA INTERNATIONAL, DAYTONA BEACH (904) 274-3880

Considered by *Golf* to be among the best new courses in the United States in 1995, LPGA International is the new home to the Ladies Professional Golf Association and to one of the LPGA Tour's richest events, the Sprint Titleholders Championship. Opened in 1994 and designed by Rees Jones expressly for the best female players in the game, LPGA International offers stategic mounding, picturesque lakes, tranquil wetlands, lots of sand, hummocky fairways, and large greens. The yardage ranges from 5131 to 7088 yards, and the rating/slope ranges from 67.1/118 to 74/134. Also planned for LPGA International is a second 18-hole course to be designed by Arthur Hills. A Radisson Hotel is set to open at the complex in 1997.

Carts: Mandatory. *Greens Fees:* Approximately $70 in high season/18 holes, including cart. *Tee Time Policy:* Can be made up to seven days in advance.

INDIGO LAKES GOLF CLUB, DAYTONA BEACH (904) 254-3607

Indigo Lakes was designed, and recently remodeled, by Lloyd Clifton. It was the former site of the LPGA's Sprint Titleholders Championship and the LPGA's qualifying school, and it has been ranked consistently by *GolfWeek* as one of the top courses in Florida. Its five tees range from 5159 to 7168 yards, and the rating/slope ranges from 69.1/123 to 73.5/128. The fairways are lined with palms and pines, and several attractive lakes make a few holes quite interesting. The greens are heavily bunkered and are fairly large, thus offering multiple pin placements.

Carts: Mandatory. *Greens Fees:* $30-$60/18 holes, including cart. *Tee Time Policy:* Can be made up to seven days in advance.

HARBORSIDE INN PALM COAST, PALM COAST (25 MILES NORTH OF DAYTONA BEACH)

Palm Coast offers five good courses: Matanzas Woods (904-446-6330) is an Arnold Palmer/Ed Seay layout that opened in 1985. It measures from 5336 to 6985 yards with a rating/slope from 71.1/126 to 73.3/132. Cypress Knoll (904-437-5807) is a 1990 design by Gary Player. It measures from 5386 to 6591 yards with a rating/slope from 69.3/117 to 71.6/130. Palm Harbor (904-445-0845) is a 1973, Bill Amick layout measuring from 5346 to 6572 yards with a rating/slope ranging from 69.2/121 to 71.8/127. Pine Lakes (904-445-0852) is another Palmer/Seay layout that opened in 1980. It measures from 5166 to 7074 yards with a rating/slope ranging from 70.6/121 to 73.5/126. The Hammock Dunes Links Course is semi-private (guests of the Sheraton Palm have limited access). It is a 1990, Tom Fazio design that ranges from 5155 to 6802 yards with a rating/slope ranging from 69.9/124 to 73.1/133. The best of the group may be the Matanzas Woods course, which winds through towering pines, palms,

and other Florida vegetation. Additionally, the course travels over and along Lake Success, the Jefferson Davis Waterway, and several other lakes and ponds. Each hole seems progessively tougher, until the thirteenth hole, which begins Matanzas Woods's version of Amen Corner. The finishing hole is a 532-yard par 5 that plays to an island green. Cypress Knoll is a hallmark Player course, with narrow fairways and small greens requiring accurate shotmaking from the tees, fairways, and from around the greens. Palm Harbor features fairways lined with tall palms, pines, and oaks that play to small, elevated greens. Pine Lakes sports 63 white-sand bunkers, water on eleven holes, and over 7000 yards of good golf. Finally, Hammock Dunes offers marvelous views of the Atlantic and winds through lakes, marshes, wetlands, pines, oaks, and palms in pure Fazio fashion.

Carts: Mandatory. *Greens Fees:* $50 January-May, $40 June-December/18 holes. *Tee Time Policy:* Harborside Inn Palm Coast guests with the golf package can reserve times up to six months in advance; non-resort guests can reserve times up to six days in advance (or earlier at Cypress Knoll and Matanzas Woods if booking through Golf Daytona Beach).

OTHER EXCELLENT AREA COURSES:

Halifax Plantation Golf Club, Ormond Beach (904-676-9600), is a par 72 course designed by Bill Amick, with tees ranging from 4971 to over 7100 yards. The course is set among century-old oaks, pines, and palms. **River Bend Golf Club**, Ormond

Beach (904-673-6000), is set along the historic Tomoka River. This 6821-yard, par 72 course was built by Lloyd Clifton. **Pelican Bay Country Club's** South Course, Daytona Beach (904-788-6496), is a par 72, Lloyd Clifton course with tees ranging from 5278 to 6630 yards. The course meanders around canals and lakes and through heavy Florida foliage. **The Golf Club at Cypress Head**, Port Orange (904-756-5449), is an Arthur Hill, 6814-yard course that winds through towering cypress trees.

ATTRACTIONS ....

TOURS

The Sea Critter **Sightseeing Boat,** at 4950 South Peninsula Drive in Ponce Inlet, gives local nautical tours. Call 904-767-7676. Similar tours are offered by **Daytona Charter Sailboat Rides**, at 3300 South Peninsula Drive in Daytona Beach. Call 904-761-2104. For both water tours and cruises, contact **A Tiny Cruise Line**, at 401 South Beach Street in Daytona Beach. Call 904-226-2343. For wildlife tours or boat rentals, try **Hontoon Landing Marina**, at 2317 River Ridge Road in Deland. Call 904-734-2474.

HISTORIC PLACES

Daytona Beach's historic district makes a nice walking tour. From the paths of **Riverfront Park**, visitors can view many old churches and buildings, as well as visit some newer shops and restaurants. The city's charm has been maintained, as the nineteenth-century buildings blend nicely with the style-conscious modern construction.

Halifax Historical Society and Museum is located at 252 South Beach Street in the stone-columned Merchant's Bank building in downtown Daytona Beach. The museum has artifacts recovered from area plantations, auto-racing memorabilia, a video presentation on Daytona's history, and a miniature replica of the Daytona Beach Boardwalk as it existed in 1938. Open Tuesday through Saturday. Admission is charged. Call 904-255-6976.

The Museum of Arts and Sciences, at 1040 Museum Boulevard in Daytona Beach, is on a 60-acre nature preserve. The major exhibits include one on the ecosystem of the coastal hummock, a collection of southeastern

Ponce de Leon Lighthouse
Photo courtesy of the FL Divison of Toursim

American fine arts from the mid-seventeenth through the early twentieth century, an exhibit on Cuban and African culture, and a planetarium. Don't miss the 13-foot-tall remains of an ancient giant ground sloth in the Prehistory of Florida wing. Open daily except Monday. Admission is charged. Call 904-255-0285.

The Casements, at 25 Riverside Drive in Ormond Beach, is a former winter home of John D. Rockefeller and is now a museum and cultural center. The Rockefeller Room has early twentieth-century memorabilia. Notable exhibits are the Hungarian Historic Room and the Boy Scout Exhibit. Open daily except Sunday. Guided tours of the estate are available weekdays from 10 A.M. to 12:30 P.M. Admission is charged. Call 904-676-3216.

Ponce de Leon Inlet Lighthouse Museum, at 4931 South Peninsula Drive in Ponce Inlet, has a museum and a restored lighthouse keeper's house. Hearty folks can climb to the top of the lighthouse to get a panoramic view of the coast. The museum has local lighthouse, maritime, and racing memorabilia. Admission is charged. Call 904-761-1821.

Ormond Memorial Art Museum and Gardens, at 78 East Granada Boulevard in Ormond Beach, houses a changing exhibit of Florida artists and historic displays. The museum is surrounded by lush gardens, nature trails, tropical gardens, gazebos, and stone fountains. Donation suggested. Call 904-676-3347.

The Southeast Museum of Photography, at 1200 International Speedway Boulevard at Daytona Beach Community College, is one of only twelve museums devoted solely to photography in the United States. Old and new photos encompass a myriad of subjects. Call for hours. Donation suggested. Call 904-254-4475.

CULTURAL OFFERINGS

Peabody Auditorium, at 600 Auditorium Boulevard, is the home of the Daytona Symphony and the Daytona Beach Civic Ballet; the facility also hosts concerts by a variety of other groups. Call 904-255-1314.

Art League of Daytona Beach, at 433 South Palmetto Avenue in Daytona Beach, has rotating exhibits by various regional artists, and sometimes holds fine-arts demonstrations. Call 904-258-3856.

The Daytona Playhouse's season is September through June, with a variety of productions. The theater is located at 100 Jessamine Boulevard in Daytona Beach. Call 904-255-2431. **The Seaside Music Theater**, at the Daytona Beach Community College, presents musical productions and a Saturday morning children's theater in summer. Call 904-252-6200 for ticket availability and schedule.

Ormond Performing Arts Center, at 399 North U.S. 1 in Ormond Beach, hosts a variety of plays and concerts. Call 904-676-3375.

RECREATION

Daytona International Speedway, at 1801 West International Speedway Boulevard, has a modern "World Center of Racing" visitors center, which gives thirty-minute guided tours (fee charged) of the track except during racing events. The center has photos, films, and other racing souvenirs, and the

Gallery of Legends profiles famous drivers and moments in racing history. The simulated video Daytona 500 in the Oldfield Grandstand is so realistic that the grandstand seats actually shake. Also be sure to check out the new **Daytona USA** entertainment facility, with hands-on exhibits about car racing and racing history (e.g., participating in a pit-crew competition, and helping to design and test a stock car). Open daily. Call 904-254-2700.

Frisbee golfers will find an 18-hole disc golf course in **Tuscawilla Park**, in Daytona Beach on the corner of Nova Road and International Speedway Boulevard. Open daily.

Horse racing and horse shows take place at the **Spring Garden Ranch**, at 900 Spring Garden Ranch Road in DeLeon Springs. Harness racing takes place November 1 through April 1; horse shows take place the remainder of the year. Call 904-985-5654.

What historic Atlantic beach resort would be complete without a boardwalk? **The Daytona Beach Boardwalk** has an amusement park with an arcade, band shell, games, and rides (including the 100-foot Skycoaster rollercoaster that makes you feel like you'll zoom down into the ocean, as well as a gondola and a skyride). A "Salute to Speed" series of plaques commemorates local racing history. Hours vary seasonally. Admission is charged at various attractions. Call 904-258-3106.

Water sports are big here. **Salty Dog**, at 700 Broadway in Daytona Beach, rents sailboards, surfboards, and boogie boards. Call 904-258-0457. For jetski rentals, try **J & J**, at 841 Ballough Road. Call 904-255-1917. Snorkelers and scuba divers can dive among the plentiful reefs and shipwrecks, including the famous *Liberty Ship* and other wartime vessels. Local fishing opportunities are great, too. Surf and pier fishing is allowed on the Ocean Pier in Daytona Beach; the Halifax River offers great freshwater fishing; and for deep-sea fishing, charters can be found at Ponce Inlet. For licensing fees and requirements, call 904-677-4050.

There are a variety of facilities available for tennis players, such as: Daytona Beach Golf and Country Club (call 904-258-3139), Derbyshire Courts (call 904-258-3106), Palm Coast Players Club (call 904-446-6360), Ormond Beach Racquet Club (call 904-676-3285), and City Island Court (call 904-258-3139).

Horseback riding along trails can be found at **Shenandoah Stables** on Tomoka Farms Road. Rides are by reservation only. Call 904-257-1444.

Stone Edge Skateboard Park in South Daytona has an outdoor skateboarding course. Call 904-761-1123. Roller-bladers and roller-skaters can head for **Starlite Skate Center** in Ormond Beach (call 904-672-0119), or **Skate City Daytona** in South Daytona (call 904-788-4401).

There's a giant maze with different entrance points and a floor plan that changes weekly at **The Castle Adventure**, located east of Volusia Mall in Daytona Beach. There's also a video arcade, snack bar, and miniature golf. Call 904-238-3887. On rainy days, more indoor play areas are available at the **Discovery Zone** in Daytona Beach (call 904-257-0404), **KidSports** in Ormond Beach (call 940-673-5437), and **KidZoo** in Port Orange (call 904-322-8500).

Daytona International Speedway, Daytona
Photo courtesy of the FL Division of Tourism

Gamble Place and Spruce Creek Preserve are in nearby Port Orange. Spruce Creek is a 150-acre wildlife preserve once owned by James Gamble (of Proctor & Gamble fame). You can obtain a map for self-guided walking tours or take a pontoon-boat trip along Spruce Creek. Visitors can view the 1907 house, a citrus packing house, and the Snow White cottage, which is modeled after the one in the Walt Disney movie. Reservations are required to visit the house, cottage, and packing house. Admission is charged. Call 904-255-0285.

SEASONAL EVENTS

Daytona's a natural spot for golf tournaments. The **Sally Invitational Golf Tournament** is in mid-January at Oceanside Country Club. Call 904-677-7200. In late April, the prestigious LPGA **Sprint Titleholders Championship** is played at LPGA International.

For ticket information, call 904-672-7900 or 7200.

Racing fans can also find plenty of excitement in Daytona Beach. The biggest event is **Speedweeks**, which runs from late January through mid-February and culminates in the **Daytona 500** NASCAR race at the Daytona International Speedway. For information, call 904-253-RACE (7223). During spring break in late March, the **Daytona Beach Spring Speedway Spectacular** is held at the Speedway (call 904-255-7355), and July brings the **Racefest Celebration** (call 904-255-0981) and the **Pepsi 400** race (call 904-253-RACE). In October, the **Championship Cup Series** motorcycle races take place at Daytona International Speedway. Call 904-253-7223 or 800-854-1234.

In April, art lovers may find the **Ormond Art Show** at the Casements of interest. Call 904-677-3454. The

Florida International Festivaland, in July and August, features performances by the visiting London Symphony Orchestra and others. Call 904-257-7790. Over Fourth of July weekend, there's the **Jazz Matazz** at the Casements and Rockefeller Gardens. Call 904-677-3454 or 904-676-3257.

For a complete schedule of events, call the Daytona Beach Area Convention and Visitors Bureau at 904-255-0415 or 800-544-0415 to request their bi-annually published calendar of events.

ACCOMMODATIONS ....

Adam's Mark Daytona Beach Resort, at 100 North Atlantic Avenue, is an exotic-looking, blue-and-white hotel that resembles a tropical villa. Rooms are all oceanfront, and there are heated indoor and outdoor pools, a health club, and several nightclubs and restaurants. This hotel also participates in Golf Daytona Beach. Call 904-254-8200 or 800-872-9269.

The recently renovated **Daytona Beach Hilton Oceanfront Resort**, at 2637 South Atlantic Avenue, has a pool, fitness center, tennis courts, oceanfront rooms, and participates in Golf Daytona Beach. Call 904-767-7350 or 800-525-7350.

Harborside Inn Palm Coast Resort (formerly the Sheraton Palm Coast) is in Palm Coast, between Daytona Beach and St. Augustine. The resort offers rooms and villas, plus tennis and other exercise-and-recreational facilities, as well as discount golf packages to the fabulous golf courses here (see Golf Information). Call 800-654-6538.

A good place for families wishing to avoid college crowds is the **Granada Inn**, at 51 South Atlantic Avenue in Ormond Beach. Rooms have private balconies with ocean views, and there's an indoor and an outdoor pool. Call 904-672-7550 or 800-228-8089.

Best Western LaPlaya Resort, at 2500 North Atlantic Avenue, is located on the beach (as its Spanish name implies). Rooms face the ocean, and the hotel has a spa, game room, and a summer children's program. It participates in Golf Daytona Beach. Call 904-672-0990 or 800-875-6996.

Daytona Inn-Seabreeze, 730 North Atlantic Avenue, has a pool, wading pool, golf privileges, rooms with private balconies and patios, rooms with kitchens, and supervised children's activities in summer. Call 904-255-5491 or 800-874-1822.

Sun Viking Lodge, at 2411 South Atlantic Avenue, has heated indoor and outdoor pools, a kiddie pool, free children's activities during certain times, an exercise facility, lawn games, balconies, and picnic tables. Call 904-252-6252 or 800-874-4469.

SHOPPING ....

Bargain shoppers may want to visit the **Daytona Flea and Farmer's Market**, at the convergence of I-4, I-95, and FL 92 in Daytona Beach. The market covers over 40 acres with more than a thousand booths and an enclosed antique market. Open Friday through Sunday from 8 A.M. to 5 P.M.

RESTAURANTS ....

Live Oak Inn and Restaurant, at 448 South Beach Street, serves great food, with popular selections being pasta dishes and velvet satin pie. This non-smoking restaurant is in the historic district. Serves lunch and dinner. Call 904-252-4667.

The Cellar, at 220 Magnolia Avenue, is a charming downtown restaurant in President Harding's former home (now on the National Historic Register). The food is outstanding, and their French pastries are wonderful. Outdoor patio dining is available. Serves lunch and dinner (dinner by reservation only). Call 904-258-0011.

Top of Daytona is located on the twenty-ninth floor of a highrise building at 2625 South Atlantic Avenue. The food here is as spectacular as the ocean views. Serves lunch and dinner. Call 904-767-5791.

Park's Seafood Restaurant, at 951 North Beach Street, offers a nice view of the Halifax River in a quiet setting. They have an extensive seafood menu, with other specialties being ribs, steaks, and kids' meals. Open daily for dinner. Call 904-258-7272.

Hungarian Village, at 424 South Ridgewood, has a decor that features an impressive display of wooden musical instruments. Specialties include Wiener schnitzel and goulash. Open daily for lunch and dinner. Call 904-253-5712.

The Clubhouse Restaurant, at 600 Wilder Boulevard, serves breakfast, lunch, and dinner selections daily in a bright setting with great views. Call 904-257-0727.

JUST FOR KIDS ....

Playgrounds are located at City Island Park in Daytona Beach and at Ormond Tomb Park, Riviera Park, and Bicentennial Park in Holly Hill. Also, several area hotels have supervised children's programs in the high seasons (See Accommodations).

Florida's answer to New York's FAO Schwartz is **Dunn Toys and Hobbies**, founded in 1904. The store has two floors packed with toys, games, puzzles, and models, with demonstrations and samples to play with. **The Riverview Coffee Shop** downstairs serves lunch and snacks, and its walls have old photos and other memorabilia of Daytona. Call 904-253-3644. **Angell & Phelps Chocolate Factory**, at 154 South Beach Street, gives half-hour tours. Call 904-252-6531.

SIDE TRIPS ....

Visitors to the **Bulow Plantation Ruins State Historic Site**, on Old Dixie Highway north of Ormond Beach, can view the ruins of this 1821 plantation. There's also an open-air museum displaying local Seminole Indian artifacts. Visitors can picnic and rent canoes. Open daily. Call 904-439-2219.

GENERAL INFORMATION ....

Contact the Daytona Beach Area Convention and Visitors Bureau at 904-255-0415 or 800-544-0415. Publications of interest available from the visitors bureau include the *Golf Daytona Beach* brochure and a calendar of events.

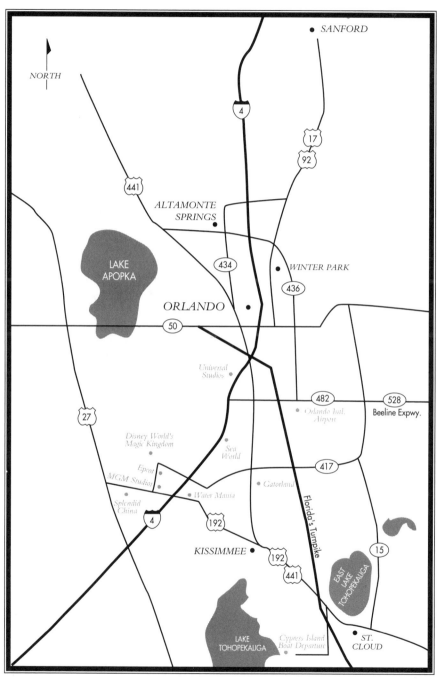

ORLANDO, FL.

Orlando

AREA CODE: 407

INTRODUCTION ....

Orlando is a place that almost needs no introduction, as it's the number-one domestic travel destination of Americans, in addition to being internationally known as a vacation capital. For the uninitiated, the city has a wide variety of theme parks and entertainment, and it is a delightful (albeit sometimes crowded) vacation spot for both adults and children. Though entire books have been dedicated to Orlando, the summary here will describe some major golf courses and attractions and provide other basic information. Attractions here are generally clustered within the cities of Orlando, Kissimmee-St. Cloud, and Lake Buena Vista.

For most visitors, the must-see sites in Orlando are the Magic Kingdom, Sea World, Epcot, and perhaps a movie theme park (Universal Studios Florida or Disney-MGM Studio). From there, the rest depends on how much time and resources are left to see other attractions. The region is quite spread out, so keep travel distances in mind. While the theme parks are mainly to the south and west areas of Orlando, the downtown section is relatively quiet and serene, as are the suburbs—like the refined Winter Park, which has been a long-time winter home of wealthy northern families and is known for its fine arts, culture, and dining.

Even before the historic day in October of 1971 when the Magic Kingdom opened its gates, Orlando was known as a land of theme parks—namely Cypress Gardens and Gatorland—which brought visitors inland from the beaches for an entertaining interlude. However, tourism is not the only industry that's been booming recently in Orlando. The city, which began as a soldier encampment during the Seminole Indian War and a trading post in the 1800s, is now a major technical and industrial center, thanks mostly to the establishment of the nearby Kennedy Space Center. Today, local electronics, aerospace, and defense industries make the community's economy a healthy one, although tourism is indeed the major economic force here.

Orlando is a popular vacation spot all year, but the largest crowds come in the summer months (which are winter months for those living below the equator), and February, March, and April. Generally, the least crowded months are May and September. Normal monthly temperatures are: January, 59.7; February, 61.2; March, 66.7; April, 71.2; May, 76.9; June, 81.1; July, 82.3; August, 82.5; September, 81; October, 75.2; November, 68; December, 62.1.

GOLF INFORMATION ....

GRENELEFE GOLF AND TENNIS RESORT, HAINES CITY (941) 422-7511

Grenelefe, on the shores of Lake Marion, features three, 18-hole courses: West, East, and South. The West is a 1971, Robert Trent Jones, Sr., design that, at 7325 yards, is one of the longest courses in Florida. The West course has long been considered one of the top public courses in the United States and Florida by *Golf Digest*. As with most of Jones's courses, this layout features long, tight fairways lined with pines, oaks, and lots of large sand bunkers. It also features very long par 5s, all over 560 yards. The tough par 4s, the first, ninth, and tenth holes, each are near 460 yards, and the par 3s are brutal—all over 200 yards, with the fourth hole reaching 230 yards. The East course is a 1978, Ed Seay/Arnold Palmer layout requiring more shotmaking than strength, which is a pleasant relief from the West course. You will enjoy the first tee on this course, which plays from the second story of the Grenelefe Conference Center, 50 feet above the first fairway. The South Course, designed by Ron Garl and PGA Tour player Andy Bean in 1983, is a 6869-yard, par 71 course with numerous lagoons and bunkers. This course requires patience and the use of most of the clubs in your bag, as well as careful thought on the greens to negotiate the many mounds, swales, and undulations.

Carts: Mandatory. *Greens Fees:* Please call, change seasonally (approximately $125 in high season/18 holes). *Tee Time Policy:* Advance reservations required. Resort guests can book up to sixty days in advance (or even farther in advance with some available packages). Non-guests can call twenty-four hours in advance.

HUNTER'S CREEK, ORLANDO
(407) 240-4653

Considered to be among the top seventy-five public courses in the United States by *Golf Digest*, Hunter's Creek may well be the longest course in Florida, stretching 7432 yards (the blue tees are 6905, the white tees are 6521, and the red tees are 5755 yards). The rating/slope ranges from 71/118 to 75.2/127. Designed by Lloyd Clifton and opened in 1986, Hunter's Creek, although relatively flat and open, has water on almost every hole and sand guarding most of its large greens.

Carts: Mandatory. *Greens Fees:* $32-$60/18 holes, including cart. *Tee Time Policy:* Advance times recommended. Can be reserved three days in advance.

WALT DISNEY WORLD RESORT,
LAKE BUENA VISTA

Consistent with its high standard of quality in everything it does, Disney offers excellent golf on its five, 18-hole courses. The Magnolia (call 407-824-2288) and Palm (call 407-824-2288) courses, which opened in 1971, and the Lake Buena Vista course (call 407-828-3741), which opened in 1972, are all Joe Lee designs. In 1992, Disney added Osprey Ridge (call 407-824-2675) by Tom Fazio and Eagle Pines (call 407-824-2675) by Pete Dye. The Magnolia, site of the PGA Tour's Walt Disney World/Oldsmobile Golf Classic, is a challenging, 7190-yard (the other tees range from 5414 to 6642 yards), par 72 course. The course rating/slope ranges from 70.55/123 to 73.9/133. Over 1500 magnolia trees line the course, several lakes come into play on ten of the holes, and there are over a hundred bunkers. The Palm, a past site of the Disney World/Oldsmobile Classic, ranges in yardage from 5311 to almost 7000 yards, with a course rating/slope ranging from 68.7/124 to 73/133. The 454-yard, par 4 eighteenth, with its tree-lined fairway and well-bunkered small green, has earned a fair amount of notoriety, ranking as the fourth-toughest hole on the PGA Tour. Lake Buena Vista, ranging from 5194 to 6819 yards with a course rating/slope ranging from 68.2/120 to 72.7/128, is a less demanding course than Magnolia and Palm, but it requires that a player execute a wide variety of shots to negotiate the lagoons and tropical vegetation. Osprey Ridge, Tom Fazio's recent addition, is ranked among the top ten courses in Florida by *Golf* (one of Fazio's four courses in the top ten) and was given 4½ stars by *Golf Digest's Places to Play.* This course, ranging from 5402 to 7101 yards with a rating/slope ranging from 68.9/121 to 73.9/135, winds through a lovely tropical wilderness of lush vegetation with palmetto, bay, cypress, pine, and scrub-oak trees. The abundant wildlife on the course includes osprey, wild turkey, tortoises, deer, armadillos, and rabbits. Finally, Eagle Pines, ranging from 4838 to 6772 yards with a rating/slope ranging from 66.3/115 to 72.3/131, has irregularly shaped fairways and vast sand beds, giving the course a unique look.

Carts: Mandatory (walking allowed sometimes on Lake Buena Vista). *Greens Fees:* Approx. $85-$120, depending on course and whether a player is a guest or non-guest of the resort/18 holes, including cart. *Tee Time Policy:* Resort guests can reserve thirty days in advance; non-resort guests can call four days in advance (seven days in advance during the offseason).

ARNOLD PALMER'S BAY HILL CLUB, ORLANDO (407) 876-2429

(Note: Open to resort guests only)

Bay Hill's Challenger/Champion course is one of the finest courses in the world, and it should be on your list of courses that must be played. Originally designed by Dick Wilson in 1961 and renovated by Arnold Palmer and Ed Seay in 1989, Bay Hill, like Palmer himself, is tough, fair, and exciting, with tees that range from 5192 to 7114 yards and a rating/slope that ranges from 70.3/120 to 74.6/141. It is equally beautiful, with colorful flowers, rosebuds, and tropical plants that sweep across 270 acres along the shores of the Butler Lakes chain. Bay Hill is the site of the PGA Tour's Nestle Invitational and of the USGA's Sectional United States Open qualifying. It was also the site of the USGA's 1991 Junior Championship won by Tiger Woods. The 441-yard, par 4 eighteenth hole, consistently ranking among the hardest holes on the PGA Tour, requires a blast of a drive followed by an approach to a double-tiered green that is fronted by a lake.

Carts: Caddie or cart mandatory. *Greens Fees:* Included in hotel package. *Tee Time Policy:* Only guests of Bay Hill Lodge can play course; advance reservations allowed for guests.

GRAND CYPRESS GOLF CLUB, ORLANDO (407) 239-4700 OR (407) 239-1904

(Note: Open to resort guests only)

Grand Cypress offers 45 holes of very fine golf on its 9-hole North, South, and East courses and 18-hole New course. The North and South courses were designed by Jack Nicklaus and Robert Cupp in 1984, and the same team collaborated on the East course which opened in 1985. Played together, the North/South courses range from 5360 to 7024 yards and feature towering grassy mounds, moguls, giant waste bunkers, sculptured sand traps, and platformed greens. Typifying the North/South combination are the two ninth holes, which share the same massive, V-shaped green. The ninth on the North is a wonderful 435-yard par 4, with water all the way up the right side. However, the right side is buffered by a huge waste area that nicely slows down the pace of a ball's search for water. The ninth on the South is a 463-yard par 4 that offers a considerably different look than its counterpart on the North. Set on the other side of the lake, the fairway borders the water on one side and has giant mounds running down the opposite side. The New course, opened in 1987, was designed by Nicklaus alone. It measures 6773 yards (tees begin at 5314 yards), is a par 72, and except for the nice warm sun and gentle breezes (rather than squalls and gale winds), you may as well be in Scotland. The New course features both large and small sand and grass bunkers, deep pot bunkers, seven double greens, and a windy burn (brook). Recently, *Golf* ranked both the New and

Jai Alai
Photo courtesy of the FL Division of Tourism

North/South courses among the top ten public courses in Florida.

Carts: Not required at New course; mandatory at other courses. *Greens Fees:* Approximately $80-$180/18 holes, including cart. *Tee Time Policy:* Open only to guests of Hyatt Regency Grand Cypress or Villas of Grand Cypress. Guests can book tee times when making room reservations.

OTHER EXCELLENT AREA COURSES:

Baytree National Golf Links, Melbourne (407-259-9060), an excellent, 1994, Gary Player layout with five sets of tees ranging from 4803 to 7043 yards, features waste areas of red shale. **Black Bear Golf Club**, Eustis (800-4BEAR-18) is a brand-new, par 72 course by P.B. Dye that sports six tees, ranging from 5100 to 7000 yards, and

offers Dye's usual unusual—sandy waste bunkers, dramatic elevation changes, wildly undulating greens, and a nineteenth "shoot-out" hole. **Eastwood Golf Club**, Orlando (407-281-4653), is a par 72, Lloyd Clifton layout, with tees ranging from 5393 to 7176 yards. Eastwood offers some of the best Bermuda-grass greens in Central Florida. **Falcon's Fire Golf Club**, Kissimmee (407-239-5445), is a 1993, Rees Jones design offering tees ranging from 5417 to 6900 yards and featuring the "Pro Shot" digital measurement system on every golf cart. **Palisades Country Club**, Clermont, 20 miles west of Orlando (904-394-0085), is a 7000-yard, par 72, Joe Lee course that overlooks Lake Minneola and features rolling terrain. **Metrowest Country Club**, Orlando (407-299-1099), is a wide-open, par 72, Robert Trent Jones course with tees ranging from 5325 to 7051 yards. **Mission Inn Golf and Tennis Resort**, Howey-on-the-Hills (904-324-3885), features the El Campeon ("Champion") course, originally designed in 1926 by C.E. Clarke of Troon, Scotland, and often considered among the top courses in Florida by *Golfweek*. This 6770-yard, par 72 course, featuring large and frequent elevation changes (some tees are actually 85 feet above the fairway), travels through old oaks, towering pines, and over and around many lakes. Also available at Mission Inn is the 6800-yard, par 72 Las Colinas course, designed by Gary Koch and opened in 1992. **Golden Ocala Golf and Country Club**, Ocala (904-622-0198), is considered among the top seventy-five public courses in the United States by *Golf Digest*. This Ron Garl course offers replica holes such as versions of the Road Hole at St. Andrews, the Postage Stamp at Royal Troon, and Augusta's Amen Corner. **Southern Dunes Golf and Country Club**, Haines City (941-421-4653), is a links-style course with tees that range from 5200 to 7200 yards. The course is built on sandhills and sports excellent, lightning-fast greens.

ATTRACTIONS ....

TOURS

Motor Tours

Pro Florida Tours, Inc., at 5401 South Kirkman Road in Orlando, offers tours to theme parks and attractions, such as the Kennedy Space Center and Busch Gardens. Free pickup is provided from many area hotels. Call 407-352-7707. **Gray Line of Orlando**, at 4950 L.B. McLeod Road, also has several tours; call 800-394-8687 for a list of half- and full-day programs available. Historic and theme tours are given by **Suncoast Sightseeing Tours** at 6149 Chancellor Drive in Orlando. Call 407-859-4211 or 800-827-0028.

Boat Tours

Cypress Island is a quiet island where exotic animals roam freely. Visitors can hike a 2-mile nature trail or take airboat gator safaris at night. Tour departs daily at 9 A.M. from the Country Store, at 1541 Scotty's Road in Kissimmee. Fee for trip, but parking is free. Call 407-935-9202.

Boggy Creek Airboat Rides, at 3702 Big Bass Road in Kissimmee, has half-hour cruises through 10 miles of unspoiled Florida wetlands, where alli-

gators, birds, and other wildlife can be seen up close. Tours run from 9 A.M. until dark daily. Call 407-344-9550. Similar airboat wildlife tours are given by **Toho Airboat Excursions, Inc.**, at 2001 Southport Road in Kissimmee, which also offers nighttime alligator safaris. Airboat tours run from 9 A.M. to 6 P.M. Call 407-931-2225.

Air Tours

Kissimmee Aviation Services, at 3031 West Patrick Street in Kissimmee, takes up to three guests per flight on one-hour and half-hour air tours. Call 407-847-9095.

Balloon Tours

Central Florida Balloon Tours in Winter Park serves guests champagne and picnic-style meals during sunrise and sunset flights. Call 407-294-8085. **Orange Blossom Balloons, Inc.**, of Lake Buena Vista serves guests champagne during flights, while a buffet meal awaits your return. Call 407-239-7677. **Rise and Float Balloon Tours** in Orlando uses Flamingo balloons. Call 407-352-8191.

HISTORIC PLACES

Osceola County Historical Museum and Pioneer Center, at 750 North Bass Road in Kissimmee, has a small museum of pioneer artifacts from the nineteenth and early twentieth centuries. There's also an 1899 Cracker House, a 1900 General Store, and a nature preserve with eight areas for picnicking, hiking, and relaxing. Open daily. Donation suggested. Call 407-396-8644.

MUSEUMS/SCIENCE CENTERS

Loch Haven Park is a science and cultural center with three major attractions: the **Orlando Science Center**, the **Orlando Museum of Art**, and the **Orange County Historical Museum**. The Orlando Science Center, at 810 East Rollins Street, is a large, kid-friendly museum with hands-on exhibit areas like the Nature Works, Waterworks, Tunnel of Discovery, and Weather Central. The facility also has a planetarium. Spectators can pet the stars of the live animal shows, from the furry to the slimy. Admission is charged. Call 407-896-7151. The Orlando Museum of Art, at 2416 North Mills Avenue, has sizeable collections of eighteenth- and nineteenth-century American art, African art, and pre-Columbian artifacts. Closed Mondays. Donations suggested. Call 407-896-4231. The Orange County Historical Museum, at 812 East Rollins Street, covers Florida's history from pre-history to the present. Fun exhibits are the General Store and a restored 1926 firehouse with antique fire trucks. Admission is charged. Call 407-897-6350.

On the landscaped grounds of Rollins College is the **Cornell Fine Arts Museum**, at 1000 Holt Avenue in Winter Park. The museum is noted for having the state's largest collection of American and European paintings, among other works. Open daily except Monday. Admission is free. Call 407-646-2526.

Charles Hosmer Morse Museum of American Art, at 133 East Welbourne Avenue in Winter Park, houses American art works. Most notable is their stained-glass collection (including Tiffany lamps), as well as their nineteenth- and twentieth-century painting, pottery, and (eye-popping) jewelry collections. Open daily except Monday. Admission is charged. Call 407-645-5311.

Flying Tigers Warbird Air Museum, at 231 Hoagland Boulevard in Kissimmee, is a museum and working restoration facility for World War II aircraft. On display are more than thirty antique planes. Open daily. Admission is charged. Call 407-933-1942.

CULTURAL OFFERINGS

The Orlando Opera Company, at 1111 North Orange Avenue, presents professional grand operas throughout the year. For information, call 407-426-1717 or 800-336-7372.

Civic Theater of Central Florida, at 1001 East Princeton Street, presents plays, musicals, and special productions. The box office is open weekdays. Call 407-896-7365.

RECREATION

Gatorland, between Kissimmee and Orlando at 14501 South Orange Blossom Trail, opened in 1949, predating Walt Disney World. The park is chock-full of gators, crocodiles, snakes, and other slimy, scaly, or bumpy reptiles. There's an observation deck where visitors can view the gator-breeding area, a small zoo with birds and mammals, a park-wide train ride, and presentations like a gator-wrestling show and snake show. Though it can seem a bit tawdry (the entrance is a large alligator jaw and the shows have melodramatic elements), Gatorland is a fun and longstanding Orlando tradition. Open daily. Admission is charged. Call 407-855-5496.

Cypress Gardens, located on

U.S. 27 off of I-4, combines entertainment (such as the popular water-skiing stunt show and the bird show) with an amusement area and a large botanical garden containing more than 8,000 international varieties of plants, as well as other attractions. Open daily. Admission is charged. Call 941-324-2111 or 800-237-4826.

Splendid China, at 3000 Splendid China Boulevard in Kissimmee, is a nice change from other theme parks. The park has realistic recreations of Chinese landmarks, from the Great Wall (not to scale, of course) to temples, buddha statues, and the Imperial Palace. Other fascinating exhibits include a fourteenth-century Chinese village. The park also features a play area for children and live entertainment like Chinese acrobatics and traditional dancers in costume. Open daily. Admission is charged. Call 407-396-7111 or 800-244-6226.

Sea World, at 7007 Sea World Drive, is the largest zoological park in the world, spanning 135 acres. Every one of its species is found in the world's oceans and their tributaries. Some of the more notable exhibits include: Terror of the Deep, where deadly sea creatures, such as piranhas, sharks, eels, and barracudas, lurk at a safe distance behind Plexiglas; the Penguin Encounter, with its fun and sometimes funny display of the little tuxedo-clad birds; Wild Arctic, featuring polar bears; and "Shamu: Close Up," the famous live show by the Shamu whale family. Additionally, there are touch-tank displays, play areas, other shows, and some live, non-fish creatures like birds, mammals, and reptiles. Admission is charged. Call 407-351-3600 extension 3625 or 800-327-2424.

Universal Studios Florida, at 1000 Universal Studios Plaza, celebrates famous movies, cartoons, and directors (mainly Hitchcock and Spielberg). The park has several unique rides and shows based on these movies, such as an *ET* ride, *Back to the Future* ride, *Earthquake* ride, *Jaws* ride, and a playground area based on the Fievel mouse *American Tail* movies. There's also a few streets patterned after famous United States city areas, from Chicago and San Francisco to New York and Hollywood. Other displays teach about special effects. Some of the rides may be too intense for young children (or less-daring adults). Admission is charged. Call 407-363-8000 or 800-232-7826.

There are many water parks in the area (admission charge for all), with pools, rides, and attractions for people of all ages and levels of daring. The major water parks are **Wet 'n' Wild**, at 6200 International Drive in Orlando (call 407-351-1800); **Water Mania**, at 6073 West Irlo Bronson Memorial Highway (call 407-396-2626); and the three at the Walt Disney Resort in Lake Buena Vista: **Blizzard Beach**, **River Country**, and **Typhoon Lagoon** (for information on these water parks, call 407-824-4321).

The theme parks at the **Walt Disney World Resort Complex** are world famous, and for good reason. For general information on Walt Disney World, including hotel reservations, operating hours, ticket information, and transportation information, call 407-824-4321. The following entries describe only the three main Disney parks (admission charge at all), although there are many other Disney attractions in the complex.

Magic Kingdom is Disney's world-renowned theme park. It's divided into several theme areas, each featuring rides, entertainment, displays, and vendors. The different theme areas include: Main Street U.S.A. a replica of a turn-of-the-century village with food, souvenir shops, and a train ride that circles the park; Fantasyland, where you'll find "It's a Small World" and several milder rides, like a carousel; Adventureland, featuring a terrific pirate ride, among other things; Frontierland, with a new Splash Mountain water ride based on *Song of the South*; Tomorrowland, which has the fast 'n' famous Space Mountain, plus futuristic displays; Liberty Square, containing the Hall of Presidents and the must-see Haunted Mansion; and for the younger set, Mickey's Starland, with a miniature village, Mickey's house, a stage show that delights youthful audiences, rides, and displays.

Epcot, the largest Disney Park, is divided into two main areas: World Showcase, which is a series of pavilions encircling a lagoon, each featuring a particular country and containing souvenirs, displays, entertainment, foods, music, and more; and Futureworld, with rides and displays centered on future technology in communications, energy, transportation, and a variety of other areas.

Disney-MGM Studios may sound a lot like Universal Studios, but they're actually quite different. Disney-MGM is divided into the following sections: Hollywood Boulevard, with the Great Movie Ride that has clips of famous movie moments; Sunset Boulevard, with the *Beauty and the Beast* stage show and a new thrill ride called the *Twilight Zone* Tower of Terror; Studio Courtyard, which demonstrates Disney animation techniques and special effects through a display on *The Lion King*, and has a *Little Mermaid* stage show; the Backlot, with the *Honey, I Shrunk the Kids!* Movie Set Adventure playground area; the Backlot Annex, with the Indiana Jones Stunt Spectacular and a simulated space ride called Star Tours (based on the *Star Wars* epics); and finally, Lakeside Circle, with displays and shows.

Leu Botanical Gardens, at 1730 Forest Avenue in Orlando, is on the former estate of citrus magnate Harry P. Leu. The house museum contains the original turn-of-the-century furnishings, and the 56-acre grounds feature a fabulous rose garden, orchid conservatory, and one of the eastern United States' largest collections of camellias. Open daily; call for hours. Admission is charged. Call 407-246-2620.

Mystery Fun House, at 5767 Major Boulevard in Orlando, is not for the meek. At the entrance is a warning that the display is 90 percent dark and contains graphic and gory scenes. With that said, the eighteen rooms have special lighting, effects, live characters, props, and sounds that create an outstanding haunted-house maze. If that isn't enough, the complex includes Star Base Omega, a laser-battle game (for a separate admission charge, you're issued a special costume and weapon), a miniature-golf course, and a video arcade. Admission is charged. Call 407-351-3355. For more haunted-house fun, check out the older and better-known **Terror on Church Street**, at Church Street and Orange Avenue in Orlando, which features a combination of live characters, special effects, and theatrics to make for a realistic haunting. Open 7 P.M. until midnight. Admission is charged. Call 407-649-3327.

Kennedy Space Center
Photo courtesy of the FL Division of Tourism

Jai Alai takes place at the **Orlando-Seminole Jai Alai**, located at 6405 South U.S. 17-92 in Fern Park, just off I-4 north of Orlando. Call 407-331-9191.

Dog racing is held from November through May at the **Sanford Orlando Kennel Club**, at 301 Dog Track Road in Longwood. Call 407-831-1600.

The Orlando Magic plays professional NBA basketball at the Orlando Arena, located at 600 West Amelia Street, 1 Magic Place. For information, call 407-839-3900.

There are many additional entertainment options for sunny and rainy days, from miniature-golf to paintball fighting (where opponents enter pretend battles with CO2 powered paintballs), laser-gun fighting, go-karts, bungy

jumping, and more. For more information, contact the Kissimmee-St. Cloud Convention and Visitors Bureau at 407-847-5000 or 800-327-9159, and the Orlando/Orange County Convention and Visitors Bureau at 407-363-5871.

SEASONAL EVENTS

February brings the **Central Florida Fair** to the area, with horses and livestock, music, entertainment, midway games, and rides. Call 407-295-3247. **The Kissimmee Bluegrass Festival** takes place in late February or early March. Call 800-327-9159. Golfers come to see the **PGA Nestlé Invitational** at the Bay Hill Golf and Country Club during the third week in March. Call 407-876-2888.

The Silver Spurs Rodeo comes in the summer and mid-winter. For information, call 800-327-9159.

In late October, the two-day **Pioneer Days Folk Festival** takes place at the Pine Castle Folk Arts Center, 6015 Randolph Street. Spectators can watch traditional crafts and skills dating from pioneer days, like syrup making, sugar-cane grinding, bluegrass music, clogging, and more. 407-855-7461.

In December, sports fans descend here for the **Florida Citrus Sports Holiday**—the events that precede and culminate in the Citrus Bowl on New Year's Day. Call 407-423-2476. Of course, major holidays like Christmas and Fourth of July bring many special festivities. For more information on these, or other, special events, contact the Kissimmee-St. Cloud Convention and Visitors Bureau at 407-847-5000 or 800-327-9159, and the Orlando/

Orange County Convention and Visitors Bureau at 407-363-5871.

ACCOMMODATIONS ....

EXPENSIVE

The Grand Floridian, at the Walt Disney World Resort Complex, is a four-star hotel on the Seven Seas Lagoon. The Victorian, gingerbread-like structure features elegant rooms, a lovely beach, an exercise room, tennis courts, and a children's program. Call 407-824-3000.

The recently opened **Disney Institute**, at the Walt Disney World Resort Complex, is best suited for adults or families with older children. Aside from terrific accommodations, this resort offers some eighty hands-on activities within nine broad categories, such as Culinary Arts and Entertainment Arts. You can choose to customize your vacation around activities like cooking, shooting videos, creating animation, canoeing through a wilderness preserve, learning to take quality photographs, and more. Call 407-282-9282 or 800-4-WONDER.

Just opened in 1996 are the **Disney Boardwalk Villas and Inn** (two separate accommodations), which feature health clubs, community halls, arcades, regular pools, and an amusement-park theme pool. For information and reservations, call 407-939-7746.

The Renaissance Hotel, at 6677 Sea Harbor Drive in Orlando, has many resort amenities, including children's programs and golf on the premises. Call 407-351-5555.

The Peabody Orlando, at 9801 International Drive in Orlando, has a lovely interior graced with a fountain, marble floors, and modern artworks. Guests enjoy pools, lounges, a health spa, golf privileges, tennis, and a children's program. Call 407-352-4000 or 800-732-2639.

Two of the area's finest golf-resort complexes only allow guests to play the courses. They are: **Arnold Palmer's Bay Hill Club**, at 9000 Bay Hill Boulevard (800-523-5999), and the **Grand Cypress Resort**, at 1 Jacaranda Boulevard, made up of the Hyatt Regency Grand Cypress (800-233-1234) and the Villas of Grand Cypress (800-835-7377). (See Golf Information.) While both resorts offer pools and tennis facilities, the Grand Cypress Resort also offers children's activities.

MODERATE

Holiday Inn Sunspree Resort, at 13351 FL 535 in Lake Buena Vista, is a great family place. Rooms have VCRs, and there's a courtyard pool, wading pool, and whirlpool. However, the real attractions are the extensive, and free, children's programs, with arts and crafts and magic shows. There are also children's suites and the special restaurant where kids eat free while parents dine in a separate room (with beeper rentals for peace of mind). Call 407-239-4500 or 800-366-6299.

All-Star Sports and All-Star Music Resorts are located at the intersection of World Drive and U.S. 192, southwest of Epcot and Disney-MGM Studios. The complex has hotels centered around sports themes (basketball, football, baseball, tennis, and surfing) and music themes (country-and-western, rock-and-roll, calypso, jazz, and Broadway), which are reflected in the landscaping, decor, and architecture. These resorts are huge, with fun surprises (like a guitar-shaped pool), as well as food courts, game rooms, pools, and babysitting services. Call 407-934-7639.

Sheraton Lakeside Inn, at 7769 West Irlo Bronson Memorial Highway in Kissimmee, is a 27-acre complex surrounding a small lake. The hit here is not the hotel's interior, but the amenities: three pools, a wading pool, tennis, boating, fishing, a children's program, and miniature-golf. Call 407-396-2222 or 800-848-0801.

INEXPENSIVE

Quality Inn Plaza, at 9000 International Drive in Orlando, allows pets. There's a game room, three pools, and an on-site restaurant. Though it's not luxurious, it's near the parks and reasonably priced. Call 407-345-8585.

Wynfield Inn-Westwood, at 6263 Westwood Boulevard in Orlando, has comfortable, cheerful rooms. There's also a game room, and two pools. Call 407-345-8000 or 800-346-1551.

Kissimmee is the best place for no-frills, small-but-adequate, inexpensive motels near the major theme parks. There are two quality motels in Kissimmee. **The Park Inn International**, at 4960 West Irlo Bronson Memorial Highway, is a Mediterranean-style motel with a pool and game room. Not luxurious, but a good value. Call 407-396-1376 or 800-327-0072. Also try **King's Motel**, at 4836 West Irlo Bronson Memorial Highway on Lake Cecile. This motel has a pool, playground, and free coffee in the lobby. Call 407-396-4762 or 800-952-5464.

SHOPPING

The following are several of the most notable shopping spots, though there's many a place to spend a buck down here. Before you head off, check for distances from where you're staying.

The Church Street Exchange, at 124 West Church Street in Orlando, is a Victorian-style complex with the feel of a theme park, where you'll find shopping, nightlife, and dining. Over fifty shops are here (including Augusta Janssen, where the kids will enjoy watching fudge being made). Across the street is the **Historic Railroad Depot**, with pushcarts and specialty shops.

The Old Town Shops is another entertainment-and-shopping complex in Kissimmee (at 5770 Irlo Bronson Memorial Parkway). It features an early twentieth-century, Floridian-village theme. Highlights include a 1909 carousel, a Ferris wheel from 1928, a Saturday night cruise, nickel Pepsi Colas, and over seventy stores and restaurants.

The Mercado, at 8445 South International Drive, is a Spanish/Mediterranean-style shopping village with over sixty stores, international foods, and a courtyard featuring live music. Orlando's Official Visitor Information Center is located here, as well.

In Lake Buena Vista, there are two noteworthy shopping districts. At **The Crossroads at Lake Buena Vista**, located at FL 535 and I-4, across from the entrance to the hotels in Lake Buena Vista, visitors can find a grocery store, pharmacy, post office, bank, and over twenty shops. The other is the **Disney Village Marketplace**, on Lake Buena Vista Lagoon, with shops selling Disney gift items, clothes and collectibles, as well as artwork, crafts, clothing, and more.

For outlet shoppers, the area's largest center, **Belz Factory Outlet World and International Design Outlet,** at 5401 Oakridge Road in Orlando, contains over 170 shops. **The Quality Outlet Center** and the **Quality Center East**, at 5409 and 5529 International Drive, have over twenty outlets, as does the **Manufacturer's Outlet Mall**, on U.S. 192 a mile east of FL 535.

The St. Cloud Historic District's antique district, at 1200 New York Avenue in St. Cloud, has more than a dozen shops with merchandise from the rare and valuable to chichi. Call 407-892-3671.

RESTAURANTS ....

DINNER THEATERS

Themed dinner theaters abound here. They tend to be pricey but, with the right frame of mind, lots of fun. Here are a few notable choices. The medieval-English **King Henry's Feast** is located at 8984 International Drive in Orlando (call 407-351-5151). The western-style **Wild Bill's Wild West Dinner Show** is at 5260 West Irlo Bronson Memorial Highway in Kissimmee (call 407-351-5151). **Arabian Nights** features trick riders and special effects (dinner is prime rib or lasagna). It's located at 6225 West Irlo Bronson Memorial Highway (call 407-239-9221 or -9223). **Medieval Times**, at 4510 West Irlo Bronson Memorial Highway, features lots of knights, jousting, and damsels in distress (call 407-396-1518). **Capone's Dinner and Show**, at 4740 West Irlo Bronson Memorial Highway, is a 1930s-style cabaret and speakeasy (call 407-397-2378). **Sleuth's Mystery Dinner Show** is at 7508 Republic Drive in Orlando (call 407-363-1985). **Mark Two**, at 3376 Edgewater Drive in Orlando, has classic Broadway musicals like *Oklahoma!* and *The King and I* (call 407-843-6275). Seaworld's **Polynesian Luau** features an Hawaiian-style dinner and entertainment. It's located at 7007 Sea World Drive in Orlando (call 407-363-2200 or 800-227-8048).

FINE DINING

Dux, at 9801 International Drive in the Peabody Hotel, Orlando, is one of the finest restaurants in the city, serving creative gourmet entrées and spectacular desserts. Call 407-352-4000.

Atlantis, at 6677 Sea Harbor Drive in the Renaissance Hotel, Orlando, specializes in gourmet seafood dishes with a regional twist. Reservations are suggested. Call 407-351-5555.

Victoria and Albert's, at the Grand Floridian Resort in the Walt Disney World Resort Complex, is an unusual fine-dining experience. Each table is served by a male-and-female pair, calling themselves Victoria and Albert, who recite the gourmet menu. The decor is Victorian, of course. Jacket required. Call 407-824-1089.

CASUAL DINING

Charley's Steak House, at 2901 Parkway Boulevard in the Parkway Pavilion Shops in Kissimmee (though there are other locations around the Orlando area), has an atmosphere straight from yesteryear, with faux tiffany lamps and old portraits. Menu selections include steaks and seafood. Call 407-396-6055.

The menu at **Cafe Tu Tu Tango**, at 8625 International Drive in Orlando, is cosmopolitan, with a variety of appetizer-size selections featuring chicken, beef, and seafood (e.g. chicken quesadillas, Cajun chicken egg rolls, etc.). The food is served on painter's palettes. The painter/artist theme is fun, and the sangria is delicious. Call 407-248-2222.

Austin's, at 8633 International Drive in Orlando, is named after Stephen Austin, first president of the Republic of Texas. Specialties include grilled and barbecued chicken, beef, fish, and shrimp, with burgers and the like to keep kids happy. Call 407-363-9575.

Kobe Japanese Steak House, at 2901 Parkway Boulevard in Kissimmee, has seafood, steaks, and sushi, as well as selections for children, all prepared tableside. There's another location at 8460 Palm Parkway in Lake Buena Vista. Call 407-396-8088.

JUST FOR KIDS ....

This entire area is a child's fantasy come true. However, be aware that a few places have attractions that may be too scary for younger kids (e.g., some of the rides at Universal Studios), although at Universal Studios and other places there are rides and/or special areas for younger children.

Many hotels have children's programs, at least during the high season, as well as babysitting services.

SIDE TRIPS ....

Kennedy Space Center is about an hour's drive east of Orlando, and well worth the trip. This active, yet historic, space center is where the *Apollo 11* lifted off on July 16, 1969, for its groundbreaking, three-man voyage to the moon. It's also where more than forty shuttle missions have been launched, in addition to satellites, Skylab missions, and more. The visitors center, with exhibits and an IMAX theater featuring a five-story screen, is called Spaceport USA. In the facility, there's a simulated futuristic space journey that lasts about forty minutes, an outside Rocket Garden with real retired rockets, a Gallery of Space Flight with real space capsules, and a moon rock. Don't miss the moving memorial to the sixteen astronauts who died during missions and/or training. Call 407-452-2121. For more space history, the **United States Astronaut Hall of Fame,** at 6225 Vectorspace Boulevard in nearby Titusville, showcases the lives and accomplishments of the United States' space heroes. It's also where the children's "Space Camp" program is located. Open daily. Call 407-269-6100.

Lake Wales, about an hour's drive south of Orlando, is home to the lovely **Bok Tower Gardens**, located at 1151 Tower Boulevard, about 3 miles from U.S. 27A. Bok Tower is a 205-foot tower of marble and coquina (a building material with a seashell base) that is situated on Iron Mountain, the highest point on the Florida peninsula. The tower has a fifty-seven-bell carillon, and its bronze doors have ornate carvings of scenes from the Book of Genesis. The visitors center shows a film of the tower's history (the film also shows the interior, which isn't open to the public). Surrounding the tower are 128 acres, and the grounds have nature trails, a bird observatory, and flower gardens. Admission is charged. Call 941-676-1408. A fine Swiss chalet–style restaurant here is **Chalet Suzanne**, at 3800 Chalet Suzanne Drive, with gourmet offerings like filet mignon and lobster Newburgh, or a seven-course prix fixe dinner. The house dessert is crepe Suzanne. Call 941-676-6011.

GENERAL INFORMATION ....

Contact the Kissimmee-St. Cloud Convention and Visitors Bureau at 407-847-5000 or 800-327-9159, and the Orlando/Orange County Convention and Visitors Bureau at 407-363-5871. Publications of interest to visitors include the *Welcome Area Guide-Map*, which can be found at visitor information centers or obtained for $1.00 from CJ Publishers, 3734 131st Avenue North, Suite 13, Clearwater, Florida 34622. Call 800-940-8626. Some good free travel guides you can find locally or call to obtain are: *The Best Read Guide*, published in Orlando (call 407-363-3600); *See Magazine* (call 407-363-7491); and *Happy Florida*, available in both English and Portuguese (call 407-354-3080). You'll find these and many other magazines and brochures at various locations like visitors centers, restaurants, motels, and other attractions.

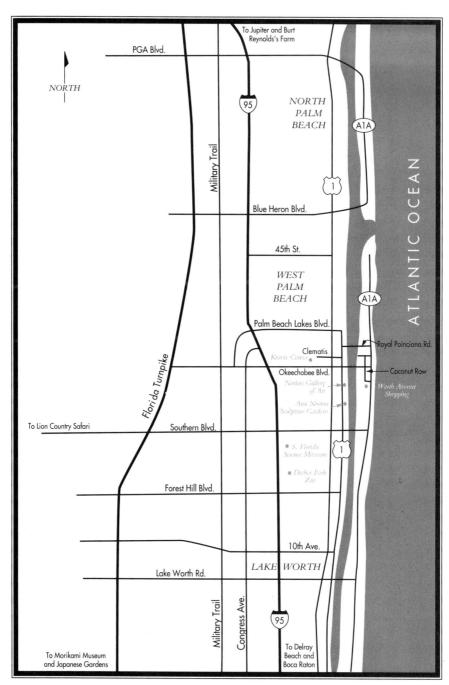

PALM BEACH AREA, FL.

Palm Beach area

INTRODUCTION ....

Known as a playground for the rich since it was founded, Palm Beach has world-renowned beaches, elegant streets lined with mansions, famous shopping districts, and plenty of museums and art galleries. The lush semi-tropical foliage makes for a perfect resort setting, much of it thanks to an 1878 shipwreck in which a cargo of coconuts, which landed on the island, sprouted roots, and literally, were fruitful and multiplied. But the main influence for turning this land of coconut groves and fishermen into an exclusive luxury resort was the railroad that Henry Flagler brought here, which connected the area to the northeast. The development of West Palm Beach, across Lake Worth on the mainland, also increased during this time. However, at that time Lake Worth was used as a place to put up the servants while their wealthy employers enjoyed the beach.

Though it still draws the well-to-do and can be quite expensive, Palm

Beach is far more accessible today than in previous eras, and recent revitalizations in the areas of arts and culture make it all the more attractive to visitors of all types. The climate and beauty also make the location ideal for enjoying beautiful beaches and for playing golf (as evidenced by the more than 150 area courses, counting private ones), and other sports, from tennis to polo.

The normal monthly temperatures, as measured in West Palm Beach, are: January, 65.1; February, 66.2; March, 70; April, 73.4; May, 77.6; June, 80.6; July, 82.2; August, 82.5; September, 81.6; October, 77.8; November, 72.3; December, 67.4. The high season here runs from November through April, with February being the peak month for visitors.

GOLF INFORMATION ....

Palm Beach has a Golf-a-round program from April to December, in which guests at about a hundred area hotels can play a free round of golf daily at one of approximately ten courses. For information, call the Palm Beach County Convention and Visitors Bureau at 561-471-3995.

EMERALD DUNES GOLF CLUB, WEST PALM BEACH (561) 687-1700

Emerald Dunes, a Tom Fazio design that opened in 1990, is probably the finest course in the Palm Beach area. *Golf* ranks it the number-eight public course in Florida (that's out of more than a thousand golf courses) and named it one of the "Top 100 You Can Play" in 1996, and *Golf Digest's Places to Play* gives it 4½ stars (a half-star below its top rating). Fazio clearly is in tune with what's fun for golfers nowadays. His courses reward good strategy but are not penal. Emerald Dunes ranges in yardage from 4676 (the Ruby tees) to 7006 (the Tiger tees) yards, and the rating/slope ranges from 67.1/115 to 73.8/133. The signature centerpiece of Emerald Dunes is the "SuperDune," which rises more than 50 feet, making it one of the highest points in Palm Beach County. The SuperDune accommodates three tees, three greens, a waterfall and cascades, and provides an exciting vantage of the entire course and the surrounding area. Like Fazio's other courses, Emerald Dunes certainly will provide you with a memorable round of golf and is a must if you are in the area.

Carts: Walking permitted but must maintain pace of play. Rates are the same for walking. *Greens Fees:* $65-$125/18 holes, including cart. *Tee Time Policy:* Must reserve thirty days in advance; can reserve up to forty-five days in advance with a $50 reservation fee.

WEST PALM BEACH MUNICIPAL COUNTRY CLUB, WEST PALM BEACH (561) 582-2019

West Palm, once a stop on the PGA Tour, boasting winners such as Arnold Palmer, Julius Boros, and Gibby Gilbert, is considered among the top seventy-five pubic courses in the country by *Golf Digest*. A Dick Wilson layout, with origins dating back to 1921, this 18-hole, par 72 championship course has tees that range from 5884 to 6789 yards and a rating/slope around 73/125. Set on 200 acres of rolling terrain, it winds among a wide variety of trees including cabbage, coconut and bottle-branch palms, Australian pines, and live oaks.

Like many older courses, it has little water and few elevated greens, and it is fairly straightforward as to the shots required. Given the quality of the course and the very reasonable greens fees, West Palm is heavily played during the peak seasons (late fall through spring). To provide all players a chance to play, it uses a lottery system to provide tee times.

Carts: Walkers are accepted after 12:30 P.M.; carts mandatory for morning starting times. *Greens Fees:* Approximately $11-$31 (varies seasonally, has twilight discounts)/18 holes; carts: $10 per person. *Tee Time Policy:* Advance tee times generally not the rule here. The club has a lottery system held each night before play; on Wednesday night, names are drawn for Saturday and Thursday times; on Thursday night, names are drawn for Friday and Sunday times.

Golf lessons
Photo courtesy of Palm Beach Convention and Visitors Bureau

PALM BEACH POLO AND COUNTRY CLUB, WEST PALM BEACH
(561) 798-7401

This resort sports two, 18-hole courses: Dunes by Ron Garl and Jerry Pate, and Cypress by Pete and P.B. Dye. There's also a 9-hole course by George and Tom Fazio. The 1984 Dunes course, considered to be among the top resort courses in the United States by *Golf Digest*, offers tees ranging from 5516 to over 7050 yards, with a rating/slope from 71.4/122 to 73.6/132. It is remarkably similar to a Scottish links–type layout, with fairways that have rolls, ripples, and swales that are bordered by extensive mounding and water. The greens are surrounded by bunkers, pot bunkers, grass traps, and waste areas. The Cypress course, which has hosted the PGA Tour's Chrysler Team Championship, measures from 5172 to over 7116 yards with a rating/slope ranging from 69.8/121 to 74.4/138. This course has many hallmark Dye features: huge bunkers, pot bunkers, lots of water, blind shots, a tree in the middle of a fairway (your approach on the fourteenth hole must contend with a cypress), sharp drop-offs to bunkers and water, and greens that range from very small to enormous (the fifteenth hole's green is more than 20,000 square feet).

Carts: Mandatory. *Greens Fees:* Approximately $75-$100/18 holes; carts: $15 per person. *Tee Time Policy:* Can be reserved two days in advance for members and guests. Non-guests must reserve at least five days in advance.

PGA NATIONAL RESORT AND SPA, PALM BEACH GARDENS (561) 627-2000 OR (800) 633-9150 (Note: Open to resort guests only). PGA National offers 90 holes of golf on its five excellent courses. Champion was designed by Tom and George Fazio and renovated by Jack Nicklaus. Haig, dedicated to Walter Hagen, and Squire, dedicated to Gene Sarazen, are also Tom and George Fazio layouts. General is an Arnold Palmer design and is dedicated to the General (of Arnie's Army) himself. Estate is by Karl Litten. Although each course possesses its own personality (for example, the 150-yard markers on the Haig course are rose bushes, so you remember "to stop and smell the roses," as Hagen always recommended), a trait common to them all is water, which comes into play on over 80 of the 90 holes—so you might want to bring a couple of extra balls. The best of the courses probably is the Champion. It was the site of the 1987 PGA Championship and 1983 Ryder Cup Matches, and it is listed among the top resort courses in the United States by *Golf Digest*. Champion ranges from 5377 to 7022 yards and the rating/slope ranges from 70.9/121 to an awesome 74.4/142. As indicated, water is a major factor on Champion, framing many of the fairways and greens. For example, the number-one handicap hole, the 444-yard, par 4 eleventh, requires a tee shot that will avoid the lake on the left side of the fairway, an approach shot that will avoid the lake on the right side of the green and a trap on the left side, and there's even more water further to the green's left—bring a life jacket.

Carts: Mandatory. *Greens Fees:* Approximately $85-$125/18 holes; cart: $20 per person. *Tee Time Policy:* Open to resort guests only; can reserve up to a year in advance.

OTHER EXCELLENT AREA COURSES: **Ballantrae Golf and Yacht Club**, Port St. Lucie (561-337-5315), is situated along the lovely St. Lucie River. This 7022-yard, Jack Nicklaus signature course has a Scottish links–type layout and lots of water. **Binks Forest Golf Course**, Wellington (561-795-0028) is a 1990, Johnny Miller layout that plays to a par 72, with tees that range from 5600 to almost 7000 yards and a rating/slope from 71.3/127 to 75/138. **Delray Beach Golf Club**, Delray Beach (561-243-7380), is a vintage Donald Ross course, which opened in 1923. It features a 6907-yard, par 72 layout. **Polo Trace Golf and Tennis Club**, Delray Beach (561-495-5301), was designed by Karl Litton and the PGA Tour's Joey Sindelar in 1989. It is an excellent links-type course that can reach almost 7100 yards.

ATTRACTIONS ....

TOURS

Old Northwood Historic District Tours gives walking tours of West Palm Beach's historic district on Sundays. Call 561-863-5633.

The Star of Palm Beach paddlewheeler takes visitors on daily sightseeing and dinner-dance cruises along the Intracoastal Waterway. It is located on Blue Heron Boulevard in Riviera Beach. Call 561-842-0882.

HISTORIC PLACES

The 1925 **Bethesda-by-the-Sea**

Church, at 141 South County Road, founded by southeast Florida's first Protestant congregation, features gothic-style architecture with a stone tower, elegant archways, and beautifully landscaped gardens. Admission is free. Call 561-655-4554.

Whitehall (also called the Flagler Museum), at Cocoanut Row at Whitehall Way in Palm Beach, is the palatial, 1901 home of railroad magnate Henry Flagler. The seventy-three rooms are an art museum in themselves, as they're filled with the family's artworks and other furnishings (including lace, dolls, silver, clothing, and a 1200-pipe organ). There's also a railroad history exhibit, and Flagler's personal railroad car is parked out behind the house. Open daily except Monday. Admission is charged. Call 561-655-2833.

MUSEUMS/SCIENCE CENTERS

South Florida Science Museum, at 4801 Dreher Trail North in West Palm Beach, contains an aquarium with touch tanks, a public observatory with the state's most powerful telescope, a planetarium, and a laser-light show. Open daily. Admission is charged. Call 561-832-1988.

Hibel Museum of Art, at 150 Royal Poinciana Plaza on Lake Worth, displays works by American artist Edna Hibel, in addition to antique furniture, books, and dolls. Admission is free. Call 561-833-6870.

CULTURAL OFFERINGS

The Kravis Center for the Performing Arts, at 701 Okeechobee Boulevard in West Palm Beach, is a huge (2200-seat) showcase theater where more than 300 music, dance, theater, and opera performances take place annually. Call 561-832-7469. For more live theater, there's the Royal Poinciana Playhouse at 70 Royal Poinciana Plaza in Palm Beach. Call 561-659-3310.

Palm Beach Opera, at 415 South Oliva Avenue in West Palm Beach, performs during winter months at the Kravis Center. Call 561-833-7888.

Norton Gallery and School of Art, at 1451 South Olive Avenue, displays mainly Chinese bronze and jade sculptures, as well as nineteenth- and twentieth-century French and American paintings. It also has an outdoor sculpture patio. Open daily. Donation suggested. Call 561-832-5194.

The prestigious Ballet Florida, at 500 Fern Street in West Palm Beach, has toured internationally, receiving high praise. Their local season is during winter months. Call 561-659-2000.

Puppetry Arts Center has puppet shows on Friday evenings and some Saturday mornings. It's located at the Cross County Mall in West Palm Beach, 4356 Ocheekobee Boulevard. Call 561-687-3280.

RECREATION

The 22-acre Dreher Park Zoo, at 1301 Summit Boulevard in West Palm Beach, has over 500 specimens, including the endangered Florida Panther. Open daily. Admission is charged. Call 561-533-0887.

The Burt Reynolds Ranch and Film Studio, at 16133 Jupiter Farms Road in Jupiter, is Reynolds's own working ranch. A bus tour of the 160-acre ranch shows visitors the house, chapel, a petting barnyard, and working film sets. Admission is charged. Call 561-747-5390.

The **Ann Norton Sculpture Gardens**, at 253 Barcelona Road in West Palm Beach, has an impressive collection of Norton's works throughout the 3-acre park (Mrs. Norton was Ralph M. Norton's second wife). Hours are inconsistent, so call first. Admission is charged. Call 561-832-5328.

Be sure to drive along the **Canyon of Palm Beach**. It's an amazing, man-made feat, since the road (Country Club Road) was cut through sandstone and limestone that was over 25 feet deep.

Spectator sports abound here. There's racing year-round (chiefly drag and motorcycle) at the **Moroso Motorsports Park** in Palm Beach Gardens, at 17047 Beeline Highway (call 561-622-1400); greyhound racing at the **Palm Beach Kennel Club**, at 1111 North Congress Avenue at Belvedere Road and at 1415 West Forty-fifth Street (Exit 54 off I-95), both in West Palm Beach (call 561-683-2222); base-ball spring training for the Montreal Expos (for tickets, call 561-684-6801) and the Atlanta Braves (for tickets, call 561-683-6100) at Municipal Stadium in West Palm Beach, 1610 Palm Beach Lakes Boulevard. The **Palm Beach Expos** (minor-league baseball) also play at Municipal Stadium. The Municipal Stadium number is 561-684-6801. Fans can watch polo at the **Palm Beach Polo and Country Club**, at 13420 South Shore Boulevard in West Palm Beach. Call 561-793-1440. **The World Cup Competition** for polo, sponsored by the Palm Beach Polo and Country Club, is held each spring at the Palm Beach Polo Stadium in Wellington. For information, call 561-793-1440. To play polo, call the **Gulfstream Polo Club**,

at 4550 Polo Road in Lake Worth, which is available for teams of certain handicaps. Call 561-965-2057.

Fishing and boating are big in Palm Beach, as are scuba diving, snorkeling, and canoeing. For divers, there's an abundance of reefs, shipwrecks, and even an underwater statue of Neptune for exploring. For information, call the Palm Beach County Convention and Visitors Bureau at 561-471-3995.

Cyclists will enjoy the miles of beautiful bike paths here, which are some of the most scenic in United States. For information, contact the Palm Beach County Bicycle Coordinator at 561-684-4170.

SEASONAL EVENTS

In mid-January, there's a seventeen-day **South Florida Fair and Exhibition**, with midway games and rides, agricultural exhibits, contests, and live entertainment. The fairgrounds are at 9067 Southern Boulevard in West Palm Beach. Call 561-793-0333 or 800-527-3247.

In February at the **Flagler Museum**, the employees don turn-of-the-century costumes and provide period refreshments, music, special events, and show special films and exhibits. Call 561-655-2833. February also brings a seafood festival to West Palm Beach. Call 561-832-6397.

In early May, the five-day **Sunfest** takes place in West Palm Beach. The festival celebrates art and jazz with live music, exhibitions, water sports, contests, and more. Call 561-659-5980. Also in May is the **West Palm Beach Celebration** on the Intracoastal Waterway, with water events, jazz, arts, and live entertainment. Call 561-659-5992.

ACCOMMODATIONS ....

EXPENSIVE

PGA National Resort and Spa, at 400 Avenue of the Champions in Palm Beach Gardens, is a fabulous golf resort (See Golf Information), with plenty for non-golfers and children. This expensive but worthwhile hotel has deluxe accommodations and a long list of amenities that even includes special mineral pools. Call 561-627-2000 or 800-633-9150.

Brazilian Court, at 301 Australian Avenue in Palm Beach, is located just two blocks from Worth Avenue's shopping district and the beach. The hotel has a heated pool, a renowned restaurant and bistro, and entertainment most nights. Call 561-655-7740 or 800-552-0335.

The Breakers, at 1 South County Road in Palm Beach, has long been a choice of the rich and famous. This oceanfront hotel, which has been rebuilt after twice being destroyed, has lovely vaulted ceilings, a private beach, tennis, spa, three dining rooms with outstanding food, and many luxurious amenities. Golfers can play the 36 holes of golf here while kids enjoy the playground, pool, and children's programs. Call 561-659-8440 or 800-833-3141.

EXPENSIVE/MODERATE

Heart of Palm Beach, at 160 Royal Palm Way in Palm Beach, has rooms with private balconies, patios, and refrigerators. The hotel accepts pets, and provides bellhops, a valet service, and a heated pool with poolside service. Call 561-655-5600 or 800-523-5377.

Worth Avenue shopping, Palm Beach
Photo courtesy of the FL Department of Commerce, Division of Tourism

Palm Beach area, FL

Holiday Inn Sunspree Resort Palm Beach Oceanfront, at 3700 North Ocean Drive on Singer Island, is an especially good choice for families, with lots of activities for both children and adults. There's a heated pool, a terrific spa, and nice additional amenities like hair dryers, refrigerators, and computer-compatible phones in rooms. Call 561-848-3888 or 800-443-4077.

MODERATE/INEXPENSIVE

Beachcomber, at 3024 South Ocean Boulevard in Palm Beach, is a beachfront motel that borders the line between inexpensive and moderate. The pool is saltwater, which is not for everyone. While small, it's comfortable, reasonably priced, and best of all, on the beach. Call 561-585-4646.

Royal Inn, at 675 Royal Palm Beach Boulevard in West Palm Beach, is on a lake, and the rooms have balconies and patios. Other amenities include a pool, restaurant, barber shop, lawn games, and in-room refrigerators. Call 561-793-3000.

SHOPPING ....

Worth Avenue in Palm Beach is world-famous for its luxury shopping, with stores like Hermes, Saks Fifth Avenue, and Van Cleef & Arpels. The more than 250 stores stretch from the beach on the east end in Palm Beach to Lake Worth on the west end.

Another popular shopping area is the strip along **South County Road**, about six blocks north of Worth Avenue.

A fashionable shopping district (and a key nightlife spot in West Palm Beach) is the up-and-coming **Clematis Street** area. You'll find nice stores as well as bars and restaurants here, with pretty landscaping and lovely waterfront parks.

RESTAURANTS ....

DINNER THEATER

Jupiter Dinner Theater, at 1001 East Indiantown Road in Jupiter, has Broadway-type productions, often with well-known stars. Call 561-746-5566.

FINE DINING

Café L'Europe, at 150 Worth Avenue (in the Esplanade) in Palm Beach, is an elegant restaurant with walnut paneling, pink banquettes, classical music, and fabulous food. Jacket required. Lunch (except Sunday) and dinner served daily. Call 561-655-4020.

Café Du Parc, at 612 North Federal Highway (U.S. 1) in Lake Park, serves specialties like beef Wellington, sweetbreads, and veal medallions, with an accent on French cuisine and decor. The restaurant is located within a restored home. Jacket and reservations required. Closed September to mid-October. Hours vary seasonally. Call 561-845-0529.

CASUAL DINING

At **Chuck & Harold's**, at 207 Royal Poinciana Way in Palm Beach, you may wind up rubbing elbows with celebrities. This attractive restaurant emphasizes pasta, fresh fish, and seafood dishes. Children's meals and outdoor dining are available. Open daily for breakfast, lunch, and dinner. Call 561-659-1440.

Basil's Neighborhood Café, at 771 Village Boulevard in West Palm Beach, has gourmet pizza and fresh seafood, and a fun mural of famous people. Open for lunch weekdays and dinner daily. Call 561-687-3801.

For an upscale casual dining experience, try the **Café Protégé** at the Florida Culinary Institute, at 2400 Metrocentre Boulevard in West Palm Beach. The restaurant offers gourmet continental selections. Serves lunch weekdays and dinner daily. Call 561-687-2433.

JUST FOR KIDS ....

There's plenty for children here, from beaches to attractions. Many hotels have children's programs, especially in summer. Contact your hotel or the Palm Beach Chamber of Commerce regarding the availability of programs.

Of particular interest to kids are the Lion Country Safari (See Side Trips), the Dreher Park Zoo, and the South Florida Science Museum. In Boca Raton, at the southern end of Palm Beach County, there's the **Children's Science Explorium**, at 131 Mizner Boulevard (call 561-395-8401); the **Children's Museum**, at 498 Crawford Boulevard, with educational hands-on

exhibits (call 561-368-6875); and the **Gumbo Limbo Nature Center**, at 1801 North Ocean Boulevard (call 561-338-1473). In nearby Delray Beach is the **Morikami Museum and Japanese Gardens**, at 4000 Morikami Road, with Florida bonsai plants, and other exotic plants. Call 561-495-0233.

SIDE TRIPS ....

Lion Country Safari is on U.S. 98/441 about 20 miles west of I-95. Its large exhibit areas have freely roaming animals you can view from your car (using the 5-mile drive area) or from a guided boat ride. There's also a petting zoo, dinosaur exhibit, paddleboats, and camping. Admission is charged. Open daily. 561-793-1084.

GENERAL INFORMATION ....

Contact the Palm Beach Chamber of Commerce at 561-655-3282, or the Palm Beach County Convention and Visitors Bureau at 561-471-3995. For Golf-a-round information or other details, ask either office for a current *Vacation Planner*.

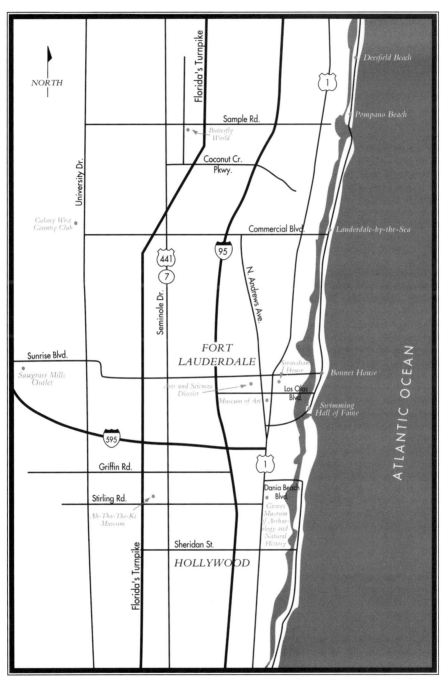

FORT LAUDERDALE and HOLLYWOOD, FL.

Fort Lauderdale and Hollywood

AREA CODE: 954

INTRODUCTION

Fort Lauderdale has been aptly nick-named the "Venice of America," as throughout the city there are over twenty miles of beaches, most dotted with red-roofed, villa-style mansions, and inland waterways with water taxis that transport residents and visitors. It's also home to world-famous spas and Port Everglades, the departure point for over one million cruise-ship passengers annually. Additionally, the city is the "Yachting Capital of the World," with well over forty thousand yachts registered here.

For those who associate Fort Lauderdale with spring-break zaniness, the area has done wonders to clean up its image. Though today it's still a popular spring-break choice (as are most affordable Florida beach resorts), it's now a family-oriented spot, with quality arts, museums, and a sophisticated nightlife.

You may wonder where the "Fort" is in Fort Lauderdale. The forts in question (three total) were built here in

1838 by Major (surprise!) William Lauderdale to protect supplies during the Seminole War. Though the name stuck around, the forts did not. However, there's plenty of history and culture to be learned here. Then again, you may have trouble uprooting yourself from the 23 miles of fine, wide beaches for a history lesson.

The main beach areas are Fort Lauderdale Beach, Pompano Beach (which has some terrific golf courses, as you'll see below), Hollywood, Deerfield Beach, and Lauderdale-by-the-Sea. Of these, Hollywood is probably the best known. It offers not only great beaches, but some additional attractions.

As for golf, there are over fifty golf courses in the Greater Fort Lauderdale area, several of which are exceptional. The palm tree–laden terrain and the great weather make for lovely scenery and ideal playing conditions.

The normal monthly temperatures for the area are: January, 67.2; February, 68.1; March, 71.7; April, 74.6; May, 78.1; June, 81; July, 82.6; August, 82.8; September, 81.8; October, 78.3; November, 73.3; December, 68.9. The most popular season is from December through April, especially the winter months.

GOLF INFORMATION ....

COLONY WEST COUNTRY CLUB, TAMARAC (954) 726-8430

Considered by *Golf Digest* to be one of the top public courses in the United States, Colony West is another excellent course designed by Bruce Devlin and Robert von Hagge (the same team that collaborated on Doral). With tees that range from 4810 to 7271 yards, and a rating/slope ranging from 71.6/127 to a hefty 75.8/138, this course provides a comfort zone or challenge for players of all levels. Although a golfer should play, and not be played by a course, Colony West, cut through towering cypress trees and featuring water on most holes, runs the show right from the first tee to the eighteenth green. The first hole is a 621-yard par 5 that requires three solid, accurate shots to a green that is more than 40-yards deep. The eighteenth is 452-yard par 4, with water cutting in front of another very deep green. You can imagine what's in-between these two excellent golf holes.

Carts: Mandatory (although walking sometimes permitted in afternoons). *Greens Fees:* Approx. $30-$75/18 holes, including cart. *Tee Time Policy:* Call three days in advance for tee times.

BOCA RATON RESORT AND CLUB, BOCA RATON (ABOUT 25 MILES NORTH OF FORT LAUDERDALE) (407) 447-3076

(Note: Open to resort guests only)

Opened in 1926, the par 71 Resort course was originally designed by William Flynn (the same designer who built Upper Cascades and Cherry Hills). It was renovated by Robert Trent Jones, Sr., in 1956, and renovated again by Joe Lee in 1988. Lee's work included the addition of a lake, reshaping traps, rebuilding seven holes, and placing new grass on most of the greens and fairways. The Resort course's tropical setting is created by a variety of palms, banyan trees, and colorful flowers and plants. The Resort course, measuring from 5259 to 6682 yards, with a rating/slope ranging from 69.2/116 to 71.5/122, boasts having Tommy

Armour (from 1926 to 1955) and Sam Snead (from 1956 to 1970) as resident pros. Also available is the 6585-yard (tees start at 5565 yards), par 72 Country Club course, which was designed by Joe Lee.

Carts: Mandatory. *Greens Fees:* $78 October–May, $46 June–September (greens fees lower after 2:30 P.M.)/18 holes; carts: $20 per person. *Tee Time Policy:* Resort guests only. Advance reservations suggested; can reserve up to a year in advance with guest-room confirmation number.

OTHER EXCELLENT AREA COURSES:

Inverrary Country Club, Lauderhill (954-733-7550), features two, 18-hole courses designed by Robert Trent Jones, Sr. The 7124-yard, par 72 East course

Scuba diving

was once a stop on the PGA Tour and produced winners such as Nicklaus, Trevino, Weiskopf, and Johnny Miller. **Crystal Lake Country Club**, Pompano Beach (954-942-1900), features two, narrow, tough, par 72 courses designed by Rees Jones. **Pompano Beach Golf Course**, Pompano Beach (954-781-0426), is a 1968, Devlin/Von Hagge facility sporting two courses. **Rolling Hills Hotel and Golf Resort**, Fort Lauderdale (954-475-3010), is a 6900-yard, par 72 course designed by William Mitchell and opened in 1963. Movie buffs might like to know that Rolling Hills is the course where the *Caddyshack* movies were filmed.

ATTRACTIONS ....

TOURS

Trolley Tours
South Florida Trolley Company gives narrated tours aboard the "Lolly Trolley," which stops at several attractions, the beach, and shopping areas. The entire loop, without disembarking, takes about ninety minutes. Call 954-768-0700 for tour routes and special excursions.

The Downtown Trolley service takes visitors to museums and other cultural attractions, and has three lines: the Red (called the Courthouse Line), Blue (the Las Olas to Courthouse), and Green (Arts and Sciences District to Las Olas) lines. The lines run at varying hours and intersect at certain points. Call 954-761-3543.

Boat Tours
The Water Taxi service is an

inexpensive and fun way to get around the city, or simply to enjoy the scenery. It covers the inland waterways between Port Everglades and Atlantic Boulevard (10 A.M. to 1 A.M.), and between Atlantic Boulevard and South Fort Lauderdale (noon until midnight). Boats make stops at many restaurants, nightclubs, hotels, and shops along the route. For information, call 954-467-6677.

The Jungle Queen gives three-hour sightseeing cruises twice daily, and there are dinner-dance cruises. Reservations are recommended. The ship departs from the Bahia Mar Yacht Basin. Call 954-462-5596.

Horse and Carriage Tours

Narrated jaunts along the downtown streets are offered by **Las Olas Horse and Carriage Tours**. Call 954-763-7393.

HISTORIC PLACES

The Riverwalk, in the downtown area, spans more than a mile along the north bank of the New River. The walkway is lined with gardens, benches, and boat landings. By the Riverwalk is the **Arts and Sciences District**, which is home to the huge Broward Center for the Performing Arts, where interactive exhibits about navigational history are on display in the esplanade area.

Stranahan House, at 335 SE Sixth Avenue in downtown Fort Lauderdale, was once a post for trading with the Seminole Indians. In 1906, the Stranahans made the house their home, and it is now a museum, still filled with their luxurious possessions. Open Wednesday through Sunday. Admission is charged. Call 954-524-4736.

Bonnet House is surrounded by a 35-acre estate featuring lush tropical gardens, standing artworks, animal carvings, and a swan pond. The mansion is a winter residence of Evelyn Bartle, who is well over a hundred-years old, yet it is open to the public. The house can be toured by reservation only and the hours are limited. Open Wednesday through Sunday, from May through November. Admission is charged. Call 954-563-5393.

MUSEUMS/SCIENCE CENTERS

Ah-Tha-Thi-Ki Museum, at 5845 South State Road 7 in Fort Lauderdale, is a new museum that explores local native Seminole Indian culture and heritage. It encompasses seven buildings that contain artworks, traditional clothing, documentary videos, and many artifacts depicting the culture and history of this tribe. Open Wednesday through Sunday. Admission is charged. Call 954-792-0745.

*Las Olas Boulevard,
Fort Lauderdale*
Photo courtesy of Greater Fort Lauderdale
Convention and Visitors Bureau

International Swimming Hall of Fame, at 1 Hall of Fame Drive (one block south of Las Olas Boulevard), has photos, film clips, memorabilia, and the medals of some of swimming's greatest legends. There are also two olympic-size swimming pools. Admission is charged. Call 954-462-6536.

The new **Museum of Discovery and Science and IMAX Blockbuster Theater**, at 401 SW Second Street in Fort Lauderdale's Arts and Sciences District, has touchable exhibits (including live animals), and the theater has a five-story screen. Admission is charged. Call 954-467-6637 for the museum, or call 954-463-4629 for the theater.

Fort Lauderdale Historical Society Museum, located at 219 SW Second Avenue on the Riverwalk, has recently been expanded. Its exhibits span from the Seminole Indian culture to the end of World War II. Open daily except Monday. Admission is charged. Call 954-463-4431.

Graves Museum of Archaeology and Natural History, at 481 South Federal Highway in Hollywood, has a large collection of ancient relics from the Grecian, Roman, and pre-Columbian eras, and more. Open daily except Monday. Admission is charged. Call 954-925-7770.

The Museum of Art, at 1 East Las Olas Boulevard in Fort Lauderdale, has permanent and temporary exhibits. The works of Native American, pre-Columbian, twentieth-century American, West African, oceanic ethnographic, and "CoBrA" (Copenhagen, Brussels, and Amsterdam) artists are all on display. Open daily except Monday. Admission is charged. Call 954-525-5500.

Seminole Native Village, at 4150 North Route 7 in Hollywood, is an Indian reservation where you can purchase handmade crafts. Call 954-961-5140 or 954-961-3220.

The New World Aquarium is scheduled to open in the area in 1998. For details, contact the Greater Fort Lauderdale Convention and Visitors Bureau at 954-765-4466.

CULTURAL OFFERINGS

Broward Center for the Performing Arts, at 201 SW Fifth Avenue in Fort Lauderdale, is a $55 million arts complex that stages Broadway plays and musicals, classical music, ballet and other dance, as well as pop performances. Call 954-462-0222.

The Greater Hollywood Philharmonic Orchestra gives pop concerts December through April at Young Circle Park in Hollywood. Call 954-921-3404.

The Gold Coast Opera gives matinee and evening performances in four locations, though it is based in Pompano Beach at 1000 Coconut Creek Boulevard. Call 954-973-2323.

RECREATION

Public parks abound in the area, and all have many activities to offer. Two which feature waterslides, swimming, camping, and boat rentals, are: **Topeekeegee Yugnee Park** (understandably, it's more commonly called T.Y. Park), on North Park Road, off the Sheridan Street exit of I-95 near Hollywood (call 954-985-1980); and **C.B. Smith Park**, in Pembroke Pines on Flamingo Road, about 20 miles west of Hollywood (call 954-437-2650). C.B. Smith Park also has miniature-golf and an outdoor amphitheater. For information on other parks, contact the Greater Fort Lauderdale Convention and Visitors Bureau at 954-765-4466.

There are several world-famous spas in the area offering massages, facials, herbal wraps, and other amenities. You may want to try: **Bonaventure Resort and Spa**, at 250 Racquet Club Road in Fort Lauderdale (call 954-389-3300 or 800-327-8090); the **Palm-Aire Spa Resort**, at 2601 Palm-Aire Drive North in Pompano Beach (call 954-972-3300 or 800-272-5624); or the **Hyatt Regency Pier 66**, at 2301 SE Seventeenth Street (call 954-525-6666 or 800-327-3796).

Butterfly World, at 3600 West Sample Road in Coconut Creek (near Pompano Beach), is a must-see tropical garden with many species of butterflies, ranging from larvae and cocoons to mature specimens. The plants and winged creatures are colorful, delicate, and beautiful, and the experience is accentuated with birds, flowers, and cascading waterfalls. Open daily. Call 954-977-4400.

Fishing and boating are popular pastimes in this area, with lots of opportunities for the sportsman. For boat owners, there are several boat ramps available. For fishermen, there are public fishing piers. Several outfits offer charter boats for fishing, boating, and diving. For charter boats in Fort Lauderdale, try the **Bahia Mar Yachting Center** at 801 Seabreeze Boulevard. Call 954-764-2233.

Diving's another big sport here, with several outfitters. Though dive sites are numerous, the most popular are the Fort Lauderdale Reef (which is artificial but spectacular) with sunken ships and houseboats; the *Mercedes I*, intentionally sunk 1½ miles offshore from Sunrise Boulevard; and the Lowrance Artificial Reef, about 1½ miles offshore from Atlantic Boulevard in Pompano Beach.

You'll find jai alai and five-star rodeos at the Davie Arena, at Sixty-fifth Avenue and Orange Drive in Dania. Call 954-384-7075 (for information on jai alai, call 954-927-2841). For dog racing, head to the **Hollywood Greyhound Track** in Hallandale, at 831 North Federal Highway. Races are run daily from December 26 through April 26 (the track has a giant flea market on weekends year-round). Call 954-454-9400. Horse racing takes place at the **Pompano Harness Track**, at 1800 SW Third Street in Pompano Beach, from November to early April. Call 954-972-2000. More horse racing takes place at **Gulfstream Park**, home of the Florida Derby, at U.S. 1 and Hallandale Beach Boulevard in Hallandale. Call 954-454-7000.

Billie Swamp Safari, located at the Big Cypress Seminole Indian Reservation about 23 miles west of Fort Lauderdale (on Alligator Alley, Exit 14 off I-75), has airboat rides or swamp-buggie adventure rides, both of which explore the wildlife of the Everglades. Visitors can also see wildlife shows and daily arts-and-crafts demonstrations. Admission is charged. Call 954-257-2134.

Flamingo Gardens, at 3750 Flamingo Road in nearby Davie, has several wildlife exhibits, including a 23,000-foot aviary, wetlands, a citrus grove, gators, crocs, otters, birds, a greenhouse, and a museum of the Everglades inside a pioneer home. There's a guided tram ride that transports you to the separate exhibits. Open daily. Admission is charged. Call 954-473-2955.

SEASONAL EVENTS

The month-long **Winterfest** is held throughout December in Fort Lauderdale. The main event is a nighttime boat parade. Winterfest's finale is **Light Up Fort Lauderdale**, with lasers and fireworks, on New Year's Eve. For information on Winterfest, call 954-767-0686.

In February, Hollywood has several notable special events. One is the four-day **Seminole Indian Tribal Fair**, with arts and crafts demonstrations, Seminole folklore, dress, foods, music, customs, a rodeo, and a competition powwow which draws competitors from tribes all over the United States. Call 954-584-0400. Also in February is the **Hollywood Festival of the Arts** at Young Circle Park, with art displays, food, and special events. In late February and/or early March, the **Florida Derby Festival** takes place at Gulfstream Park in Hallandale, culminating in the Florida Derby at the racetrack.

In May, there's the spectacular **Shell Air and Sea Show**, on Fort Lauderdale Beach, which attracts around 800,000 people in one weekend. In October, there's a **Jazz Festival** in Young Circle Park in Hollywood. Call 954-921-3404. Visitors also won't want to miss Fort Lauderdale's annual **International Boat Show** in October. Events and displays take place at the Bahia-Mar Yacht Basin, the convention center, and the Hyatt Regency Pier 66. Shuttles are available between locations.

ACCOMMODATIONS ....

EXPENSIVE

Hyatt Regency Pier 66, at 2301 SE Seventeenth Street in Fort Lauderdale, just underwent a $4 million renovation. The hotel has a fabulous spa, in addition to a revolving rooftop lounge. Hotel guests have special golf privileges at the Inverarry Country Club (see Golf Information). Call 954-525-6666 or 800-327-3796.

Marriott's Harbor Beach, at 3030 Holiday Drive in Fort Lauderdale, is a deluxe beachfront hotel with pools, massage service, tennis courts, a children's program, a terrific fitness center, and a large beach area. Call 954-525-4000.

Bonaventure Resort and Spa, at 250 Racquet Club Road in Fort Lauderdale, is a palatial, four-diamond

Broward Center for the Performing Arts, Fort Lauderdale
Photo courtesy of Greater Fort Lauderdale Convention and Visitors Bureau

resort with a deluxe spa, children's program, pools, concierge service, lawn games, roller skating, and much more. Golfers will enjoy the two 18-hole golf courses (See Golf Information). Call 954-389-3300.

The golf course at **Rolling Hills Hotel and Golf Resort**, at 3501 West Rolling Hills Circle in Fort Lauderdale, is where the *Caddyshack* movies were filmed, and the resort is where the Miami Dolphins make their home during spring training. Aside from the terrific golf course, there's a large pool and two tennis courts. Located in a relatively quiet and uncrowded area. Call 954-475-0400.

The Westin Cypress Creek, at 400 Corporate Drive in Fort Lauderdale, is a lovely, blue-tiled building surrounded by palms, a waterfall, and a lake. There's tennis and golf, exercise facilities, concierge service, and a free shuttle to the beach. Call 954-772-1331.

Holiday Inn Sunspree Resort, at 2711 South Ocean Drive in Hollywood, is great for families. This beachfront hotel has a heated pool, children's programs, and other special perks, and plenty of on-site entertainment for both children and adults. Call 954-923-8700.

The Sheraton Yankee Clipper, at 1140 Seabreeze Boulevard in Fort Lauderdale, has three heated pools, a lounge, and a restaurant. Call 954-524-5551.
The Sheraton Yankee Trader, also in Fort Lauderdale at 321 North Atlantic Boulevard, has a bridge connecting the hotel to the beach, two heated pools, a whirlpool, and more. Call 954-467-1111.

Days Inn Fort Lauderdale, at 1595 West Oakland Park Boulevard (west of I-95), has an outdoor pool and allows pets. This is a comfortable stay for a reasonable rate, though it's not on the beach. Call 954-484-9290.

The Oceanside Days Inn, at 435 North Atlantic Boulevard (east of I-95), is also a good choice, although despite its name, it's not on the beach. Call 954-462-0444.

Howard Johnsons Hollywood Beach Resort, at 2501 North Ocean Drive in Hollywood, is right on the ocean, and rooms have balconies and patios with beach views. There's also a restaurant, pool, and lounge. Call 954-925-1411.

SHOPPING

For bargain hunters, there's a large indoor flea market with some six hundred vending booths at the **Festival Flea Market**, located at 2900 West Sample Road in Pompano Beach. Open daily except Monday.

Sawgrass Mill, at Flamingo Road and Sunrise Boulevard in Sunrise, is the largest outlet mall in the world, with over 250 shops. Shuttles are available from many hotels. Call 954-846-2350 or 800-356-4557 to arrange pick-up.

The Shops of Las Olas, along East Las Olas Boulevard, include art galleries, specialty shops, and cafés. This is where the rich-and-famous have been known to shop. The shops are fun, even if you are just browsing or people watching.

Butterfly World, Pompano Beach
Photo courtesy of Greater Fort Lauderdale
Convention and Visitors Bureau

RESTAURANTS ....

FINE DINING

Mark's Las Olas, at 1032 East Las Olas Boulevard in Fort Lauderdale, offers tropical Florida *nouvelle cuisine*, from seafood to pasta. Many dishes feature creative, flavorful sauces. Call 954-463-1000.

Yesterday's, at 3001 East Oakland Park Boulevard in northeast Fort Lauderdale, serves new American cuisine and south Florida specialties in a beautiful waterfront setting. Open daily for dinner. Call 954-563-4168.

CASUAL DINING

Mistral, at 201 South Atlantic Boulevard on Fort Lauderdale Beach, faces a promenade along the beach and serves fresh Florida cuisine. There's also live entertainment on weekends. Open daily for lunch and dinner. Call 954-463-4900.

Martha's, on the Intracoastal Waterway at 6024 North Ocean Drive in Hollywood, serves American continental cuisine with an emphasis on seafood, and there's beef and other selections for landlubbers and kids. The decor is tropical. Open daily for lunch and dinner. Call 954-923-5444.

JUST FOR KIDS ....

Young at Art Children's Museum, at 801 University Drive at the Fountain Shoppes in Plantation, has fun displays. It sponsors arts projects on various themes using sculpture, painting, crafts, and graphics. Open daily except Monday. Call 954-424-0085.

Story Theater, at the Parker Playhouse on U.S. 1 and Sunrise Boulevard in Fort Lauderdale, gives professional live performances for children. *Beauty and the Beast* and *The Lion, the Witch, and the Wardrobe* were part of the 1995 series. Call 954-763-8813.

GENERAL INFORMATION ....

For more information, contact the Greater Fort Lauderdale Convention and Visitors Bureau (which covers Broward County from Hollywood to Deerfield Beach) at 954-765-4466, or call 800-227-8669 to request a visitor information packet.

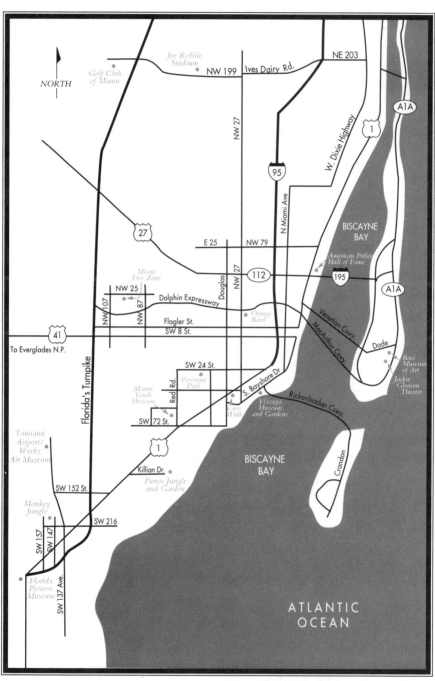

MIAMI and KEY BISCAYNE, FL.

Miami and Key Biscayne

AREA CODE: 305

INTRODUCTION

Miami is a major southern metropolis—a sort of tropical Manhattan, yet somehow brighter and, for the most part, cleaner. But unlike most of Manhattan, Miami has a distinct, ubiquitous Latino flavor. Billboards and street signs are often in Spanish and English, and several older buildings have Spanish-influenced architecture. While around half the city's population is Hispanic, there are many other international influences in Miami, as there are also sizable numbers of Jamaicans, Haitians, and other groups here. In fact, when downtown, one is often unlikely to find a majority of the people conversing in English, and instead will hear most conversations in Spanish, Portuguese, Japanese, and a variety of other languages.

Like other large cities, Miami has a lot to offer visitors. Tourists will find centuries-old buildings juxtaposed beside spanking new ones, and great wealth in addition to bleak poverty. After recent bad publicity over crimes directed at tourists, the city has taken some effective measures to lower these incidents; nevertheless, there are areas of the city that should be avoided. However, any such negative publicity has hardly deterred tourism—evidenced by the fact that more than 8 million people continue to visit Miami annually to savor its unique offerings. Overall, these tourists will find an exciting, cosmopolitan, pan-American city with a warm, tropical flare.

Although taking in many of the interesting attractions away from the beaches (and getting to some of the fabulous area golf courses, unless staying at a golf resort) requires having a car, Miami is a relatively easy city to find your way around. It is divided into four main sections: northwest, northeast, southwest, and southeast. It is also intersected and divided east and west by Miami Avenue and north and south by Flagler Street.

Miami Beach, a separate entity on the east side of Biscayne Bay, off the shores of Miami, is made up of seventeen islands. The majority of visitors to the Miami area come to Miami Beach, where they enjoy the sun-drenched beaches and its lovely South Beach area, which features a newly renovated, upbeat Art Deco district that has drawn plenty of celebrities (Madonna, Sylvester Stallone, and others have recently bought homes here), as well as the glamour and attention that goes with them. Also offshore from Miami is Key Biscayne, which has fabulous beaches and one of the country's prettiest and highest rated golf courses.

The normal monthly temperatures are: January, 67.2; February, 68.5; March, 71.7; April, 75.2; May, 78.7; June, 81.4; July, 82.6; August, 82.8; September, 81.9; October, 78.3; November, 73.6; December, 69.1. The most popular times to visit Miami are from late February through October, and many come to the beaches during the summer (though this is not a popular season for golfers).

GOLF INFORMATION ....

DORAL GOLF RESORT AND SPA CLUB, MIAMI
(305) 592-2000 OR (800) 713-6725

Doral, recently named among *Golf's* "Top 100 You Can Play," might be the finest golf facility discussed in this book. It has five 18-hole courses, named Blue, Gold, Red, Silver, and White, as well as a 9-hole course, named Green. Also here is the Jim McLean Golf School, arguably the best in the country. The school has an excellent staff and is well organized and operated. But the main attraction is the Blue course, nicknamed the "Blue Monster." Designed by Dick Wilson and Robert von Hagge in 1961, renovated by Bruce Devlin in 1971, and undergoing renovation again by Raymond Floyd as of the spring of 1996, the Blue is an incredible golf course. It is the site of the PGA's Doral Ryder Open, which has been won by the very finest players, including Jack Nicklaus, Billy Casper, Lee Trevino, Raymond Floyd, Tom Weiskopf, Tom Kite, Lanny Wadkins, Ben Crenshaw, Greg Norman, and Nick Faldo—making true the adage that great players win on great courses. Norman holds the course record with a 62 (normal players would still have a long walk to the clubhouse if they stopped at 62). A par 72 that ranges in yardage from 5786 to

6939 yards, the Blue can be extremely tough, especially from the twelfth hole all the way to the clubhouse. The twelfth is an excellent, 591-yard par 5 with sand in each landing area—from the tee, on the lay-up, and around the green. The par 3 thirteenth usually plays into the wind, and that can be a problem with 246 yards to traverse to the green. Then there is the 425-yard, par 4 eighteenth, a slight dogleg left. Hugging a lake from tee to green, the hole requires a long and accurate tee shot (Nick Faldo hooked his drive into the water in the 1995 Doral Ryder Open) and an accurate approach (Norman almost hit the floating scoreboard in the same year) to a very long green that sits on an angle along the lake. A par here is quite an accomplishment.

Carts: Walking occasionally permitted. *Greens Fees:* $50-$150/ 18 holes. *Tee Time Policy:* Resort guests can reserve when they reserve room; others can reserve a day in advance, sometimes three days in advance.

GOLF CLUB OF MIAMI, MIAMI
(305) 829-8456

The West course at the Golf Club of Miami is a 7017-yard (6389 yards from the whites and 5690 yards from the reds), par 72 course designed by Robert Trent Jones, Sr. The course has an exciting history: its original club pro was Arnold Palmer; Jack Nicklaus played his first tour event on the course; and Lee Trevino won his first professional event here. Recently it has hosted the Senior PGA Tour qualifying school.

Downtown Miami
Photo courtesy of the FL Department of Commerce, Division of Tourism

Miami and Key Biscayne, FL

Photo courtesy of the FL Department of Commerce, Division of Tourism

The course features water on every hole in some form or another. It is heavily bunkered and has large, contoured greens. Witness the sixth hole, a ghoulish, 461-yard par 4, with water on the right and out of bounds on the left. The Golf Club of Miami also offers the 6300-yard, par 70 East course, and the executive 5400-yard South Course.

Carts: Mandatory. *Greens Fees:* Approximately $40-$75/18 holes, including cart. *Tee Time Policy:* Can be reserved three days in advance.

THE LINKS AT KEY BISCAYNE, KEY BISCAYNE (305) 361-9129

The Links is another excellent layout by the prolific Bruce Devlin/Robert von Hagge tandem. Opened in 1972, it has long been considered among the best courses in the United States by *Golf Digest*, is rated 4½ stars by *Golf Digest's Places to Play*, and is the site of the Senior PGA Tour's Royal Caribbean Classic. The course, ranging in yardage from 5690 to 7070 yards and rating/slope from 71/129 to 72.7/138 (the Ladies' Forward tees are 74/128), plays through coconut palms, mangroves, and an assortment of subtropical vegetation, as well as along and over the beautiful Biscayne Bay. Walking is permitted after 1 P.M. and such rare rights should be used in order to enjoy the lovely landscape. Also, a computerized reservation system is available to make tee times seven days in advance over the telephone.

Carts: Walking sometimes permitted. *Greens Fees:* Approximately $45-$75/18 holes (less for county residents). *Tee Time Policy:* Can book up to seven days in advance, and as little as one day in advance.

TURNBERRY ISLE RESORT AND CLUB, AVENTURA (NORTH MIAMI)
(305) 932-6200

(Note: Open to resort guests only).

Turnberry Isle, opened in 1970, offers two 18-hole courses, North and South, designed by Robert Trent Jones, Sr. The par 72 South course was the site of the 1981–83 Senior PGA Championship and was a regular stop on the LPGA Tour. Currently, it is the site of the Raymond Floyd-Turnberry Isle Junior Golf Classic. The South course measures from 5581 to 7003 yards with a rating/slope ranging from 71.3/116 to 73.7/136. An exciting hole on this course is the 545-yard, par 5 eighteenth. The tee shot must avoid a long lake that borders the right side of the fairway. The green sits on an island, so reaching this hole in two is risky. Therefore, a lay-up to a narrow fairway often is required, leaving an approach to a wide green fronted by a gaping bunker. The par 70 North course measures from 4991 to 6348 yards with a rating/slope ranging from 67.9/107 to 70.3/127. This course, while obviously shorter, requires accurate shots to avoid the many water hazards and bunkers.

Carts: Mandatory. *Greens Fees:* Approximately \$35–\$103/18 holes, including cart. *Tee Time Policy:* Resort guests only; can be reserved at time room reservation is confirmed.

ATTRACTIONS ....

TOURS

Motorized Tours

The following companies offer a variety of sightseeing trips around Miami, as well as shopping tours, nightlife tours, and out-of-town day trips: in Miami, try **ACC Tours**, at 444 Brickell Avenue (call 305-579-8688); or **Go America Tours**, at 16375 NE Eighteenth Avenue (call 305-945-7036). In Miami Beach, try **Suntours**, at 1111 Lincoln Road (call 305-538-6080); or **Miami Nice Excursions**, at 19250 Collins Avenue (call 305-949-9180).

Walking Tours

For ninety-minute walking tours of Miami Beach's Art Deco district, join the **Miami Design Preservation League** for their Saturday morning and Thursday evening tours. Their office is located at 1001 Ocean Drive. Call 305-672-2014. More walking tours are offered by **Deco Tours**, located at 420 Lincoln Road, Suite 412, in Miami Beach. Call 305-531-4465.

Boat Tours

Beginning at 10 A.M. daily, water taxis transport passengers throughout the downtown area, making stops at several area hotels, restaurants, and attractions. The taxis also go to the Miami Beach area on weekdays. The water taxis help eliminate the need for a designated driver for nighttime activities. For information, call 954-467-6677.

Ninety-minute sightseeing cruises around the city and islands aboard *The Island Queen* depart daily from Bayside Marketplace and the Hyatt Regency Hotel, located at 400 SE Second Avenue. For a schedule and information, call 305-379-5119.

For airboat tours of Florida's famous, watery ecosystem known as the Everglades, contact **Coopertown Boat**

Ride, which has given airboat tours of the Everglades since the 1940s. There is a two-person minimum. Call 305-226-6048. Another choice is **Buffalo Tiger's Florida Everglades Airboat Ride**, which offers airboat tours (with a three-person minimum) that include a stop at an Indian camp. Call 305-559-5250. **Everglades Gator Park** also offers forty-five-minute airboat tours. Visitors can also see the "Gator Pit" and a Native American village. Call 305-559-2255.

HISTORIC PLACES

The lovely **Coral Castle,** at 28655 South Dixie Highway, was built entirely of coral and has a fascinating history. Open daily. Call 305-248-6344.

South Beach's **Art Deco District**, which lies between Lenox Court and Ocean Drive and runs from Sixth to Twenty-third Street, is a charming national historic district with, naturally, many Art Deco structures, as well as other architectural styles.

Miami Sea-quarium, at 4400 Rickenbacker Causeway on Virginia Key, was the home of "Flipper" of television (and now movie) fame. The facility is a combination garden and aquarium, with plenty of sea creatures on display and daily animal shows. Admission is charged. Call 305-361-5705.

Vizcaya Museum, at 3251 South Miami Avenue in Coconut Grove, is the Italian renaissance–style home of the late industrialist James Deering. The house contains European fine arts and decorative arts dating from the first through the nineteenth centuries. The 10 acres of gardens feature sculptured statues and fountains. Open daily. Admission is charged. Call 305-250-9133.

Weeks Air Museum in Tamiami Airport, at 14710 SW 128th Street, has restored aircraft from World Wars I and II. Admission is charged. Call 305-233-5197.

Bass Museum of Art, at 2121 Park Avenue in Miami Beach, has an eclectic display of European and American paintings. Open daily except Monday. Admission is charged. Call 305-673-7530.

Historical Museum of Southern Florida, at 101 West Flagler Street at the Metro-Dade Cultural Plaza in downtown Miami, showcases the region's culture and history. Open daily. Admission is charged; donations suggested on Mondays. Call 305-375-1492.

The Museum of Science, at 3280 South Miami Avenue in Coconut Grove, features exhibits on the human body, physical sciences, biology, and technology that will delight both adults and children. The complex also has an observatory and a planetarium with astronomy and laser-light shows. Open daily. Admission is charged. Call 305-854-4247.

American Police Hall of Fame and Museum, at 3801 Biscayne Boulevard, is dedicated to the United States police officers who have been killed in the line of duty since 1960. It also has exhibits on firearms, special equipment, weapons used in notorious crimes, and execution equipment. Open daily. Admission is charged; free admission for police personnel and their families. Call 305-573-0070.

Gold Coast Railroad Museum, at 12450 SW Fifty-second Street, has steam locomotives and passenger railroad cars on display, including cars used by Roosevelt, Truman, and others for campaigning, as well as photos and other artifacts. Call for hours. Admission is charged. Call 305-253-0063.

CULTURAL OFFERINGS

Jackie Gleason Theater of the Performing Arts, at 1700 Washington Avenue in Miami Beach, presents several high-caliber plays and other entertainment each year. Call 305-673-7300. Other quality performing arts theaters include: the **Colony Theater**, at 1040 Lincoln Road in Miami Beach, which presents classic and experimental dramas, dance, and music (call 305-674-1026); the **Dade County Auditorium**, at 2901 West Flagler Street in Miami, with opera, musicals, and more (call 305-547-5414); the lovely **Gusman Center for the Performing Arts**, at 174 Flagler Street in Miami, presenting concerts, ballets, and plays (call 305-372-0925); and the **Coconut Grove Playhouse**, at 3500 Main Highway, which presents dramas, plays, comedies, musicals, and more from October through June (call 305-442-4000).

Several quality theater companies are located in Miami. Some suggestions are: **Acme Acting Company**, at 955 Alton Road in Miami Beach, which presents cutting-edge and experimental theater productions in winter and spring (call 305-372-9077); **Actor's Playhouse**, at 280 Miracle Mile in Coral Gables, which produces several children's plays (call 305-444-9293); **Area Stage**, at 645 Lincoln Road in Miami Beach, which presents off-Broadway shows (call 305-673-8002); and the **Florida Shakespeare Festival**, at 2304 Salzedo Avenue in Coral Gables, which does a Shakespeare play each year but also produces modern works (call 305-446-1116).

The Miami City Ballet, at 905 Lincoln Road in Miami Beach, is among the nation's finest dance companies, and it presents many New York City ballet productions as well as original creations. Call 305-532-7713.

The Florida Grand Opera, at 1200 Coral Way in Miami, is another cultural jewel, hosting luminaries like Domingo and Pavarotti (who made his American debut with this company) each year. Call 305-854-7890.

The New World Symphony's season runs October through May. For information on performances, call 305-673-3331. **The Friends of Chamber Music** arranges performances by internationally acclaimed artists, both professionals and students. For information, call 305-372-2975. More area classical performances are coordinated by the **Concert Association of Florida**, with offices at 555 Hank Meyer Boulevard in Miami Beach. Call 305-532-3491.

The South Florida Arts Center, at 924 Lincoln Road in Miami Beach's Art Deco district, exhibits works by local artists. Call 305-674-8278. Another upscale gallery in Miami Beach's Art Deco district, with works by Latin American and other artists, is the **Barbara Gillman Gallery**, located at 939 Lincoln Road. Call 305-534-7872.

RECREATION

Miami Metrozoo, at 12400 SW 152nd Street in greater Miami South, is a 290-acre zoo. Its nearly 1,000 specimens represent almost 250 species. Open daily. Admission is charged. Call 305-251-0400.

Fruit and Spice Park, at 24801 SW 187th Avenue, has more than five hundred species of fruits, nuts, herbs, and spices (which are also for sale) growing on 20 acres that visitors can tour. Picnic areas are provided. Open daily. Call 305-247-5727.

Parrot Jungle and Gardens, 11000 SW Fifty-seventh Avenue in Miami, is a bird sanctuary, wildlife habitat, and gardens. Bird species include native flamingoes and parrots; other animals include reptiles, tortoises, and apes. For kids, there's a petting zoo and playground. Open daily. Admission is charged. Call 305-666-7834.

Monkey Jungle, at 14805 SW 216th Street in Miami, is a lot like it sounds: a tropical, jungle–like park where hundreds of monkeys roam free. The twist is that the facility is built to appear as though the humans are on display for the primates, though there is caging for safety purposes. There's also a rich fossil deposit in the park. Open daily. Admission is charged. Call 305-235-1611.

The Venetian Pool, at 2701 DeSoto Boulevard in Coral Gables, is a lagoon of carved coral. Visitors can explore and swim this landmark pool surrounded by waterfalls, bridges, and Venetian buildings. There's also a new café with a lunch menu. Open daily except Monday. Admission is charged. Call 305-460-5356.

Bill Baggs Cape Florida State Recreation Area, at 1200 Crandon Park Boulevard, has public beaches and bike paths. Admission is free. Call 305-361-5811.

Jai Alai is played year-round at the Miami Jai-Alai Fronton, located just east of Miami Airport at 3500 NW Thirty-seventh Avenue. For times and information, call 305-633-6400. The **Miami Dolphins** play professional football at JRS (Joe Robbie Stadium), located at 2269 NW 199th Street. For ticket information, call 305-620-2578. The **Florida Panthers** play NHL hockey at the Miami Arena, at 701 Arena Boulevard in Miami. For information, call 305-577-4328. Auto racing fans won't want to miss the **Toyota Grand Prix**, usually held in February or March. For information, call Miami Motor Sports at 305-230-5200.

Horse racing takes place at the **Calder Race Course**, located at 21001 NW Twenty-seventh Avenue in Miami, from late May through early January. For dates and post times, call 305-625-1311. Dog racing is held at the **Biscayne Greyhound Track**, at 320 NW 115th Street in Miami Shores (call 305-754-3484), and at **Flagler Greyhound Track**, at NW Thirty-seventh Avenue and Seventh Street in Little Havana (call 305-649-3000).

For windsurfing, try **Sailboards Miami** at 1 Rickenbacker Causeway in Key Biscayne. Call 305-361-7245. For scuba diving, try **Bubbles Dive Center**, 2671 SW Twenty-seventh Avenue in Miami (call 305-856-0565), or in Key Biscayne, try **Divers Paradise of Key Biscayne**, at 4000 Crandon Boulevard (call 305-361-3483). Boating and fishing are also available at marinas throughout the area. For more information, contact the Greater Miami Chamber of Commerce at 305-350-7700 or the Miami Beach Chamber of Commerce at 305-672-1270.

The following places offer tennis facilities (assuming your hotel doesn't have courts): in Miami Beach, go to the **Flamingo Tennis Center**, at 1000 Twelfth Street (call 305-673-7761); in Key Biscayne, try the **Tennis Center at Crandon Park**, at 7300 Crandon Boulevard (call 305-365-2300); and in Coral Gables, go to the **Biltmore Tennis Center**, at 1150 Anastasia Avenue (call 305-460-5360).

SEASONAL EVENTS

In early January, the **Orange Bowl** parade and football game are held, the crowning events of two weeks' worth of celebrations throughout the city. In 1997, the game itself will move from the famed Orange Bowl to Joe Robbie Stadium. For information, call 305-620-2578.

In early to mid-January, the **Art Deco Weekend** takes place, with special lectures, tours, and other events. For information, call the Miami Preservation Society at 305-672-2014.

Early February brings the **Festival of the Arts** to Miami Beach, on Collins Avenue between Forty-ninth Street and Fifty-third Street, with art displays and sales, music, and theater performances.

In mid-February, the **Coconut Grove Arts Festival** features some three hundred artists who come to showcase and sell their work. Call 305-447-0401. Winter also brings the **Royal Caribbean Classic** golf tournament to the Links at Key Biscayne (See Golf Information). Call 305-365-0365. Another big winter event is the **Homestead Rodeo**, which takes place at Doc Demilly Rodeo Arena, located at U.S. 1 and SW 312th Street (in Homestead, south of Miami). Call 305-247-3515. In mid-February or early March, the

Doral Ryder Open PGA golf tournament takes place at the Doral Resort and Country Club (See Golf Information). Call 305-477-4653. Also about this time of year is the **Grand Prix of Miami** auto race, which takes place in downtown Miami. Call 305-379-RACE.

In early March, the **Calle Ocho** (8th Street) **Festival** (also called Carnaval Miami), takes place in Little Havana. The festival features a parade, entertainment, music, foods, and more. Call 305-644-8888.

The **Italian Renaissance Festival** is in mid-March at the Vizcaya Museum and Gardens in Coconut Grove. The festival takes place in a recreated, medieval Italian village and includes foods, reenactments, crafts, and entertainment. Call 305-250-9133 extension 2250.

Late March on Key Biscayne brings the two-week-long **Lipton Championship** tennis tournament, at the Tennis Center at Crandon Park, 7300 Crandon Boulevard. Call 305-442-3367.

In late December or early January, representatives from several Indian tribes come to the **Indian Arts Festival** at the Miccosukee Indian Village to display dances, music, and other Native American customs. Call 305-223-8380.

ACCOMMODATIONS ....

EXPENSIVE

Doral Golf Resort and Spa, at 4400 NW Eighty-seventh Avenue in Miami (call 305-592-2000 or 800-22-DORAL), and the **Doral Ocean Beach Resort Hotel**, at 4833 Collins Avenue in Miami Beach (call 305-532-3600 or

800-22-DORAL), offer beautiful surroundings and first-class amenities like spas, pools, fine restaurants, a social director with entertainment and activities for adults and children, private patios and balconies, refrigerators, and free transportation between both properties. The country club features some of the country's best golf (See Golf Information).

Fountainebleau Hilton Resort and Towers, at 4441 Collins Avenue in Miami Beach, is a huge (1,146 rooms!), glitzy hotel. There's an 18-hole golf course here, as well as a health club, supervised children's programs, tennis, pools (including both fresh and saltwater pools), restaurants, private beach, windsurfing, boating, and parasailing. Call 305-538-2000 or 800-548-8886.

Turnberry Isle Resort and Club, at 1999 West Country Club in Aventura (north Miami), is a lovely, tranquil resort nestled on 300 tropical acres. The resort has pools, exercise equipment, tennis, luxurious rooms, on-site entertainment, and of course, world-class golf (See Golf Information). Call 305-932-6200 or 800-327-7028.

The Biltmore Hotel, at 1200 Anastasia Avenue in Coral Gables, is a multitiered castle—a landmark of old-time elegance (tours of the hotel are given on Sundays). Facilities include a championship golf course, a huge health spa, pools, and tennis courts. Call 305-445-1926 or 800-727-1926.

Sonesta Beach Hotel and Tennis Club, at 350 Ocean Drive in Key Biscayne, has been entirely rebuilt after Hurricane Andrew destroyed it. Most rooms have fabulous views, and there's great artwork throughout the hotel. The private beach is beautiful, and there's

windsurfing, tennis, golf privileges, children's programs, aerobics classes, massage service, and a pool. Call 305-361-2021 or 800-766-3782.

The Courtyard by Marriott, at 15700 NW Seventy-seventh Court, located east of downtown Miami, has free airport transportation, exercise facilities, balconies, and a heated pool. Call 305-556-6665 or 800-321-2211.

At the **Silver Sands Motel**, at 301 Ocean Drive in Key Biscayne, all the rooms are suites. They're smaller than luxury suites, but they're comfortable and reasonably priced. Call 305-361-5441.

Fairfield Inn by Marriott, at 3959 NW Seventy-ninth Avenue, west of downtown Miami, has a heated pool, free breakfast, and airport transportation. Call 305-599-5200.

SHOPPING ....

The Falls Shopping Center, at U.S. 1 and SW 136th Street in the Kendall area, is located in a lovely tropical setting of walkways, waterfalls, and bridges. The center has over sixty stores (like The Polo Store, Banana Republic, The Gap, Victoria's Secret, etc.), as well as restaurants, theaters, and cafés. Open daily. Call 305-255-4570. **The Bal Harbour Shops**, at 9700 Collins Avenue in Bal Harbour, include stores like Gucci and Neiman Marcus. **Cocowalk**, at 3015 Grand Avenue in Coconut Grove, has several restaurants and specialty shops.

Manatee
Photo courtesy of Naples Area Chamber of Commerce

For antiques and European home furnishings, head to the **Alhambra Antiques Center**, at 3640 Coral Way in Coral Gables. Call 305-446-1688. For more antique shopping, check out the **Homestead Antique District**, along Krome Avenue in Homestead (see Side Trips).

For outlet shopping, try the **Florida Keys Factory Shop**s, with more than fifty-five outlet stores. Its located at 250 East Palm Drive in Florida City (east of Homestead, which is south of Miami and Coral Gables). Open daily. Call 305-248-4727.

The huge, three-story **Miami Free Zone,** at 2305 NW 107th Avenue, sells goods to the public at wholesale prices. If sending goods outside the United States, you can buy duty-free; for domestic use, you pay duty but will still save money on clothes, electronics, liquors, cosmetics, computers, and more. Open weekdays. Call 305-591-4300.

For bargain clothes shopping, you can't beat the fashion district in Miami, at Fifth Avenue between Twenty-fifth and Twenty-ninth Streets.

RESTAURANTS ....

Dining in Miami is like dining in New York: the choices are almost endless, with fine cuisine by world-class chefs as well as unique casual choices, and over a hundred different cultures providing a variety of ethnic dining that is matched by few cities.

FINE DINING

Le Pavilion, at 100 Chopin Plaza in downtown Miami, has a leather-and-mahogany English club atmosphere. The cuisine is gourmet, and selections include fish, chicken, lamb, and veal. The desserts are fabulous. Jacket required; reservations recommended. Dinner served daily except Sunday; brunch served on Sunday. Call 305-577-1000 extension 4494 or 4462.

Dominique's at the Alexander Hotel, on 5225 Collins Avenue in Miami Beach, serves exotic, gourmet cuisine, with offbeat appetizers like gator tail and buffalo sausage. Specialties are the rack of lamb and fresh seafood. Serves breakfast, lunch, and dinner. Call 305-865-6500.

CASUAL DINING

Burt Reynolds's **Backstage at The Park Central and Imperial Hotel**, at 640 Ocean Drive in Miami Beach, is decorated with memorabilia from Reynolds's movies. House specialties are breast of duck, pastas, and steaks. Outdoor dining available. Reservations are recommended. Serves lunch and dinner. Call 305-673-6181.

While we're dropping names, **Dan Marino's Sports Bar and Grill,** at 3015 Grand Avenue at CocoWalk in Coconut Grove, serves basic continental selections (there's no dolphin on the menu). It's a lively place with forty TVs, cutting-edge video games, and electronic darts. Serves lunch and dinner. Call 305-567-0013.

The Purple Dolphin, in the Sonesta Beach Resort at 350 Ocean Drive in Key Biscayne, is nice and casual, with sandwiches and salads for lunch and Florida/continental selections at dinner. Most evenings, dinner is accompanied by piano music. Serves breakfast, lunch, and dinner. Call 305-361-2021.

Centro Vasco, at 2235 SW Eighth Street in Little Havana, has classic Spanish cuisine such as paellas and tapas, and traditional Spanish and Cuban entertainment. Serves lunch and dinner. Call 305-643-9606.

JUST FOR KIDS ....

The Miami Youth Museum, at 5701 Sunset Drive, is an art museum with hands-on exhibits where kids can learn by participating in projects. Open daily. Call 305-661-ARTS. There's also the **Junior Orange Bowl Festival** (the country's largest youth festival) from November through January, with sports and cultural activities for children and teens.

You'll also find children's programs at resorts and hotels, especially in Miami Beach. In addition, most major area hotels here provide babysitting services to guests for reasonable fees.

SIDE TRIPS ....

Homestead, about 35 miles south of Miami, has a variety of attractions. **Everglades Alligator Farm**, at 40351 SW 192nd Avenue, has gators, snakes, and other reptiles. They offer airboat tours of the Everglades and snake and other animal shows daily. Call 305-247-2628. Nine miles east of Homestead is the **Biscayne National Underwater Park**, at the east end of SW 328th Street, where visitors can snorkel, scuba dive, and view marine life through a glass-bottomed boat. Open daily. Call 230-1100.

GENERAL INFORMATION ....

Contact the Greater Miami Convention and Visitors Bureau at 305-539-3063 or 800-283-2707, the Greater Miami Chamber of Commerce at 305-350-7700, or the Miami Beach Chamber of Commerce at 305-672-1270. Ask for a current copy of *Miami Visitors Guide*. For information on Miami Beach's Art Deco District, call or stop in at the Art Deco Welcome Center at Tenth Street and Ocean Boulevard in Miami Beach. Call 305-531-3484.

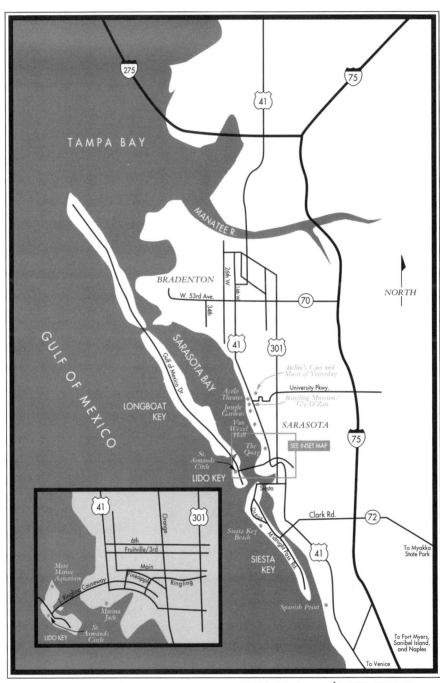

SARASOTA and VICINITY, FL.

Sarasota and vicinity

AREA CODE: 941

INTRODUCTION ....

The city of Sarasota is known for its arts, museums, and fine dining. A few glamorous skyscrapers dot Sarasota's skyline, but the majority of buildings are low and pastel colored. Many of the city's attractions are located on or near a main drag, the Tamiami Trail, so finding your way around is fairly easy. Like many Florida resort areas, Sarasota harbors a strong association with a legendary captain of industry and philanthropist. In Sarasota's case, the wealthy

philanthropist who left a cultural legacy in the city was John Ringling (of Ringling Brothers, Barnum and Bailey fame). In past eras, his circus made Sarasota its summer home, and today, the majority of Ringling's cultural contributions can be found within the Ringling complex located on his former estate.

Causeways connect Sarasota to a series of sea islands (or "keys"), which are renowned for beaches covered in soft, white sand, called "sugar sand," and shores that sparkle with the crystal blue waters of the Gulf of Mexico. In fact, nearby Siesta Key was selected in a 1987 International Sand competition as having the softest and whitest sand in the world. The main islands in the area are Lido Key, St. Armands Key, Longboat Key, and Siesta Key. These keys possess varying degrees of glamour, with perhaps the most famous upscale district being St. Armands Circle (known for its high-end shopping and dining). However, deluxe resorts can also be found on Longboat Key, known chiefly for its golf and tennis (See Golf Information), and Lido Key (connected with St. Armands). For nice beaches, though, you can't go wrong with any of the keys.

Sarasota has been a resort area for decades. Additionally, it is literally Florida's "cradle of golf," since the state's first course, consisting of four holes, was built here in 1886. Today, there are more than three dozen courses in the area, several of them fine choices. Sarasota is also reasonably close to Tampa and St. Petersburg (See Tampa and St. Petersburg chapter) and the Fort Myers, Sanibel Island, and Naples areas (See Side Trips), which have more great golf and beaches.

The normal monthly temperatures, as measured in Venice, are: January, 61.8; February, 62.7; March, 67.2; April, 71.1; May, 76.1; June, 80.2; July, 81.7; August, 81.9; September, 81; October, 75.5; November, 69.3; December, 64.1. October through April is the chief tourist season.

GOLF INFORMATION ....

UNIVERSITY PARK COUNTRY CLUB, UNIVERSITY PARK (813) 359-9999

Opened in 1991, University Park is a Ron Garl design that is considered one of Florida's best courses by *Golfweek*. It was given 4 stars by *Golf Digest's Places to Play*. With lots of mounds, moguls, and swales, the course has a lunar feel to it. If you find yourself on the wrong side of these obstacles, or in one of the many sand, pot, or waste bunkers, recovery is not easy. The course offers five sets of tees ranging in yardage from 4914 to 6951 yards. It has a rating/slope ranging from 67.8/114 to 73.4/132.

Carts: Walking occasionally permitted. *Greens Fees:* Approximately $50-$85/18 holes. *Tee Time Policy:* Call two days in advance.

THE RIVER CLUB, BRADENTON (941) 751-4211

Considered to be among the best new courses in the United States in 1989 by *Golf Digest*, this Ron Garl design is a delight. The front nine is somewhat open, with rolling, rippling fairways, while the back nine winds through dense woodlands. As with most Garl courses, accuracy is a must due to the prevalent water, sand, and other score-threatening obstacles. The course features five sets of tees that range from 5157 to 7026 yards and a rating/slope ranging from 69/119 to 73.6/133. An exciting hole is the 416-yard, par 4 sixteenth, a slight dogleg left. It requires an accurate tee shot to a fairway bordered on the right by a lake. This lake then must be traversed to a green that is totally enveloped by the water, with the green sitting on a peninsula.

Carts: Mandatory. *Greens Fees:* $50 before 1 P.M., $40 after 1 P.M./18 holes, including cart. *Tee Time Policy:* Call two days in advance.

(Note: Open to resort guests only)

The Islandside course is one of those courses that you can not go wrong on (no matter what your score), given its absolutely beautiful setting. Designed by William Mitchell and measuring from 5198 to 6792 yards, with a slope ranging from 121 to 138, this wind-blown course travels through thousands of palm trees, and over and around a seemingly equal number of lakes and lagoons (water is a factor on every hole). Greens tend to be large, which can be comforting on holes like the second, a 500-yard par 5 where water flanks the green front, right, and back.

Carts: Mandatory. *Greens Fees:* $100/18 holes, including cart. *Tee Time Policy:* Open to resort guests only; should be reserved three or more days in advance.

OTHER EXCELLENT AREA COURSES:

Serenoa Golf Club, Sarasota (941-925-2755), is a 6270-yard, par 72 course designed by David Alden, with water as a factor on every hole. **Tatum Ridge Golf Links**, Sarasota (941-378-4211), was designed by Ted McAnlis and is a 6757-yard, par 72, links-style course that opened in 1989. **Tara Golf and Country Club**, Sarasota (941-758-7961), was also designed by Ted McAnlis and is a 6900-yard course that winds through numerous lakes. **Bobby**

Jones Golf Complex, Sarasota (941-955-8097), has historical significance since the American course was designed by Donald Ross in 1927. Its course record of 62 is held by Paul Azinger.

ATTRACTIONS

TOURS

Marina Jack II, located at 2 Marina Place, is a 100-foot boat used to take passengers on lunch, dinner, and dancing cruises. For a schedule, call 941-366-9255.

The Gator Gal, which is located at 13207 S.R. 72 in Sarasota, is the world's largest airboat. It takes visitors on narrated wildlife lake cruises daily within the Myakka State Park and Wilderness Preserve (See Recreation). Call 941-361-0100.

HISTORIC PLACES

At **Historic Spanish Point**, located on U.S. 41 in Osprey, along Little Sarasota Bay, you can glimpse remnants of local history. Sites include a Native American burial mound, ruins of a late nineteenth-century homestead, a Victorian estate and gardens, a cemetery, and a chapel. Admission is charged. Call 941-966-5214.

MUSEUMS/SCIENCE CENTERS

The Ringling Complex, at 5401 Bay Shore Road, is a must-see area attraction. An admission ticket includes entry to all buildings on the grounds. **The John and Mable Ringling Museum of Art** is among the largest draws here. This columned, Italian Renaissance–style building contains one of the country's finest collections of baroque art and European tapestries. The grounds themselves have beautifully manicured gardens lined with fine sculptures, chiefly Grecian and Roman, one of which is a replica of Michelangelo's *David*. Also on the grounds is the Ringling residence, named **Ca'd'Zan** ("House of John"), which was built in the late 1920s when Ringling decided to bring the circus here during summers. It's an Italian Renaissance mansion modeled after a doge's palace in Venice. Inside, there's a wonderful art collection containing paintings, tapestries, marble floors, and exquisite detailing. A marble terrace outside leads to the water, which once held Mable Ringling's Venetian gondola. Circus fans will love the **Circus Galleries**, which contain historic photos (including one

of the real Tom Thumb), costumes, posters and artworks, calliopes, a miniature model of a big-top circus, and other memorabilia from the circus. The complex is open daily. Admission is charged. Call 941-355-5101.

Near the Ringling complex is **Bellm's Cars and Music of Yesterday**, at 5500 North Tamiami Trail. The collection has over two hundred restored antique cars, including Rolls Royces and Pierce Arrows. The music-box collection has over twelve hundred items, and there's a 30-foot Belgian organ, as well as a penny arcade with antique games. Open daily. Admission is charged. Call 941-355-6228.

Mote Marine Aquarium, at 1600 City Island Park, just south of Longboat Key on City Island, displays marine life. Sharks, manta rays, and exotic fish are

Ca'd'Zan, Sarasota
Photo courtesy of FL Department of Commerce, Division of Tourism

Golf Vacations Even Non-Golfers Will Enjoy

all on display. The facility is the site of cutting-edge marine research. One popular feature for kids is the 30-foot touch tank, which holds crabs, rays, sea urchins, whelks, and more. Open daily. Admission is charged. Call 941-388-2451.

CULTURAL OFFERINGS

Florida Studio Theater, at 1241 Palm Avenue in Sarasota, is ranked as the top theater in the state by the Florida Arts Council. Productions of contemporary plays and musicals run from December through August. Call 941-366-9796. **The Lemon Bay Playhouse**, at 350 West Dearborn Street, produces eight different productions between September and June. Call 941-475-6756. **The Asolo Theater Company**, at the Ringling Complex, presents several plays, lectures, and other programs during the year. The theater's beautiful decor consists of antique objects brought from Asolo, Italy. For schedule information, contact the theater at 941-351-8000. **Theater Works, Inc.**, is a professional group that performs a variety of shows, including musicals and comedies. Call 941-952-9170. Another local theater where plays, ballets, and other works are performed is the lovely **Van Wezel Performing Arts Hall**, at 777 North Tamiami Trail, which was designed by the Frank Lloyd Wright foundation. Call 941-953-3366.

The Sarasota Opera Association, located at 61 North Pineapple Avenue, is among the state's best, though the season only runs February to March. Their annual repertoire consists of four full operas and some miscellaneous concerts. Call 941-953-7030 or 941-366-

8450. **The New Gloria Musicae Singers** perform music of varying styles from the last four centuries, including harmony jazz and orchestral accompaniments. For information, call 941-954-4223.

The area has three symphony orchestras. The most prestigious is the **Florida West Coast Symphony**, with offices at 709 North Tamiami Trail, which presents concerts, often with renowned guest musicians. The orchestra gives both classical and pops performances. A string quartet, piano quartet, wind quintet, and a brass quintet are affiliated with the orchestra. Call 941-953-4252. **The Venice Symphony** performs pops and classical concerts from December through April and during a November music festival. For information, call 941-488-1010. **The Sarasota Concert Band**, with offices at 75 South Palm Avenue, is a fifty-piece professional band which presents series like the "Music for the People," monthly performances at the Van Wezel Performing Arts Hall, located at 777 North Tamiami Trail in Sarasota, and a summer series in area parks. Call 941-955-6660.

The Sarasota Ballet of Florida performs six ballets between September and April. Call 941-366-6740.

RECREATION

Fishing of all types can be found around Sarasota and its sea islands. There are around twenty boat ramps and marinas offering access to the waters. In addition, more than twenty-five local captains work as fishing guides; they are listed in *Sarasota: Florida's Mild Side*, distributed by the Sarasota Convention and Visitors Bureau. Call 800-522-9799.

The **Chicago White Sox** spring training takes place in Sarasota from March through early April at the Ed Smith Sports Complex, at Twelfth Street and Tuttle Avenue. For information, call 941-954-7699 extension 232.

The 35,000-acre **Myakka State Park and Wilderness Preserve**, about 9 miles east of Sarasota on S.R. 72, is a state-owned land area in Florida. The park has wetlands, woodlands, and prairies, as well as a river, a lake, and plenty of native plants and wildlife (most notably alligators, birds, and deer) in their natural habitats. There's an airboat tour, a natural history museum, hiking trails, a bird walk, camping, fishing, and boating areas. Open daily. Call 941-361-6511.

Marie Selby Botanical Gardens, overlooking the bay at 811 South Palm Avenue (off U.S. 41), has a splendid orchid-and-display garden filled with plants. On the grounds is the Christy Payne Mansion, home of the Museum of Botany. Open daily. Admission is charged. Call 941-366-5730.

Sarasota Jungle Gardens, at 3701 Bayshore Road, about a mile south of the Ringling complex, is a 10-acre jungle. Its tropical gardens have nature trails, a butterfly and shell museum, bird and reptile shows, and a petting zoo. Open daily. Admission is charged. Call 941-355-5305.

Pelican Man's Bird Sanctuary, on City Island across the parking lot from the Mote Marine Aquarium, is devoted to the rescue and rehabilitation of local birds. Open daily. Admission is free. Call 941-388-4444.

SEASONAL EVENTS

Golf fans come in late February for the **Senior Golf Classic Cup** tournament, part of the Senior PGA Tour. For information, call 941-925-8687.

In early March, the **Renaissance Festival** comes to the Ringling Complex, with medieval games like jousting, jesting, juggling, and a human chess game, as well as period costumes, crafts, and foods. Call 941-355-5101. The Saturday preceding March 17, a **Saint Patrick's Day Parade** is held in Venice, with over a hundred floats and local musicians, and a big turnout. In late March through early April, the **International Chamber Music Festival** comes to the Sarasota area, showcasing internationally renowned artists.

In April, the **Sarasota Jazz Festival** is held at the Van Wezel Performing Arts Hall. Recent artists have included Tito Puente and Steve Allen. Call 941-366-1552. Also in April, the **Siesta Fiesta on Siesta Key** features exhibits by more than 250 artisans and craftsmen, an International food fair, and children's events. Call 941-962-0388. Wine lovers will enjoy Sarasota's **Florida Winefest and Auction**, also in April, where vintners, chefs, and wine experts gather to showcase, judge, and sell fine wines. Call 941-952-1109.

In May, the **Longboat Key Islandfest**, featuring samples of local cuisine, live entertainment, and children's activities, is held on Longboat Key. Call 941-383-2466.

June brings the two-week-long Sarasota Music Festival, in which up-and-coming and established classical and chamber musicians present concerts throughout the area. Call 941-952-9634.

July brings a fireworks festival and the **Offshore Grand Prix** boat race, the crowning event of many festivities that include marching parades, a children's fishing tournament, a boat parade, and more.

August brings the **Sharks Tooth Festival** in Venice, with displays of sharks' teeth, games, food, a kite competition, crafts, and live music. Call 941-488-2236.

The Pioneer Days Festival begins the week before Labor Day and honors the early settlers of this area. Celebrations include golf and tennis tournaments, games, barbecues, crafts, a parade, beauty pageants, and the Labor Day weekend grand finale: the **Sarasota Sailing Squadron Labor Day Regatta**. Call 941-474-5511.

In October, local restaurants showcase their best dishes at the **Taste of Sarasota**. Other activities for the event include an ice carving contest, races among local waiters, a petting zoo, and rides. Call 941-355-1447. Also in October, the **St. Armands Art Festival** draws over two hundred international artists. Call 941-962-0388.

The Sandy Claws Arts and Crafts Festival is in early December, and is a fun-filled festival geared toward families. Call 941-349-7981.

ACCOMMODATIONS ....

EXPENSIVE

The Resort at Longboat Beach Club, at 301 Gulf of Mexico Drive on Longboat Key, is a four-star resort located on the beach noted for its spectacular 45 holes of championship golf (See Golf Information). It also has tennis facilities, a spa, activities for children, and great restaurants. Call 941-383-8821.

The Colony Beach and Tennis Resort, at 1620 Gulf of Mexico Drive on Longboat Key, has luxury beachfront villas, a fitness center and spa, a children's program during the high season, and tennis courts (which draw international tennis stars). There's also an award-winning restaurant. Call 941-383-6464 or 800-4-COLONY.

MODERATE

Siesta Sands Beach Resort, at 1001 Point of Rocks Road on Siesta Key, has luxury condominiums on Crescent Beach, with private beachfront balconies, dining rooms, kitchens, and heated pools. Call 941-349-8061 or 800-331-7293.

Holiday Inn/Holidome Longboat Key, at 4949 Gulf of Mexico Drive on Longboat Key, has large rooms overlooking the water, a private beach for guests, indoor pool, tennis, sailing facilities, and a beachside bar. Call 941-383-3771 or 800-HOLIDAY.

Coquina on the Beach Resort, at 1008 Ben Franklin Drive on Lido Key, is within walking distance of St. Armands Circle. There's a heated pool, a barbecue-and-picnic area with a beach view, and comfortable spacious rooms. This is a good place for families, and they accept pets. Call 941-388-2141.

MODERATE/INEXPENSIVE

Islander Inn, at 1725 Stickney Point Road, at Siesta Key Bridge, is a two-story motel with relatively low rates. Amenities include a whirlpool and sauna, and a location near the gulf. Call 941-923-5426.

Surfview Motel, at 1121 Ben Franklin Drive on Lido Key, is located across from the beach. Rates here are

The John and Mable Ringling Museum of Art, Sarasota
Photo courtesy of FL Department of Commerce, Division of Tourism

reasonable for rooms, efficiencies, and suites, and the motel is within minutes of St. Armands Circle. Call 941-388-1818.

SHOPPING ....

St. Armands Circle, on St. Armands Key, is perhaps the most famous shopping area in the region due to its circular layout and upscale retail establishments (not to mention the smattering of fine restaurants). For information, call 941-388-1554.

For antiques, art galleries, and interior designer's showrooms, head to **Palm Avenue** located off lower Main Street in Sarasota, where you'll find several such shops clustered together. For information, call 941-955-9495.

Sarasota Quay is a peach-colored, villa-style complex located on the waterfront, with lovely arched walkways and stone fountains. Throughout the facility are shops and restaurants, and there's also a large nightclub. Call 941-957-0192.

On Longboat Key, part of Gulf of Mexico Drive is known as the **Avenue of the Flowers**, with pretty gardens, clothing boutiques, art galleries, and gourmet food shops.

RESTAURANTS ....

DINNER THEATER
Venice Golden Apple Dinner Theater, in the Best Western Resort Inn at 447 U.S. 41 Bypass in nearby

Venice, serves a buffet followed by a professional stage show. Call 941-484-7711. There's another **Golden Apple Dinner Theater** in Sarasota at 25 North Pineapple Avenue. 941-366-5454.

FINE DINING

Cafe L'Europe, at 431 St. Armands Circle on St. Armands Key, serves creative European cuisine, with an emphasis on seafood and veal selections. They also offer beef, chicken, and other dishes. Lunch and dinner are served. Call 941-388-4415.

The Summerhouse Restaurant, at 6101 Midnight Pass Road on Siesta Key, is one of the area's finer eating establishments and there's live music nightly. Call for an entertainment schedule and come for dinner if your budget allows. Serving lunch and dinner. Call 941-349-1100.

CASUAL DINING

Café of the Arts, in a quaint little building at 5230 North Tamiami Trail in Sarasota, serves French and continental cuisine. The pastries are terrific. Serves breakfast, lunch, dinner, and Sunday brunch. Call 941-351-4304.

Primo, at 8076 North Tamiami Trail in Sarasota, specializes in Italian veal, seafood, and pasta dishes. All the baking and desserts are done on the premises. Open daily for dinner. Call 941-359-3690.

Sugar and Spice, at 1850 South Tamiami Trail in Sarasota, may not catch your eye from the outside, but the inside has a casual, homey, Dutch-Amish theme and serves hearty homestyle food like shoo-fly pie, chicken dishes, and homemade breads. Serves lunch and dinner. Call 941-953-3340.

JUST FOR KIDS ....

Gulf Coast World of Science, at 8251 East Fifteenth Street in Bradenton, is designed for school-age children, and occasionally has Saturday morning programs. Open daily except Monday. Admission is charged. Call 941-359-9975. Other exhibits of interest to kids include the petting zoo at the Jungle Gardens, touch tank at Mote Marine Aquarium, and Circus Galleries at the Ringling complex.

SIDE TRIPS ....

Fort Myers, Sanibel Island, and Captiva Island, approximately 80 to 100 miles south of Sarasota, are other gems of Florida's west coast favored by beach and golf lovers, some of whom wouldn't stay anywhere else.

The palm tree–lined streets of Fort Myers once contained the winter homes of Thomas Edison and Henry Ford. In fact, a major attraction in Fort Myers is their side-by-side winter homes (Ford's "Mangoes" and Edison's "Seminole Lodge"), known as the **Edison-Ford Complex**, which comes complete with laboratories and gardens. The complex is located at 2350 McGregor Boulevard. Open daily. Call 941-334-3614. Other attractions in Fort Myers include **Echo**, at 17430 Durrance Road, which is a farm that experiments with plants that can thrive in third-world environments (call 941-543-3246); the **Fort Myers Historical Museum**, at 2300 Peck Street, which features a collection of local artifacts nestled inside an old train depot (call 941-332-5955); and a three-hour, narrated jungle cruise through the Everglades leaving from the City

Yacht Basin at Lee Street (call 941-334-7474). There's also spring training for the Boston Red Sox (call 941-334-4700) and the Minnesota Twins (call 800-28-TWINS). Golfers may want to try **Eastwood Golf Course** in Fort Myers (call 941-275-4848), which is a 6772-yard, par 72 layout designed by Bruce Devlin and Robert von Hagge. The course is considered among the top public courses in the United States by *Golf Digest*. Another excellent course in Fort Myers is the **Gateway Golf and Country Club** (call 941-561-1010). This Tom Fazio layout is a 6974-yard, par 72, links-style course that has hosted a variety of tournaments since its opening in 1989 and features "Cape Cod" mounded bunkers.

Fort Myers Beach, off the coast from Fort Myers, runs along Estero Island, a thin strip of land wedged between the Gulf of Mexico and Estero Bay. This beach is not only gorgeous, but is considered the safest beach in Florida.

Sanibel Island and Captiva Island are about 25 miles away from Fort Myers and are also popular beach resorts. Sanibel Island may be preferable to golfers as it has two golf courses, one of which is the highly regarded **The Dunes Golf and Tennis Club**, at 949 Sandcastle Road on Sanibel Island. Call 941-472-2535. This course is associated with several hotels owned by the South Seas Company; the number to call for information or reservations at one of their affiliated properties is 800-554-5454.

There are several good hotels and fine restaurants on Sanibel and Captiva Islands. For information, contact the Lee County Visitors and Convention Bureau at 941-335-2631.

Many vacationers describe **Naples**, approximately 40 miles south of Fort Myers, as one of the most beautiful areas in Florida. Ironically, it once was mere swampland that has now been artificially drained. Since the 1950s, it has became an increasingly popular resort area. Named for the Italian city, a highlight here is the lovely Bay of Naples. The city is known for upscale (and abundant) shopping, a scenic historic area, and fun attractions for the kids. The most notable kid friendly attractions are the **Teddy Bear Museum of Naples**, at 2511 Pine Ridge Road, with over 1500 bears (call 941-598-2711) and **Jungle Larry's Zoological Park**, a botanical gardens with animal shows, boat rides, and more (call 941-262-5409). Of course, the beaches are popular here, mainly Bonita Beach near North Naples and Marco Island, south of Naples. In all, there are ten miles of beaches in the Naples area.

For golfers, Naples is a veritable treasure trove. Marco Island is home to the highly regarded **Golf Club at Marco Island**, which is a resort hotel with a golf course. The course is a tight, 6900-yard, Joe Lee design set among hundreds of acres of pines, palms, and mangroves. Call 941-793-6060 (for the course) or 800-438-4373. Additionally, the area is home to the following fine courses.

LELY FLAMINGO ISLAND CLUB, NAPLES (941) 793-2223

Lely Flamingo, opened in 1990, is a Robert Trent Jones, Sr., layout. The assortment of tees range from 5377 to almost 7200 yards, and the rating/slope ranges from 70.6/126 to 73.9/135. The course winds through an assortment of lagoons and lakes, as well as sable palms and other miscellaneous Florida vegetation. Additionally, most of its fairways are well guarded by bunkers and waste areas. As is Jones's trademark, Lely Flamingo has excellent par 3s, the 210-yard fourteenth probably being the best of the bunch. It sits on a piece of land best described as a backwards "C" that is surrounded by water on all sides. All that's necessary is that you grab your 2 or 3 iron; ignore the water short, left, and long; and make a perfect swing. In case this is not quite enough, the green has three tiers and a couple of bunkers on the right.

Carts: Mandatory. *Greens Fees:* $120 during A.M. hours, $75 during P.M. hours in high season/18 holes, including cart. *Tee Time Policy:* Can be reserved three days in advance.

PELICAN'S NEST GOLF CLUB, BONITA SPRINGS (15 MILES NORTH OF NAPLES) (941) 947-4600 OR (800) 952-NEST

Pelican's Nest offers four separate 9-hole courses—Gator, Hurricane, Panther, and Seminole—that can be played in any combination. Tees generally range from 5200 to 7000 yards, with rating/ slope ranging from 69/120 to 75/140. Designed by Tom Fazio, these layouts feature fairways lined by mounds, bunkers, oaks, palmettos, and pines, as well as a fair number of lakes, streams, and creeks. The greens come in a multitude of shapes and sizes, including some that are as shallow as 20 yards and some that are almost 50 yards deep. Like most, if not all, Fazio layouts, the Nest has a lot of variety from hole to hole. It requires an assortment of shots, some sort of a game plan, and is just good fun to play.

Carts: Mandatory. *Greens Fees:* $90 during A.M. hours, $50 during P.M. hours in high season/18 holes, including cart. *Tee Time Policy:* Can be reserved two days in advance.

For more information on golf or other attractions in Naples, call the Naples Area Chamber of Commerce at 941-262-6141.

GENERAL INFORMATION ....

Contact the Sarasota Convention and Visitors Bureau at 800-522-9799. Ask them for a free copy of *Sarasota: Florida's Mild Side.*

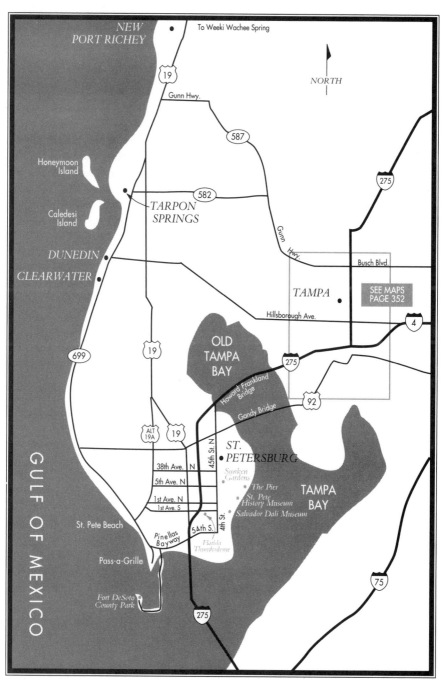

TAMPA and ST. PETERSBURG, FL.

Tampa and St. Petersburg

AREA CODE: 813

INTRODUCTION

Tampa and St. Petersburg lie across Tampa Bay from one another like two claws jutting out from Florida's mainland. These cities tempt vacationers in a number of ways, mainly with their fabulous beach areas, their great golf courses, and their large variety of theme parks and museums. It's also convenient to Orlando (about an hour's drive away), and many vacationers come to take in the Tampa/St. Petersburg area's beaches and Orlando's attractions in the same trip. Recently, the city has also become a destination for many business travelers, since Tampa has a sizeable amount of industry and serves as headquarters for several large companies.

As for golf, despite unpredictable and sometimes nippy bouts in winter, the season runs year-round. The mild climate, coupled with sprawling tropical flatlands, knobby hills, and occasional small bodies of water, make for some great layouts that attract serious amateurs on vacation, as well as many professionals seeking winter or year-round homes. However, some of the area's great courses are a fair distance from the beaches (e.g., World Woods), so you'll need to keep distances in mind when making plans to play. Beach lovers shouldn't despair, though, since there are some great courses closer to the beach (like Innisbrook and Dunedin), making it possible to play a round and ride the waves all in the same day.

You should also keep distances in mind when planning trips to non-golf attractions, as the area is fairly spread out and travel between locations can be slow (and confusing if you don't stick to major thoroughfares). However, that's not to say visitors should simply stay on the beaches, as it would be a shame to miss the many terrific and unique attractions, from Busch Gardens to the Salvador Dali Museum to Tampa's Ybor City, and many others.

The normal monthly temperatures for Tampa/St. Petersburg respectively, are: January, 59.9/60.7; February, 61.5/62; March, 66.4/67.1; April, 71.2/72.6; May, 77.2/78.2; June, 81/82; July, 82.1/83.1; August, 82.1/83; September, 81/81.6; October, 74.9/76.2; November, 67.6/69; December, 62.2/63.1. Visitors come in greatest numbers between January and April for Tampa, and between March and October for St. Petersburg.

GOLF INFORMATION ....

INNISBROOK RESORT AND COUNTRY CLUB, TARPON SPRINGS
(813) 942-2000

Innisbrook sports 63 holes of excellent golf—the 18-hole Copperhead and Island courses and the 27-hole Sandpiper course. Both the Island and Sandpiper courses are ranked 4 stars by *Golf Digest's Places to Play*, and the Island course (a personal favorite of the author) was the site of the 1990 NCAA Championship. The gem here, however, is the Copperhead course. Designed by E.L. Packard and opened in 1972, Copperhead consistently ranks among the top courses in the United States and Florida according to *Golf Digest* and *Golf*, and since 1990, it has been the site of the J.C. Penney Mixed Team Championship (featuring stars from the PGA and LPGA tours). It is narrowly cut through a lovely pine forest, with many hills and dales (not often found in Florida). In addition, you will find as much water and sand on the course as you will on the nearby beaches. The course's yardage ranges from 5506 to over 7087 yards, and its rating/slope from the back tees is a solid 74.4/140.

Carts: Mandatory. *Greens Fees:* Approximately $60-$175 depending on season, course played, and whether a resort guest or not/18 holes, including cart. *Tee Time Policy:* Can be reserved four days in advance.

WORLD WOODS, BROOKSVILLE
(904) 796-5500

Tom Fazio's Pine Barrens and Rolling Oaks courses at World Woods have burst upon the United States golf scene in the last year, grabbing about every accolade and award available. *Golf Digest* and *Golf* each consider both courses among the top new courses in the United States. *Golf Digest* includes Pine Barrens among the top hundred courses in the world, *Golf* ranks both courses among the top ten courses you can play in Florida, and *Golf Digest's Places to Play* gives each course 4½ stars. Once again, Fazio has demonstrated his genius in laying out courses that every level of golfer will get a thrill in playing. Both courses wind through tall pines, oaks, and cypress on terrain with gentle rolling hills that is more akin to Georgia's Augusta or courses in the Carolinas than to Florida. The fairways are open and invite the player to swing away. Approaches, however, require accuracy and, in some instances, courage. The greens come in all sizes. They are often elevated, and generally, they will dictate to the wise player what side to miss on. True to form, Fazio offers a wide variety of holes, requiring a player to properly execute most of the shots in his or her bag. The par 3s range from 150 to 230 yards, the par 4s from 330 to 470 yards, and the par 5s from 490 to 570 yards. The par 71 Pine Barrens course ranges in yardage from 5301 to 6902 yards, and the rating/slope ranges from 70.9/132 to 73.7/140. The par 72 Rolling Oaks course ranges in yardage from 5245 to 6985 yards, and in rating/slope from 70.7/128 to 73.5/136. World Woods also features the 9-hole Short course, the 3-hole Practice course, and a circular range.

Carts: Mandatory. *Greens Fees:* $60 weekdays, $75 weekends/18 holes, including cart. *Tee Time Policy:* Can be reserved up to thirty days in advance.

SEVEN SPRINGS GOLF AND COUNTRY CLUB, NEW PORT RICHEY (813) 376-0035

The Championship course at Seven Springs is a Ron Garl, 6566-yard (tees start at 5250 yards), par 72 layout. With water in play on 17 holes, and cypress, live oaks, and Florida pines lining most of the fairways, this course puts a premium on shot placement. Although accurate, aggressive play will be rewarded, the risk of landing in an unrecoverable hazard is great. The 378-yard, par 4 eighth is a dogleg left that serves as the signature hole. A tee shot of 200 yards is required—anything longer or pulled slightly left will risk going into lakes which skirt both sides of the fairway. An approach of about 170 yards then must be played to a green protected by a lake on the left and cypress trees to the back and right.

Carts: Mandatory. *Greens Fees:* $50/18 holes, including cart. *Tee Time Policy:* Can be reserved a day in advance.

BLOOMINGDALE GOLFERS CLUB, VALRICO (813) 685-4105

(Note: On weekends, this course is closed to non-members.)

A golfer's club is an accurate description of what you will find at Bloomingdale. From the time you enter the parking lot, which provides spaces for its champs, as well as for PGA, LPGA, and Senior PGA residents (such as Lee Janzen, Steve Stricker, Michael Bradley, and Vicki Goetz), to when you first step onto the giant putting green, range, and practice area, you will get the feeling that this course is for serious golfers. Consistently ranked among the top courses in Florida and rated 4 stars by *Golf Digest's Places to Play*, Bloomingdale, designed by the prolific Ron Garl, opened in 1983. It offers five sets of tees ranging from the 5397 to 7165 yards. Most of the fairways are lined with trees, and the large, multishaped (including clover leaf–shaped) greens are undulating and tiered. The finishing holes on each side are fascinating. The ninth is a 546-yard par 5 that is kind of "S" shaped. Depending on the wind, a player can have a go at the green in two, but beware—it sits on a peninsula surrounded almost completely by water. The lay-up seemingly is horizontal to the green, and the approach obviously requires a good degree of accuracy. The eighteenth is a 409-yard par 4 that doglegs left over a marsh. The tee shot must be long to even get a look at the green, for a dense forest protects the left side of the fairway all the way up to the corner of the dogleg. The green is wide, shallow, and sloped back to front.

Carts: Mandatory. *Greens Fees:* $40-$55 in high season/18 holes, including cart. *Tee Time Policy:* Open to guest-play all day Monday-Thursday, and before 11:30 A.M. on Fridays. Guests are required to make a reservation six days in advance.

DUNEDIN COUNTRY CLUB, DUNEDIN (813) 733-7836

Dunedin is a Donald Ross course that opened in 1928. Over the years it has hosted a variety of professional events, several of which were won by the "Squire," Gene Sarazen. By modern standards, the course is not very long—the blue tees reach 6565 yards, while the whites and reds are 6245 and 5726 yards, respectively. The story of this course, however, is the classic Ross design. The tees are elevated and rectangular, like those at Ross's Pinehurst Number 2 or Siwanoy (the host of the first PGA Championship in 1916). The fairways are sprawling and rolling, and defined by palms, live oaks, pines, streams, and lakes. Finally, the greens are vintage Ross—and the key to scoring

well at Dunedin. Generally, each green is small and slopes toward the middle like a saucer. Additionally, the greens are elevated, with steep banks on each side. Therefore, well-struck, accurate shots will hold the greens, while all others will bound down the slopes—leaving the player with a brutal chip or lob back up onto the green. Possessing all of the above characteristics is the 439-yard, par 4 second, a dogleg left. Teeing off from elevated tees, the player is given vast room to the right of the fairway. And the player must use that room to avoid being blocked by a huge oak sitting on the corner of the dogleg. (The whole left side of this hole is lined with 300- to 400-year-old, massive oaks, with boughs reaching to the ground). The approach plays slightly uphill to a narrow, deep green protected with bunkers front right and front left. A par here is an excellent score.

Carts: Walking permitted in the afternoons. *Greens Fees:* $35 members, $40 nonmembers/18 holes, including cart. *Tee Time Policy:* Can be reserved two days in advance.

THE EAGLES GOLF AND COUNTRY CLUB, ODESSA (813) 920-6681

Having recently added the 9-hole Islands course, designed by Gary Koch, The Eagles now offers 36 holes of excellent golf. The other 9-hole courses are Oaks, Lakes, and Forest. The Eagles is set upon more than 1000 wooded acres with oaks, maples, pines, and cypress, and over thirty lakes, ponds, canals, and creeks are found on the courses. Since more than half of the club's acreage is devoted to nature preserves, wildlife on and around the course is abundant and active. The Oaks and Lakes courses make up the club's original 18 holes, and in and of themselves, they are quite a bit of golf. A testimony to their challenge is the Lakes's eighth. It is a 241-yard par 3 that plays over a pond to a massive, rolling green, which has three putts written all over it if you don't land your shot close to the hole. The new Island nine features a reachable par 4 with a green set in an island surrounded by sand, a double dogleg par 5, and a par 3 with an island green (this time surrounded by water). Each nine features four sets of tees, the back tees for each combination stretching to over 7000 yards and having a rating/slope of 70.3/130.

Carts: Walking sometimes permitted. *Greens Fees:* $50 weekdays, $55 weekends/18 holes, including cart. *Tee Time Policy:* Can be reserved up to four days in advance.

OTHER EXCELLENT AREA COURSES:

Seville Golf and Country Club, Weeki Wachee (See Side Trips) (904-596-7888) is a par 72, Arthur Hills course that can reach over 7100 yards. It features a natural, rolling terrain and waste bunkers that utilize local sand. **Saddlebrook Golf and Tennis Resort**, Wesley Chapel (813-973-1111), has a lovely countryside setting. The resort features a par 70, Arnold Palmer/Dean Refram course reaching 6600 yards, and an Arnold Palmer/Ed Seay course that stretches 6469 yards with a par of 71. **Bardmoor North Golf Club**, Largo (813-397-0483), was once the site of the PGA/LPGA Tour's J.C. Penney Mixed Team Classic. This 6960-yard, par 72 course features small, elevated greens. **Tournament Players Club of Tampa Bay**, Lutz (813-949-0091), is a 6900-yard, par 71 course

Tarpon Springs
Photo courtesy of the FL Department of Commerce, Division of Tourism

which is the site of the Senior PGA Tour's annual GTE Suncoast Classic, won in 1996 by Jack Nicklaus. **Westchase Golf Club**, Tampa (813-854-2331), features a Lloyd Clifton design. This 6710-yard, par 72 course winds through lakes, woods, and conservation areas. **Fox Hollow Golf Club**, New Port Richey (813-376-6333), is a 1994, Robert Trent Jones, Sr., design with a par of 71, featuring six sets of tees ranging from 4454 to 7138 yards.

ATTRACTIONS ....

TOURS

Walking Tours

In Tampa's **Ybor Square** (See Historic Places), free guided walking tours are given on Tuesday, Thursday, and Saturday at 1:30 P.M. Ybor Square is located at 1901 Thirteenth Street.

Motorized Tours

Around the Town Tours, at 3450 West Busch Boulevard, offers tours to attractions in Tampa and Tarpon Springs (call 813-932-7803), as does **Tampa Tours**, 5805 North Fiftieth Street (call 813-621-6667), and **Gulf Coast Gray Line**, which also has tours of St. Petersburg and the major theme parks in Orlando, like Disney World, Sea World, etc. (call 813-535-0208).

In Ybor, the **Tampa-Ybor Trolley** takes passengers around the downtown district from 7:30 A.M. to 5:30 P.M. For information, call 813-254-4278.

Air Tours

Suncoast Helicopter's Tampa Bay area tours depart from the Tampa International Airport. Call 813-872-6625.

Boat Tours

Sightseeing lunch and dinner tours aboard the **Lady Anderson** cruise along the St. Petersburg Causeway. The tours begin at 3400 Pasadena Avenue in St. Petersburg Beach. Call 813-367-7804. **The Starlite Majesty** gives boat tours that leave from Clearwater Beach Marina. Call 813-462-2628.

HISTORIC PLACES

Historic **Ybor** (Ee-bore) **City** in Tampa is a Cuban enclave, with a reputation for wild nightlife, terrific cigars, microbrewed beers, rich history, and cutting-edge arts. Plus, there's plenty of classic culture and old-world architecture added to the mix. The area is quaint, with some cobblestone streets and wrought-iron balconies, and in some spots, the air is filled with the smell of cigars being made. Some chief points of interest include: **Ybor Square** (on the National Register of Historic Places), at 1901 Thirteenth Street, was once a booming cigar factory in the 1800s and now houses restaurants and shops. Open daily. Call 813-247-4497. **The Ybor City State Museum**, at 1818 East Ninth Avenue, provides a solid historical orientation on Ybor City. Admission is charged. Call 813-247-6323.

MUSEUMS/SCIENCE CENTERS

The Tampa Museum of Art, at 601 Doyle Carlton Drive, contains over 7,000 artworks, chiefly from the classical periods in Greece and Rome, and twentieth-century American works. There are also children's exhibits. Admission is charged. Call 813-223-8130.

The Museum of Science and Industry, at 4801 East Fowler Avenue in Tampa, has a great planetarium plus hands-on exhibits on flight (including a simulated flight), natural phenomenon (there's a hurricane room), insects (including a butterfly garden with free-flying butterflies), wildlife, and more. Open daily. Admission is charged. Call 813-987-6300 or 800-998-MOSI.

The Florida Aquarium, at 300 South Thirteenth Street, in Tampa, is a new complex with an 84-foot glass dome housing more than 4,000 specimens of fish and marine animals, and over 500 native plant species. The aquarium's four major areas represent different aquatic habitats: springs and wetlands, bay and barrier beach, a coral reef, and the Gulf Stream and the ocean. Also of note is a full-scale coral reef in a tank and a nighttime cave exhibit. Open daily. Admission is charged. Call 813-273-4020 or 813-273-4000.

Salvador Dali Museum, at 1000 Third Street in St. Petersburg, is the world's largest collection devoted solely to the works of Dali, the amazing Spanish surrealist. The collection includes paintings, sketches, drawings, and sculpture. Open daily. Admission is charged. Call 813-823-3767.

Florida International Museum, at 261 Second Avenue North in St. Petersburg, hosts many important international historic exhibits and has some permanent exhibits. Some recent exhibits include the "Splendors of Ancient Egypt," with over 170 objects by ancient skilled craftsmen and an exhibit on Alexander the Great. Admission is charged. Call 813-822-3693.

St. Petersburg Museum of History, at 335 Second Avenue, focusing on the history of this booming coastal city, has both permanent and changing exhibits. Open daily. Admission is charged. Call 813-894-1052.

Great Explorations!, at 1120 Fourth Street in St. Petersburg, is an interactive museum for the young and young-at-heart, with exhibits on the body and health, a crawl-through maze, and an area where touch, color, and music can be explored (featuring a moog synthesizer which allows you to "see" sounds). Open daily. Admission is charged. Call 813-821-8885.

Museum of Fine Arts, at 255 Beach Drive NE in St. Petersburg, has artworks from America, Europe, the Far East, and the pre-Columbian era, and a sizeable collection of photographs. Open daily except Monday. Admission is charged. Call 813-896-2667.

CULTURAL OFFERINGS

Tampa Bay Performing Arts Center, at 1010 W.C. MacInnes Place, is a 290,000-square-foot complex with a playhouse, theater, and a festival hall. Productions include ballet, drama, opera, concerts, and special events. Call 813-221-1045 or 800-955-1045.

In Clearwater, the **Ruth Eckerd Hall**, at 1111 McMullen Booth Road, holds a variety of performances—from plays, classical music, and ballet, to jazz and pop concerts. Call 813-791-7400.

The **Mahaffey Theater** in St. Petersburg's Bayfront Center, at 400 First Street South, has a variety of performances throughout the year. Call 813-893-7211. For dancing, try the **Coliseum Ballroom**, at 535 Fourth Avenue North in St. Petersburg, which is a landmark 1924 theater with one of

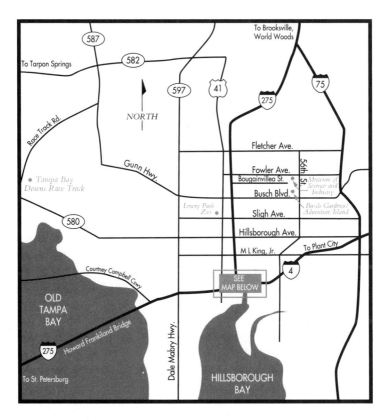

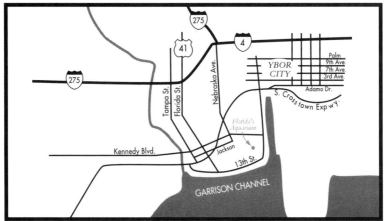

TAMPA, FL.

the nation's largest dance floors. Call 813-892-5202.

Fans of quality ballet will enjoy the **Tampa Ballet** (call 229-7827), and the **St. Petersburg Concert Ballet** (call 813-892-5767).

For concerts, including big-name bands, check local listings for events at the **Sun Dome**, located at 4202 East Fowler Avenue in Tampa. Call 813-974-3111.

RECREATION

Lowry Park Zoo, 7530 North Boulevard in Tampa, is a 105-acre park with animals from several continents. It includes a monkey exhibit, bird house, and petting zoo. Kids will enjoy the amusement park, the statuary of nursery rhyme characters carved in marble, the playground, and the boat launch. Parents appreciate the children's Safety Village museum, which teaches bicycle safety. Open daily, with varying hours. Admission is charged. For information, call the park at 813-223-8230; the zoo at 813-932-0245; or the museum at 813-935-8441.

Spectator Sports are numerous here. Fans can see **Tampa Bay Buccaneers** NFL football at Tampa Stadium, located at 4201 Dale Mabry Highway. For ticket information, call 813-879-2827; to reach the stadium, call 813-673-4300. The **Tampa Bay Lightning** plays NHL hockey at 401 Channelside Drive in Tampa. Call 813-223-4919. For professional baseball, there are several choices. The area is home to the **Grapefruit League**, a collection of major league teams who head here for spring training in March and April. The Orioles and Cardinals train in St. Petersburg, the New York Yankees at Leg-

ends Field in Tampa, the Cincinnati Reds in nearby Plant City, the Pirates in Bradenton (south of Tampa), and the Blue Jays in Dunedin (near Clearwater). For information, call 904-488-0990. In 1998, the **Tampa Bay Devil Rays** will begin playing major league baseball at the St. Petersburg Thunderdome (for more information, call the St. Petersburg Chamber of Commerce at 813-821-4069). Also, the **Tampa Bay Mutiny** plays major league soccer at Tampa Stadium. Call 813-289-6811.

You can watch jai alai at the **Tampa Fronton**, on South Dale Mabry Highway at Gandy Boulevard, in the evenings (except Thursday and Sunday), and on Monday, Wednesday, and Saturday afternoon. Call 813-831-1411.

Clearwater has drag racing from March 1 through November 29 and stock-car racing from February 27 to November 26 at the **Sunshine Speedway**, located at 4500 Ulmerton Road. Call 813-573-4598.

Horse racing takes place at **Tampa Bay Downs**, off FL 580 on Race Track Road in Oldsmar, where thoroughbreds race from mid-December through early May. Call 813-855-4401. Dog racing can be seen from January through June at **Derby Lane**, located at 10490 Gandy Boulevard in St. Petersburg (call 813-576-1361), and July through December at **Tampa Greyhound Track**, at 8300 North Nebraska Avenue (call 813-932-4313).

Sunken Gardens, at 1825 Fourth Street North in St. Petersburg, is a tropical paradise within the city. It has large botanical gardens with tropical and subtropical plants and wildlife. There's also a wax museum. Admission is charged. Call 813-896-3186.

Busch Gardens, at Fortieth Street and Busch Boulevard, is about 8 miles north of Tampa off I-275. This theme park, encompassing some 300 acres, is a combination zoo and amusement park. There are eight exotic regional theme areas (e.g., Timbuktu) and lots of rides (including the famous "Kumba" roller coaster). The collection of animals from several continents constitutes the fourth-largest zoo in the United States. A tram ride travels through some of the roaming animal exhibits, while visitors can walk through other exhibit areas— like the alligator exhibit. Live entertainment is scheduled daily. This is a must-see for families. Admission is charged. Call 813-987-5082.

Adventure Island, at 4500 Bougainvillea Avenue (less than a mile from Busch Gardens), is a water park with almost 40 acres of wave pools, waterslides, and standing pools. Open daily from March through November. Admission is charged. Call 813-987-5660.

Public tennis courts can be found at **City of Tampa Tennis Complex**, at Hillsborough Community College in Tampa (call 813-870-2383), and at McMullen Park, on 1000 Edenville Avenue in Clearwater (call 813-462-6144).

Fort DeSoto Park in St. Petersburg can be reached from Pinellas Bayway off I-275 or from St. Petersburg Beach. This park encompasses over 900 acres and is spread over six keys (islands). The fort, built during the Spanish-American War, still stands at the end of Mullet Key, the largest island in the group. There are several nice, unspoiled

Salvador Dali Museum, St. Petersburg

Photo courtesy of the FL Department of Commerce, Division of Tourism

Golf Vacations Even Non-Golfers Will Enjoy

beaches, as well as areas for fishing and camping. There's a small toll for the bridges.

Caladesi Island State Park is an unspoiled barrier island located about 3 miles off the coast from Dunedin (20 miles north of Clearwater), which is accessible only by ferry. There's a beach on one side, which was voted second-best in the United States in 1995, and plenty of wildlife along the nature trails. You can swim, boat, fish, collect shells, and picnic (there's a snack bar on the island). Rangers answer questions and distribute fact sheets about local wildlife. The ferry departs hourly from Honeymoon Island, off the Dunedin Causeway, and from the Drew Street Dock in downtown Clearwater, between 10 A.M. and 5 P.M. daily (weather permitting). The park is open from 8 A.M. until sunset. There is a fee for the ferry ride. Call 813-734-5263.

SEASONAL EVENTS

For information on current events, call the visitor's information line at 813-223-2752 or 800-44TAMPA.

Football fans flock to Tampa for the **Outback Bowl** on New Year's Day at Tampa Stadium, and there are other special celebrations around town leading up to the event.

In February, the **Florida State Fair**, at the Florida State Fair and Expo Park in Tampa, has agricultural and husbandry exhibits, contests, an orchid show, industrial expo, a midway area with games and rides, and other entertainment. Call 813-621-7821.

In early February through late March, the **Gasparilla** (Pirate) **Festival** comes to Tampa. This month-long celebration features a mock pirate in-

vasion, a parade, a special play presentation, and more. For information, call 813-272-1939.

Also in early March is the ten-day **Florida Strawberry Festival and Hillsborough County Fair**, which has live country music, plenty of foods with strawberries, and a strawberry-shortcake contest. The festival takes place in nearby Plant City. Call 813-752-9194.

In St. Petersburg, several events occur in March. The **International Folk Fair** features exhibits and demonstrations, music, dancing, and food. **The Renaissance Festival** has jousting, maidens, royalty, foods, exhibits, and unique merchandise with a Merry Olde English theme. The two-week **Festival of States** features a huge parade, concerts, a coronation and ball, concerts, sports competitions, art shows, and more. For more information about these events, and other events held in St. Petersburg throughout the year, contact the St. Petersburg/Clearwater Area Convention and Visitors Bureau at 813-582-7892 or 800-345-6710.

ACCOMMODATIONS ....

EXPENSIVE

The 1,000-acre **Innisbrook Hilton Resort**, on U.S. 19 in Tarpon Springs near Clearwater Beach, is a first-rate resort with three championship golf courses that rank among the country's finest resort courses (See Golf Information). The all-suite accommodations range in size and price, but all are nicely furnished. The resort has a children's program, health club, tennis, restaurants, miniature-golf, and a nightclub. Call 813-942-2000.

Saddlebrook Golf and Tennis Resort, at 5700 Saddlebrook Way in Wesley Chapel, 15 miles north of Tampa, is known for tennis more than golf (See Golf Information), but has fine facilities for both. The resort is surrounded by woods, and the accommodations are comfortable and roomy. The resort includes pools, health club facilities, restaurants, and fishing. Call 813-973-1111 or 800-729-8383.

The Don CeSar Resort and Spa, at 3400 Gulf Boulevard in St. Petersburg Beach, is a beautiful, pink, palatial hotel that is about the first thing you notice as you're coming into St. Petersburg Beach. This spectacular landmark is elegant both inside and out. Guests are pampered with a private beach, jetskiing, boating, parasailing, children's programs, tennis, a spa with cutting-edge technologies, and fine dining. Call 813-360-1881.

Renaissance Vinoy Resort, at 501 Fifth Avenue NE in St. Petersburg, is the newly renovated landmark Vinoy Park Hotel (circa 1925). The spacious rooms have several amenities, from blow dryers and bathrobes to multiple televisions. Other perks include a terrific 18-hole golf course on the premises (designed by Ron Garl), tennis courts, pools, a fitness center, lawn games, restaurants, and lounges. Call 813-894-1000.

MODERATE

Holiday Inn Busch Gardens, at 2701 East Fowler Avenue in Tampa, is conveniently located (if the theme park is your destination). There's a pool with a poolside bar, pets are allowed, and free shuttles are provided to Busch Gardens. Call 813-971-4710.

Colonial Gateway Inn is located at 6300 Gulf Boulevard on the beachfront in the St. Petersburg Beach area. The hotel has a pool bar, restaurants, lounges, and comfortable rooms, many with kitchens. Call 813-367-2711 or 800-237-8918.

Holiday Inn Sunspree Resort on Gulf Boulevard, at 5250 Gulf Boulevard in St. Petersburg Beach, is a beautiful, modern, tower-like structure on the beach, with a pool, a revolving rooftop lounge, and beautiful spacious rooms. Call 800-HOLIDAY.

Comfort Inn, at 3580 Ulmerton Road in Clearwater, features a center courtyard surrounded by the motel. The rooms are modern, and there's a pool and a fitness center. Call 813-573-1171.

INEXPENSIVE

Tahitian Inn, at 601 South Dale Mabry Highway in Tampa, is reasonably close to Tampa's main attractions, like Busch Gardens. The small but comfortable motel has a pool and a restaurant. Call 813-877-6721.

Days Inn Marina Beach Resort, at 6800 Sunshine Skyway Lane on the bay in St. Petersburg, has a private beach area. Guests can enjoy sailing, fishing, the two pools, poolside service, a playground, and private balconies and patios. Call 813-867-1151.

Sea Captain Resort, at 40 Devon Drive in Clearwater Beach, is a small, non-smoking motel on the bay, with a dock area for boats and fishing, and a swimming beach two blocks away. Guests enjoy a heated pool, lawn games, and a picnic area. Call 813-446-7550.

SHOPPING ....

Old Hyde Park Village, on Swan Avenue near Bayshore Boulevard in Tampa, encompasses about seven blocks of buildings with specialty shops tucked inside them. Along the bay in St. Petersburg, **The Pier**, at 800 Second Avenue NE, is a five-story building that looks like an inverted pyramid. Inside are shops, restaurants, and entertainment spots.

At Madeira Beach, along the coastal islands in St. Petersburg, is **John's Pass Village and Boardwalk**, a collection of shops resembling an old fishing village. The shopping center is located at 12901 Gulf Boulevard.

The Big Top Flea Market, at 9250 Fowler Avenue in Tampa, has several oblong sheds housing more than 600 vendors. Some vendors sell new items while others sell used ones—from clothing to guns, toys, magazines, and even steak and live lobsters in season.

RESTAURANTS ....

FINE DINING

Armani's, in the Hyatt Regency Westshore at 6200 Courtney Campbell Causeway in Tampa, emphasizes northern Italian cuisine, with specialties like veal Armani and lobster ammiraglia. The antipasto bar and the fresh pasta are spectacular. Jacket and tie required. Dinner served Monday through Saturday. Call 813-281-9165.

Donatello, at 232 North Dale Mabry Highway in Tampa, also serves northern Italian cuisine and is ranked among the state's best restaurants. Specialties include fresh pastas, seafood, veal chops, and duck. Reservations required.

Open for lunch and dinner. Call 813-875-6660.

Mauritania Grille, at the Don CeSar Beach Resort at 3400 Gulf Boulevard in St. Petersburg Beach, serves gourmet selections like wine-glazed filet mignon and poached grouper. The service is impeccable, and the dining room is peacefully decorated with aquariums. Reservations recommended. Open for dinner only. Call 813-360-1882.

Bern's Steak House, at 1208 South Howard Avenue in Tampa, has a reputation for serving the best steaks in Florida, and the wine list is staggering (the most expensive selection runs about $10,000). The aged prime rib and the other steaks are exquisite, as is the service and the decor. Open for dinner only. Call 813-251-2421.

CASUAL DINING

Columbia, at 2117 East Seventh Street in Tampa's Ybor City, is a Spanish-style restaurant with live flamenco dancing and a decor that reflects the local Cuban culture. Since the turn of the century, the restaurant has served delicious paella, black-bean soup, and other Spanish delights. Serves lunch and dinner. Call 813-248-4961.

Cactus Club, at 1601 Snow Avenue in Old Hyde Park Village in Tampa, is a southwestern restaurant serving good fajitas, quesadillas, and pizza. Open for lunch and dinner. Call 813-251-4089.

Nick's on the Water is an Italian restaurant located at 800 Second Avenue NE on the St. Petersburg Pier. They have pasta dishes with specialties like rigatoni in vodka sauce, cream sauce flavored with prosciutto, and pizzas with offbeat toppings like barbecued chicken.

Open for lunch and dinner daily. Call 813-898-5800.

Bob Heilman's Beachcomber, at 447 Mandalay Avenue in Clearwater Beach, has great steaks, salads, and seafood. The beachcombing theme is depicted in scenic murals. Open daily for lunch and dinner. Call 813-442-4144.

JUST FOR KIDS ....

Many hotels have children's programs and babysitting services. However, the main draws for children, besides the beaches, are the water and theme parks like Adventure Island and Busch Gardens in Tampa, and Buccaneer Bay at Weeki Wachee (See Side Trips). Other good choices are Lowry Park's zoo, park, and children's museum, and hands-on museums like Great Explorations! and the Museum of Science and Industry (see Museums/Science Centers).

Celebration Station, at 24546 U.S. 19 North in Clearwater, has rides, go-carts, bumper boats, miniature-golf and more. Call 813-791-1799.

SIDE TRIPS ....

Tarpon Springs, about 20 miles north of Clearwater on U.S. 19, is a small, but famous, Greek community near the water. The main cornerstone of the economy here is sea sponges. The Greek immigrants dive for the sponges in local waters, and visitors can purchase them in all sizes and shapes for reasonable prices. Another popular attraction are the several tour boats located on the right-hand side of Dodecanese Boulevard that take passengers on cruises along the Anclote River (which eventually empties into

the Gulf of Mexico). Tarpon Springs is also the home of the 1943 Grecian-marble **St. Nicholas Orthodox Cathedral**, which has lovely stained-glass windows and is the home of a famous Epiphany ceremony reenacting Christ's baptism. The cathedral is located at 36 North Pinellas Avenue. (Note: *Please* don't pop into the church if you're improperly dressed.) Call 813-937-3540. There's also a deep-sea mini-museum on sponge diving, with a film and exhibits (call 813-942-3771), and several little shops and restaurants specializing in Greek food and goods. One famous eatery is **Pappas**, at 10 West Dodecanese Boulevard. This spacious, popular restaurant serves Greek specialties and pastries, as well as prime rib and seafood. Open daily for lunch and dinner. Call 813-937-5101. A popular event in Tarpon Springs is the **Not Just a Seafood Festival** in May. Call 813-937-6109. Also in Tarpon Springs is the fabulous golf resort, the Innisbrook Resort and Country Club (See Golf Information).

Weeki Wachee Spring, at U.S. 19 and FL 50, about 60 miles north of St. Petersburg, has an underwater show that has been around for decades, and in earlier days attracted celebrities like Bing Crosby, Elvis Presley, and others (evidenced by the photos of the stars posing with mermaids that deck the walls of the snack bar). The underwater show features real people in mermaid costumes. The actors pause to breathe through small tubes occasionally, but young kids will leave thinking the mermaids are real. After the show, kids can be photographed with a mermaid on a little dock. Behind the dock, you can see the water park, **Buccaneer Bay**, which has a couple of waterslides that cascade into a fresh-water bay. There's also a sandy beach and a swim area for little ones. Buccaneer Bay is a separate charge from Weeki Wachee (though combination tickets are available) and entrance to the latter includes a birds-of-prey show and a narrated river cruise exploring local wildlife. Weeki Wachee Spring is open daily; Buccaneer Bay has seasonal hours. For information, call 904-596-2062. There is a terrific golf course here, the Seville Golf and Country Club. It's also a reasonable distance from the World Woods golf course in Brooksville (See Golf Information).

GENERAL INFORMATION ....

For information on Tampa, contact the Greater Tampa Chamber of Commerce at 813-228-7777 and ask for a free copy of their Tampa visitor's guide, or call the current events line at 800-44TAMPA. For St. Petersburg, contact the St. Petersburg Chamber of Commerce at 821-4069 or contact the St. Petersburg/Clearwater Area Convention and Visitors Bureau (at the Thunderdome) at 582-7892 or 800-345-6710 and ask them for a free area visitor's guide.

Appendix

SPECIAL CHECKLISTS ....

TRAVEL/TOUR COMPANIES OFFERING GOLF PACKAGES AND NON-PROFIT GOLF ORGANIZATIONS

The following companies specialize in golf travel and can assist in making arrangements for golfers and non-golfers traveling together. These listings are followed by listings for non-profit organizations that help promote golf in their area. Most of these non-profit organizations will send golf and accommodations information to prospective visitors, who can then contact hotels and arrange money-saving packages directly. The advantage of using either for-profit or non-profit organizations is that they will generally save you money on hotels and greens fees. Also, in many cases, they will provide you with greater access to certain golf courses and/or preferred tee times not offered to non-guests or those without golf-package arrangements. Some companies even offer discounted airfare. Call the companies that serve areas you wish to visit to compare prices and select a company that deals with courses you wish to play.

Tour Companies

Coastal Golfaway
6987 Market Street
Wilmington, NC 28405
(910) 791-8494 or
(800) 368-0045
Area(s) Served: Wilmington and the Cape Fear Coast, North Carolina
What they do: Offer discount golf packages at several area courses and accommodations in downtown Wilmington and nearby beach areas.

Disney World Golf Packages
Disney Central Reservations Center, PO Box 10,
Lake Buena Vista, FL 32830
(407) 827-7200
Area(s) Served: Orlando, Florida (Walt Disney World Resort Complex)
What they do: Offer golf packages and secured tee-time reservations at the resort's great courses, as well as other specialized packages and add-ons to Walt Disney World visitors (e.g., meal plans, etc.).

The Golf Connection, Inc.
650-C Page Street
Pinehurst, NC 28374
(800) 255-4653 (ALL GOLF)
Area(s) Served: Pinehurst, North Carolina
What they do: Offer discount airfare, condominium rentals, car rentals, and tee-time reservations at many area golf courses.

Golf Digest Golf and Travel Club
P.O. Box 4011
Harlan, IA 51593
(800) GD-EAGLE
Area(s) Served: entire United States
What they do: For an annual membership fee, members can book discount golf vacations through the *Golf Digest* travel agency. Members receive a newsletter and discounts on over 2,000 golf courses and 1,500 hotels throughout the United States and can take advantage of discounts on airfare, accommodations, car rentals, and other travel-related expenses. However, you may have better luck reaching them by mail than by telephone.

The Golf Group of the Carolinas
P.O. Box 3246
Pinehurst, NC 28374
(800) 845-3402
Area(s) Served: Pinehurst, North Carolina
What they do: Arrange packages with a choice of eight area hotels (including Holiday Inn, Hampton Inn, and the Foxfire) and discounted golf rounds at many Pinehurst courses. Arranges rentals of condominiums and town houses, some overlooking the Pinehurst Resort. Offers preferred tee times at many of the area's great courses—like The Pit, Talamore, and Legacy (with the exception of the Pinehurst Resort's courses, which are open to non-guests on a same-day basis only, making it extremely difficult for non-guests to get tee times)—without surcharges. Also offers up-to-the-minute course conditions for these courses.

The Golf Travel Shop

13400 Riverside Drive

Sherman Oaks, CA 91423

(800) GOLF-USA (465-3872)

Area(s) Served: North Carolina, South Carolina, and Florida

What they do: This company, sponsored by *Golf*, is an amalgam of American Express Travel and Golf Reservations of America, Inc. They also work with National Car Rental. It offers all-inclusive, custom-tailored golf packages at competitive rates for hundreds of locations. There are two format types available: the "golf around" package, in which you choose an accommodation and then play at various courses available within 30-45 miles of your lodging; or the "stay and play" package, where you choose an accommodation and play the courses there (or resort hop, if you wish to play other home courses).

Golfpac

P.O. Box 162366

Altamonte Springs, FL 32716-2366

(800) 327-0878

Area(s) Served: Florida, including Jacksonville, St. Augustine, Orlando, Kissimmee, West Palm Beach, Fort Lauderdale, Miami, Naples, Fort Myers, Sarasota, St. Petersburg, and Clearwater; Pinehurst, North Carolina; Myrtle Beach; two resorts on Hilton Head Island, and Kiawah Island, South Carolina

What they do: Offer packages at a variety of hotels and motels, including many familiar chains, and at a variety of golf courses. Visitors can choose from a list of courses and hotels in each area, and then add together the room rates and greens fees to arrive at golf-package prices. They also offer all-inclusive

packages at several resorts, as well as arrange car rentals.

Great Golf Getaways

3225 South MacDill #307

Tampa, FL 33629

(800) 644-8440

Area(s) Served: Florida

What they do: This is as close to having a personalized travel agency in Florida as it gets. Owned by Bruce and Jean Crawford, a couple with over twenty years experience in the travel industry, this company performs a variety of services, including arranging discount airfare from several cities in the United States (mainly in the Northeast and Midwest). The Crawfords work closely with approximately a hundred golf courses statewide (all handpicked by Bruce Crawford with the help of a PGA professional) and forty hotels and resorts in those areas. In addition to saving you money and helping you select quality courses, they work to assure that your stay will be comfortable, including staying up to date on a weekly basis with the courses to be sure they are in top shape.

Great Golf Resorts of the World

111 Presidential Boulevard, Suite 222, Bala Cynwyd, PA 19004

(800) 442-4479

Area(s) Served: Exclusive upscale golf resorts around the world. In the Southeast, resorts offered are mainly in Georgia, North Carolina, South Carolina, and Florida.

What they do: Arrange golf packages and accommodations with some of the world's most prestigious golf resorts.

Great Times Out

314 South Burrowes Street
P.O. Box 948
State College, PA 16804
(800) 877-5006

Area(s) Served: Myrtle Beach and Hilton Head Island, South Carolina; Jekyll Island, Georgia; Jacksonville and Tampa, Florida

What they do: Arrange accommodations (mainly at upscale and moderate hotels and resorts) and tee times at golf courses. Clients can review courses and accommodations listed in a brochure, then call to make all arrangements needed for individuals or groups. They also arrange airfare with USAir and car rentals through Hertz.

Mr. Golf, Inc.

4 Sawgrass Village, Suite 110
Ponte Vedra, FL 32082
(800) 216-4PAR

Area(s) Served: Focus on Jacksonville, Amelia Island, Ponte Vedra, and St. Augustine, Florida. They also have quality listings in Orlando, Florida; Myrtle Beach and Hilton Head, South Carolina; and Pinehurst, North Carolina.

What they do: Work with many prestigious area golf resorts and offer golf package rates. They are affiliated with over twenty courses (including some non-resort courses). All customers receive free enrollment in Mr. Golf's travel club. Aside from offering great courses and hotels at low prices, the company has forty years of experience and stays in constant contact with affiliated courses regarding current course conditions. Custom-tailored packages are available.

Outer Banks Golf Getaways

P.O. Box 2007
Kitty Hawk, NC 27949
(919) 255-1074 or (800) 916-OBGG

Area(s) Served: The Outer Banks of North Carolina

What they do: This company is owned by a local realty company and offers accommodations packages at rental homes and condominiums. Each night's accommodation includes a round of golf at one of four area courses (Sea Scape, Nags Head Links, The Pointe, and Goose Creek).

PGA Travel

3680 North Peachtree Road
Atlanta, GA 30341
(800) 283-4653

Area(s) Served: Kiawah Island, South Carolina, and PGA National, Florida

What they do: Offer discount golf/accommodations packages at these selected resorts, both of which have world-renowned golf courses.

Preferred Golf

2134 Tremont Center
Columbus, OH 43221
(614) 481-8845

Area(s) Served: Entire United States

What they do: Arrange golf packages, including discounted greens fees, accommodations, and airfare.

Southern Living Travel Service

1760 Peachtree Road NW
Atlanta, GA 30309
(800) SL-TRIPS

Area(s) Served: Several popular Southeastern destinations, including Myrtle Beach, Charleston, Hilton Head Island,

South Carolina; Asheville, North Carolina; Callaway Gardens, Georgia; Orlando, Florida; and others.

What they do: Though golf packages aren't this company's emphasis, unique, romantic, and classy vacation packages are, and they do handle golf arrangements.

Talamore Golf and Travel
1595 Midland Road
Southern Pines, NC 28387
(800) 552-6292

Area(s) Served: Pinehurst, North Carolina

What they do: This company is part of the Talamore Golf Club in Pinehurst (known for great golf and their unique llama caddies). It offers discount golf packages through Talamore and other Pinehurst area golf courses, including help in arranging accommodations (though no lodging is available at Talamore).

Tee-Times, Inc.
2030 Eastwood Road
Wilmington, NC 28403
(910) 256-8043 or (800) 447-0450

Area(s) Served: Wilmington and the Cape Fear Coast, North Carolina

What they do: Arrange golf packages with over forty area courses and several area accommodations, both in Wilmington and in the beach areas. They also arrange discount airline reservations.

Tee Times USA
P.O. Box 641
Flagler Beach, FL 32136
(904) 439-0001 or (800) 374-8633
(374-TOFF)

Area(s) Served: Florida

What they do: For those who don't need golf packages, they will reserve advance tee times at courses throughout Florida at no charge, help you decide which courses are right for you, and send you a tee-time confirmation with printed directions, score cards, and brochures for your selected courses. They also offer discount packages at several quality courses and hotels, motels, and resorts in many popular Florida cities.

World of Golf, Inc., Tours
255 Semoran Commerce Place
Suite 103
Apopka, FL 32703
(407) 884-8300 or (800) 729-1400

Area(s) Served: Florida, including Orlando, Tampa, Sarasota, Fort Lauderdale, West Palm Beach, Miami, Fort Myers, Naples, Daytona Beach, and Jacksonville; Hilton Head and Myrtle Beach, South Carolina

What they do: Offer inclusive packages including accommodations and greens fees, carts, and preconfirmed tee times at many courses throughout the areas served in Florida and South Carolina. Several courses they work with are among the best and most prestigious in each area. They also offer golf-only packages for certain Florida destinations. Customers get a five percent discount if they book airline travel through the company.

Non-profit Organizations

The following organizations provide golf and golf package information or provide other free services to prospective area visitors.

Florida's First Coast of Golf, Inc.
P.O. Box 52086
Jacksonville, FL 32201-2086
(800) 877-PUTT

Area(s) Served: Amelia Island, Jacksonville, Ponte Vedra, and St. Augustine areas, Florida

What they do: Send a glossy magazine listing the twenty-six accommodations and twenty-two golf courses that participate in this association, including detailed information on golf packages offered at area accommodations. Visitors can choose accommodations and then phone them directly to make reservations and tee times at golf courses of their choosing. Many of the great public and semi-private courses (except certain resort courses, such as the TPC course at Sawgrass) participate.

Golf Daytona Beach
P.O. Box 265222
Daytona Beach, FL 32126
(800) 881-7065

Areas Served: Daytona Beach, Florida

What they do: This organization was recently formed to help promote Daytona Beach as a golf destination. They will send visitors detailed information on golf courses and accommodations. Visitors then contact hotels directly to make room reservations and book tee times at chosen courses. There's also information about Daytona Beach's free golf program, where visitors staying a minimum number of nights at certain accommodations during designated dates can choose a free round of golf at participating local golf courses, provided they tee off in the afternoon after 1 P.M.

Information on restaurants and a few other attractions and services is also included.

Hilton Head Central Reservations
P.O. Box 5312
Hilton Head Island, SC 29938
(800) 845-7018

Area(s) Served: Hilton Head Island, South Carolina

What they do: This centralized agency makes reservations at more than forty hotels and approximately twenty courses. They also provide unbiased and helpful information, from best times to save money to available babysitting services. They help visitors find exactly what they're looking for in their vacation to Hilton Head Island.

Masters Housing Bureau
PO Box 211416
Augusta, GA 30917
(706) 855-8898 or (800) 244-4709

Area(s) Served: Augusta, Georgia (during Masters Week only)

What they do: Arrange local accommodations (including private home rentals, usually from residents fleeing this annual invasion of tourists) for spectators of April's annual Masters Tournament.

Myrtle Beach Golf Holiday

609 Seaboard Street, P.O. Box 1323
Myrtle Beach, SC 29578
(800) 845-4653

Area(s) Served: Myrtle Beach, South Carolina

What they do: This is an association of over ninety local accommodations and over seventy-five golf courses (representing the majority of courses in the area). Call to receive a comprehensive, magazine-style vacation planner, which has detailed information on golf packages, courses, and accommodations. Once you choose where you want to stay and the courses you wish to play, call the accommodations directly and arrange tee times with the hotel. The planner includes a special section listing airlines with discounts and information on arranging travel.

Williamsburg Golf Association

c/o Williamsburg Hotel and Motel Association (WHMA), P.O. Box 1515
Williamsburg, VA 23187
(800) FOR-GOLF

Area(s) Served: Williamsburg, Virginia

What they do: This recently formed association includes several area hotels and all eleven area golf courses, including the two newest ones. They will send a color brochure detailing the area golf courses, participating accommodations, and golf package information. Visitors call the hotel they choose and arrange their room reservations and tee times directly.

MAJOR CHAIN HOTELS WITH QUALITY GOLF ....

HILTON
(800) HILTONS

South Carolina

Hilton Head Island
Hilton Resort

P.O. Box 6165, 23 Ocean Lane
Hilton Head Island, SC 29938
(803) 842-8000

Golf Information: This resort has 54 holes of championship golf. Discount packages are available to resort guests. It also features a Hilton Vacation Station family program.

Myrtle Beach Hilton
Oceanfront Golf Resort

10000 Beach Club Drive
Myrtle Beach, SC 29572
(803) 449-5000

Golf Information: Affiliated with the Arcadian Shores championship 18-hole golf course. Guests of the resort don't receive priority on tee times but do receive discount greens fees via golf packages.

Georgia

Lake Lanier Island Hilton Resort

7000 Holiday Road
Lake Lanier, GA 30518
(770) 945-8787 or (800) 768-5253

Golf Information: This resort has a fine 18-hole course. Guests can save on greens fees with discount packages offered through the resort. It also features a Hilton Vacation Station family program.

Florida

Hilton at Walt Disney World Village

1751 Hotel Plaza Boulevard
Lake Buena Vista, FL 32830
(407) 827-4000

Golf Information: This resort has five 18-hole courses. Resort guests have priority on tee times and can reserve times much farther in advance than non-resort guests. Discount packages are available through the resort. Guests receive free shuttle to golf courses.

Innisbrook Hilton Resort

P.O. Box 1088
Tarpon Springs, FL 34688
(813) 942-2000; for reservations,
call (800) 456-2000

Golf Information: This resort has 63 holes of golf and is located a convenient distance from Clearwater Beach and St. Petersburg Beach. Discount golf packages and a golf instruction institute are available through the resort (tennis packages are also offered) with a three-night minimum stay.

HYATT
(800) 233-1234

Florida

Hyatt Regency Grand Cypress
One Grand Cypress Boulevard
Orlando, FL 32836
(407) 239-1234

Golf Information: This resort has 45 holes of championship golf and a 9-hole pitch-and-putt course. Only resort guests can book tee times, and only one

tee time can be booked in advance. However, golf packages are available through the resort. Courses are also affiliated with Sterling Group's The Villas of Grand Cypress (see below).

MARRIOTT
(800) 228-9290

Virginia

Marriott's Manor Club

101 St. Andrews Drive
Williamsburg, VA 23187
(757) 258-1120

Golf Information: This resort has 36 holes of championship golf and offers a "Villa Package" that includes discounted greens fees.

Georgia

Chateau Elan Resort and Winery

100 Rue Charlemagne
Braselton, GA 30517
(770) 932-0900 or (800) 233-9463

Golf Information: This gorgeous, French chateau–style resort (managed by Marriott) has three golf courses and offers special golf and spa packages to guests; there's also a *Golf Digest* school on the premises.

Florida

Marriott at Sawgrass Resort

1000 TPC Boulevard
Ponte Vedra Beach, FL 32082
(904) 285-7777 or (800) 457-GOLF

Golf Information: This deluxe resort has two championship golf courses. Discount golf packages are available to resort guests. Guests also can book advance tee times when making firm reservations.

Marriott Orlando World Center
8701 World Center Drive
Orlando, FL 32821
(407) 238-8660
Golf Information: This resort has an 18-hole golf course and is located near the area theme parks and other golf courses. Golf packages are available through the resort.

Marriott's Marco Island Resort and Golf Club
400 S. Collier Boulevard
Marco Island, FL 33937
(800) 438-4373
Golf Information: This resort has an 18-hole golf course, and golf packages are available to resort guests. Guests can reserve thirty days in advance (while non-guests must reserve just forty-eight hours in advance).

STERLING HOTEL GROUP (800) 637-7200

Virginia

The Homestead
U.S. 220 North, P.O. Box 2000
Hot Springs, VA 24445
(540) 839-5500 or (540) 839-7994 for the golf course
Golf Information: Discount golf packages and preferred tee times are available to resort guests.

North Carolina

Pinehurst Resort and Country Club
Carolina Vista Drive
Pinehurst, NC 28374
(800) IT'S GOLF (for reservations) or (910) 295-8141 (for golf course)
Golf Information: There are now a total of eight 18-hole courses at this resort (the newest being the Centennial course, opened March 21, 1996). Discount packages are available only to resort guests, as are preferred tee times (tee times available to non-guests only on same-day basis).

Florida

Grenelefe Golf and Tennis Resort
3200 State Road 546
Haines City, FL 33844
(941) 422-7511 or (800) 237-9549
Golf Information: Three championship 18-hole courses are offered at this resort. Depending on the golf package chosen, resort guests can book tee times from a year to ninety days in advance. Some advance tee times also include discounted greens fees.

PGA National Resort and Spa
400 Avenue of the Champions
Palm Beach Gardens, FL 33418
(407) 627-2000 or (800) 633-9150
Golf Information: This resort has five 18-hole championship courses. The prestigious Academy of Golf is also here. Resort guests can reserve tee times up to a year in advance and can book special discount golf packages. The spa and tennis facilities are also internationally known (combination spa and golf packages are available).

The Villas of Grand Cypress
One North Jacaranda
Orlando, FL 32836
(407) 239-4700
Golf Information: This resort has two 18-hole championship courses (also affiliated with the Hyatt Regency Grand Cypress, see above). Only resort guests can receive tee times; discount golf packages are available to guests.

RENAISSANCE
(800) 468-3571

Georgia

Renaissance Pine Isle Resort
9000 Holiday Road
Lake Lanier Island, GA 30518
(770) 945-8922 or (800) 468-3571
Golf Information: Discount golf packages are available for resort guests. Guests can make advanced tee times when they make confirmed room reservations, while outside players can only call a week in advance.

Florida

Renaissance Vinoy St. Petersburg
501 Fifth Avenue NE
St. Petersburg, FL 33701
(813) 894-1000
Golf Information: The resort offers a 18-hole golf course; golf and tennis packages are available.

Renaissance Orlando
6677 Sea Harbor Drive
Orlando, FL 32821
(407) 351-5555
Golf Information: This hotel has qual-ity golf, and guests enjoy golf packages and special golf privileges.

WESTIN HOTELS AND RESORTS
(800) 228-3000

South Carolina

The Westin Resort
Two Grasslawn Avenue
Hilton Head Island, SC 29928
(803) 681-4000
Golf Information: The resort has three championship 18-hole golf courses. Golf packages are available to guests.

Florida

The Biltmore Hotel
1200 Anastasia Avenue
Coral Gables, FL 33134
(305) 445-1926
Golf Information: One 18-hole championship golf course is at the resort; golf packages are available to guests.

Walt Disney World Swan
1200 EPCOT Resorts Boulevard,
Lake Buena Vista, FL 32830
(407) 934-3000
Golf Information: The resort has five championship golf courses which are part of Walt Disney World's Magic Linkdom. Guests receive advance tee time privileges on the courses and complimentary transportation to theme parks and golf courses.

Index

Tullie Smith Farm, 238
Turnberry Isle Resort and Club, 323, 328
Turtle Point Golf Course at Kiawah Island Resort, 166
Tuscawilla Park, 278
Tweetsie Railroad, 142-43
Tybee Island (Ga.), 200, 207
Tybee Island Lighthouse, 207
Typhoon Lagoon, 290
Tysons Corner, 13-14, 16

Underground Atlanta, 237, 242
United States Army Transportation Museum, 47
United States Astronauts Hall of Fame, 296
United States Customs House, 202
United States Open, 107
United States Senior Open, 107
United States Women's Open, 107
Universal Studios, 283, 290, 296
University of North Carolina Botanical Gardens, 115
University of Virginia, 66, 69
University Park Country Club, 334
Unto These Hills, 120
Uptown Music Jam Festival, 229

Valentine Museum, The, 24
Van Wezel Performing Arts Hall, 337
Vanderbilt, George, 112, 114, 115
Vantage Championship at Tanglewood Park, 131
Venetian Pool, 326
Venice (Fla.), 334, 339
Venice Golden Apple Dinner Theater. *See* Golden Apple Dinner Theaters.
Venice Symphony, 337
Veteran's Day Parade, 240
Victorian Christmas at Biltmore Estate, 114
Village Shops, 268
Villas of Grand Cypress, 287, 293, 369
Virginia Air and Space Center, 47
Virginia Beach (Va.), 42-53
Virginia Dare Day Celebration, 83
Virginia Discovery Museum, 72
Virginia Horse Center, 59
Virginia Living Museum, 48
Virginia Marine Science Museum, 48
Virginia Military Institute, 56, 59, 61
Virginia Military Institute Museum, 59

Virginia Museum of Fine Arts, 24
Virginia Oaks Golf and Country Club, 8
Virginia Opera, 48-49
Virginia Stage Company, 49
Virginia State Fair, 25
Virginia State Library and Archives, 22
Virginia Symphony, 49
Virginia Zoological Park, 49, 52
Vizcaya Museum and Gardens, 324, 327

Waccamaw Shopping Outlet Center. *See* Outlet Park at Waccamaw.
Wade's Mill, 61
Wake Forest University, 127-28, 129, 133
Walking Tours of Old Savannah Gardens, 205
Walt Disney World Resort, 285-86, 290
Walt Disney World Resort golf courses, 285-86
Walt Disney World Swan, Orlando, 369
War Memorial Museum of Virginia, 47
Warm Springs (Ga.), 231
Warm Springs Village, 231
Washington (D.C.), 5-6, 9, 10, 12, 15, 16
Washington and Lee University, 56
Washington Bullets, 12
Washington Capitals, 12
Washington Dolls' House and Toy Museum, 15
Washington, George, 6, 10, 11, 12, 22, 35, 39, 56, 169
Washington Redskins, 12
Water Country USA, 36
Water Mania, 290
Water Taxis: Fort Lauderdale, 311-12; Miami, 323.
Waterford (Va.), 10, 11
Waterfront Shops, 84
WaterFun Park, 182
Watermen's Museum, 35
Waterside, The, 51
Waterside Theater, 82
Wax Museums. *See* Potter's Wax Museum; Myrtle Beach National Wax Museum.
Weatherspoon Art Gallery, 130
Weeki Wachee Spring, 358-59. *See also* Buccaneer Bay.

Weeks Air Museum at Tamiami Airport, 324
Wells Theater, 49
West End Dinner Theater. *See* Alexandria's West End Dinner Theater.
West Palm Beach (Fla.), 299-307
West Palm Beach Celebration, 304
West Palm Beach Municipal Country Club, 300-301
Westchase Golf Club, 350
Western North Carolina Nature Center, 116
Westin Golf Resorts, 369
Westin Resort, The, 183, 369
Westville Village, 231.
Wet 'n' Wild, 290
Weymouth Center, 106
Weymouth Nature Preserve and Museum, 106
White Columns Golf Club, 234-35
White Water Park, 239, 244
White shrimp, 268
Whitehall, 303, 304
White's Ferry, 9
Wicked Stick Golf Links, 155
Wickham House. *See* Valentine Museum.
Wild Bill's Wild West Dinner Show, 295
Wild Dunes Resort, 164-65, 172
Wild Water and Wheels Water Park, 157
Wild Wing Plantation Golf Courses, 154
Willbrook Plantation at Litchfield Beach and Golf Resorts, 155
William Byrd Park, 25
Williamsburg (Va.), 28-41, 44, 199
Williamsburg Doll Factory, 39
Williamsburg Golf Association, 31, 366
Williamsburg Hotel and Motel Association, 37, 41
Williamsburg National Golf Course, 34
Williamsburg Soap and Candle Factory, 39
Willoughby-Baylor House and Garden, 46
Willowcroft Farm and Vineyards, 11
Wilmington (N.C.), 88-99
Wilmington Railroad Museum, 96
Wilton, 23
Windsor Parke Golf Club, 262-63
Winkler Bakery, 133